COMPUTERS,
COMMUNICATIONS,
AND THE
PUBLIC INTEREST

This volume originated in a series of lectures and discussions sponsored by The Johns Hopkins University and the Brookings Institution in 1969–70. The series was supported by grants from the Alfred P. Sloan Foundation and the American Federation of Information Processing Societies.

MARTIN GREENBERGER
EDITOR

COMPUTERS, COMMUNICATIONS, AND THE PUBLIC INTEREST

THE JOHNS HOPKINS PRESS
BALTIMORE AND LONDON

Copyright © 1971 by Martin Greenberger
All rights reserved
Manufactured in the United States of America

The Johns Hopkins Press, Baltimore, Maryland 21218
The Johns Hopkins Press, Ltd., London

Library of Congress Catalog Card Number 74-140671
ISBN 0-8018-1135-X

CONTENTS

PREFACE	vii
INTRODUCTION Martin Greenberger	xi
1. LARGE TIME-SHARING NETWORKS	1

  Speaker: John G. Kemeny
  Discussant: John E. Bertram
  Discussant: Alan J. Perlis
  Moderator: Lee A. DuBridge

2. DESIGNING ORGANIZATIONS FOR AN INFORMATION-RICH WORLD	37

  Speaker: Herbert A. Simon
  Discussant: Karl W. Deutsch
  Discussant: Martin Shubik
  Moderator: Emilio Q. Daddario

3. COMPUNICATIONS IN THE NATIONAL DECISION-MAKING PROCESS	73

  Speaker: Anthony G. Oettinger
  Discussant: Ithiel de Sola Pool
  Discussant: Alain C. Enthoven
  Moderator: David Packard

4. EDUCATION IN MODERN SOCIETY	115

  Speaker: James S. Coleman

Discussant: EUGENE G. FUBINI
Discussant: PATRICK SUPPES
Moderator: DAEL WOLFLE

5. CIVIL LIBERTIES AND COMPUTERIZED DATA SYSTEMS   149

Speaker: ALAN F. WESTIN
Discussant: CHARLES L. SCHULTZE
Discussant: RALPH NADER
Moderator: DAVID L. BAZELON

6. PROPERTY RIGHTS UNDER THE NEW TECHNOLOGY   189

Speaker: RALPH S. BROWN JR.
Discussant: BENJAMIN KAPLAN
Discussant: DAN LACY
Moderator: CARYL P. HASKINS

7. DEVELOPING NATIONAL POLICY FOR COMPUTERS AND COMMUNICATIONS   225

Speaker: NICHOLAS JOHNSON
Discussant: LEE C. WHITE
Discussant: RICHARD POSNER
Moderator: KINGMAN BREWSTER JR.

8. MAN AND THE MACHINE: PROSPECTS FOR THE HUMAN ENTERPRISE   259

Speaker: GEORGE WALD
Discussant: DANIEL BELL
Discussant: HARVEY BROOKS
Moderator: JAMES B. FISK

BIOGRAPHICAL NOTES   295

INDEX   303

PREFACE

This volume is an edited record of the lectures and discussion in a series of symposia held jointly by The Johns Hopkins University and The Brookings Institution in Washington, D.C., during the period of September, 1969 to May, 1970. Some readers may be curious about how the series came about.

I had organized a similar series of lectures in 1961 as part of a celebration of the one hundredth birthday of MIT. Its theme was "Management and the Computer of the Future," and it was well attended by a responsive audience from the Boston-Cambridge area. A book covering this earlier series was published first in hard covers and later as a paperback under the title *Computers and the World of the Future*. As the titles suggest, the spotlight played on the future: where computer technology was headed and what meaning it had for our lives. Among the interesting papers was the first technical account of time sharing in the sense we use the term today.

In the years since 1961, the computer has fulfilled and surpassed many of the expectations expressed in the MIT lectures. Still there have been disappointments, and the technology cannot be said to have helped in alleviating many of the pressing problems facing the country. The disappointments have not been for lack of progress in hardware development. They have resulted from unanticipated complexities and organizational difficulties in programming for large systems and from social, economic, and political factors that are only now beginning to receive the attention they deserve.

Several friends and colleagues encouraged me to organize a follow-up to the MIT series. Much had happened in computing since 1961, and the end of the sixties and beginning of the seventies seemed a good time for serious reflection. In 1968 Paul Armer, then president of the American Federation of Information Processing Societies (AFIPS), asked me to explore possible activities this organization might undertake in the social sphere. I recommended a series of symposia on "Computers, Communications, and the Public Interest" that would emphasize the public policy questions posed both by the technology's rapid progress and by its unmet potential—looking backward as well as forward, examining the mistakes and false hopes as well as the successes and the problems they have created.

Because of the emphasis on public policy matters, Washington was an ideal site for the symposia. Brookings, a distinguished Washington institution for public policy studies, was a logical cosponsor with my home base, The Johns Hopkins University. President Kermit Gordon of Brookings and President Lincoln Gordon of Hopkins gave their active support to the project, as did Caryl Haskins, president of the Carnegie Institution of Washington, and Dael Wolfle, executive officer of the American Association for the Advancement of Science. These four men joined with me to form an organizing committee for the symposia. The AFIPS Board of Directors voted a grant to help finance the endeavor, and the Alfred P. Sloan Foundation made a complementary grant. Bruce Gilchrist of AFIPS and Nils Wessell and Larkin Farinholt of the Sloan Foundation took personal interests in the project and gave us helpful encouragement.

We decided to follow the format of the earlier series: eight lectures, each with a main speaker, moderator, two discussants, and general discussion peppered with questions from the audience. The first order of business was to select the eight most worthwhile topics. To help with this important task we convened a planning group at Brookings on January 9, 1969. Members of the group were:

Donald Baker, Department of Justice; *John Brademas*, House of Representatives; *William M. Capron*, Brookings; *James Coleman*, Hopkins; *John Cunniffe*, International Business Machines Corporation; *Kenneth Cox*, Federal Communications Commission; *Bruce Gilchrist*, AFIPS; *Kermit Gordon*, Brookings; *Martin Greenberger*, Hopkins; *Warren House*, National Academy of Sciences; *Nicholas Johnson*, Federal Communications Commission; *William K. Jones*, Columbia University; *Francis Keppel*, General Learning Corporation; *William T. Knox*, McGraw-Hill; *L. E. McMahon*, Bell Telephone Laboratories; *Harold Orlans*, Brookings; *Joseph Pechman*, Brookings; *Henry Riecken*, Social Science

Research Council; *Eugene Rotberg*, World Bank; *Charles L. Schultze*, Brookings; *James Shannon*, National Academy of Sciences; and *Sam Zagoria*, National Labor Relations Board.

The topics proposed by this group were mailed to a larger number of advisers for an expression of their preferences on possible speakers as well as topics. This was the basis for the selections we subsequently made.

As in the previous series, the discussants received the main paper ahead of the lecture. This time, however, we invited a small group of representatives of government, business, education, and law who were concerned in their daily occupations with the issues being treated to join with the participants in informal discussion at dinner. The dinner discussions followed the lectures (except in the last session) and provided us with an opportunity to pursue the subjects at greater length. The dinner discussions have been condensed and included with the main papers, discussants' remarks, and general discussions in the present volume. All of these parts have been edited for clarity and meaning with the help of the participants.

The symposia were held at the Johns Hopkins School of Advanced International Studies (SAIS), and the dinner discussions took place across the street at Brookings. The lectures were free and open to the public. Audiences ran to over a thousand people, well in excess of the capacity of the SAIS auditorium. We accommodated the overflow with closed-circuit television hookups in the SAIS lobby, cafeteria, and lounge. One of our enterprising student-helpers strung a coaxial cable across the street to provide television reception in the Brookings auditorium also, but since the cable seemed to be a safety hazard we removed it and settled for audio reception there through a service provided by the telephone company.

At the suggestion of Larkin Farinholt and Nils Wessell of the Sloan Foundation, we collected statistics on the composition of the audiences at all but the first session. We used prepunched cards to accomplish this. The computer industry's representation at the symposia ranged from about 10 to 20 percent of the total audience, with the largest percentages coming at the Coleman and Westin sessions. The Brown session drew the most lawyers (over 18 percent) and also the largest proportion of people from distances greater than 140 miles from Washington (10 percent). Administrators and managers appeared to favor the Simon session by a slight margin (20 percent), public officials were drawn to the Johnson session (9 percent), and programmers and analysts came out in greatest relative force to the Westin session (22 percent). The government contingent (including the military) comprised a consistent 50 percent of the audience except at the Coleman and Wald sessions, where it dropped to around 40 percent. The relative magnitude of the university contingent (including students) had an inverse relation to the relative size of the government group, rising from 9 percent at the Oettinger session to 29 percent at the Wald session. The military representation was highest at the Oettinger session (over 14 percent) and lowest at the Wald session (6 percent), exactly opposite to the student pattern of 2 percent at the Oettinger session and over 15 percent at the Wald session.

The reader can draw his own conclusions from these figures. They seem to suggest among other things that Oettinger's subject was as uninteresting to the students as it was interesting to the military. But this is not the whole story. By an unfortunate turn of events, the date originally selected for the Oettinger session coincided with the day chosen by the students to begin their November 1969 Vietnam Moratorium, a national antiwar movement centered in Washington, D.C. The students labeled the combination of Oettinger, Packard, Enthoven, and de Sola Pool "DOD," and they were said to be making elaborate plans to bus hundreds of protesters to the session for a disruptive demonstration and confrontation inside the auditorium. The crowds at our two prior sessions had already seriously overtaxed the facilities, and we felt that this new development might result in a very nasty and potentially dangerous situation. We rescheduled the session for May of 1970. We cannot know exactly what would have happened if we had gone ahead with the original November date, but of one thing we can be sure—there would have been considerably more students in attendance!

Many people helped run the series and prepare this volume. Steadfast throughout were my secretaries Virginia Crum of Brookings and Joan McKibbin of Hopkins, who were extremely effective in coordinating with each other across the Baltimore-Washington axis and with participants, committee members, and advisers across the country. Jack Goellner of The Johns Hopkins Press and Charles Pepper provided valuable editorial assistance; Fisher Howe and Francis O. Wilcox facilitated our use of the SAIS auditorium; Robert F. Hewes, Thomas Kleis, Michael L. McGrael, and Arthur R. Mitchell helped with publicity; and my students Terry Easton, Thomas V. Hoffman, and Stephen C. Lloyd took care of arrangements for the audience and the audio and video facilities, aided by student ushers from SAIS, members of radio station WAMU in Washington, and Russell E. Wolford of The Johns Hopkins Applied Physics Laboratory.

The unmentioned friends and colleagues who assisted me in various ways are many in number. Several fellow committee members, participants in the series, and outside advisers provided me with more cooperation and counsel than I can begin to acknowledge. They know who they are. I thank them sincerely and hope they have experienced at least a portion of the pleasure and gratification I have felt in all phases of this very enjoyable project. I believe the reader will find the value of their contributions clearly reflected in the following pages.

MARTIN GREENBERGER

INTRODUCTION

MARTIN GREENBERGER

As recently as 1962 we compared the computer to a growing youngster.[1] Today this would be inappropriate. That the computer is still young goes without saying, since it first appeared on the scene in its modern form less than thirty years ago. But its place in our life is now established and its importance unquestioned.

The computer's development in a few brief decades has given rise to an imposing industry in the United States with a composite revenue in 1970 estimated at over twelve billion dollars, growing at roughly 19 percent per year.[2] For comparison, consider the much more senior but hardly senile electric power industry, whose revenue in 1969 stood at somewhat over twenty billion dollars and was increasing at a rate of 8.4 percent per year.[3] If these growth rates were to hold relatively constant during the next few years (and that is a big *if*), we would see computers and related products overtaking electric power by 1976. Telephone service, at just under nineteen billion dollars in 1969 and growing at 11.6 percent per year, would be passed a year or two later.[4]

Revenue figures aside, the vast and important assortment of uses to which the computer has already been put fully earns adult status for it among today's technologies. Yet its physical capacities continue to expand at a relentless pace and its prospects still dazzle the imagination. But we can no longer afford to be dazzled. The issues raised by the computer's accomplishments and assured position in today's world require our clear-headed attention.

As if to recognize the computer's maturity, we have come to speak in recent years of its marriage with communications. Communications, although several times older than computers, is also a fast-growing technology and some of its most exciting advances will become visible only later in the decade. Many of these advances depend on the computer and on the same semiconductor technology that computers use. Together computers and communications make possible applications of wide scope and deep social significance. We may rejoice at their wedding, so long as we do not succumb to our elation and become romantics.

With this caveat before us, let us consider one possible example in medicine of computers and communications joining forces for the public good. There are computers today that can analyze electrocardiograph (EKG) signals to help a physician make a diagnosis. In the original application, the signals were recorded on tape, then converted to digital form and fed to a computer for processing. In a more current version, the live signals go to a computer sitting alongside the patient's bed and the computer can produce an analysis on the spot. But the value of the analysis is limited by the fact that the computer does not have access to past EKG readings and other information about the patient.

Now consider a computer that is centrally located and able to receive EKG signals directly by telephone. A physician examining the patient sets up a portable EKG device equipped with a telephone interface, calls up the computer, identifies the patient, and transmits the EKG signals from the patient directly to the computer via the switched telephone network. The physician may wait a few minutes and transmit a second set of EKG signals. He then receives back from the computer by voice or visually an extensive analysis and factual account of the patient, all in less than twenty minutes from beginning to end. During this period the computer has searched through a directory file to secure calling instructions to another computer where the complete medical history of the patient under observation is stored. It uses this history (including any past EKG readings of the patient) along with the present EKG signals to work out its detailed analysis and select relevant information about the patient to help the physician render a diagnosis and prescribe treatment.

Such a system is *not* operational today in its entirety. The portable EKG device for remote data acquisition by telephone is commercially available and is being used. But much more difficult is the task of getting medical records consolidated, structured, coded, and stored in a form usable by the computer.[5] Moreover, the computer still has trouble spotting certain rhythmic irregularities in the heart from EKG data. These fundamental problems are compounded by questions of an institutional and economic nature. Will the powerful medical establishment and the individual physician accept the changes in medical practice and doctor-patient relationship implied by such a system? Will they go along with the standardizations that may be necessary in format and procedure? What are the costs of the system's development and implementation to the nation—to the patient? Do the benefits really justify these costs?

The moderating effect of the real world upon technology's promise is not found only in medicine. In education, one might imagine a national or regional communications network that connects video and computer facilities at universities to homes and classrooms in local communities, thus providing the physical apparatus for a major revision of the school system. Each university, for example, might conceivably make available its special strengths in fields for which its intellectual and other resources best equip it and defer to its sister institutions in fields for which they are better suited, without feeling the need for comprehensive coverage that today often leads to intellectual inflation, depreciated values, and a waste that universities can ill afford. Adult centers, community colleges, high schools, primary schools, and homes would be the primary sites of learning, and instructional materials using the new technologies could supplement and supplant the printed media. Formal education might then no longer be just a single chapter in one's life. The citizenry could be students "from cradle to coffin," yet productive workers as well in possibly two or three occupations over a lifetime. With different generations studying together and sharing a common and continuing learning experience, there might even seem to be hope of closing the generation gap that so concerns us these days.

It is a sweet dream. But why have books failed to bring it about? Certainly not for want of their effective distribution. Andrew Carnegie believed that public libraries would become the university of the people. Others have seen in radio, films, and most recently television the makings for a revolution in education. Yet the university system still functions along medieval lines. Some say it is more susceptible to change today than ever before. Suppose a new system could be developed outside of the traditional institutions by concentrating initially on continuing education. Could we find the necessary incentives and mechanisms for producing and distributing materials that utilize the full potential of the new technologies? Can these technologies provide the critical interpersonal and motivational factors that former technologies by themselves have lacked—that only the classroom has supplied? Or are we in danger of deluding ourselves once again?

Consider now the interests of the consumer. Ralph Nader has pointed out that one of the most serious imperfections in the functioning of our free-market economy is the inadequacy or inaccuracy of the information publicly available on products.[6] The consumer is uncertain about just what he can buy, where he can find it, its quality, and its price. He has no good mechanism for communicating his preferences to the producer or for stimulating competitive excellence. A computerized buyer's information service could help, but it would be difficult for any central administration to keep the information complete and up to date. One might reason that the problem would become tractable if remote communication terminals to the computerized system were made accessible to shoppers for obtaining information and rating products and to vendors for inserting changes, all in a decentralized manner. Were the vendors to derive a benefit from the service along with the consumers—from their use of it as buyers themselves and also from the advertisement it afforded their products—it might appear that the system would not only be feasible and socially beneficial but a thumping commercial success as well. That is, unless the commercial allurements worked to subvert the basic purpose of the system or the system became unmanageable because of its complexity and scope.

Nader also sees a potential use for computers and communications in the fight against pollution. He would have a network of real-time computers and odor sensors or *sniffers* assisting government authorities in detecting pollutants, pinpointing the offenders, and determining their shares in the abuse. Since offenders often pollute in combination, to make each of them legally accountable is a complicated problem that Nader feels must be solved if any real progress is to be made. The sniffer network might also provide guidance for measures that could be taken to correct an abuse before its effects have reached dangerous proportions. The sniffers have yet to be perfected, however, and until they are, the idea must remain speculative, since no sound estimate of system cost can be made.

A point almost too obvious to mention is that a great deal of what goes on between individuals and organizations in our society consists essentially of the transfer and processing of information. This is why computers and communications offer us so many possibilities. No longer novel is the vision of a financial information network keeping the accounts and conducting the transactions of individuals and firms over a wide geographic area.[7] Such a network would offer hope for converting the present litter of cash, checks, certificates, and other paper forms into a tidier transmission of electrical signals. Or another possibility in the financial area is a decentralized automated system for trading investment securities, a logical extension of the automated system for price quotations that has existed for several years. This could conceivably bring many of the advantages of membership in the exclusive and expensive stock exchanges to the average investor and at the same time produce a substantial improvement in the efficiency and breadth of the market operation. Indeed, some automated systems are already being used for block trading and are planned for more general use. But interests with a stake in maintaining the present operation constitute a major inertial force opposing change. It is just as naive and self-defeating to discount this fact of life as it is to ignore the organizational perturbations invariably created by transition to automated systems and the considerable marketing and educational efforts that successful transition demands.

The possibilities sketched are not new. Why are they still only possibilities? Has the computer let us down? No, just the opposite. We tended to view our precocious computer during its early years with awe and adulation. We treated it as something special—a thing apart—because of its unique abilities and great promise. We would have done better to spend more time looking at the world into which our prodigy had to fit. We would have done better to have prepared it (and ourselves) more adequately for the role it had to play. We have been unfair to the computer, and we have shortchanged ourselves in the process.

This problem is a matter for public concern. It is discussed in the chapters that follow, along with another important aspect of public concern. As computers and communications become ever more a part of our daily lives, how can we protect our traditional values and rights as citizens and human beings? How can we improve the still imperfect mechanisms we have for taking account of the public interest when applying the new technologies? These are serious questions and they do not have easy answers.

Nowhere is the gap between the computer's promise and present performance so marked, and nowhere is the public interest so much at issue, as in the development of large systems with a personal touch and a social goal: systems to help unemployed workers to find jobs, students to select colleges, pupils to learn, needy people to gain assistance, physicians to obtain medical advice, shoppers to locate goods, managers to make decisions, readers to browse through stacks of information, and so on. We need these systems, and much of the required technology is available. But the critical commercial or intellectual incentives often are lacking, and so perhaps are the proper organizational forms. John Kemeny addresses the problem in chapter 1 in the context of developing large time-sharing networks, and he makes some concrete recommendations for policy and action. In the process he examines how computer systems have been designed in the past, and he pleads for much more emphasis in future design objectives on the achievement of a better life for people.

A great deal has been written in recent years about the information flood that allegedly threatens to engulf us. Many well-intentioned people have looked to the computer for relief, but their use of it to create large new data banks just swells the tide, an illustration of how misguided application of the computer can be unfair to its potential. Herbert Simon takes a fresh look at this problem of information surplus in chapter 2, turning it inside out (in effect) and into a problem of attention scarcity that suggests an unconventional solution. His concept of information storage is refreshingly different in these days of massive magnetic memories, and the conclusions he draws are both novel and provocative.

One type of information system that has caused more than mild disillusionment about the computer's magic, especially among executives who should know better, is the so-called management information system (MIS). Some early hopes for MIS were inflated and misdirected, and it should come as no great surprise that they are still far from realization. Management, the intended clientele, is not known for its enduring patience, and many skeletons of MIS projects now line the trails. In light of such disappointments, we might reasonably ask whether computers and communications really have anything substantial to offer decision makers. Anthony Oettinger gives an affirmative answer in chapter 3, but with some strong reservations that ally him with Herbert Simon in an interesting way (despite their basic disagreement on the outlook for intelligent programs). Oettinger studies the need for information systems throughout all levels of government hierarchies, including the top echelon. This leads him to formulate two operating principles that he considers essential. Both principles run counter to current practice in Washington, and their appearance in print will doubtlessly fire as much spirited discussion and debate as did their oral presentation.

Education is another area where early ambitions have tended to surpass actual successes. Research efforts under the rubric of computer-aided instruction (CAI) seem to have had more than their share of misfirings. James Coleman could have fixed his sights in chapter 4 on CAI, critically reviewing its successes and failures as an experienced sociologist and a discerning outside observer. He prefers to take it for granted that CAI's stock will grow during the coming years and asks instead the deeper question of what this development along with the blossoming of television and the other technologies that make us an information-rich society will mean for the future of schools. He finds the current school system obsolete and sees in the demise of certain social institutions and traditional values an urgent requirement for reform. He believes the needs that schools once filled are no longer applicable, but perceives an entirely new set of needs taking their place. Coleman's thoughtful analysis leads him to propose that more economic power be given to students and parents, as customers of the new education, and increased reliance be placed on the private commercial sector, as suppliers. School boards would do well to take note—and systems designers, too.

The systems designer cannot afford to ignore any aspect of the world into which his technology fits, whether it be social tensions, the play of economic forces, or political subtleties. The popular stereotype of the computer scientist or engineer is that of a person preoccupied with his devices and theories and oblivious to the world about him, especially its political nature. At the time of the congressionally ignited explosion a few years ago over the prospect of a national statistical data bank being put on a computer, some of the outraged may have assumed that the suggestion originated with politically naive computer technicians. In fact, the proposal came via the Bureau of the Budget from experienced social scientists well versed in the ways of the world. The outcry surprised them. They had not adequately recognized the latent concerns that exist over possible threats to privacy and civil liberties, whether real or imagined. Herein lies an important lesson for the systems designer.

Alan Westin examines the complex subject of civil liberties and computers in chapter 5, directing his attention to several varieties of government information systems—those used for administrative and intelligence functions as well as those intended for statistical purposes. After placing the issues in historical perspective, Westin surveys a range of current and planned systems, then lays out a set of possible judicial, organizational, legislative, and regulatory measures for protecting the citizen's rights of privacy and due process during the next five-year phase in the computerization of data files. He argues convincingly that the present is the critical time for decision and action on these measures.

In some areas of computer application where progress has seemed sluggish, careful examination reveals that incentives are missing or insufficient. Despite years of developmental work in CAI by universities and research institutions, for example, there is still a relative paucity of good learning material for use at computer terminals. A teacher or research worker can get royalties and prestige for writing a book but often only administrative headaches for running a project to develop a programmed interactive learning system. If he does persevere, chances are that he has not geared his product adequately for export or adaptation outside of his group. Or if he has, he is not eager to add to his headaches by taking on the task of marketing the product. He might attract the interest of a business enterprise with greater motivation and talent for this sort of thing but, as of now, only on a hit-and-miss basis.

Our economy traditionally has sought to spur the creation and dissemination of innovative work by providing legal protection for the property rights of the innovator and distributor. Patent and copyright are the two standard mechanisms for doing this. Ralph Brown, from his vantage point as a copyright scholar, analyzes the appropriateness of these two mechanisms for the new technologies in chapter 6. His broad purview covers computer programs as well as textual materials stored in computers. As the best means for protecting most computer programs, Brown's vote is for a modified form of copyright with an application right attached; but patent lawyers disagree. The exchanges between the two camps are lively and illuminating for the layman as well as the lawyer. Perhaps the Supreme Court may someday find them interesting, too.

Another obstacle to progress, according to many computer companies, has been the inability of the communications industry to meet the computer companies' special needs for data transmission in the area of time sharing and remote computing. The marriage of computers and communications has its squabbles and incompatibilities. This has been of concern to the Federal Communications Commission (FCC), the country's watchdog over the communications carriers. The practice of calling time-sharing networks "information (or computer) *utilities*,"[8] a term that Western Union and a number of new companies have adopted in their advertising and shareholder reports, has reinforced the FCC's interest. The regulatory agency became so interested, in fact, that it initiated a formal public inquiry in 1966 on a series of issues arising from the growing interdependence of computers and communications. Nicholas Johnson reviews the background and conduct of this major inquiry in chapter 7 and raises some basic questions about the FCC's ability to function effectively here as well as in its traditional jurisdictions. He leaves no doubt that the regulatory apparatus needs strengthening—except perhaps in the minds of those who ask whether the regulatory apparatus is needed at all.

And then there are those who ask whether technology is needed. There may, in fact, be more of this kind of questioning today than at any time since the Luddite hysteria of the early nineteenth century or the acute anxiety after World War II about nuclear weapons. Many find it profoundly disturbing when, in their eyes, they see the country become a city and the city a social sore; nature's waters turned to waste and the air to ashen smog; the hopelessness of war and a world population out of control. They ask, What is technology's role in this modern tragedy, satan or savior? These preoccupations were in many minds during the discussions recorded in this volume. They come up explicitly in chapters 2 and 7 as peripheral concerns, and they show up again in chapter 8 as the central subject. George Wald urges us in the final chapter to examine what we are and whence we came before taking our next technological step. And he challenges us to consider whither we want to go as a civilized race and as a biological species. Wald may be guilty as charged of speaking more like a poet than like a scientist, but we shall not rest easy until we think through the issues he puts before us. Technology may be our crutch and our cane, but we are still masters of the feet that take us forward. That is, we had better be.

REFERENCES

1. Martin Greenberger, ed., *Computers and the World of the Future*, MIT Press, paperback ed., 1964, preface.
2. P. J. McGovern, ed., *EDP Industry Report*, vol. 5, no. 20, September 9, 1970.
3. *Statistical Year Book*, Edison Electric Institute, New York.
4. Courtney S. Snyder, comp., *Statistics of the Independent Telephone Industry*, vol. 1, United States Independent Telephone Association.

5. Lawrence L. Weed, *Medical Records, Medical Education, and Patient Care*, Case Western Reserve University Press, 1969.
6. Ralph Nader, keynote speech, annual meeting of the Association for Computing Machinery, August 1970.
7. Martin Greenberger, "Banking and the Information Utility," *Computers and Automation*, vol. 14, no. 4, April 1965.
8. Martin Greenberger, "The Computers of Tomorrow," *Atlantic*, vol. 213, no. 5, May 1964; reprinted in *Perspectives on the Computer Revolution*, ed. Zenon W. Pylyshyn, Prentice-Hall, 1970.

LARGE TIME-SHARING NETWORKS

Speaker   JOHN G. KEMENY
*President of Dartmouth College and
Albert Bradley Third Century Professor*

Discussants   JOHN E. BERTRAM
*Corporate Staff
International Business Machines Corporation*

ALAN J. PERLIS
*Head of the Computer Science Department
Carnegie-Mellon University*

Moderator   LEE A. DUBRIDGE
*Former Science Adviser to the President
United States Government*

DuBridge. A moderator should be neutral and not known for any prejudiced views on the subject being discussed, and he should be sufficiently devoid of such views so as not to insert his own remarks too volubly into the proceedings. At the moment I am well qualified on both counts, but perhaps this will change by the end of the session.

I asked John Kemeny how he happened to have the title of Albert Bradley Third Century Professor. I wondered why a professor celebrating the third century would be concerned with computers. Professor Kemeny informed me that his title refers to the third century of Dartmouth College, which recently passed its two hundredth year.

Kemeny. My presentation will be divided into four parts: (1) the feasibility of large time-sharing networks; (2) what society can expect in the way of new services from such networks; (3) some probable long-range effects of the combined computer-communications revolution on the structure of society; (4) recommendations for actions to remove bottlenecks and significantly speed up progress.

Feasibility of Large Time-Sharing Networks

So that we can have the benefit of common terminology, let me begin by defining *time sharing*. The traditional mode of operating high-speed computers, known as *batch processing*, dates back to the time when computers were scarce and very expensive. Batch systems are designed to maximize the use of a computer, so that it can accomplish a wide variety of different tasks with a minimum waste of computing time. Typically, a *batch* of job requests is put on magnetic tape and fed to the computer quickly and serially. As each job is processed, answers or error messages are written on an output tape, which is removed and printed off-line when the batch is completed. Batch operation is extremely efficient in machine utilization and provides excellent service when turnaround times of an hour or more are acceptable.

The major disadvantage of batch processing is that even users requiring a minimum amount of service must wait the standard interval for their answers. But a user debugging a complex program, for example, is ordinarily much better off when he can have many fraction-of-a-second runs in rapid succession to correct a number of errors in one session at the computer. In an educational environment, moreover, a delay of one or more hours makes it very difficult for an inexperienced user to acquire competence on a high-speed computer. In addition, many applications require real-time interaction (i.e., *conversational mode*) between user and computer, which is impossible under batch processing.

Time sharing was designed to overcome these shortcomings.[1] In a typical time-sharing system, the user communicates with a small intermediate computer that has simultaneous conversations with many different people. It interrupts a larger central processor only when a user needs computing service, customarily for a very brief period of time. The central processor's time is divided into small time slices, and a user can obtain a quick shot of processing on demand. In a well-organized system, the average user can expect response within ten seconds and as many as a dozen servicings within the span of fifteen minutes. Thus, time sharing allows the user effectively to interact with his program.

The time-sharing user sits at a terminal device such as a typewriter, teletypewriter, or cathode-ray display having both input and output facilities. He types his problem in a natural manner and receives error messages and answers. In a modern system, as many as one hundred users may receive excellent service simultaneously, with each one having the illusion of exclusive use of the computer.

Time-sharing systems are by now widely employed in both educational and commercial environments. The ease of using a typewriter device, coupled with the availability of several simple high-level computer languages for time sharing (including BASIC and versions of FORTRAN), have opened up modern computing (by one or two orders of magnitude) to a vastly larger number of users than ever participated in batch-processing systems. Universities have found time sharing an excellent, economical way to teach hundreds rather than dozens of students in the use of high-speed computers. Faculty members and research workers have recognized time sharing as an invaluable research tool. A time-sharing system combines the convenience of a desk calculator with the power of a modern computer. The inversion of a ten-by-ten matrix can be as simple and fast on a time-sharing system as taking a square root on a desk calculator. Businesses maintaining their files within a time-sharing system have achieved remote-inquiry capabilities never before possible.

There are hybrid systems in existence that combine some of the best features of batch processing and time sharing, but for purposes of simplicity I shall ignore them in the following discussion. I shall call time-sharing systems with ten to thirty users *small*, a hundred to two hundred users *medium*, and over a thousand users *large*. There are a vast number of small systems in use, quite a few medium systems, but no large systems at the present time. I shall present the case for the design and implementation of large time-sharing networks and argue that it is both feasible and desirable for us to develop several of them within the next decade.

It is sad but true that even the best central processors now in commercial use cannot handle more than two hundred customers at a time. Our experience at Dartmouth College on the GE 635 system indicates that the ratio of terminal to central processor time is about a hundred sixty to one. Thus, a hundred sixty users would completely flood the central processor even if the system ran with zero overhead. I have said a large time-sharing system must accommodate over a thousand users.

There are at least three approaches to the design of a large time-sharing system: (1) a much larger, more powerful central processor; (2) several central processors of the present type within one system; (3) a telephone hookup of several medium systems in a single network.

I am personally skeptical about the first approach. Reliability and continuity of service are crucial requirements in any time-sharing system. A single mammoth processor seems to me like putting all our eggs into one shaky basket—in other words, bad design. Both the second and third possibilities, however, appear highly attractive.

Let me start with the second approach and suggest how a large system might be assembled on a single site. My favorite system is shown in figure 1. In the middle of the room is a huge block of core memory connected to a number of processors of different types. One good fast processor is designated as the boss. It makes the decisions and keeps track of everything. I do not believe you can run a large computing system by having each processor make part of the major decisions. There has to be one key decision maker. There are also a number of extremely simple-minded slave processors whose function may be merely to work on a problem in core for fifty seconds or fifty milliseconds at a time.

A large data file is needed for storing programs, including the system programs, and maintaining the enormous data banks existing today and the even larger ones expected in the future. The data file is managed by some inexpensive but efficient special-purpose processors, also connected to the core.

Last, there are communication processors that enable the system to talk to the outside world. There are many fine communications processors on the market today that can talk to a thousand people at a time and also communicate with peripheral equipment.

So here is one feasible design: a large core memory, a master processor, slave processors, file processors running the file system, and communications processors talking to the outside world and managing peripheral equipment. I would estimate that such a large time-sharing system is entirely practical within five years, and perhaps even three years, assuming some major computer manufacturer is willing to commit itself to the very significant software development and new hardware design required.

The system could offer a wide variety of services of interest to all kinds of users. If fully loaded, its cost could be brought down to about two dollars per hour spent *at the terminal*, plus terminal and communication costs. If we can assume that communication will be via local telephone, and that the many current efforts devoted to the development of new terminals will produce at least one attractive and inexpensive terminal, then time sharing will come within the reach of even modest-sized businesses. Eventually costs will reach the point where most homes will have time-sharing terminals.

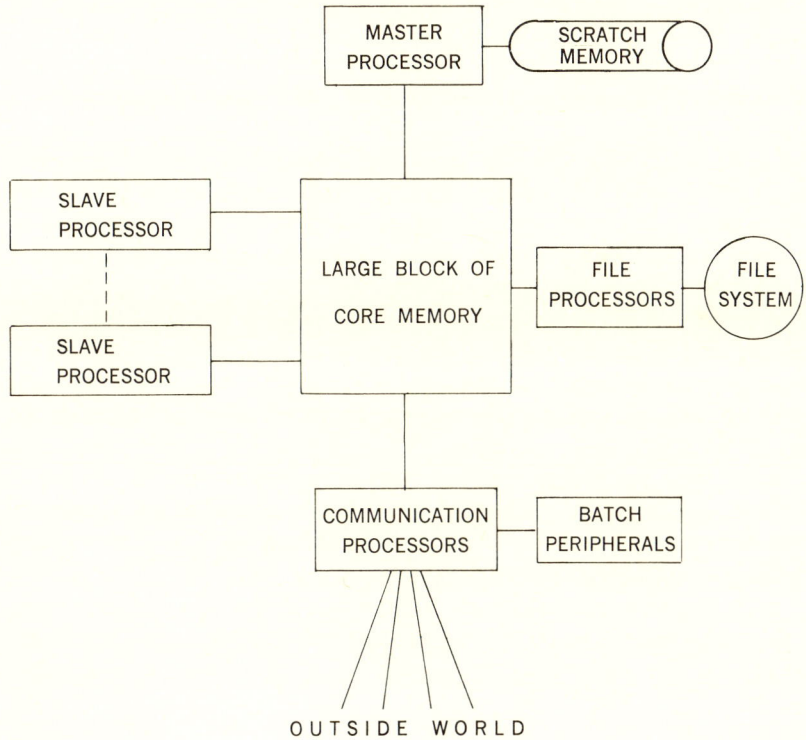

Figure 1. Several processors in one large time-sharing system

Still further economies and efficiencies may be achievable by hooking together a number of large time-sharing systems into a national network. The engineering and software techniques for doing this are already known. Then an installation could lay off an overload on a sister installation and use it for back-up. A user in any part of the country could have access to distant files and tie into the system at a relatively modest communication cost no matter where he is located. He should not have to know which computer maintains which data bank. The system should "do the walking" through the Yellow Pages for him.

I shall personally be quite shocked if we do not have several national networks of large time-sharing systems by 1980. A number of companies are already engaged in establishing national networks of medium-sized time-sharing systems. Networks of large systems are both technically and economically feasible, given one or more major organizations dedicated to the task.

Future Services

After reviewing the first two decades in the history of modern computers, I come to a very depressing conclusion. While the high-speed computer is man's most powerful intellectual tool, most of its past uses have been designed either to improve efficiency, save costs, or perform previously impossible tasks. Little effort has been expended thinking up new services to make life better. This may be one reason why the man in the street feels resentment toward computers.

Numerous large companies, for example, use computers for billing and customer accounting, which may be simpler and less expensive for the company but harder for the customer. Many an entertaining story tells of the customer who repeatedly receives incorrect bills but cannot get his complaints past the computer. The fault is in the design. The designer was probably told to save the company as much money as possible rather than heed the customer's interests. Given modern technology, it would cost little to modify billing programs so that a supervisor is notified when a customer complains twice about the same bill. I have estimated that for many systems the cost difference between an almost unacceptable (though highly efficient) service and one that makes customers happy is as little as 5 percent; but the operation cannot be by conventional batch processing.

By way of contrast, I can cite two well-designed systems that do keep customers happy. One is the airline reservation system and the other is a time-sharing system designed for university students. I hope that a primary design criterion in the construction of national time-sharing networks will be to provide new services that make life better for all of us.

For example, a perennial problem of society is finding jobs for millions of human beings. The current means of filling jobs is inefficient, archaic, and degrading. Finding a job in New York City is a miserable experience. Let us imagine how a large time-sharing system could be applied to the problem, assuming that the primary criterion is to make human beings happy.

Each employer of sufficient size has his own input terminal to the system. He periodically registers and briefly describes the available jobs and indicates when a job has been filled, so that an applicant does not have to journey across town just to learn this. Small employers enter their job listings through city offices, and employment agencies have terminals to the system to assist job applicants. An applicant can walk into any employment agency in town and have access to all available jobs in the city. He fills out a form indicating his qualifications and preferences, and a clerk types this information into the system. Then a conversation takes place between computer and job seeker with the clerk as intermediary. The computer asks questions in real time. If no jobs of the kind requested are available, the computer asks the applicant to specify which of his criteria are least important. Or if there are too many possibilities, the computer suggests more conditions until a small list of possible jobs is finally identified. The computer then automatically schedules interviews for the candidate and notifies the firms of his qualifications.

This system is entirely feasible today, although it requires a large design and software implementation project. A substantial subsidy might be needed to sustain the system until the fees from employers and employees made it self-financing. If a statistical record were kept of all interactions within the system, it might help the mayor deal with his employment problem by suggesting a need for new industry or retraining programs. The system could also notify candidates automatically when a job opens up. With local employment services connected in a national network, the federal government could get early warning on geographical shifts in population and employers and thereby relieve or avoid major unemployment in the country.

I have read that the city of Baltimore has a modest batch-processing service that runs off lists of available jobs quickly and efficiently for fifteen city employment agencies. This is a significant improvement over past practices, but it falls far short of what is possible. A plumber looking for a job must still have a clerk in the employment agency look through the entire listing to pick out suitable positions. The clerk is not likely to have the time or computational ability to take into account such complex factors as distance or available transportation to the worker's residence. A hundred people still may show up for a single job, and it may already have been filled. I am not criticizing the Baltimore system; it is no doubt a major step forward. I am simply saying that with today's technology we should be doing a great deal more.

A system similar to the one outlined for filling jobs could help new residents of a community find housing. A national network could be a significant weapon in fighting crime, with police forces all over the country obtaining almost instantaneous information on criminal records and motor-vehicle registration. A major municipal time-sharing system could be used on a large scale for the control of traffic signals, as is beginning to happen in New York and other cities, and at the same time accumulate statistical information for a simulation model of traffic flow designed to test improvements and plan future highway construction—without using people as guinea pigs.

All of these applications require large time-sharing systems, but not necessarily a national network. There are important applications, however, which do. A national advisory system, for example, could help guidance counselors give better advice to high school seniors applying to college. Few counselors can keep up with current developments at over two thousand institutions of higher education, and they do not have the time or energy to match student qualifications and interests against college offerings. As a result, some of the advice given by college counselors today is hair-raising.

An advisory system operating in conversational mode would be fairly easy to design. The counselor types in relevant data about the student's qualifications and preferences. The system answers with information about the colleges that seem most appropriate. If the list is too long, the system asks questions such as, "Which sports does the student like?" The reply, "He loves soccer," might eliminate two-thirds of the schools. At the other extreme, if no colleges were left, the system says, "Look, the student wants too much; which of the following five things is he willing to give up so he can go to college?"

Even more important would be a consultant service for the medical profession. Many interesting experiments have been conducted in the use of computers to help advise physicians; some of them were spectacularly successful. Suppose each general practitioner, no matter where he is located, were tied by terminal into a national network and could obtain instantaneous advice on a difficult case by means of a program and data bank constructed under the supervision of the most eminent physicians in the country. He could excuse himself, walk into the next room, and get the advice he badly needs. This would help bring the latest medical findings to the doctor long since out of medical school and would constitute a major improvement to medical service in the United States.

Someday most homes will have terminals connected to time-sharing systems. The terminal at home will be used to provide valuable shopping information to housewives, such as which nearby stores carry size 7½ AA ladies' shoes and what they charge for them. It will list information on entertainment, such as the movies at the local theaters and when the next show begins. It will serve as an automated newspaper, and a customer who subscribes will have printed out at his terminal news items on topics of particular interest to him. Municipal and state governments will be able to poll the population on questions of public policy from these terminals at home.

Nor should we overlook the tremendous recreational potential of a time-sharing system, which can be used for playing a variety of games economically. At Dartmouth College a number of terminal users can share the same program and play competitive games simulated and refereed by computer. In the future, time-sharing terminals may include visual devices that display movies, and they may in the long run become one of the principal sources of entertainment. By 1990 I envision two people sitting at terminals quarterbacking opposing football teams in highly realistic matches simulated by computer and displayed with appropriate visual and sound effects. This will enable television stations to increase audience participation. The Columbia Broadcasting System on one of its famous national quizzes could have millions of viewers answering questions in real time, with cash prizes awarded directly.

For better or worse, the coming of television has permanently changed the structure of society. Time-sharing systems, vastly more flexible than television and allowing much more active participation, will have a considerably greater impact on society. Consider, for example, the possibilities for combining the powers of television and time sharing in adult education: lectures over TV, and students using their terminals for doing homework or library research. No one can foresee all of the incredible opportunities being opened up by computer and communications technology. The applications will continue, as they have in the past, to go far beyond our hopes and imagination.

Probable Effects on Society

Computers have already had a significant impact on society. Much first-rate research carried on today would have been inconceivable a decade ago. Businesses are operated more efficiently and provide new customer services. Dartmouth College is a much better educational institution than five years ago, and a medium-sized time-sharing system is one major reason why. Man could not have landed on the moon without computers. And yet I feel that we have not even begun to experience the real effect of this technology on society.

When there were just a few telephones in the country, they were hardly more than amusing toys of limited usefulness. Today, the general ability to call anyone anywhere in the world has made the telephone essential to society. Similarly, while it is significant that the President of the United States can fly to any point of the globe within a day, what is much more important for society is that millions of human beings are able to fly great distances cheaply and efficiently. The impact of television on society zoomed when it reached the stage where nearly every American had easy access to it daily.

Computers, originally designed for high-speed computation and phenomenal at this task, are equally useful as sources of information, tools for education, and means of entertainment. I think the ultimate effect of computers on society will not be really felt until computer terminals are available not only in business, research, and educational institutions but also commonly in the home.

At the MIT Centennial Celebration in 1961, I proposed the establishment of an automated National Research Library for the United States by the year 2000 A.D.[2] My goal was to head off the incredible cost increases taking place in university libraries. We hardly have space to put the exploding numbers of books and journals. In my plan, only reference items in every day use and books for browsing and pleasure reading were in conventional libraries. The enormous volume of other material that is at times essential for research projects but that does not justify cluttering up thousands of libraries resided in the National Library. I hoped that establishment of this library could make a major impact on the incredibly complex problem of identifying and retrieving information.

I recently reread that article, and I find that the technical details and basic philosophy are still sound. I am sorry to say, however, that in the intervening eight years essentially no progress has been made on implementing such a plan. I am not surprised. I chose the date of 2000 A.D. not because it would take forty years to build the automated library but because I felt it would take twenty years for anyone to assume the initiative (there is another twelve years to go).

I still believe that an automated research library is essential and inevitable and that its services should be available through national computer networks. Sitting in our homes we could have at our fingertips all the reference materials of the entire world. The impact on research and the ability of the average man to keep himself informed is beyond imagination.

Let us next consider the effect of computer networks on business. The history of the recent past is one of centralization and movement to major cities, with resulting congestion, traffic problems, and slums. A few manufacturers have been moving their industrial plants outside city complexes, but concentration continues to be a major tendency. Most white-collar workers and professionals find it necessary to work within the city while preferring to live in the suburbs, and the problems this causes are well known to all of us.

I should like to consider a radical solution to the problems of the city. Arrange businesses so that suburban dwellers can *stay* in the suburbs; that is, remove the necessity for their going to the city.

Let us try to analyze in schematic form why a man must get up early in the morning to drive an hour to his office and then battle back through a traffic jam in the evening. One reason is to consult with colleagues and clients. But soon videophones will make face-to-face communication over long distances economical. I certainly hope this will remove the excuses for calling conferences (such as the committee meetings of mathematical societies) where people from all over the country travel several days to speak together for a few hours.

Another reason why a man goes to his office is because that is where his secretary is. But he could equally well have a small local office with secretarial aid, and before very long dictated letters will be automatically transcribed by computer.

More important, his files are at his office, and it is not efficient to have a large number of small offices all keeping files. Here is where time-sharing systems can help. Within a decade it will be practical for firms to maintain their files within a national computer network so that they may be consulted and updated by any authorized employee no matter where he is located.

Will everyone have his office at home? I doubt this, partly because men like company and partly because wives cannot stand having their husbands home all day. Rather, I predict that large firms will consist of hundreds of small branch offices whose locations are chosen for convenience of the employees, typically in suburbs or small towns.

The decentralization of business and the availability of computer terminals in the home will have an extremely important by-product for women. Millions of women well trained for a productive career in the past have not been able to make significant use of their education. A typical pattern is a career interrupted for fifteen to twenty years to raise children, with skills atrophying due to neglect and knowledge becoming hopelessly out of date. In future years women will have an opportunity for continued education in the home and a choice of meaningful part-time employment either at home or nearby. For the first time a woman will be able to keep up with her profession without sacrificing her role as wife or mother.

I see an unparalleled opportunity for social planning during the next few decades. The combination of videophones and time-sharing networks will remove most reasons for congregating millions of people in the city during the working day. There will be enormous economic incentive for firms to decentralize. A company that can offer its executives and white-collar workers ten minutes' commuting in an area of their choice will have an incredible advantage over a centralized competitor. For the first time in years we shall be able to do something meaningful about the traffic problem. We shall have an opportunity to clean up our large cities, make them attractive, and possibly dispense with the megalopolis altogether.

No doubt there will be new problems. What worries me most, however, is that our plans for improving life in the United States may implicitly assume that the fundamental structure of society will not change in the near future. This assumption is dangerously wrong. Current social planning must be concerned with life in the 1980's, since large-scale social measures require a decade or more to take effect. If we add to the vast strides being made in transportation and communication the revolutionary effect of national computer networks, we must conclude that the society of the 1980's will differ drastically from that of the present day, and I do not just mean more people. This has got to be well understood by social planners.

Recommendations

What are the roadblocks to progress in developing large national time-sharing networks, and what can be done to remove them?

Let me first consider the dependence of time sharing on communications. This subject lies outside my general area of competence, but I accept the conclusion of those more informed that in the long run over half the load on our national communications system will be generated by computers or inputs to computers.[3] This requires a fundamental rethinking in national policy and a reorientation of planning in the communications industry.

Procedures and rates designed primarily for voice communication often impose significant hardships on computer users. Dartmouth College operates a regional educational computing center, for example, and users beyond a hundred miles from Dartmouth sometimes pay more for communication than for computing. Phone companies impose rate structures that discriminate against computer users, and their facilities in many parts of the country already appear overloaded. Their development plans may not be based on realistic estimates of computer needs. In facing the problem, we must consider even drastic solutions, such as development of a separate communication network providing special, less expensive facilities for teleprocessing.

As a case history, when Dartmouth College switched from a small to a medium-sized time-sharing system we fortunately gave the New England Telephone Company a year's notice; otherwise we would have put long-distance service completely out of business in northern New England. Even with a year's lead time the company did not seem well equipped to handle our greatly increased load in this remote area.

I conclude that we need much better forecasting of future communications loads and vastly accelerated expansion of facilities, perhaps by a new supplier of communications for time-sharing networks. The Federal Communications Commission should completely reconsider rate structures and the rules governing use of communications networks by computers.

On the highly controversial issue of regulation of computer networks,

I agree that the existing communications network must be protected. Careful ground rules should be laid down on how computers gain access to the network, but other rules may be premature. It will take at least a decade to learn what time-sharing services are likely and worthwhile in the long run. An unfortunate rule laid down too early could inhibit progress. Nor is it easy to specify when a computer network is providing communications. In most time-sharing systems, for example, the user may store data which is reached by another user from a different location. At Dartmouth, several users can be actively tied to the same computer program. This presents exciting possibilities for research, experimentation, and entertainment. As long as the system does not degrade communication for other users, I believe such ties should be permitted.

In the future, interconnection between separate time-sharing networks will be desirable, and the Federal Communications Commission can perform a major service by mediating the question of what code formats and data structures are appropriate to ensure compatibility. A user should be able to switch from one national time-sharing network to another as easily as he now switches from CBS to NBC on a TV set.

I next wish to cite a report of the President's Science Advisory Committee published in February of 1967, which made a completely convincing argument for federal support of computers in higher education.[4] The report recommended "that colleges and universities, in cooperation with the federal government, take steps to provide all students needing such facilities with computing services at least comparable in quality to that now available at the more pioneering schools." To accomplish this, annual expenditures in the range of a hundred to two hundred million dollars were proposed. But the National Science Foundation, given the mandate of implementing the report's recommendations, has actually been provided with only about twenty million dollars per year. This level of support is totally inadequate.

At Dartmouth College 85 percent of all students now know how to use a computer. We have found that the availability of a time-sharing system causes a qualitative change in the attitude of students and faculty. Vast numbers of people can be trained efficiently and economically through on-line experience with computers. Unless the federal government is willing to spend at least five times the current rate to help higher education obtain large-scale computer services, we cannot hope to improve significantly the acceptance of computers or the availability of technically qualified programmers throughout the country.

I therefore strongly urge the federal government to increase the budget of the National Science Foundation by at least a hundred million dollars per year to support computing in higher education. I predict that within a decade the resulting revenue to the government from expansion of the economy will make this a most profitable investment.

So much for the long run. I shall now make a recommendation directed at helping state and local governments use computers *in the immediate future;* in fact, *tomorrow,* given that the President's Science Adviser is kind enough to be listening. (He says it takes money, but you will be surprised how little this recommendation calls for.) Individual state and local governments cannot afford the large expenditures required to develop time-sharing networks for their purposes, nor can they recruit the necessary software experts. No state or city should be expected to bear by itself the cost of development of a system that could be equally useful to many other states or cities. This suggests a cooperative endeavor by federal, state, and local governments to construct software systems for common use.

I propose the immediate establishment of a National Computer Development Agency (abbreviated NCDA) as a federally subsidized private agency. An annual seed appropriation of five million dollars per year would suffice to support the initial staff and computer system for preliminary research and development. State and local governments and other organizations would acquire participating memberships in the NCDA by paying a per capita fee of as little as five cents per constituent per year. The NCDA then would have the funds and prestige necessary to attract outstanding software people from all over the country. I am quite certain that many bright, young idealists (and there are a surplus of them today) would join such an organization in the hope of making a contribution to society.

The NCDA's mandate would be to develop hardware-software systems useful on a national scale but too complex or otherwise costly to attract commercial interest. The job-placement service described earlier might be an example. State and local governments, as members and participants in the NCDA, would be able to influence the design of systems and become ready to use them once they were fully tested and approved.

I would limit the activity of the NCDA to design, development, and testing of new systems on an experimental basis, as well as training of employees of member organizations to help with installation of adopted systems. The existence of the NCDA would have several benefits. First, it would encourage development of highly desirable but currently neglected systems. Second, it would spread development costs among many states and cities so that the burden on any one would be minimal. Third, it would encourage standardization and thereby facilitate interconnection into a national network.

While the primary customers of the NCDA are likely to be state and local governments, other customers might include the American Medical Association, on a consultant service for physicians; the Office of Education, on a college advisory service for high school counselors; and the Library of Congress, on an automated reference library.

It is a fact that well-designed time-sharing systems, no matter what their specific area of application, have a great deal in common. Over the years the NCDA would acquire a general expertise that would represent an advance in the art of developing large user-oriented software packages. Each new system would be easier than the one before, and much waste and duplication would be eliminated.

Might the NCDA favor one computer manufacturer over another, and would it not be subject to immense sales pressure? The dangers are reduced if its programming systems are written in user-oriented languages such as FORTRAN, BASIC, or COBOL. They are then almost universally usable on the equipment of practically any manufacturer. I realize that this principle does not always hold in practice, since computer languages are not yet truly standardized. But the NCDA might be instrumental in effecting such standardization and thereby perform an invaluable service to users all over the world. Indeed, I would require that any new system be run successfully on the equipment of at least three different manufacturers before acceptance, to assure that the software is machine-independent. In addition, a national conference of staff members of the NCDA and representatives of computer companies and various user groups could agree on simple specifications that a large time-sharing system must satisfy in order to accommodate complex applied software systems. Then any manufacturer with suitable time-sharing systems could compete for the business of the NCDA and its members. Each member would be free to choose its own hardware configuration for implementation of any system developed by the NCDA.

I am convinced that the main reason why computer systems for improving society are not now being developed is that the know-how is in the wrong places. On the one hand, it is with major computer companies, which naturally enough are profit motivated and give priority to commercial applications. At the other extreme, it is with the universities, which are busy with teaching and basic research. A prestigious agency with sufficient financing and a strong commitment to attack social problems would have an immense impact. The bottleneck is not the operating cost of the systems needed but rather their development cost, the lack of necessary expertise, and plain inertia. The existence of the NCDA would go far to overcome these obstacles.

I am not naive enough to think that computers alone will solve the problems of society, but neither do I believe we can solve these problems without computers. I urge the *immediate* establishment of a National Computer Development Agency. It is a rare opportunity for the federal government to take an imaginative, effective, and yet inexpensive step in the right direction.

We are now at the crossroads. Modern technology will make it possible to restructure society to make life more pleasant and meaningful for man. We cannot afford to ignore this opportunity.

PANEL DISCUSSION

BERTRAM. I agree with most of Kemeny's observations and suggestions. Specifically, I am convinced that large time-sharing networks with a thousand or more concurrently active terminals could be operational by 1980, perhaps even sooner. I agree that the existence of such networks, given the proper development of applications, could make a significant and lasting improvement to life in our society. But I think Kemeny underestimates (or at the very least does not emphasize sufficiently) the problems involved in realizing such a functioning network, particularly the theoretical and practical software problems.

Let me take up my concerns in the order they arose in reading Kemeny's paper. First, to service a thousand or more users and supply the range of data-base applications suggested requires an on-line file capacity on the order of 10^{11} to 10^{12} bits at the very minimum. This means that the files must be resident on archive devices with a low cost per bit, which in turn implies a slow access time, probably measured in seconds, although some believe new technologies will reduce this to milliseconds. To service a thousand concurrent users from files resident in such archive devices requires a storage hierarchy. There must be sophisticated software to control the staging of files from the archive level up through the hierarchy to the highest level, where programs are executed, and back down again. Efficient software for this task does not yet exist. Nor is it likely to be developed if we follow Kemeny's proposal to hook together via telephone communications several time-sharing systems in a single network with distributed data bases.

Furthermore, the goal of two dollars per terminal-hour seems incompatible with Kemeny's idea of using several central processors of the present type with a large block of core. Today, time-sharing systems without large data bases cost at least three times this amount, and with data bases they cost at least four or five times as much. Price reductions are possible only when the higher levels of the storage hierarchy and the central processor are time-shared. Using n processors in a multiprocessing system does not yield n times the performance of a single processor because of programming overhead and memory interference.

The design approach that Kemeny discarded—a single large central processor—seems the most promising to me for a number of reasons. First, the cost of a processor only goes up as the square root of performance, to a first approximation. Second, the software problem is much simpler for a single processor, and the recovery and restart problem is less complex. Finally, processors of the power required are feasible, if not already available, and they are reliable. Solid hardware failures account for less than 5 percent of today's system incidents, and central processors represent only a small fraction of that 5 percent. Freedom from system incidents and software simplicity go hand in hand.

Given all this, I too would be quite shocked if at least one large national time-sharing network were not in existence by 1980; but I predict it will be of the single-processor type.

The second area of my concern relates to the many new services Kemeny suggests for large time-sharing networks. Each of these applications requires the creation and maintenance of data bases, often large and dynamic. The programming attendant to these data bases is spoken of as *data management*. Currently, data mangement consists of a nonhomogeneous mixture of poorly defined methods with little or no theoretical structure. As a result, the cost of data-base systems tends to be high, the performance less than satisfactory, and the rate of revision very rapid. A still unrealized goal is to be able to write efficient programs that are completely independent of the format and structure of the data bases and to allow for convenient modification of these data bases. Much more work needs to be done in this area.

It is fair to say that all of the services proposed by Kemeny for large time-sharing networks are or have been investigated by commercial organizations. Ideally, the large development expense should be spread over a broad range of customers; but each customer wants a custom design. For example, IBM has built and tested an on-line student guidance system similar to the one proposed by Kemeny to assist high-school guidance counselors. Since not all students go to college, the data base must contain material for vocational guidance as well. IBM constructed and tested such a system and data base, in conjunction with Columbia Teachers College, at Montclair, New Jersey, this past year. It was thought that a general data base, not customized to the geographical area, would suffice. While the test was a great success and highly accepted by both students and teachers, the desire for local information was apparent. In fact, the first sales query from a Midwestern city school system asked for a vocational data base related to its geographical region.

The value of creative market planning in our society is too often ignored. A program product and data base must have sufficiently widespread acceptance or applicability built in so that each user's share of the cost of creating the product is commensurate with the benefits he receives from its use. Creative market planning is a skill found primarily in industry. This leads me to question seriously Kemeny's suggestion of a federally subsidized National Computer Development Agency charged with the development of application systems to be used by a large percentage of state and city governments. If such an agency were to be set up, I believe it would better use its resources to attack directly the problem of high development costs by finding new tools and concepts. I believe that major responsibility for development should remain with private industry, with at most occasional exceptions for purpose of experimentation by the agency.

KEMENY. Dr. Bertram is an expert on hardware, and his guesses are likely to be better than mine. I have a reputation, however, for being an incurable optimist. When we set out to develop a time-sharing system several years ago at Dartmouth, if we had known the task was not possible with the kind of staff we had (as everyone else knew), we certainly would not have succeeded.

I am not frightened by a memory size of 10^{11} to 10^{12} bits. I believe a 10^{12}-bit memory is now commercially available with access times of a fraction of a second. It is not even an IBM product, so that presumably even better memories will soon be announced.

Bertram said I oversimplified the difficulties, and I am sure I did. But I still would like to argue for the federally subsidized independent agency. Private industry can only attack great social problems if there is some assurance that enough customers will sign on the dotted line. Large companies labor under a major handicap of enormous software development costs. They develop a complex software system, and a small company with very little overhead comes along and pirates it. This may seem unfair, but it is a fact of life. I therefore think that large computer companies in general will not find the development of huge user-oriented systems profitable, particularly when the customers are politically oriented city and state governments that must count every penny they spend. This is why I feel an independent, neutral agency, motivated by social concern rather than profit, should assume the cost and responsibility.

DUBRIDGE. The earlier references to 1980 reminded me of a recent experience I had at a meeting of the Environmental Quality Council in San Clemente. An announcement was made that the government wants to get rapidly to work to develop new kinds of automobile engines to reduce the smog. I pointed out that if we had a perfect automobile engine in an experimental form today, or even in production, it would take ten years to junk all the old cars now on the streets and highways. Action today cannot possibly take full effect until 1980. Whereupon certain newspaper writers said, "The council is delaying things again; nothing is to be done until 1980." I think the point has been brought out here also: to get something done by 1980, a start needs to be made immediately.

PERLIS. I too concur, by and large, with Kemeny's statements and recommendations, but maybe I can shed some light on why things are not what they ought to be today. I shall comment both on what Kemeny did say and on what he did not say.

Time-sharing networks are clearly feasible. They are being used every day. Both university and commercial systems abound. *Large* networks do not yet exist, but certainly there are no technical barriers to their realization.

Batch systems also exist, and are extensions of the way computers have been managed for years. In fact, there is no fundamental difference between batch processing and time sharing at the present time. Sad to say, the same languages are used for both. The main dissimilarity seems to be whether the internal computer monitoring places a higher value on system efficiency or the convenience of the external user.

Programming in the time-sharing environment has the potential of being much simpler than in batch processing. Errors are easily and quickly corrected, programming need not be complete before execution is attempted, and so on. But many of the advantages are still more promise than reality.

What Kemeny did not say is that the really successful time-sharing systems have been dedicated, or limited, systems providing only a narrow band of useful and faithful services. They have been efficient in operation and relatively inexpensive to build, whereas general-purpose systems capable of offering great variability in modes of service have been enormously expensive to build and also generally unresponsive to quality control in design and operation. Yet it is the general-purpose system which Kemeny has in mind for large networks. No one is really sure why these systems became so expensive, and everyone hopes the phenomenon is temporary, but some pessimism is called for. The refractory period may be at least a decade, which puts us in 1980 again.

Some of the problems are not hard to identify. Each such system is a social and engineering extension of its predecessors. It is full of new ideas and techniques artfully (but not mechanically) integrated into a highly subjective unity organized for objective purposes. (Such a system seldom works.) It is built using labor of the worst kind: poorly trained and highly paid. As the effort grows, it sucks off appreciable numbers of the untrained into management positions, making for exponential propagation of chaos, delay, and unrealistic and wistful expectations.

Nevertheless, programming has the potential of being the most perfectly engineered of all complex activities. Once we set our attention to engineering large hardware-software systems and training the needed engineers, we can expect these systems to come under more perfect control and attain desired goals more easily than any of our other artificial systems.

There are, in my opinion, effective alternatives to time sharing for purposes of undergraduate education. I refer to high-speed batch processing as practiced at Case Western Reserve and Waterloo universities, with turnaround times on the order of five or six minutes. The service to students is not really inferior to time sharing, and it is substantially cheaper (at less than twenty dollars per student per year). I believe that at the present stage of computer and software development, this express batch service is probably the best way to service very large universities (of which Kemeny's school, like mine, is not one). Not everybody can be served in bed; some must eat in cafeterias!

I agree with Kemeny that very little effort is being applied to use computers to improve the quality of human life. Computer applications have been dominated by the desire to improve efficiency, cut costs, and support an increased need to know in this ever more complex world. We are all gluttons at a continuing banquet of data.

Computer systems tend not to increase the sublimity of the human component but rather to bend it to the will of the system. Kemeny cites the airline reservation system as an exception, but this is, of course, because pleasant human contact is an important part of the function airlines are optimizing. Kemeny suggests computerizing the local employment register as a good example of what might be done. It is a very different thing, however, to provide a person a seat on an airplane and to find him a job which will match his skills and make him socially comfortable. The problems are by no means comparable.

We can already see time-sharing computer services being commercialized to exploit the possibilities raised by Kemeny. Additional services on the horizon include glorified pinball machines and remote motel billing services using credit cards. We may expect enormous numbers of such services in the very near future, but all commercially oriented. Much more work is in order on intellectual aids for which the computer is so badly needed and well suited.

One of the major possibilities for time sharing is the development of what might be called an instantaneous updating system: a system that can be quickly updated by the addition of only marginal information, without requiring complete recalculation. In symbolic terms, if a data base P has indices $i_1, i_2, \ldots, i_n$, then each change to the data base, ΔP, should lead to a new set of indices, i_k', by the differential calculation

$$i_k' = i_k + \Delta i_k \, (\Delta P)$$

rather than *in toto* from the complete data base by

$$i_k' = i_k' \, (P + \Delta P).$$

As an illustration, some time ago a company headquartered in Pittsburgh was engaged in extensive labor negotiation. The process that took place at the bargaining table was of the following kind. The union proposed x. After running the entire data base of the corporation through its computer to learn the effect of x, management came back next day with its answer, $f(x)$. This was followed by the union's proposing x', and management once again marching the entire data base through the computer to compile $f(x')$. So it went, at tremendous computing expense.

A differential data system does not yet exist in the files of this company, nor in the files of very many other organizations today. Until we learn how to build such systems well, I am afraid that the uses of the data bases required for Kemeny's applications are going to be terribly inefficient and expensive.

The automated newspaper is a great idea, as anyone knows who recognizes that almost all the news the *New York Times* prints is not meant to be read by most of its readers. But it will require enormous work to bring this idea to fruition. Computers can be very effective in catering to differential interests and could radically improve the badly groaning publication cycle in science. Instead of the scientific journal, uniform to all and unread in its entirety by almost all, we could have a cheap, highly coded newspaper able to be scanned by computer. Complete documents would be obtainable upon individual request, and the formal editorial hierarchy would be replaced by a large number of separate groups interested in specific technical issues. Their findings would be audited by comprehensive reviews and summations.

The computer can increase choice while it decreases cost; this dual effect is the source of its value to society. But exercising choice burdens the mind and requires mental discipline. Many people just might not want the new options that computers make available.

Kemeny's major and important point is that the real effect of the computer on society will be felt only when saturation is attained. As is the case with other saturations, however, we may expect a new set of problems, identified as information pollution problems, to arise when vast networks come into existence. Too much information makes Jack neurotic. Information tends to accumulate, and the more the accumulation, the less the impact and value of incremental data. The networks could become conservative and self-serving. It may be erroneous to assume that access to data increases personal happiness, except for the small, happy breed (always a minority) that equates joy with knowledge. Do most people have that much interest in being well informed? Are there really large files of data they wish to peruse? I have not seen these assumptions substantiated of late.

One important consequence of widespread time-sharing networks will be the emergence of still another service elite engaged in the support and protection of society: those who police the archives and access to them. The automation of services for the many puts more burdens on a few.

Those in power have always been required to show responsibility for those whom they lead. As we begin to rely on the silent and selfless functioning of time-sharing networks, those on whom technical responsibility is thrust must be given additional social power. They are not likely otherwise to choose to perform in a socially responsible way from within these anonymous systems.

Kemeny argues for improved communication facilities, more support for computing in higher education, and a center for system planning and development. These are highly desirable goals. We must be sure that universities provide appropriate education in computing, with realistic objectives. While a great deal is already being done, the surface has just been scratched. We still do not know how to teach computing properly to nonprofessionals.

The National Computer Development Agency that Kemeny requests is much like the Systems Development Corporation that the Department of

Defense has supported over the years (until very recently). It would have many benefits, although there has been great opposition to the idea in the past.

In the computer field, each crisis has been diffused. Our sense of urgency has arisen as from a slow sinking into quicksand rather than the thrust of a knife. Everything is being done, but on an insufficient scale, in petty disorder, and with little overall professional guidance. There is no solid computer profession as yet. If we do not follow Kemeny's suggestion, our mishandling of the computer's promise will probably not kill us, but it will give rise to questions in the future as to why intelligent and coordinated action was not carried out by a wealthy society devoted to the advancement and freedom of man.

KEMENY. I want to be the first subscriber to Perlis' personalized scientific journal, but I would like it to have one additional feature for us poor mathematicians. I would like it to print out not only the latest theories, but also their counterexamples. It would save a great deal of time.

I thoroughly agree that we really do not have a science of computing yet. Much of the development of particular software systems is hit and miss, and it is important to discover more systematic approaches. But the problems of society cannot wait for a theoretical foundation to be found. They are too urgent.

The major point on which I disagree with Perlis is his advocacy of the inexpensive batch system with five- or six-minute turnaround. I am very tempted to say, "cheap is cheap." I have seen seven hundred students a year learning enthusiastically about computing at Dartmouth College for the last five years. The student sitting down to write his first program is absolutely guaranteed to make twelve logically separate mistakes. If he has to stand around for five minutes to get his first error message (and that is very good service for batch processing), it may be one and a half hours before he receives his last error message. That student is going to be thoroughly disgusted with computing.

PERLIS. The Waterloo batch processing system runs twenty-four hours a day, at its worst with a six-minute turnaround, and most of the time with a one- or two-minute turnaround. Furthermore, when you commit twelve errors in a program, you do not correct them sequentially: the first, then the second, and so on. If you do, you do it only once. And by the way, the students at Waterloo are not turned off by computing. Indeed, there are about eleven hundred of them in the Department of Computer Science.

I do believe that time sharing is the ultimate way to use a computer, but we still cannot provide it to all of the (say) forty thousand students at the University of Minnesota. It is urgent that these students have some contact with computers. In order to get large numbers of students trained, not in 1980, but this year and next, we have to depend on large-scale batch processing (if the universities are going to be able to afford it). A batch-processing system for a university of thirty thousand can be run for about five hundred thousand dollars a year. This is impossible today under time sharing.

DUBRIDGE. Martin Greenberger will now present questions from the audience.

GREENBERGER. Here are two questions on the National Computer Development Agency proposed by Kemeny. Barry Talsky, with the Department of Defense, asks if the NCDA should not *administer* projects rather than *implement* them. By letting out contracts and signing up customers, could it not still yield many of the advantages Kemeny suggests without either requiring subsidies or encroaching upon free enterprise?

The second question, by Richard E. Barry, director of the Education Institute of Computer Command and Control Company, is whether we might not expect a very negative reaction from Congress, which presumably would be the key funder of the NCDA, because of the Big Brother syndrome. Would such a concern be well founded?

KEMENY. I think that the NCDA should do more than just administer projects. We need well-trained, experienced, first-rate programmers to do this job, and they are very scarce at present. A primary mission of the NCDA would be to develop a highly competent professional staff internally. As the staff becomes more experienced, it would turn out better and better software systems.

On the second question, I do not dare guess how Congress would react to my proposal with Dr. DuBridge here. Since I do not have the federal government dictating policy, however, I see no explosive political issues. But I may be quite naive.

DUBRIDGE. Thanks for the compliment in suggesting I have become an expert on Congress during my first few months in Washington. Actually, I am still trying to understand Congressional attitudes. I can assure you, however, that getting a bill through Congress to create a new agency, especially an operating agency with laboratories and development machinery, would be extremely difficult—to say nothing of getting the agency into the budget and funded. It would seem better to find an existing agency, like the National Bureau of Standards, with existing laboratories and the talent with which to build the development program. Would you agree?

KEMENY. I completely agree. I have been taking a cowardly position by suggesting a *new* agency, because I did not dare single out any particular existing one. The National Bureau of Standards would provide an ideal nucleus.

GREENBERGER. Here are three technical questions which any of the panelists could address. The first one, by Mrs. Billie J. Pease of the U.S. Geological Survey, Department of the Interior, agrees with the use of high-level languages to implement large software systems. But Mrs. Pease asks whether at present it is not so that there are only two standard languages, COBOL and FORTRAN, both unsuitable for use with large dynamic data bases, and neither one ever implemented in pure form as defined.

The second question, by David A. Negrin of IBM, inquires if the problem of converting existing data into computer form suitable for establishing file-oriented time-sharing systems may not be formidable, and even prohibitive.

The third question, by Robert Hershey of Bolt, Beranek, and Newman, asks what size data base should have its own time-sharing system rather than be part of a large common system.

PERLIS. There *are* other languages besides COBOL and FORTRAN, although perhaps not as standard. The Multics time-sharing system, developed by MIT and Bell Laboratories, was written in a variant of PL-1. I have heard some very satisfying figures regarding the effectiveness of doing a large software system in a high-level language like PL-1.

KEMENY. At Dartmouth we are developing a fairly large data management, retrieval, and statistics program for social scientists. We hope to have hundreds of students gaining access to, and doing statistical analysis on data bases with millions of numbers. The first version, written in the BASIC language, is now running.

DUBRIDGE. At Cal Tech we have a combination of time sharing and batch processing for the campus and nearby colleges. One of our social scientists developed a data bank on economic and social institutions containing statistics from various parts of the world. He would sit down at the terminal and ask, "What product is produced in the most countries?" and the computer would answer, "Beer." Then he would ask, "What is the annual production of beer in Nigeria?" whereupon the computer would answer immediately, "x many barrels." This requires only a modest system, but it contains an enormous amount of economic, trade, and social data from all United Nations countries.

KEMENY. The question on the size of the data base for a dedicated system is difficult to answer the way it was asked. It seems to me to depend on the size of the time-sharing system. With a very small time-sharing system, a relatively small data base needs a dedicated system, whereas a large time-sharing system can accommodate several significant data bases.

BERTRAM. It seems to me less a function of the size of the data base than the statistics of inquiries to the data base. On the question of how to create the data bases, development of character-recognition equipment is needed far beyond what we have today.

KEMENY. Is IBM about to announce a new product along that line (I hope)?

BERTRAM. No, I am afraid there are fundamental problems to be solved first.

GREENBERGER. The next question is from Stanley Weintraub, a physicist. Would a communications network on a nonprofit basis for government and educational computer uses be a good idea?

PERLIS. Anything on a nonprofit basis which provides services is a good idea, at least the first time around. But a communications network requires continuous maintenance and modernization. It does not come into full being all at once and then remain static forevermore. There is evidence in some countries that communications systems installed by the government do not tend to change very rapidly or well.

GREENBERGER. This last question could be addressed to any one of the panelists, and is on many minds these days. David Crawford, a lawyer at the Securities and Exchange Commission, asks if it is possible to protect a time-sharing network adequately from unauthorized access. May a user, for example, gain information from one terminal which has been entered through another?

KEMENY. Yes, in answer to the last part of the question. It does not matter through which terminal you enter information. But this is the easy part of the question. The hard part is what protection can be provided against unauthorized access to a private file. I think this is a function of how high a price you are willing to pay. Protection is one of the outstanding features by which the MIT time-sharing system has been better than our system at Dartmouth College. With the kind of use we have on our system, privacy is not as crucial to us as it is to others.

I think that if you can stop people from physically gaining access or electronically tapping certain crucial pieces of equipment, you can build reasonably safe protection systems. But you can never be absolutely sure that the really first-rate systems programmer will not break your code.

PERLIS. The problem is not just a hardware-software problem. Ultimately it will find its solution in the courts, and a set of laws will be developed and precedents established concerning the sanctity of information as it relates to the Bill of Rights and common law. No system we build can guarantee by mechanical means that information will be seen only by the persons concerned or authorized.

DINNER DISCUSSION

GREENBERGER. Charles Holt has a point to raise with Kemeny.

HOLT. Perlis suggested there was a qualitative difference between the airline reservation problem and the job-placement problem, after Kemeny

Participants: Paul Baran, Institute for the Future; John Bertram, International Business Machines Corporation; Edward E. David, Jr., Bell Telephone Laboratories;

gave the impression that all we had to do was bring the computer to bear on the one as we did the other. Sometimes the computer is an essential part of a solution; but it is not at all obvious that we know enough about the job-placement problem, nor the student-counseling problem, to separate software from substantive aspects.

KEMENY. I have a point of view which is practically heresy in mathematics. Mathematicians look for optimum solutions; but in applying computers, I am ready to accept some meaningful advance over present methods.

A boy wanting to major in oceanography could not receive useful guidance from most high-school counselors; they generally have only a vague idea of the relative strength of various institutions. We once lost a brilliant prospect in mathematics to a school that did not have a single faculty member in the Mathematical Association of America, let alone one with a master's degree. But some counselor told the student this school had a great mathematics department, meaning he knew somebody who taught mathematics there.

Boys from city schools are sometimes routinely and incorrectly advised that they have no chance of getting into an Ivy League college. Or students are encouraged to apply to a school when they should be discouraged.

To achieve a really sophisticated counseling system, we would have to use psychology, sociology, and many other things; but I think a computer system can produce a great improvement over what we do today in just making facts available.[5]

DUBRIDGE. I agree. Students select colleges for the most trivial and irrelevant reasons. Usually the counselor only knows about schools within a fifteen-mile radius. If he is acquainted with somebody at a given school, he recommends it without concern for the student's interests or capacities.

We continually find students who did not apply to College X because their counselor told them they could never get in, despite their being at the top of their class and getting the highest College Board scores. No counselor can possibly know much about more than ten of the two thousand widely varying institutions in the country. If a push of the button could provide essential and factual information, that would be very useful, yet have little to do with psychology or sociology.

Lee A. DuBridge, Office of Science and Technology; B. O. Evans, International Business Machines Corporation; Robert M. Fano, Massachusetts Institute of Technology; Larkin H. Farinholt, The Alfred P. Sloan Foundation; George Feeney, General Electric Company; Lincoln Gordon, The Johns Hopkins University; Herbert R. J. Grosch, National Bureau of Standards; Charles C. Holt, The Urban Institute; Glenn Ingram, National Science Foundation; John G. Kemeny, Dartmouth College; Rep. Charles A. Mosher, House Committee on Science and Astronautics; Alan J. Perlis, Carnegie-Mellon University; Lawrence G. Roberts, Advanced Research Projects Agency, Department of Defense; James E. Rowe, Computer Applications Incorporated (formerly at Union Carbide Corporation); George Sadowsky, The Urban Institute; Bernard Strassburg, Federal Communications Commission; Dael Wolfle, University of Washington; Martin Greenberger, chairman, The Johns Hopkins University.

KEMENY. My own story might be of interest. I was a first-generation immigrant in a New York City high school, and not a very good one, but the guidance counselor took an interest in me. I knew I wanted to be a mathematician.

The counselor told me that to be a mathematician, I obviously must go to MIT. (At the time, MIT's mathematics department was at a relatively low point, not nearly as good as it is today.) But the counselor also gave me a most alluring and effective sales talk about the liberal education. She advised me to go to a university that did not specialize in things like mathematics; I could read philosophy and literature as an undergraduate, then go to MIT as a graduate student. That is how I happened to go to Princeton. At the time, Princeton had without doubt the greatest mathematics department in the world.

PERLIS. Some time ago, two gentlemen from the RAND Corporation published a mating algorithm in the Mathematical Monthly.[6] Each male or female lists his or her preferences in order. The algorithm provides an optimal set of mates, in the sense that everybody gets the best he or she could hope for in the competition.

If a computerized college placement service is really to be meaningful, once a student selects a school he should be dynamically and instantly notified that he is or is not yet accepted. Just providing information which could be obtained by opening a book is not enough. The student should be able to express his preferences and shift from one preference to another until he finds the school he most wants that will have him.

GORDON. This is close to what is done today to assign interns and residents to hospitals.

PERLIS. The universities must continually feed correct information into the data bank of the system. Harvard must make known in 1970 the distribution of students it accepted in 1969—the number from the East, Midwest, Far West—and the other imponderables that characterize the freshman class. What good is it for the student to know the best mathematics department is at Princeton if he does not have a chance of getting in?

HOLT. The point is there is more involved than just computers. There has been a tremendous effort already to build software systems for cities. Some people argue that city governments captured by the glamour of computers used these systems to accumulate low-quality, irrelevant data, not at all oriented to the important problems. The argument runs that the effort to automate has set cities back several years by misdirecting their energies. You cannot leave development of these systems to computer specialists. There are many horrible examples where the need was misconstrued. They were automating or computing when they should have been analyzing.

GREENBERGER. Let us consider the communications problem. Mr. Strassburg is involved with both sides of the communications industry.

STRASSBURG. Yes, I like to feel I represent the telephone company as well as its customers. The Federal Communications Commission is identified both with the companies it regulates and with the consumers in whose behalf it regulates.

FANO. Kemeny said that people using his time-sharing system from a moderate distance were paying more for communications than for computing. What is the problem?

KEMENY. Also, New England Telephone is completely incapable of handling a large regional computing center.

DUBRIDGE. Is there any telephone company in the country that is able to?

DAVID. I have heard that the Triangle Universities Computing Center in North Carolina has been extremely well handled by Southern Bell. Whether the communications cost is fair compared to the computing cost depends on whether the required computer and communications capital equipments are comparable. It is not self-evident that the communications facilities are somehow much less expensive than the computing facilities.

ROBERTS. The time-sharing user is paying for a facility which was not designed for him and is expensive to maintain. In the process, he is overloading the central exchange and costing Bell money. But there are ways to use the facilities efficiently. Leased lines, for example, can be very effective, if you use them properly. In the Advanced Research Projects Agency (ARPA) network, our own leased-line system costs under 10 percent of the total computer budget. We can send a thousand words anywhere in the country within a second for a penny.[7]

DUBRIDGE. How about the picturephone system, which allows us to see our secretary and colleagues on the phone? Is not an enormous communication investment required? Is it going to become cheap and reliable in a few years? Or is it a long-term proposition? How many telephone lines are needed to provide one picturephone channel?

DAVID. Three hundred, in round numbers; about one megahertz of bandwidth, according to present designs now being tried between New York and Pittsburgh.

DUBRIDGE. So it costs three hundred times as much for picturephone transmission as for regular phone service?

DAVID. No, nowhere near that. The cost will depend upon the FCC and the Bell company.

STRASSBURG. If I recollect Bell's estimates, by 1980 there will be a million picturephone subscribers.

ROBERTS. And transmission costs are going down rapidly.

FANO. Right, but the cost of switching worries me. We need a technology that makes it economically possible to charge by the bit actually transmitted. This requires fast message switching. The only extensive research done on this very difficult technical problem for large systems was by Paul Baran several years ago.[8] The ARPA network must be kept small, from my understanding, because each communication processor in it has a map of the entire system. This does not work for a large system, and techniques must be found for routing messages locally. The amount of research done on this problem has been minimal.

BARAN. The major communications cost of time sharing is not in short calls or local lines. It is the high tariffs and poor line utilization of calls to a computer more than fifty miles away. By gathering traffic together from many geographically distributed users, the ARPA system allows a potentially low overall system cost for communications.

It is odd that no entrepreneur has attempted to become the data-transmission common carrier of the future by sending short packages of bits between arbitrary points in the country at a low cost per package. Each large time-sharing system is already multiplexing its own lines. But a full economy of scale is impossible unless many time-sharing services concentrate their traffic. In Middletown, Connecticut, I can rent a terminal and a computer service from Stamford, Connecticut, for about six dollars an hour, whereas the telephone line costs about nine dollars an hour. There is room for improvement here.

GREENBERGER. This country is not known for the timidity of its entrepreneurs. Why have so few entered the data-communications business?

FANO. The entrepreneur's capital is relatively small. It disappears during the lengthy legal procedures.

GROSCH. The shape of the communications industry depends more on social than on technical considerations. One possible set of rules could maximize the creation of new businesses, another could encourage extension of the communications network to the Appalachian valleys, and a third could advance new technology (as Kemeny wants). No entrepreneur has any right to complain about the rules that existed when he went into business.

DAVID. I believe Bell ought to provide adequate data services. It could, in principle, take over the ARPA wide-band communication network idea and do something with it. But what would Western Union say?

STRASSBURG. Western Union would probably not be enthralled by the prospect, but let us make no mistake; Western Union is not under a protective umbrella of the Federal Communications Commission. Any private entrepreneur should be able to act as middleman in data communications.

FEENEY. Bunker-Ramo tried to be an entrepreneur and went down in flames.

STRASSBURG. If an entrepreneur cannot do it, the telephone company should, without a middleman, assuming efficient use can be made of existing communication facilities by a sharing arrangement. This requires breaking down the rate-making traditions of the Bell System, which is happening. The telephone companies are becoming responsive to the growing demands for more flexible, economical use of communication facilities, with some very deliberate prodding from the FCC.

GREENBERGER. B. O. Evans, what are your reactions?

EVANS. I think the problems are much deeper than Perlis or Bertram enumerated, but Kemeny's dissertation turns me on. He raises possibilities that I know are not being pursued by the computer industry, and I think we are going to see tremendous progress in unforeseeable forms many years sooner than anybody is predicting. I agree with Kemeny's thesis that we can plant seeds, fertilize them, water them, and they will grow into big trees. I personally believe the laws of supply and demand and the responsibilities of industries and the institutions can solve the problems a lot faster than we think. I also believe improvements in communications will come at a rapid pace.

GORDON. One of the examples used by Kemeny was the library and Dartmouth's growing bills. At Johns Hopkins, I am finding the bills very painful. Kemeny promoted his idea for an automated library at the MIT Lecture Series in 1961. Since then, eight years have passed out of the first twenty in which he anticipated nothing would happen. Why, precisely, has nothing happened?

KEMENY. When no one is charged with the responsibility for taking the initiative, nothing happens. There is no competent, funded group in the country whose charge it is to establish an automated library and apply computer technology to the solution of social problems.

DAVID. There has been an attempt to automate the reference process in the medical field, but it has not been wildly successful. It seems to me the real problem with the automated library is not technological; it is substantive—indexing, classifying, and so forth.

PERLIS. No, sir. Why do people write so many books that are not read? In the book store, 30 percent of the books never sell. In the library, 80 percent of the books have not been taken out for five years. Johns Hopkins does not need the books at Johns Hopkins, if it has information on where to get them. Now, if you have books centrally located, they have to be automatically scanned and therefore should be written to facilitate automatic scanning. We need books with large abstracts where the author anticipates and codes the questions readers will ask. He will have to learn to write in an artificial language. Otherwise, the system is going to fail. It will spend all its time scanning characteristics at very low rates of success and very large costs. People are going to have to give way to the system. The book business cannot remain as it is today.

GROSCH. Why should the most affluent society in the world have a computer system at its heels? We need a central receiver of information, but we also need the Firestone Library at Princeton, and other places where we can browse and enjoy real books with leather bindings.

KEMENY. My proposal was not to abolish university libraries, but just to cut them back to reasonable size. I think two hundred fifty thousand books (a fourth of the present Dartmouth library) is quite enough for browsing.

GREENBERGER. Jack Bertram, what are the prospects for a cheap time-sharing terminal?

BERTRAM. The television set is a terminal IBM has provided in some applications recently, and it is inexpensive by comparison with things used in the past. The keyboards are much cheaper than formerly, and very reliable. When you start talking about cheap terminals, however, you must decide whether you want them maintained or not.

ROWE. At Union Carbide, we have need for two classes of terminals: the slow-speed individual terminal, like the teletype, and the high-volume output terminal, like the line printer. They are both still too expensive.

FANO. I feel terminals must have graphic capabilities. One developed at MIT is now being sold commercially for nine thousand dollars. It is quite adequate but costs too much. It is all electronic and has no mechanical parts. With electronic equipment, mass production makes the difference. A television set is a complicated piece of equipment, but mass production makes it inexpensive. The terminal cannot be in mass production, however, until there is enough demand for it; and the demand will not grow until many people have used it to do useful things. The problem is how to break this vicious circle. It takes time, but I am not worried about having cheap terminals in the long run.

At MIT people have been writing papers directly into the computer from a time-sharing system. They can permit other people to read them, limit their use, or make them available to everybody. There is no need for printing. It may not be long before it is cheaper to store English text in computer mass memory than on paper. Once there are systems that permit access to many people, the demand for such memories will develop and costs will descend.

GREENBERGER. Dael Wolfle is the publisher of the very successful magazine *Science*. What do you think about the idea of doing away with printing?

WOLFLE. We have considered the possibility of selective distribution of material for *Science*. It is pretty costly, partly because so many elements of existing systems are geared to the old-fashioned standard method of publication. I doubt that it would cost the Post Office any more for us to send the reader a packet tailored to his interests, but under existing rules we can mail the magazine at second-class postal rates whereas individual mail costs more.

There is also the consideration of dividing the cost as widely as possible. The gas company used to send me a bill in an envelope with a return envelope enclosed. All I had to do was write a check. Now the bill comes on a post card and I have to hunt for an envelope. It costs the gas company a little less but me a little more.

The cost of handling *Science* the way we do is widely distributed over many people who contribute time instead of dollars. We can send all subscribers the same issue of *Science* once a week for twelve dollars a year. Advertisers are willing to pay a good deal of the cost. If we were to send *Science* on tape to the library, I do not know what the charge would be, but the subscription list would go down drastically and we would get no advertising. There is much inertia built into the system, and this argues for continuation of the present magazine format. We are considering alternatives, but they do not look very attractive.

GORDON. Law reporting is a field which occupies considerable space in both general and private libraries. The abstracting is already taken care of, and there is no advertising problem. The lawyer only wants the case that Shepard's Citations tells him is relevant, and classification indexing is highly developed.

I spent a day recently looking up some legal terms at the Johns Hopkins library. We have no law school nor law students, but we have a fully equipped law library. (I intend to ask our librarian why.) I was delighted that we had it on that day, but I would have been just as happy at a computer terminal connected to the law library at the University of Maryland or the Library of Congress. Has anyone tried to automate the referencing of law reports?

GROSCH. Project LITE [Legal Information Through Electronics] is now available inside the government.[9] It makes available through machines all of the Federal Code, and also state and specialized regulations.

FANO. The cost bottleneck will be broken by having automatic instead of physical transmission of information and a time-sharing system providing a great number of different services, like the telephone. It would be uneconomical to have one telephone for calling the doctor and another for calling the office. This is the reason for a network; each installation can specialize in a different service.

GREENBERGER. Robert Fano believes that a general-purpose time-sharing network is the economic answer. Does everyone agree?

EVANS. I do not agree at all. I think it might migrate to that in a hundred years or so, but it is starting with selective applications that are profitable and meaningful.

KEMENY. Surely you agree there would be great economy in having the same information-retrieval system for all fields.

EVANS. I am not certain. As a matter of fact, it might be the formula for failure. I think applications will be specialized and constantly evolving, and we are going to see dedicated systems for a long time.

FEENEY. This sounds very reminiscent of the discussion of special-purpose computers about twelve years ago.

GROSCH. Except now the discussion is about special-purpose software.

EVANS. We need general-purpose computers, general-purpose communication lines, and even general-purpose terminals. We also need some general-purpose software and a lot of dedicated software. I am simply saying the equation for success is not one giant network for all applications.

KEMENY. President Gordon would never spend the university's funds for an expensive terminal and network if all he could do was search for law precedents. But he might if the same terminal and network could be used for looking up books in mathematics, chemistry, and political science.

FANO. At MIT the physicists have found Myer Kessler's information-retrieval system for physics quite useful.[10] Before long they were asking if they could do some simple arithmetic on it; and they could, because it was embedded in a general-purpose time-sharing system. There are really no boundaries between information retrieval and other intellectual activities. You have to be very careful not to inject barriers.

GREENBERGER. Evans may be thinking primarily about commercial applications rather than intellectual activities.

ROBERTS. Does Evans envision many consoles in his office (one for each system), or a single console that reaches all systems?

EVANS. I think it feasible and proper for a single console to serve medicine, education, and law, if that is the way the user's requirement develops. But I think this is not going to be the case. The lawyer or doctor with a terminal in his office will be inquiring into the network for his particular specialty.

FANO. The issue is one of compatibility. It should be possible for the user to bring things from different fields to bear on his problem.

HOLT. We ought really to be talking about standards. At present, there is a tremendous amount of parallel, overlapping, low-quality, undocumented software that cannot be transferred from one computer to another. To put together a national network would require much more standardization than is now in sight.

KEMENY. One of the first things the National Computer Development Agency should do is sponsor a national conference of computer manufacturers and major users to agree on standards. The standards do not have to be elaborate: a code for communications, and two or three standard languages, like FORTRAN. We do not have to agree on a common machine language, nor on a physical format. The place for standards is at the user interface.

ROBERTS. Why do you need standards at all?

KEMENY. Because I think the political factor to which the agency would be most sensitive is the impression of favoring a given manufacturer. Each large city will probably have its own dedicated system, and it should be able to choose its own vendor.

ROBERTS. A network does not require that a machine be duplicated for different locations (which is where the manufacturer gets an edge). One system can be accessible from everywhere. In the kind of network I envision, the computer can be a thousand miles away or next door. A local computer with an interface program admits the user into the network and connects him to any system. It is a common mistake to assume that machines or languages have to be similar. Standards are almost impossible to enforce, and they are not necessary.

DAVID. What we are discussing is the transfer of programs and data bases from one machine to another. The right way to go about it depends on what we are trying to accomplish. In the telephone system, for example, we find it cheaper to let subscribers make free long-distance calls to remote cities for information service (now called directory assistance) than to keep all telephone books at each location.

If you want to transfer a program from one computer to another, the right way to do it is probably not by setting rigid standards but by applying modern technology. People at Bell Laboratories have used a macroprocessor written in FORTRAN to put the ALTRAN system into a form where it can be bootstrapped on any machine having at least a minimal FORTRAN-IV compiler.[11] Even though the macroprocessor can be written in a very inefficient, simplified form, the program it produces (for example, the ALTRAN compiler) is fine.

GROSCH. There are bright people contributing to the voluntary standards program in ANSI [American National Standards Institute, formerly called USASI]. They are backed up by laboratory work and administrative forces, and they still have difficulty. The committee goes home and everything stops until the next meeting.

FANO. Standards begin to take effect when people are interested in working together. In the past, there have not been standards because people preferred to go their own way, and there was little incentive to collaborate. Standards are created when people gain more from cooperation than competition. One of the advantages of Kemeny's suggestion is that it creates a vested interest in cooperation.

HOLT. We have had several years of free-wheeling evolution, and from where I sit as a computer user it has resulted in an utter shambles.

KEMENY. In spite of all the confusion, some standards have been enforced very effectively. The outstanding example was IBM's FORTRAN. People used it either the way IBM wrote it, or not at all; it was the best thing around.

Now it seems to me if you produce large software systems and say to the cities, "All right, if you want to use this, here it is; if not, go write your own," that is going to be very effective. You do not have to get total agreement.

HOLT. Bertram reacted negatively to Kemeny's proposal for a National Computer Development Agency. I wonder if he could elaborate on his position.

BERTRAM. I did not react negatively to the agency, but I did suggest that its role should be more one of reducing the cost of producing systems and developing tools and concepts rather than creating packages of software. Very little is being done on what I call software engineering. Let us contrast, for example, the production of software and hardware. For hardware, we have good design automation. We do much of the design in a high-level computer language like PL-1, and it is checked automatically for us. A small group of designers can do a great deal of work. But for software development, we go back to the most primitive computer language and start from the ground up. It has been said that programming is the only branch of engineering where instead of standing on our predecessor's shoulders we stand on his toes. People who produce large software systems are firmly convinced that they cannot write an efficient system in a high-level language. I think they are wrong. I think they could and should.

FANO. I have seen the electronics field mature from a time (1939) when attitudes in it were the same as in programming. World War II made the difference. People were forced to make things work, and they developed discipline in their engineering. This is going to happen in programming also.

BERTRAM. I think it is going to come, and it has got to come quickly; but let me make a point. The agency, if it existed, could establish a high-quality, high-level language suitable for building large software systems. There is already a certain amount of experience in this area. Subsets of PL-1 and extensions of FORTRAN have both done rather well. Eventually there will have to be a language that has optimizing features.

KEMENY. I completely agree that there is a need for a powerful, flexible, high-level language for systems programming. With annual funding of ten million dollars instead of five million, perhaps the agency could develop one. I would love to see it. On the other hand, I feel we cannot wait until it is developed to get started. I was trying to give the agency an easier job. Whether or not the agency turns out lovely software in the first two or three years is not important. There is no software for cities and states today, and that is a problem for society.

REFERENCES

1. John G. Kemeny and Thomas E. Kurtz, "Dartmouth Time-Sharing," *Science*, 162 (1968): 223–28; John McCarthy, "Time-Sharing Computer Systems," in *Computers and the World of the Future*, ed. Martin Greenberger, MIT Press, 1964.
2. John G. Kemeny, "A Library for 2000 A.D.," in *Computers and the World of the Future*, ed. Martin Greenberger, MIT Press, 1964.
3. Stanford Research Institute, *Report on the FCC Computer/Communications Inquiry*, vol. 1: *Policy Issues*, PB 183612, National Bureau of Standards Clearing House for Scientific and Technical Information, May 1969.

4. *Computers in Higher Education,* Report of the President's Science Advisory Committee, Panel on Computers in Higher Education, U.S. Government Printing Office, February 1967.
5. J. F. Cogswell and D. P. Estavan, "Explorations in Computer-Assisted Counseling," TM-2582, Systems Development Corporation, August 1965.
6. D. Gale and L. S. Shapley, "College Admissions and the Stability of Marriage," *American Mathematical Monthly,* 69 (1962): 9–15.
7. L. G. Roberts, "Resource Sharing Computer Networks," *IEEE International Convention Digest,* March 27, 1969.
8. Paul Baran et al., *On Distributed Communications,* vols. 1–13, The RAND Corp., August 1964. These are a series of RAND memoranda. Unclassified volumes are RM-3420-PR, RM-3103-PR, RM-3578-PR, RM-3638-PR, RM-3097-PR, RM-3762-PR, RM-3763-PR, RM-3764-PR, RM-3765-PR, RM-3766-PR, and RM-3767-PR.
9. "LITE, Legal Information Through Electronics," *JAG Law Review,* Special Issue 86, November-December 1966, pp. 1–51.
10. M. M. Kessler, "The M.I.T. Technical Information Project," *Physics Today,* March 1965.
11. W. S. Brown, "Software Portability," North Atlantic Treaty Organization Conference on Software Engineering, Working Papers, October 1969.

Editor's note: In August 1970 it was announced that Edward E. David, Jr., of Bell Telephone Laboratories would replace Lee A. DuBridge as Science Adviser to the President and director of the Office of Science and Technology.

DESIGNING ORGANIZATIONS FOR AN INFORMATION-RICH WORLD

Speaker   HERBERT A. SIMON

Richard King Mellon Professor of Computer Science and Psychology Carnegie-Mellon University

Discussants   KARL W. DEUTSCH

Professor of Government Harvard University

MARTIN SHUBIK

Professor of the Economics of Organization Yale University

Moderator   EMILIO Q. DADDARIO

Chairman of Subcommittee on Science, Research, and Development U.S. House of Representatives

DADDARIO. I was attracted to participate in this series by the appropriateness of the theme, *Computers, Communications, and the Public Interest*. Perhaps the title of the present session should be "Designing Organizations for an Information-Rich, *Communications-Poor, Problem-Overwhelmed World*." If anything characterizes the current age, it is the complex problems of our technological civilization and the unpleasant physical and mental trauma they induce. John W. Gardner and other social critics warn us that a nation can perish from internal strains: indifference, unwillingness to face problems, incapacity to respond to human suffering, failure to adapt to new conditions, and the waning energy of old age. Gardner speaks of the "waxwork of anachronisms" in government and the "impenetrable web of vested interests" in unions, professions, universities, and corporations. He argues for "a society (and institutions) capable of continuous change, continuous renewal, and continuous responsiveness."[1]

I see no room for complacency by the growing community devoted to communications and information processing in the face of the obvious needs of our society. Today we exchange a growing proportion of knowledge in new ways: via magnetic tapes, remote consoles wired to computers, national and international information networks, and large data banks. Expansion is so rapid, it is hard to document what is happening.

What concerns many of us is what I expect our speaker and discussants will be addressing in part. The creation of powerful computerized information systems, unless we take precautionary steps, may spawn new systems in Parkinsonian abandon, leading to quality-poor scientific and technical information. Furthermore, science can only flourish when it is untrammeled and open-ended. We must be careful not to institutionalize our information systems in such a way that they inhibit or interfere with this necessary freedom.

Herbert Simon is a member of the distinguished Panel on Technology Assessment of the National Academy of Sciences. I owe the panel a personal debt of gratitude for an outstanding report it recently completed on technology assessment.[2]

SIMON. If men do not pour new wine into old bottles, they do something almost as bad: they invest old words with new meanings. "Work" and "energy" are venerable English words, but since the Industrial and Scientific Revolutions they have acquired entirely new definitions. They have become more abstract and divorced from directly sensed qualities of human activity; and they have become more precise, finding expression in quantitative units of measurement (foot-pound, erg) and exact scientific laws (Conservation of Energy). The word "energy" uttered in a contemporary setting may represent quite different concepts and thought processes from the word "energy" uttered in the eighteenth century.

Old word meanings do not disappear; they tend to persist alongside the new. This is perhaps the most insidious part of what C. P. Snow has dubbed the problem of the two cultures. To know what a speaker means by "energy" it is not enough to know what century he is speaking in, but also whether his talk belongs to the common culture or the scientific culture. If the former, his words should not be credited with the quantitative precision that belongs to the latter; and if the latter, his words should not be interpreted vaguely or metaphorically.

Old Words in New Meanings

All of this is preliminary to raising a difficulty I must hurdle to communicate. I intend to use familiar words like "information," "thinking," and "organization," but not with the meanings that the common culture has attached to them over the centuries. During the past twenty-five years these words have begun to acquire new, increasingly precise and quantitative meanings. Words associated with the generation and conversion of information are today undergoing a change of meaning as drastic as that experienced by words associated with the generation and conversion of energy in the eighteenth and nineteenth centuries.

Within the common culture, one cannot carry on a twentieth-century conversation about energy with a physicist or engineer. Similarly, it is increasingly difficult to carry on a twentieth-century conversation about information with a social scientist who belongs to the humanistic rather than scientific subculture of his discipline. The difficulty does not stem from jargon but from a complete disparity of meanings hidden behind a superficially common language.

What do I mean when I say: "Machines think"? The word "machine" seems obvious enough: a modern electronic digital computer. But "machine" has all sorts of unintended humanistic overlays. A machine, in the common culture, moves repetitively and monotonously. It requires direction from outside. It is inflexible. With the slightest component failure or mismanagement it degenerates into senseless or random behavior.

A computer may exhibit none of these mechanical properties. While retaining the word "machine" in the scientific culture as a label for a computer, I have revised drastically the associations stored with the word in my memory. When I say "Machines think," I am *not* referring to devices that behave repetitively and inflexibly, require outside guidance, and often become random.

The word "think" itself is even more troublesome. In the common culture it denotes an unanalyzed, partly intuitive, partly subconscious and unconscious, sometimes creative set of mental processes that sometimes allows humans to solve problems, make decisions, or design something. What do these mental processes have in common with the processes computers follow when they execute their programs?

The common culture finds almost nothing in common between them. One reason is that human thinking has never been described, only labeled. Certain contemporary psychological research, however, has been producing computer programs that duplicate the human information processing called thinking in considerable detail.[3] When a psychologist who has been steeped in this new scientific culture says "Machines think," he has in mind the behavior of computers governed by such programs. He means something quite definite and precise that has no satisfactory translation into the language of the common culture. If you wish to converse with him (which you well may not!) you will have to follow him into the scientific culture.

As the science of information processing continues to develop, it will not be as easy to sequester it from the main stream of managerial activity (or human social activity) as it was to isolate the physical sciences and their associated technologies. Information processing is at the heart of executive activity, indeed at the heart of all social interaction. More and more we are finding occasion to use terms like "information," "thinking," "memory," and "decision making" with twentieth-century scientific precision. The language of the scientific culture occupies more and more of the domain previously reserved to the common culture.

Make no mistake about the significance of this change in language. It is a change in thought and concepts. It is a change of the most fundamental kind in man's thinking about his own processes—about himself.

The Scarcity of Attention

My title speaks of "an information-rich world." How long has the world been rich in information? What are the consequences of its prosperity, if that is what it is?

Last Easter, my neighbors bought their daughter a pair of rabbits. Whether by intent or accident, one was male, one female, and we now live in a rabbit-rich world. Persons less fond than I am of rabbits might even describe it as a rabbit-overpopulated world. Whether a world is rich or poor in rabbits is a relative matter. Since food is essential for biological populations, we might judge the world as rabbit-rich or rabbit-poor by relating the number of rabbits to the amount of lettuce and grass (and garden flowers) available for rabbits to eat. A rabbit-rich world is a lettuce-poor world, and vice versa.

The obverse of a population problem is a scarcity problem, hence a resource-allocation problem. There is only so much lettuce to go around, and it will have to be allocated somehow among the rabbits. Similarly, in an information-rich world, the wealth of information means a dearth of something else: a scarcity of whatever it is that information consumes. What information consumes is rather obvious: it consumes the attention of its recipients. Hence a wealth of information creates a poverty of attention and a need to allocate that attention efficiently among the overabundance of information sources that might consume it.

To formulate an allocation problem properly, ways must be found to measure the quantities of the scarce resource; and these quantities must not be expandable at will. By now, all of us have heard of the *bit*, a unit of information introduced by Shannon in connection with problems in the design of communication systems.[4] Can we use the bit as a measure of an information-processing system's capacity for attention?

Unfortunately, it is not the right unit. Roughly, the trouble is that the bit capacity of any device (or person) for receiving information depends entirely upon how the information is encoded. Bit capacity is not an invariant, hence is an unsuitable measure of the scarcity of attention.

A relatively straightforward way of measuring how much scarce resource a message consumes is by noting how much time the recipient spends on it. Human beings, like contemporary computers, are essentially serial devices. They can attend to only one thing at a time. This is just another way of saying that attention is scarce. Even the modern time-sharing systems which John Kemeny described are really only doing one thing at a time, although they seem able to attend to one hundred things at once.[5] They achieve this illusion by sharing their time and attention among these hundred things. The attention-capacity measure I am proposing for human beings applies as well to time-sharing systems and also to an organization employing many people, which can be viewed as a time-sharing system.

Scarcity of attention in an information-rich world can be measured in terms of a human executive's time. If we wish to be precise, we can define a standard executive (IQ of 120, bachelor's degree, and so on) and ask Director Lewis Branscomb to embalm him at the National Bureau of Standards. Further, we can work out a rough conversion between the attention units of human executives and various kinds of computers.

In an information-rich world, most of the cost of information is the cost incurred by the recipient. It is not enough to know how much it costs to produce and transmit information; we must also know how much it costs, in terms of scarce attention, to receive it. I have tried bringing this argument home to my friends by suggesting that they recalculate how much the *New York Times* (or *Washington Post*) costs them, including the cost of reading it. Making the calculation usually causes them some alarm, but not enough for them to cancel their subscriptions. Perhaps the benefits still outweigh the costs.

Having explained what I mean by an information-rich world, I am now ready to tackle the main question. How can we design organizations, business firms, and government agencies to operate effectively in such a world? How can we arrange to conserve and effectively allocate their scarce attention?

I shall proceed with the help of three examples, each illustrating a major aspect of the problem of organizational design. I make no attempt to cover all significant problem areas, and any fancied resemblance of my hypothetical organizations to real organizations, living or dead, in the city of Washington, are illusory, fortuitous, and the product of the purest happenstance.

Information Overload

Many proposals for eliminating *information overload* (another phrase to describe life in an information-rich world) call for a new computing system. There is good precedent for this. The Hollerith punched card is a creative product of the Census Bureau's first bout with information overload, and a series of crises in the central exchanges of the phone company led to the invention of automatic switching systems.

Today, some argue that the postal service is doomed to collapse from information overload unless means are found to automate the sorting operations. This cannot be so. There is no reason why mail-sorting costs should increase more than proportionally with the volume of mail, nor why unit costs should rise with volume. A major cause of the problem is that certain information-processing services are almost free, resulting in an explosive demand for them. The Post Office is not really prepared to provide this implicit subsidy and reneges by performing the services badly, with insufficient resources. The crisis in the Post Office does not call for computers; it calls for a thoroughgoing application of price and market mechanisms.

This is not to argue that any particular manual Post Office operation, such as sorting, cannot be made more economical by computer. This kind of technical question is settled by cost-benefit analysis within reasonable limits of error and debate. But there is no magic in automation that allows it to resolve dilemmas posed by an organization's unwillingness or inability to allocate and price scarce information-processing resources, whether the resources are sorting clerks or electronic devices. Free or underpriced resources are always in desperately short supply. What is sometimes alleged to be technological lag in the Post Office is really failure of nerve.

A computer is an information-processing system of quite general capability. It can receive information, store it, operate on it in a variety of ways, and transmit it to other systems. Whether a computer will contribute to the solution of an information-overload problem, or instead compound it, depends on the distribution of its own attention among four classes of activities: listening, storing, thinking, and speaking. A general design principle can be put as follows:

An information-processing subsystem (a computer or new organization unit) will reduce the net demand on the rest of the organization's attention only if it absorbs more information previously received by others than it produces—that is, if it listens and thinks more than it speaks.

To be an attention conserver for an organization, an information-processing system (abbreviated IPS) must be an information condenser. It is conventional to begin designing an IPS by considering the information it will *supply*. In an information-rich world, however, this is doing things backwards. The crucial question is how much information it will allow to be *withheld* from the attention of other parts of the system.

Basically, an IPS can perform an attention-conserving function in two ways: (1) it can receive and store information that would otherwise have to be received by other systems, and (2) it can transform or *filter* input information into output that demands fewer hours of attention than the input.

To illustrate these two modes of attention conservation, let me talk about some of the information needs of a nation's Foreign Office. (Since the United States has a State Department and not a Foreign Office, I am obviously talking about some other country.) The bulk of information that enters a system from the environment is irrelevant to action at the time of entry. Much of it will never be relevant, but we cannot be sure in advance which part this is.

One way to conserve Foreign Office attention is to interpose an IPS (human, automated, or both) between environment and organization to index and store information on receipt. A second way is to have an IPS analyze, draw inferences from, and summarize the information received, then index and store the products of its analyses for use by the rest of the system.

This proposal has a familiar ring about it. I have simply described in unconventional language the conventional functions of a conventional intelligence unit. Moreover, I have solved the information-overload problem simply by adding information processors. I eliminated scarcity by increasing the supply of scarce resources. Any fool with money can do that.

But the very banality of my solution carries an important lesson. The functional design an IPS must have to conserve attention is largely independent of specific hardware, automated or human. Hardware becomes a concern only later in economic considerations.

My proposal, however, is actually far less conventional than it sounds. If the IPS is to be even partly automated, we must provide precise descriptions (in the language of the scientific culture) of the processes denoted by vague terms like "analyze" and "summarize." Even if we do *not* intend to automate the process, the new information-processing technology still will permit us to formulate the programs of human analysts and summarizers with precision so that we can predict reliably the relation between inputs and outputs. Looking more closely at the structure and operation of the IPS, we see it really will not resemble a traditional intelligence unit very closely at all. (My thinking on this problem has benefited greatly from acquaintance with the analyses that have been made over the past several years of information-processing requirements in the U.S. State Department.

These planning activities have been laudably free from premature obsession with automated hardware.)

The purpose of the intelligence IPS I have proposed is not to *supply* the Foreign Office with information but to *buffer* it from the overrich environment of information in which it swims. Information does not have to be attended to (*now*) just because it exists in the environment. Designing an intelligence system means deciding: when to gather information (much of it will be preserved indefinitely in the environment if we do not want to harvest it now); where and in what form to store it; how to rework and condense it; how to index and give access to it; and when and on whose initiative to communicate it to others.

The design principle that attention is scarce and must be preserved is very different from a principle of "the more information the better." The aforementioned Foreign Office thought it had a communications crisis a few years ago. When events in the world were lively, the teletypes carrying incoming dispatches frequently fell behind. The solution: replace the teletypes with line printers of much greater capacity. No one apparently asked whether the IPS's (including the Foreign Minister) that received and processed messages from the teletypes would be ready, willing, and able to process the much larger volume of messages from the line printers.

Everything I have said about intelligence systems in particular applies to management information systems in general. The proper aim of a management information system is not to bring the manager all the information he needs, but to reorganize the manager's environment of information so as to reduce the amount of time he must devote to receiving it. Restating the problem this way leads to a very different system design.

The Need to Know

That brings me to the question of *the need to know*. How do we go about deciding where information should be stored in an information-rich world and who should learn about it?

Those of us who were raised during the Great Depression sometimes do not find it easy to adapt to an affluent society. When we ate potatoes, we always ate the peel (which my mother insisted was the best part of the potato). Nonreturnable containers seem to us symbols of intolerable waste.

Our attitudes toward information reflect the culture of poverty. We were brought up on Abe Lincoln walking miles to borrow (and return!) a book and reading it by firelight. Most of us are constitutionally unable to throw a bound volume into the wastebasket. We have trouble enough disposing of magazines and newspapers. Some of us are so obsessed with the need to know that we feel compelled to read everything that falls into our hands, although the burgeoning of the mails is helping to cure us of this obsession.

If these attitudes were highly functional in the world of clay tablets, scribes, and human memory; if they were at least tolerable in the world of the printing press and the cable; they are completely maladapted to the world of broadcast systems and Xerox machines.

The change in information-processing technology demands a fundamental change in the meaning attached to the familiar verb "to know." In the common culture, "to know" meant to have stored in one's memory in a way that facilitates recall when appropriate. By metaphoric extension, "knowing" might include having access to a file or book containing information, with the skill necessary for using it.

In the scientific culture, the whole emphasis in "knowing" shifts from the storage or actual physical possession of information to the process of using or having access to it. It is possible to have information stored without having access to it (the name on the tip of the tongue, the lost letter in the file, the unindexed book, the uncatalogued library); and it is possible to have access to information without having it stored (a computer program for calculating values of the sine function, a thermometer for taking a patient's temperature).

If a library holds two copies of the same book, one of them can be destroyed or exchanged without the system's losing information. In the language of Shannon's information theory, multiple copies make the library *redundant*. But copies are only one of three important forms of redundancy in information. Even if a library has only one copy of each book, it still has a high degree of informational overlap. If half the titles in the Library of Congress were destroyed at random, little of the world's knowledge would disappear.

The most important and subtle form of redundancy derives from the world's being highly lawful. Facts are random if no part of them can be predicted from any other part—that is, if they are independent of each other. Facts are lawful if certain of them *can* be predicted from certain others. We need store only the fraction needed to predict the rest.

This is exactly what science is: the process of replacing unordered masses of brute fact with tidy statements of orderly relations from which these facts can be inferred. The progress of science, far from cluttering up the world with new information, enormously increases the redundancy of libraries by discovering the orderliness of the information already stored. With each important advance in scientific theory, we can reduce the volume of explicitly stored knowledge without losing any information whatsoever. That we make so little use of this opportunity does not deny that the opportunity exists.

Let me recite an anecdote that illustrates the point very well. We are all aware that there is a DDT problem. DDT is one of technology's mixed blessings. It is very lethal to noxious insects, but uncomfortably persistent and cumulatively harmful to eagles, game fish, and possibly ourselves. The practical problem is how to enjoy the agricultural and medical benefits afforded by the toxicity of DDT without suffering the consequences of its persistence.

A distinguished chemist of my acquaintance, who is a specialist neither in insecticides nor biochemistry, asked himself this question. He was able to write down the approximate chemical structure of DDT by decoding its name. He could recognize from general theoretical principles the component radicals in the structural formula that account for its toxicity. The formula also told him on theoretical grounds why the substance is persistent and why the molecule does not decompose readily or rapidly. He asked, again on theoretical grounds, what compound would have the toxicity of DDT but decompose readily. He was able to write down its formula and saw no theoretical reason why it could not easily be produced. (All of this took ten minutes.)

A phone call to an expert in the field confirmed all his conjectures. The new compound he had "invented" was a well-known insecticide, which had been available commercially before DDT. It is not as lethal as DDT over as broad a band of organisms but is nearly so, and it decomposes fairly readily. I do not know if the new-old chemical "solves" the DDT problem. The durability of DDT was intended by its inventors to avoid frequent respraying and reduce the costs of treatment. There may be other economic issues, and even chemical and biological ones.

What the story illustrates is that good problem-solving capacities combined with powerful (but compact) theories (and an occasional telephone call) may take the place of shelves of reference books. It may often be more efficient to leave information in the library of nature, to be extracted by experiment or observation when needed, than to mine and stockpile it in man's libraries, where retrieval costs may be as high as the costs of recreating information from new experiments or deriving it from theory.

These considerations temper my enthusiasm for using new technology to store and retrieve larger and larger bodies of data. I do not mean to express a blanket disapproval of all proposals to improve the world's stores of information. But I do believe we must design IPS's with data-analysis capabilities able to keep up with our propensities to store vast bodies of data.

Today's computers are moronic robots, and they will continue to be so as long as programming remains in its present primitive state. Moronic robots can sop up, store, and spew out vast quantities of information. They do not and cannot exercise due respect for the scarce attention of the recipients of this information. Computers must be taught to behave at a higher level of intelligence. This will take a large, vigorous research and development effort.

In a knowledge-rich world, progress does not lie in the direction of reading and writing information faster or storing more of it. Progress lies in the direction of extracting and exploiting the patterns of the world so that far less information needs to be read, written, or stored. Progress depends on our ability to devise better and more powerful thinking programs for man and machine.

Technology Assessment

Attention is *generally* scarce in organizations, *particularly* scarce at the tops, and *desperately* scarce at the top of the organization called the United States Government. There is only one President. Although he is assisted by the Budget Bureau, the Office of Science and Technology, and other elements of the Executive Office, a frightening array of matters converges on this single, serial, human information-processing system.

There is only one Congress of the United States. It can operate in parallel through committees, but every important matter must occupy the attention of many Congressmen. Highly important matters may claim the time and attention of all.

There is only one body of citizens in the United States. Large public problems such as the Vietnam War, civil rights, student unrest, the cities, and environmental quality (to mention five near the top of the current agenda) periodically require a synchrony of public attention. This is more than enough to crowd the agenda to the point of unworkability or inaction.

Congressman Daddario has devoted a great deal of thought in recent years to improving the procedures in society and government for dealing with the new technology we produce so prodigiously. At the request of his House Subcommittee on Science, Research, and Development, a panel of the National Academy of Sciences on which I served recently prepared the report on technology assessment to which he referred.

Technology assessment is not just a matter of determining the likely good and bad effects of new technological developments. Even less is it a matter of making sure, before new technology is licensed, that it will have no undesirable effects. The dream of thinking everything out before we act, of making certain we have all the facts and know all the consequences, is a sick Hamlet's dream. It is the dream of someone with no appreciation of the seamless web of causation, the limits of human thinking, or the scarcity of human attention.

The world outside is itself the greatest storehouse of knowledge. Human reason, drawing upon the pattern and redundancy of nature, can predict some of the consequences of human action. But the world will always remain the largest laboratory, the largest information store, from which we will learn the outcomes, good and bad, of what we have done. Of course it is costly to learn from experience; but it is also costly, and frequently much less reliable, to try through research and analysis to anticipate experience.

Technology assessment is an intelligence function. If it operated perfectly, which it is certain not to, it would do two things for us. First, it would warn us before our taking action of the really dangerous (especially the irreversibly dangerous) consequences possible from proposed innovations. Second, it would give us early warning of unanticipated consequences of innovations as they became visible, before major irreversible damage had been done. In performing both of these functions, technology assessment would be mindful of the precious scarcity of attention. It would put on the agenda only items needing attention and action (including the action of gathering information to evaluate the need for further attention).

A phrase like "technology assessment" conjures up a picture of scientific competence and objectivity, deliberateness and thoughtfulness, concern for the long run, and a systems view that considers all aspects and consequences. But these desirable qualities of a decision-making system cannot be imposed without considering the organizational and political environment of the system.

As our scientific and engineering knowledge grows, so does the power of our actions. They have consequences ramifying over vast reaches of space and time. The growth of knowledge allows us to recognize consequences we would have been ignorant of or ignored before. We are able to make bigger waves and at the same time have more sensitive instruments to detect the rocking of the boat. Today we sterilize and quarantine everything that travels between earth and moon. Less than five hundred years ago we diffused tuberculosis, smallpox, and syphilis throughout the Americas in happy ignorance.

The injunction to take account of *all* effects conjures up the picture of an integral stretching out through space and time without ever converging. We must assume, as mankind has always assumed, that a reasonable allocation of our limited attention and powers of thought will solve the crucial problems facing us at least as fast as new ones arise. If that assumption is wrong, there is no help for us. If it is right, then technology assessment becomes part and parcel of the task of setting an agenda for society and government.

To bring the notion of technology assessment out of the realm of abstraction, let me go back to the example of DDT. Although I have not researched the history of DDT, I believe it was introduced on a large scale without thorough (or at least adequate) study of its potential cumulative danger in the atmosphere and in organisms (especially predators). It was hailed for its agricultural and medical benefits as one of technology's miracles. Now, some decades later, we learn that the miracle has a flaw.

The possible adverse effects of DDT have been known to specialists for some time. They were probably even known, but ignored, at the time DDT was introduced. If so, this would underscore my fundamental theme of the scarcity of attention.

Suppose the dangers of DDT were not known beforehand but were discovered only in the laboratory of nature. Then, with apologies to eagle lovers, I am not sure that we (or even the eagles) have suffered unconscionable or irreversible loss by letting actual use tell us about DDT rather than trying to anticipate this experience in advance. Technology assessment has been (and is being) made by the environment. We are getting signals from the environment calling attention to some of its findings, and these signals are strong enough to deserve and get our attention. The DDT issue has been claiming attention intermittently for some months, with the loudest environmental signal being the detection of DDT in Great Lakes game fish. The issue is now high enough on the agenda of newspapers, courts, and committees to bring action.

I know this sounds complacent, and I really do not feel complacent. But it serves no useful social purpose to treat with anguish and hand-wringing every public problem which by hindsight might have been avoided if we had been able to afford the luxury of more foresight. Now that we *know* the problems, we should address them rather than hold inquests about who should have seen the problems earlier.

Our information about the effects of DDT and of long-continued diffuse contamination is in many respects unsatisfactory. (So is our information about almost any issue of public policy.) But this does not mean we could improve the situation by massive collection of data. On the contrary, we mainly need carefully aimed, high-quality biological investigations of the cause and effect mechanisms underlying the diffusion and metabolism of DDT. After we understand better the chemistry and biology of the problem we might make sense of masses of data, but then we probably would not need as much.

First-rate biologists and chemists capable of doing the required research are in as short supply as most other high-quality information-processing systems. Their attention is an exceedingly scarce commodity, and we are unlikely to capture much of it soon. The practical question, as always, is how to deal with the situation given the scrappy, inadequate data we now have.

We begin to ask questions like these: Assuming the worst possible case for the harmful effects of DDT, what is the magnitude of the effects in human, economic, and ecological terms, and to what extent are these effects irreversible? In the same terms, what would it cost us to do without DDT? What is the next best alternative?

These are common-sense questions. We do not have to know anything about the technology to ask them, although we might learn something about it from the answers. The most effective IPS for getting answers consists of a telephone, a Xerox machine (to copy documents the telephone correspondents suggest), and some very bright professionals (not necessarily specialists) who do know something about the technology. With this retrieval system, just about anything in the world now known on the problem can be extracted in a few man-weeks of work. (The time required goes up considerably if hearings and briefings are held or a research project is organized.)

There are numerous locations inside and outside the federal government where the questions may be asked. They may be asked by the Office of Science and Technology, the National Academy of Sciences, the National Academy of Engineering, the RAND Corporation, Resources for the Future, or a Congressional committee. (An excellent example of the last is the recent series of reports on steam-powered automobiles.)

The location of the investigating group is significant from only one standpoint, which may be crucial. The location of the group can determine the attention it commands and the legitimacy accorded its findings. These are interdependent but by no means identical matters.

Legitimacy may sometimes be achieved (and even attention secured) by the usual credentials of science: the right degrees, professional posts, and reputations. But many an impeccable report is ignored, and many a report without proper credentials gains a high place on the agenda. The Ralph Naders of the world demonstrate that writing and speaking forcefully, understanding the mass media, and being usually right about the facts can compensate for missing union cards and lack of access to organizational channels. Rachel Carson showed that even literary excellence is sometimes enough to turn the trick.

I agree with Congressman Daddario that we can and should strengthen and make more effective the processes of technology assessment in our country. We shall still need the world itself as a major laboratory, but we may be able to substitute foresight for hindsight to a modest extent. Did we have to wait until all Los Angeles wept before doing anything about automobile exhausts? Well-financed institutions for technology assessment should be spending a hundred million dollars a year instead of ten million to find out whether the steam automobile offers a long-term solution to the smog problem. Our current measures are temporary expedients at best.

Strengthening technology assessment means improving our procedures for setting the public agenda. It does not mean pressing more information and problems on an already burdened President, Congress, and public. In an information-rich world, there is no special virtue in prematurely early warnings. Let the world store information for us until we can focus attention and thought on it.

Assessing Information-Processing Technology

The final issue I should like to address is itself a problem in technology assessment. The science and technology of information processing is only a quarter-century old, and we have merely the faintest glimmerings of what it will be like after another quarter-century. How shall we assess it and make sure it develops in socially beneficial ways?

The most visible and superficially spectacular part of the technology is its hardware: computers, typewriter consoles, cathode-ray tubes, and associated gadgets. These devices give us powerful new ways for recording, storing, processing, and writing information to improve and replace the human IPS's with which we had to make do throughout man's history.

By itself, the hardware does not solve any organizational problems, including the problems of attention scarcity. The hardware boxes will begin to make inroads on these problems only as we begin to understand information-processing systems well enough to conceive sophisticated programs for them—programs that will permit them to think at least as well as man does.

Each step we take toward increasing our sophistication and scientific knowledge about the automated IPS also increases our sophistication and scientific knowledge about the human IPS, about man's thought processes. What we are acquiring with the new technology is something of deep significance—a science of human thinking and organization.[6]

The armchair is no more effective a scientific instrument for understanding this new technology than it was for previous technologies. If we are to understand information processing, we must study it in the laboratory of nature. We must construct, program, and operate many kinds of information-processing systems to see what they do and how they perform.

Our first systems have performed and will perform in all sorts of unexpected ways (most of them stupid), and by hindsight they seem incredibly crude. They will never pass a cost-effectiveness test on their operating performance, and we shall have to write them off as research and development efforts. From their behavior, we may learn that the new technology contains dangers as well as promises. There already is considerable concern about threats to privacy that the new technology might create. Such concerns will be mere armchair speculations until they are tested against a broad base of experience.

Very early in the computer era, I advised several business firms not to acquire computers until they knew exactly how to use them and pay for them. I soon realized this was bad advice. Computers initially pay their way by educating large numbers of people about computers. They are the principal forces for replacement of the vague, inadequate common-culture meanings of words in the information-processing vocabulary by the sharp, rich, scientific meanings these words must have in the future.

I think this points to a clear public policy for understanding and assessing the new technology. We need greatly increased public support for research and development efforts of as varied a nature as possible. They should certainly include network experiments of the sort John Kemeny envisages. They should include data-bank experiments. Above all, they should include experiments in robotry, large-scale memory organization, and artificial intelligence, leading to a basic foundation for a science of information processing.

Past experience suggests that a program pursued in the experimental spirit I have indicated will have valuable by-products. List processing is an esoteric development of computer-programming languages that was motivated initially about fifteen years ago by pure research interests in artificial intelligence. Today, its concepts are deeply imbedded in the design of large programming and operating systems regularly used in accounting and engineering computation.

The exploration of the moon is a great adventure. After the moon, there are objects still farther out in space. But man's inner space, his mind, is less well known than the space of the planets. It is time we establish a national policy to explore this inner space systematically, with goals, timetables, and budgets. Will you think me whimsical or impractical if I propose that one of these goals be a world-champion chess-playing computer program by 1975; and another, an order-of-magnitude increase by 1980 in the speed with which a human being can learn a difficult school subject, such as a foreign language or arithmetic?

If we are willing to dedicate ourselves to national goals of this kind (if you do not like my two, substitute your own), set deadlines for them, and commit resources to them (as we have committed resources to exploration of outer space), I think we soon shall have an understanding of both the information processors we call computers and those we call man. This understanding will enable us to build organizations far more effectively in the future than has ever been possible before.

PANEL DISCUSSION

DEUTSCH. The speaker has given us an example of a good information-processing program by his own definition. His remarks represent a program which does not immediately produce all the answers, but sets into motion a process which eventually may well generate them. He has done this by giving us some highly simplified versions of his important and profound thought. But they seem overly simple on two points.

Simon has suggested that information overload could be relieved by better pricing policies. I think he implied that when anything is offered free, the demands for it become infinite. I do not know what goes on at the water cooler in his office, but I shudder at the vision of money being charged for drinking water, and licenses for breathing oxygen being marketed among the more affluent citizens of Los Angeles! Social scientists, including Simon, know cases well where the price mechanism is neither the only nor the best way to distribute a good. At zero cost, if the supply of a good is well ahead of the demand, demand does not automatically grow to infinity. It may increase, but the rate of increase is a matter of empirical fact, and it need not be very fast.

The second notion that disturbed me even more for professional reasons was the splendid and provocative way Simon put before us a general theory of knowledge of a "try and see" type. He was obviously thinking of computers when he advised us not to be quite so fearful of the possible damages but to experiment and see what happens. If things go a little wrong, we will learn from the damage. After all, even DDT may have done more good than harm during the decades of its first application.

I do not know enough about DDT or ecology to have an opinion on this point. But one of my special interests is the study of international politics, and I tremble when I translate Simon's advice into this field. There we developed many interests in distant countries and strange peoples, together with supposedly adequate methods for gathering and evaluating information about them. We thought we had an adequate political intelligence system in the broadest sense, military and civilian, perhaps because of our fascination with a technology which permits faster transmission of mistaken estimates and faster transportation of misinformed officials. Our government acted on what it thought was information about Southeast Asia. We sent half a million men there, and back came some more information; also forty thousand bodies in plastic bags.

In foreign policy, at least, I should warn of the old-fashioned approach to pragmatism that says, "Let's go in and try and see what happens." I remember too readily the story of the man who fell off the top of the Empire State Building and on passing the second floor said, "On pragmatic grounds, so far things have been going well."

To make the case more general, if relatively little power is involved, the amount of damage possible from neglecting early warnings or not making forecasts is limited. The more powerful an operation, the more foresight becomes necessary to avoid fatal damage. The faster an automobile, the farther ahead must its headlights cast their beam.

As modern technology becomes more powerful, we need what my colleague John Platt calls anticipatory or crisis research:[7] determining at which point current problems are likely to reach critical mass. I think Simon himself is one of the people who is very likely to contribute to this work, but under the pressures of speaking quickly and popularly he is in danger of giving an impression of cheerful pragmatism, telling all the "nervous Nellies" not to worry. Political scientists would not agree.

Having been critical, let me say how delighted I am with the important intellectual contributions which I think are made in Simon's paper. I believe there are four major contributions:

1. the economy of attention is itself put into the focus of the analysis;
2. attention economy is proposed as a design criterion for large organizations;

3. knowledge is defined as access to information, or the procedure of its retrieval, rather than its storage;
4. emphasis is put on producing information-recreating programs, programs whose economically small number of units and operating rules can regenerate information more cheaply and perhaps more quickly than storage and retrieval of the information itself.

Simon has put before us the problem of attention overload. The population of the world doubles every thirty-five to forty years. Since most of these people want to be heard from, information will increase proportionately to the population. Simon says this is all it will increase. I beg respectfully to differ.

The per capita income of people in the world goes up 2 percent a year, and the richer they get, the more they spend on services involving information. The total information load, therefore, goes up not 2 percent a year with population, but 4 to 5 percent a year with income. That is, it doubles about every eighteen years. In addition, almost 1 percent of the work force in the United States in recent years has shifted from production-line labor or material handling into knowledge-handling or symbol-manipulating occupations.

I have recently seen a curve telling the same story for Czechoslovakia from 1929 to 1965. The curve shows that the change-over to a Communist regime did not seem to make the slightest difference in this trend. The shift from proletarians to paper shufflers goes on under Communism as much as anywhere else! The tendency toward knowledge handling increases all the time.

Finally, about every four or five years in the last quarter-century a critical threshold has been broken, demanding new thinking. Examples include nuclear energy, the mass culture of television, interplanetary transportation, footprints on the moon, the change of universities from elite to mass institutions, and many others.

For these reasons, there will be much more information overload in the future than there has been in the past. The information pressure will at the very least, in my estimation, double every twelve to fifteen years.

There are, to be sure, various ways of dealing with overload:
1. skipping;
2. delay or forming waiting lines;
3. chunking, or doing things in large batches;
4. doing things in a shoddy way, or quickly, and accepting a large measure of error;
5. (the method which Simon prefers) filtering or reducing the information.

With filtering, once again in my own field I am frightened of the results. Lyndon B. Johnson was one of the best-filtered chief executives this country has ever had. He had secretaries, White House staff, and an environment that very carefully gave him largely one kind of information. When a man like George Ball sometimes got the thankless task of serving as the devil's advocate, the devil got relatively little prime time and very little backing!

We run large risks of failure in coping with the problems of our cities, the poor, the races, international politics, arms control, verterans' systems, and all the rest, if our main preoccupation is to save executives from looking at too much uncongenial information. The uncongenial information may be the vital information.

This leads to the question of filter design. How do you make a filter intelligent enough to understand what to let through and what to screen out? The only approach I know is to analyze the operations involved in "attention." There are six:

1. *recognize* loosely what it is one should pay attention to (the target), such as things unfamiliar, strangers, or things that do not fit;
2. *track* the object of attention, and keep attention on it;
3. *interpret* the object and ask what it resembles;
4. *decide which response* to the object is most appropriate, and what should be done about it;
5. *carry out* the response;
6. *accept feedback,* and learn from the results of the response whether it was the right one and how future responses should be corrected.

All six are needed, but this means we cannot build good filters without delegating to them part of our *memories.* Filters without memories are primitive filters. Delegating memories means decentralizing decision-making capabilities and accepting some redundancy by building more capabilities, thereby increasing the total stock. We must ask whether the cost of errors of filtering our response is larger or smaller than the capital cost of building more response capabilities. The information-processing patterns of the future may not be the star or the wheel with the single hub, but rather the network where loads can be referred from one nodal point to another.

I would like to end with three small pieces of outlook.

1. The future of mankind in the advanced countries will become more intellectualized, not less, because of the shift toward knowledge-producing occupations. In the United States early in the century an eighth of the population was in knowledge-producing jobs. It is now a third, and by the end of the century it will be more than a half. The same goes for national income, given the present trends. It, too, will be allocated in an increasing proportion to the processing of information.
2. We will need much more innovation. It is impossible to carry on a great many of our past practices in either industry or politics without running into diminishing returns. The answer is to change the production function and find new ways that get around old, critical bottle-

necks. Creativity will be a matter of life and death for civilization in the coming decades.
3. There will be a great need for decentralization, shorter feedbacks, faster turnaround times, and better fits between decentralized memory and nature.

I think an intellectualized, innovative, more decentralized future is coming. We shall vitally require the contribution of computers, and even more, the contribution of creative human scholars like Simon.

SIMON. Professor Deutsch can disagree with me, but that does not force me to disagree with him! And there are really very few things I want to disagree with him about.

I will plead guilty to hyperbole. I will cheerfully plead guilty to cheerful pragmatism. Frankly, I think we could use some more of it in this country at the present time.

Without enlarging on my reasons, I will take exception to Deutsch's example. However one diagnoses our failures in Vietnam, I find it hard to interpret them as failures of technology assessment. This seems to me a very peculiar diagnosis.

On filtering, I think we can move toward appropriate decentralization and operate partly in parallel, but we shall still require some serial and synchronous operation for which we do need to ask how we filter. How will the people who stand at the apexes of decision systems receive an appropriately filtered range of considerations bearing on the decisions they have to make? Nothing we can do will change the organization of the United States government so that there will be seven Presidents instead of one. We have to find ways to allow that one President to operate as intelligently as possible on the basis of the best information obtainable.

SHUBIK. In Lewis Carroll's *The Hunting of the Snark,* the bellman (who is the central character) says, "What I have said three times is true." Even though Herbert Simon may have said three times that man is a one-at-a-time, sequential, data-processing animal, I think the question is still wide open. As a matter of fact, I offer as a mild piece of counterevidence that at precisely the same time that I was listening to Simon discuss the meanings of the word "know" I noted two eminent Old Testament experts in the audience also discussing the meaning of the word "know."

My remarks, which are variations on some of the themes of Simon, might be subtitled "How to be data rich and information poor, or let's bury ourselves with the facts." Consider the following three quotes:
1. "Don't confuse me with the facts. My mind is made up."
2. "It isn't what you know. It's whom you know."
3. "Why should I read his paper? I can prove the results more quickly myself."

Should these statements be regarded pejoratively? Not necessarily. Since data are expensive to handle, interpret, and turn into useful information, it is often good that somebody does not intend to gather further facts but has his mind made up.

A human society may be regarded as a data-processing system. Information is stored in institutions, books, brains, statistical tables, computer libraries, and elsewhere. The knowledge of who knows what, or where the information is, may frequently be more valuable than deep, narrow knowledge of a few subjects themselves.

In accordance with Simon's remark that various words used in everyday conversation sometimes take on completely different technical meanings, I wish to differentiate between *raw data* and *information*. When a communications engineer talks about information he refers to an abstract concept defined in terms of messages sent through a transmission system. Whether or not the messages make sense to the listener is of no concern so long as they are heard. A Shakespearean sonnet and a group of random noises can contain the same amount of information under this definition. The difference comes in the interpretation by the listener.

In human decision-making systems we distinguish between messages containing gibberish and messages containing significant information. A key unsolved problem is how to measure the contextual or semantic information content of a message in a social system. The technical definition of information does not help much.

In operating a communications network, the costs and techniques of data transmission are important. In a social system two added features are critical. These are the determination of the best way to use symbols or words to convey meaning and translation of the message into information of importance to decision making. The key word in coding and decoding messages in a social system is *evaluation*.

Many of us, despite Simon's "timely" warning, spend too much time reading the *New York Times*. I am reminded of the *Harvard Lampoon's* observation that the slogan of the *Times* should be, "All the News that Fits We Print." At least this sensory system provides us with some preselection. We live in a data-rich world, with the costs of transmission, storage, and reproduction declining rapidly. Wise men can now spend more time and resources decoding and evaluating more easily obtainable data. Less wise men run the danger of confusing their lack of understanding of the ever-mounting volume of data with being better informed.

An optimum information system is not necessarily the one which processes the most data. An optimum system for protecting the average stockholder does not supply him with full, detailed financial accounts. In fact, one can easily swindle the unwary by supplying them with financial details and footnotes they do not understand. It is now possible to bombard a generally uncomprehending public with myriad details on pollution, the pros and cons of insecticides, the value and dangers of irrigation schemes, on-the-spot reports of rioting and looting, televised moon landings, suicides, murders, and historical prices of thousands of stocks and commodities.

The computer and modern communications technology are to the study of man and society as important as the telescope and the microscope were to astronomy and the biological sciences. But the lyrical descriptions of technologists often omit consideration of limited human time and capability. The data-rich world may appear to make the millenium around the corner. But unorganized data are not knowledge, and modern communications contain the potential to confuse as well as educate.

How much time can the man on the street devote to politics? As population grows and the world becomes more complex, how can society keep the individual supplied with the right information for making political decisions and preserving his freedom? The problem is not the speed of generation or transmission of bits of raw data per second. It lies at the far more fundamental level of interpretation and understanding. Within a few years it may be possible to have a virtually instant referendum on many political issues. This could represent a technical triumph—and a social disaster if instability resulted from instantaneous public reaction to incompletely understood affairs magnified by quick feedback.

Consider some of the possible dangers. What is the first great TV, time-sharing demagogue going to look like? How will he put to use such extra features of modern communications as virtually instantaneous feedback? When will a TV screen with the appropriate sensory feelings be able to portray the boss behind his mahogany desk (two thousand miles away) who fires or chastises his employee, and makes him feel just as small, and his palms just as clammy with sweat, as if he were in the room with him? When will the first time-shared riot occur? Orson Welles came close in the thirties with a fairly good radio panic. Current techniques for mob control require physical proximity. In the Brave New World, will we still regard a mob as a great number of closely packed people, or will isolated mobs interacting via TV consoles and operating over large areas be more efficient?

We are moving into an era of large data banks and mass data handling. There are still many technical problems to be solved, but they are minor in comparison to the sociotechnical problems of designing organizations for a data-rich world. If we are to avoid the organizational nightmares depicted in Borges' library or Kafka's courtrooms, we must improve our design and understanding of man-machine organizations. The answers lie more in educating man to process data into better and more relevant information than in shaving microseconds off processing times.

Simon has suggested that working on prima facie impractical problems such as a program to play championship chess may provide us with valuable insights and important applications. I agree, and would like to extend his remarks. We must know more about ourselves as data processors and decision makers; but knowledge of ourselves is expensive. People do not have billions of man-hours to expend in controlled experiments. The electronics age, however, provides us with devices to observe ourselves as we function.

As one example, we could wire the chess boards at all chess clubs and sensitize the chess pieces so that a computer could immediately record each game played. Someone who knew the right questions to ask could extract information and then destroy the data, in case retrieval and storage costs exceeded the expected value of keeping the raw data.

As a second illustration, a way to charge people far more equitably than at present for automobile driving and parking would be to attach a small transmitter to each car and have a central computer bill the owner every month according to times spent in various zones. These data would also permit study of traffic movement and driving behavior, although many of us might argue against having Big Brother keep track of every move of our personal cars.

I think that Simon's interest in chess games and artificial intelligence is legitimate and terribly important, but it omits social intelligence, which may be extremely different from individual intelligence. It may be easier to build an artificial player in some social situations involving pure competition than an artificial player for chess. How do you construct a nice guy? How do you construct a stable individual? Artificial players with these properties in social situations do not have to be terribly bright to be reasonably effective.

I would like to suggest that our organizations and many of our activities be looked at as experiments. We must work out how to make on-line observations with computers and still preserve individual freedom and privacy. If we do not, we run the extreme risk of never learning enough about ourselves and our organizational abilities to be able to cope with the complexities of the world ahead.

The generation and transmission of raw data with speed and economy provides twentieth-century man with the necessary conditions for survival. The conditions are not sufficient, however, without man's studying himself. The new technology has provided us the needed medicines, but we must be our own doctors.

SIMON. I am very much in accord with Shubik's final suggestion that the big job ahead is to use the new information-processing technology to understand ourselves better.

On the question of whether a human being is a serial processing device, the lesson I drew from Shubik's counterevidence was that clearly I was not saying enough per minute to load his channel! By the way, I am obviously not a Biblical scholar or I would not have used the particular definition of "knowing" that I did.

I would like to express rather sharp disagreement with Shubik on the Orwellian tones of some of his remarks. I think he underestimates human beings as receivers of information. Even before television, we lived in an environment of information mostly conveyed by our neighbors, including some pretty tall tales. We acquired a variety of techniques for dealing with information overload. We know there are people who can talk faster than we can and give us an argument on almost any topic. We listen patiently, because we cannot process information fast enough to refute them; that is, until the next day, when we find the hole in their argument. A relevant rule that my father taught me was, "Never sign in the presence of the salesman." By adopting such rules and their extensions, we allow ourselves the extra processing time needed to deal with the information overload.

I am not really worried about Big Brother booming over the air waves. I think that at all levels of intelligence, human beings have common sense protecting them from the worst features of their information environment. If information overload ever really gets the best of me, my last resort is to follow the advice of Gertrude Stein in the opening pages of *The Autobiography of Alice B. Toklas.* "I like a view, but I like to sit with my back turned to it."

DADDARIO. During this interesting exchange, we have seen some harsh sniping by Shubik, and a charge by Deutsch that Simon has been a little too simple! We now come to the question period, if Martin Greenberger will take the podium.

GREENBERGER. In the interests of efficiency, I shall group the questions. The first set of three should have special interest to Congressman Daddario, as well as to Herbert Simon.

William Moore asks if restricting scientific research and thereby slowing down the process of change would not have the good effect of reducing disruption and social revolt, as alleged by historian Arnold Toynbee.

Quentin Ludgin, a laboratory chief at the Bureau of the Census, inquires whether Simon's opposition to premature early-warning methods recognizes the possibility that the ecology may be endangered by rapid and soon irreversible changes. Is not an early-warning network desirable?

Phil Hirsch, Washington editor of *Datamation,* wonders if technology does not carry an inherent probability or certainty of danger, given its present development and rapid advance. Should not information scientists and technicians, as citizens and taxpayers, apply their expertise to this problem, even if it means expressing controversial opinions?

DADDARIO. I would answer the first question in the negative. We should not restrict scientific research, or we would certainly have a sterile society which is unable to cope with its complex problems.

Combining the next two questions, could our technology become irreversible, does it carry dangers, and are we doing enough? I would say we are not doing enough. There is a risk that some of the tendencies becoming set in our environment are so subtle and complicated that they could in fact be irreversible and difficult to determine until they are exceedingly dangerous. The answer is to do more than we are: establish within our society the capability to anticipate these dangers, develop mechanisms to cope with them, and make positive rather than negative the results of our technical and scientific society to meet the challenge.

SIMON. My answers are very nearly identical with Congressman Daddario's. I do not think we should or can restrict scientific research. A number of our problems are going to be solved only if we have more knowledge, not less.

Whether an early-warning network is desirable depends on what is meant by such a network. With the large number of people in our country knowledgeable about large numbers of things, we already have an early-warning network. The real problems are the bottlenecks of attention. How do you get knowledge to the appropriate points in the network? How do you decide which of two things is more alarming?

I think information technologists have the same responsibility that all knowledgeable people in a democracy have: to devote some time and energy to understanding and trying to explicate the social significance, importance, and possible consequences of things about which they are knowledgeable. A good many people with whom I am acquainted do devote a considerable part of their energy to this kind of activity. In fact, I believe that is one of the important things this whole series of lectures is about.

GREENBERGER. The next question is from Stephen J. Tauber, chief of the Information Sciences Section of what he calls "Branscomb's Executive Embalming Service," namely the National Bureau of Standards. He asks if the information supply and demand problem really is not one largely of an ever-increasing demand function and a time lag in the supply function before the new equilibrium can be established. Also, William M. Hornish, a manager at Western Union, inquires how information can be organized so that its use is meaningful to our individual experiences.

SHUBIK. It is again the problem of what we mean by "information." People who insist on mistaking raw data for information see the demand for information as getting bigger and bigger. Some retailers, for example, suggest putting a card on every dress to obtain immediate notice of stock-out. It is easy to obtain new stacks of data; but what is often forgotten is how to analyze the extra data.

I will tell a story that is germane. It is the story of the owl, who is regarded as the wisest beast in the forest, and the centipede, who comes to the owl with ninety-nine sore feet and asks, "What am I going to do?" The owl looks at the centipede and says, "It is simple. You walk an inch off the ground for the next two weeks." The centipede thinks about it and becomes convinced that sure enough, it would give its pads time to heal. Then the centipede says to the owl, "How?" and the owl replies, "I have solved your conceptual problem. Don't bother me with the technical details."

This is the fundamental dilemma of data generation in our society. We are too ready to request a big sample without worrying about how to analyze it. That is a technical detail.

GREENBERGER. Perhaps Mr. Hornish's question was asked in the spirit of the owl and centipede story. Simon spoke of the need for computers to organize, filter, and make information more meaningful and easier to digest. Mr. Hornish may be seeking further advice on what really can be done to help the busy executive with his scarcity of attention.

SIMON. I think that is at the very heart of the question. As long as we use the vast power of computers to spew out data in forms which human beings then have to process extensively, we obviously are not using that capacity very intelligently. Each step we take, on the other hand, toward making computers able to carry out the kind of processing, analysis, and condensing of data that is called "thinking" in people, the more people and computers will be able to work in fruitful symbiosis.

GREENBERGER. The next question is from Professor Eliezer Naddor of The Johns Hopkins University, and is really an assertion rather than a question. He states that computers should not be programmed to make decisions, but only to assist humans make better decisions. Hence, he disagrees with the 1975 goal to have a computer be world chess champion, preferring the goal of having a computer assist Herbert Simon to become champion.

SIMON. I should enjoy being world chess champion, but the joy would be tarnished if the computer had to stand at my back while I was playing. The national goal of developing a computer world chess champion would force us really to discover some fundamental things about how human beings think and solve certain classes of problems. The reason for setting the task is to permit the needed research and investigation.

The sweeping statement that computers should not make decisions baffles me very much indeed. Whenever I fly into an airport nowadays, I ask myself whether the plane is being landed by a pilot or computer. I hope it is being landed by a computer, but I suspect it is being landed by a pilot. When it affects my personal safety, I want computers to make all decisions they can make better than men.

GREENBERGER. The final question is from David Foster, who is a programming analyst with the General Electric Information Networks Department. He requests comment on Marshall McLuhan's thesis that the growth of information technology, as opposed to mechanical technology, is causing a trend away from narrow specialization toward more generality and synthesis.

DEUTSCH. My impression from the history of science is that periods of cross-disciplinary work tend to alternate with periods of advance in special disciplines. I do not think the coming of computers will change that. To insist only on cross-disciplinary activity might require that every specialty slow down its advance to the speed of the rest of the regiment. This is the demand of the humanist who would have everything be intelligible to every well-educated man.

Within a specialization, on the other hand, the problems that can be solved with the intellectual resources of that field alone tend to get solved relatively soon, and then the field becomes stagnant until somebody brings in additional information from somewhere else. Then new questions get asked, new resources are applied, and there is another creative period, either in the old field that has somewhat changed or in a new field at its border.

The alternation between specialization and cross-disciplinary work reminds me of the process of breathing out and breathing in. They are part of the same long-term production cycle of knowledge, even though they may extend over generations of scientists.

DINNER DISCUSSION

GREENBERGER. A question that I know is bothering some people concerns the title of Simon's paper, "Designing Organizations for an Information-Rich World." Did you ever really get to the subject of designing organizations?

SIMON. Well, it is a little like Shubik's story of the owl and the centipede. I stated the general principles. Anybody who wants to, can apply them.

Seriously, we often ask what information the decision maker in an organization should have in order to make decisions, without considering his limitations as an information processor and the kind of system he is part of. In postulating attention as a scarce resource, I do think I was dealing with a central problem of organizational design.

PECHMAN. Lyndon Johnson, according to the newspapers, got himself into a position where he did not receive certain information on developments in Vietnam. How does an executive ensure that information he does not like to see will still filter through?

Participants: Andrew Aines, Office of Science and Technology; John Buckley, Office of Science and Technology; Karl Deutsch, Harvard University; Lincoln Gordon, The Johns Hopkins University; Nicholas Johnson, Federal Communications Commission; Anthony G. Oettinger, Harvard University; Joseph A. Pechman, The Brookings Institution; John Platt, University of Michigan; Martin Shubik, Yale University; Leonard Silk, New York Times (formerly at The Brookings Institution); Herbert A. Simon, Carnegie-Mellon University; Joseph Weizenbaum, Massachusetts Institute of Technology; Martin Greenberger, chairman, The Johns Hopkins University.

SIMON. I do not know any way we can get the President of the United States to accept information that he really does not want. But he can organize himself so that he has at least one information channel from each of the different points of view on a question. That does not eliminate the problem of getting information in usable form, given the very limited time at his disposal. He cannot make the day longer than twenty-four hours.

GORDON. I suspect Julius Caesar also may have suffered from listening to only what he wanted to hear. Eisenhower was a classic example of the screened President, but Lyndon Johnson was not. I saw something of his working methods firsthand and had a strong impression that a great deal of information got to him. Johnson used to take home a vast stack of reading material. He did not need much sleep, and would wake up at 5 A.M. for two consecutive, uninterrupted hours of reading. Whenever one of my memos got to him, he acted on it the same or the next day.

JOHNSON. In my own personal experience with Lyndon Johnson, I found him to read widely and seek advice wisely. He would deliberately set up debating societies before him (in effect) to hear all points of view. He also read outside normal channels. This is what I do in my own life, and I suspect most of us do. I sample a wide spectrum of material so as not to become a prisoner of my own screening system.

OETTINGER. By coincidence, Simon's paper and mine dovetail very well,[8] although I happen to have a strong disagreement with him on the desirability of programming chess. Simon has offered three very deep, important, fundamental principles that shed light on things I had not perceived clearly:
1. attention is a scarce commodity;
2. information technology allows effort to be displaced from possession, storage, and accumulation of information to its processing, even if the information is located in the world itself rather than in the file;
3. filtering and organizing the environment for persons whose attention is scarce are critical.

It remains for others to apply these general principles to particular organizations and explore their political and economic implications.

WEIZENBAUM. There is a student at MIT currently working on what it means for a computer to "know." He took a short story about Mary and Jane being invited to a party. Mommy said they could go but their three-year-old sister could not. Mary and Jane are seven and nine years old. The little sister wants to go, and she cries. Mommy tries to comfort her. That is the story.

What the student is trying to do is get the computer to "understand" the story. He is trying to write down all of the knowledge that the four characters in the story must have to operate in their tiny little framework—knowledge about children, parties, and so on. This has already taken about seventy pages. It is very difficult.

A short time ago Joel Moses wrote a Ph.D. thesis at MIT on symbolic

DESIGNING ORGANIZATIONS FOR AN INFORMATION-RICH WORLD 65

integration.[9] His program can integrate symbolic expressions probably better than any living mathematician. Now mathematicians from all over the world write to him with difficult integrations for his program; sometimes he finds a mistake in the standard tables. This program has more "knowledge" about symbolic integration than any single person and certainly more than its author. But its intelligence lies within an isolatable compartment of human knowledge. One can draw very strict boundaries around it and say, "So what? It knows all about integration, but what else does it know?" This boundary has to be broken; there are students working on breaking it; but there is a long way to go yet.

As far as organizations are concerned, I am impressed with a problem posed by a vice president of General Electric who complained that he was often put on the spot by not having information when he needed it. An admiral might call him about a steam turbine on an aircraft carrier that was six months late and ask what he was going to do about it. This would be the first time he had even heard of the contract. What he wanted was an early-warning system about everything going on in the General Electric Company that might get to such a point. Well, everything going on in the General Electric Company is far less than everything going on that the President of the United States should know about.

SIMON. That vice president did not really want to know about the problem. He wanted a way of dealing with it. And he thought the way of dealing with it was to know about it. He should have told the admiral that he would call him back.

PLATT. In the days of Socrates, the total number of volumes in the library at Alexandria was on the order of a hundred thousand. There is no evidence that Socrates ever read anything. He probably based his reasoning on a very small fraction of the totality of human knowledge.

The same is true of Aristotle, who really tried to know everything. The total number of book-length manuscripts that he could have read in his lifetime (or by the time he wrote his great encyclopedia) was not more than five thousand. So it is obviously possible to make enormous strides forward in human thinking and organization by methods of filtering known a long time ago.

SILK. In a certain sense, my fifteen years at *Business Week* were spent filtering. Simply defined, the editorial function is filtering, although it can be done badly. A typical Sunday *New York Times,* for example, weighs five and a half pounds and contains enough words to take the human eye four days to read, if it read every one; not a very good filtering performance.

Why does the press not filter better? I think some of its distortions result from the kind of institution it is. The press recruits very differently from universities or large corporations, as a hangover from an earlier period when it had a more localized function. The filtering it does is not based on what are the most important things to know but rather on what is the sexiest thing to print, although the degree varies from page to page and department to department.

If you take a Jungian conception of personality types, the good editor knows that his public does not consist of just "thinking" types. He is writing for a broad spectrum of personality types and is appealing to them in a gut as well as rational way.

SIMON. I sense that the press recruits people with a deep urge to inform the public. Perhaps if publishers just relaxed and settled on "making a buck" some of the problems would disappear. There is a serious incongruity between trying to be a major source of public information and education and getting out a publication at periodic intervals (like every day). Most of what people should take in (if they really were going to inform themselves) does not occur on a daily basis. In fact, the world is terribly redundant. Much of what happened today could have been predicted from what happened yesterday and did not need to be published.

SHUBIK. I was in Chile at the time of Project Camelot, and I think one of the reasons it blew up was that the Communist organization in Chile has a daily newspaper which delights in good headlines. The story of Project Camelot supplied the Communist newspaper with headlines for about three weeks. Each day the newspaper slapped another section of the Camelot secret report in the center of the front page and wrote a little critique around it. It was a newspaperman's dream—three weeks of free front pages!

GORDON. Justice Holmes disposed of the daily paper nicely when he compared reading it to watching the second hand of a clock!

I want to divert the conversation for a moment to an aspect of Simon's paper which has not been mentioned. As I understood his presentation, one of the elements in designing organizations for an information-rich, communication-poor world is leaving large amounts of information either in nature or the minds of friends, to be drawn on when needed.

I have two questions on this point. First, if you really knew that some experiment in nature would produce the particular results needed, have you not in a sense already verified the experiment and gone a step beyond leaving information in nature?

My second question is about the index to information. I suppose a purpose of the educational process should be to instruct students in the development of their own indices. Obviously, it should not be to put vast amounts of information into their heads for retention there indefinitely. But how is the person in an organization sure that he has the right index? This seems to me to be a very important design problem.

SIMON. Your first question centers in a technical sense on a point of logic. I do not agree that designing a question which will elicit a "yes" or "no" answer is the same as knowing whether the answer is "yes" or "no." I may understand how to pose the question without yet knowing the answer.

There are many situations where we do not want to pose the question until we need to know the answer. The best example of this is in computer technology itself. Howard Aiken's Mark I computer at Harvard University was constructed in large part because people felt they needed better mathematical tables. But after thinking about it a while, they realized they did not want the tables at all. What they really wanted were subroutines and programming languages that allowed them to get entries in the tables on demand.

On the second question, we may not have to know what the best way is but just the change required from what we do now. We need to worry much less about storing facts in people and much more about storing indexes in them. I do not know the best way to do it, but I do know that we should give people better capabilities for moving around the world, acquiring information.

GREENBERGER. Karl Deutsch has been politely silent. May we have your thoughts?

DEUTSCH. Simon dealt with attention as a scarce commodity but did not explore its purpose or function. What *goals* does an organization seek? What state of affairs is it trying to preserve? What will get a President reelected? What will keep a university happy and working; what will make it blow up? The answers to such questions would help determine the objectively relevant information input.

Relevance depends on goals and needs—functional requirements. Goals and needs, in turn, depend on organizational structure. In order to interpret relevance, we must think about knowledge not only as access to information but as the entire cycle of obtaining, storing, and processing information.

We have to know some facts in order to derive general rules from which more facts can be derived. With too few facts, we cannot derive such rules; if we did derive them we would not know what we had. Our capacities for recognition depend upon our stock of memories. We need a basis of memories of facts to recognize new information and even our own ideas.

I have reservations about Simon's enthusiasm, in the name of simplification and economy of thought, for throwing out vast amounts of what universities now teach. Much of what we learn in social science used to be interpreted against our knowledge of history. If we throw out too much historical data, many of our abstractions may lose meaning. A critical design problem for education is to determine the amount of memories from the past needed for producing and interpreting new information.

If we could build general models of the *expected distribution* of outcomes, we could then pay special attention to events falling outside the distribution. We would not expect a single outcome from a process but (for example) results fitting a bell-shaped curve. If some results fall outside the curve, we might suspect our image of the process and turn up the magnification to examine the reason for the deviation.

This use of expected distributions could be applied to surveillance or early-warning systems. Students will always gripe, and there will always be some campus conflicts and even attempts at suicide. But if too many of these things happen (outside the expected distribution curve), we might become alarmed soon enough to make institutional or organizational changes. (We might also find that the frequency of tragedies or sufferings accepted as normal was, in fact, incompatible with our values.)

Simon warned against excessive fear of unforeseen consequences. He feels experience with DDT may have been the cheapest way of learning about its dangers. This leads to the problem of which warnings to take seriously. Among the many Cassandra calls, which ones are worth heeding?

Statistical background data can help decide such matters. With regard to population explosion, we can now find out the number of people and the countries involved. Do the increases really take place as predicted? What is happening to the food supply? How fast are human reproduction habits changing, and under what conditions? Where, when, and to what extent is there a real danger?

We may not have enough information, on the other hand, for assessing the danger to the atmosphere of the CO_2 or greenhouse effect, which allegedly could change the temperature balance of our planet. The urgency of this danger is therefore presumably less. A lack of knowledge increases the risk of error but does not make it impossible to judge.

When factual knowledge and predictions are unclear, we must fall back on ethics. I think ethics is essentially a set of rules on where the *burden of proof* belongs. If the evidence is incomplete or dubious in a criminal case, Anglo-American ethics says the defendant is innocent until proven guilty. Other legal systems, from France to Russia, treat him as guilty until he proves his innocence. If we must err, on which side would we rather err?

I agree with Simon on the need for cheerful experimentation whenever the value of new experience exceeds the risk of unexpected damage. If irreversible damage results, however, such as when people get killed, we need something better and safer than discovering the consequences by experience. To be sure, there are cases when nonaction can kill more people than action. In 1939 nonaction against Hitler killed more people than action would have killed. But in such cases the evidence should be very strong before irreversible action is taken. As Edmund Burke said, the statesman should be in nothing so economical as in the production of evil.

When we take action, can we make it self-correcting? Can we set up continuous feedbacks to correct our behavior again in the light of its results? Can we make sure that it is not disloyal to discover the action was wrong? We may have to shift Simon's priorities. Instead of going ahead now and learning from experience, instead of mainly seeking to conserve attention, it may be better to stress the continuous processing of information in self-correcting feedback systems.

PLATT. It is just possible that, in the course of correcting our present instability, we might freeze ourselves into a tightly integrated system where a small error will speedily propagate like an East Coast power failure. We need to be very careful to leave lots of looseness, diversity, and lax coupling in the system, even while trying to stabilize it.

AINES. Gentlemen, we actually live in a strangely different world from the one being discussed here. It is a world in which we observe the proliferation of information systems in science and technology. Some are manual, some are computerized, but all are growing.

Sometimes they appear not to be based upon user needs or demands, but on a desire of (for example) the American Chemical Society to refurbish its information programs and create new and more efficient ways of communication. Sometimes they grow because of international competition. There is a tremendous current of international ferment visible in the development of information systems.

In the United States we lack planning and policy entities to guide this development. Yet the proliferation continues resolutely, sometimes disregarding logic and evident need. There are already about five hundred systems in the fields of astronomy, behavioral and social sciences, biological sciences, chemistry, environmental science and related technology, electronics, electrical engineering, and medical and health sciences. These systems are beginning to function. Some are federal, some national, and some international.

What I hoped I would hear discussed (and this in no way faults what has been discussed) is that we must begin to look at some of the organizational problems related to these developments. I see no such activity, even though we are seeking very hard to stimulate interest. The information systems, though growing like crystals in a favorable solution, do not necessarily appear as an integrated or harmonious array. The resulting duplications and inefficiencies in the long run may be terribly costly to society.

BUCKLEY. I cannot see these information systems affecting any real decisions, although I look at the government from the same office that Aines does. But then, I deal with the President and a number of Cabinet officers specifically on environmental problems and have a very limited view of how decisions are made, except in a pragmatic way.

It seems to me that the screens for information turn out to be very largely human ones, carefully arrayed so that there is a diversity of inputs and backgrounds. The pesticide problem did not get the attention of the President and Cabinet, despite two agency reports and a staff input (with different screens applied), until it was covered by the *New York Times* and *Washington Post*. The President commented that there was no way to keep from the top level of government those things that appear in the daily paper. Given these realities, I am afraid what Aines talks about may well lead to a waste of funds.

AINES. Let me focus on the environmental quality area. Some of us feel that the many information activities that operate in this area do not communicate effectively with each other. There is no such thing as a data system for environmental quality. It seems to me that pollution cannot be controlled until we establish a data baseline so we know specifically what we are trying to improve.

The same comment applies to the urban area. People in urban-renewal research and other programs are active all over the country, and many of them do not know what the other chap is doing. The information systems at city, state, and federal levels are relics of a previous age. We need something better.

BUCKLEY. What I feel I need more than anything else is a link in the Bell Telephone System. I have a very good list of telephone numbers, both within the government and outside. I sincerely feel that in less than five phone calls I can get the best piece of information on any subject available any place in the world. I do not worry about not having all the data. I do not have the capacity to deal with it. But I do have the capacity to find it when I need it. Therein lies my utility to the President and to Dr. DuBridge.

GREENBERGER. Nicholas Johnson, may we have your thoughts?

JOHNSON. I will make four points. First, I think we should emphasize more in our thinking the absolutely crucial importance of television as an information medium in our society. Next to the hours they spend at work and in bed, American people spend most time watching television. The average man of sixty-five will someday have spent nine full years of his life, twenty-four hours a day, three hundred sixty-five days a year watching television.

As one example, *TV Guide* has the greatest circulation of any magazine in the United States (even when we read, we read about television). An article that I wrote for *TV Guide* produced fifty to seventy-five letters.[10] In contrast, an appearance that I made on "Face the Nation" (which was nationally advertised to appear half an hour after the actual time of broadcast, thus assuring that those interested would miss it) produced twenty times as much mail.

More than 60 percent of the American people say they get most of their information and opinions from television. Our society does have an information system for adult and child education—television. It is not doing very well, but it is there. I think we cannot make a serious effort to address society's information problem without considering television and the totality of its impact.

The second point I want to make is about pricing. In setting telephone rates, my operating theory is that we ought to make communications as cheap as possible to give people potential access to a maximum of information. We need to develop better devices for selection, but if we can make a Xerox copy or a long-distance call cheaper than we can now, we should do it.

Deutsch's water-cooler example has its analogue in the local telephone system where the incremental cost of placing a call is zero. We make local telephone calls not on the basis of their cost but rather on the basis of whom we want to talk to and what else we have to do with our time. I see no reason why long-distance service should not operate on the same principle. With domestic satellites all calls go forty-four thousand miles—twenty-two thousand up and twenty-two thousand back down. It makes no difference whether the two ground stations are a thousand miles or thirteen thousand miles apart. Why base price on distance in this kind of system?

Next, I think Aines' effort to speak in specific terms is constructive. Let me offer one example, which I call the personalized journal. Many government agencies now have a morning clip service, which is an effort to survey and select from a large number of magazines and newspapers for a particular specialty. The Federal Communications Commission has a very useful service on communications items which provides me with input from many sources on a regular basis.

Bell Laboratories, IBM, and other companies have selective dissemination systems which make selections according to the user's interest, whether it be by author, subject matter, or journal. Xerox copies of the relevant items are delivered to the user on a weekly basis. I think we are going to see a great deal more of this. There is no reason why it cannot be extended with added technology to closed-circuit television presentations for executives in the morning. It could include sections from books and short courses that the user wishes to view.

My last point concerns calling up people for information. I do it, too, and agree it is now the most efficient information retrieval system. But we must keep in mind the distinction between things we call others for and things for which they call us. This imposes an obligation on us to keep some information of our own on hand, at least if we happen to be at the working staff or executive level. Otherwise, suddenly one day everyone will be calling everyone else, and no one will know anything. That will be great only for the telephone company.

PLATT. I am curious if this procedure leads to closed loops: someone calling you in order to find out something about which you asked someone else.

SHUBIK. I am reminded of the old psychiatrist and the young psychiatrist who are going down in the elevator together. The young psychiatrist is all haggard after a dreadfully tough day, yet he knows that the old psychiatrist (who is completely composed) had four times as many patients. He says, "Doctor, how do you do it?" And the old psychiatrist replies, "Who listens?"

SIMON. This story almost makes my point. We have developed all kinds of information sources: the systems Aines was discussing, the free telephone that Johnson proposes, and so on. Now it is time for us to shift our attention to the people at the receiving end and ask how they really filter all of this information.

[*Added by Simon during editing.*] On rereading the discussion and questions, I am struck with how strongly they reflect the prevailing mood of distrust of technology and of panic in the face of contemporary problems. I cannot share that mood and must reaffirm the optimism of my paper, based on some premises that seem to me supportable by good empirical evidence and logic.

First, while technology demonstrably generates some problems, and these problems have to be dealt with (using that same technology!), technology is man's one best and only hope to escape from the curse of Adam. We need more technology, not less.

Second, the information overload is in the mind of the reader. Information does not have to be processed just because it is there. Filtering by intelligent programs *is* the main part of the answer.

Third, inaction is also action, and experimentation on the real world is not as risky as it sounds, at least no more risky than that form of experimentation which consists of doing nothing new or different until all the facts are in. Life requires us to balance risks; it does not permit us to avoid them altogether. Moreover, it is easy to exaggerate how irreversible our experiments on nature are. I find it hard to come by genuine examples of important irreversibility.

Fourth, most science fiction about Big Brother *is* science fiction precisely because it ignores Big Brother's information overload. Lack of information, real or manufactured, has never been the limiting factor on the operations of political police, and I see no reason to believe that the availability of television or computers tilts the balance in their favor.

REFERENCES

1. John W. Gardner, "What Kind of Society Do We Want?", *Reader's Digest,* September 1969.
2. National Academy of Sciences, *Technology: Processes of Assessment and Choice,* Report to the Committee on Science and Astronautics, U.S. House of Representatives, Government Printing Office, July 1969.
3. Edward A. Feigenbaum and Julian Feldman, *Computers and Thought,* McGraw-Hill, 1963.
4. Claude Shannon, *Mathematical Theory of Communication,* University of Illinois Press, 1949.
5. John G. Kemeny, "Large Time-Sharing Networks," this volume.
6. National Academy of Sciences, *Technology*; Herbert A. Simon, *The Shape of Automation,* Harper & Row, 1965; Herbert A. Simon, *The Sciences of the Artificial,* MIT Press, 1969.
7. John Platt, "What We Must Do," *Science,* 166 (1969), 1115–1121.
8. Anthony G. Oettinger, "Compunications in the National Decision-Making Process," this volume.
9. Joel Moses, "Symbolic Integration," MAC-TR 47 (thesis), Project MAC, Massachusetts Institute of Technology, AD662666, December 1967.
10. Nicholas Johnson, "The Silent Screen," *TV Guide,* July 5, 1969, pp. 6–13.

COMPUNICATIONS IN THE NATIONAL DECISION-MAKING PROCESS

Speaker   ANTHONY G. OETTINGER

                Chairman of the Computer Science and Engineering Board of the National Academy of Sciences

Discussants   ITHIEL de SOLA POOL

                Professor of Political Science Massachusetts Institute of Technology

                ALAIN C. ENTHOVEN

                Vice President Litton Industries (formerly Assistant Secretary of Defense for Systems Analysis)

Moderator   DAVID PACKARD

                Deputy Secretary of Defense

PACKARD. The subject of discussion is of great interest to me because of my current position in government and also because my professional background has involved communications and computer technology. I believe the participants share my view that we cannot completely mechanize the decision-making process due to the need for people at all of its stages. I am reminded of an old librarian at the London School of Economics who observed on the application of mathematical principles to economics that

$$(A + B)^2 = A^2 + 2AB + B^2$$

except when A is stronger minded than B, and then

$$(A + B)^2 = A^3 + B.$$

I have had the good fortune to know something about Anthony Oettinger during the last several years through my son at Harvard. Professor Oettinger's involvement in the field of computers and communications has ranged very widely, and his observations are certain to be important and thoughtful.

OETTINGER. National decision making, a complex and vital process in our civilization, critically depends on a vast and heterogeneous flow of data of which there is both too much and yet not enough that is relevant and timely. The spectacular growth of *compunications* fortunately has given us powerful tools and techniques for the quick handling of masses of data. (Computers and communications have long since become inseparable. It is time to reflect this union in the fusion of their names.) How might these tools and techniques best be brought to bear on national decision-making processes? The need for such help is evident from President Nixon's belief, shared with most of his recent predecessors, "that the old ways are no longer adequate, and that much of the old machinery is obsolescent if not obsolete."[1]

I deliberately speak of help, for few of us would knowingly tolerate having vital choices (for instance about war and peace) made solely by automatic systems. Art Buchwald's gallows humor neatly expresses this widespread popular feeling: "The beauty of having a computer for a president is that we no longer would have to worry about human error. It's true, we still would have to worry about a computer erring, but on the other hand, if a computer erred, we wouldn't have to worry about it very long."[2]

Taken literally, the threat envisaged in the popular nightmare of computers running the country is pure nonsense. The danger of unwanted delegation of Constitutional responsibilities is far more real. Nearly ten years ago Richard Neustadt pointed out that "technology has modified the Constitution: the President perforce becomes the only elected man in the system capable of exercising judgment under the extraordinary limits now imposed by secrecy, complexity, and time." And so Neustadt concludes that, "as a matter . . . of preserving the essentials in our democratic order, a President these days is virtually compelled to reach for information and to seek control over details of operation deep inside executive departments." Only by doing so is there "a fleeting chance—sometimes the only chance—to interject effective judgment."[3] Under our Constitution, vital judgments on war and peace devolve upon an elected President and Congress. Art Buchwald correctly senses that these judgments are now the President's alone; he fears further delegation to a second lieutenant or computer.

An official's reach for information in his daily routine affects the balance of powers not only within the executive branch but also among the other branches of government. How government officials at all levels are informed is therefore a deeply political matter vital to the public interest. If compunications is to realize its extraordinary potential usefulness, its integration into the machinery of government cannot be left to salesmen and technicians as is now mainly the case.

Nor can so vital a matter be left to those neo-Luddites who see in technology nothing but a scapegoat. A simple example of an indispensable automatic decision-making system will show what valuable assistants compunications systems have become in one form of decision making. By calling attention to essentials common to all decision-making systems, this example will help us in understanding the less obvious and more critical national processes in which compunications can and do play useful roles.

The decision to turn the heat on or off in millions of homes is made daily and routinely by a straightforward system. Few of us would want it any other way. The homely thermostat is so simple an analog machine that it barely deserves to be called a computer. It is a far cry from the complex digital machines that process checks or guide spaceships, but it makes decisions all winter long. When room temperature reaches the level at which the thermostat is set, it shuts off the heat; when the temperature drops, it turns the heat on again.

Like more elaborate computers, the thermostat is both a source and receiver of messages. Contacts in the thermostat in the living room close the circuit actuating the furnace in the cellar. The furnace communicates with the thermostat through the ambient air, heating a bimetallic element in the thermostat to open the contacts again. Like all significant messages, these signals alter the behavior of their receiver. The messages link the furnace and thermostat in a closed feedback loop that inextricably binds together the actions of the one with the other in a typically endless chain of cause and effect.

So it is for a President and for all other men in government. A man reaches for information that will inform him and widen the choices he has available. He changes the world when he makes his influence felt, and it in turn feeds him new information about new situations. Getting information is one major piece of this endless chain and using it effectively is another.

On the ground of expediency, I shall limit my remarks to information flow *toward* officials. The President, accountable to the Congress, obtains information through the agencies of the executive branch. At all levels of the hierarchies, there are chiefs reaching for information from among their Indians, acting on it, and passing some of it on to their own chiefs. Throughout any hierarchy there is a fundamental common condition of dual upward responsibility and downward authority and a common participation in the same endless chain.

Hence whatever assistance compunications might give, it must give to all levels of a hierarchy. That it must be so is generally missed by those who speak glibly of *management* information systems. They see only the mirage of dramatic decisions explicitly made at the apex of a hierarchy and overlook the diffuse, interdependent, and often implicit decision making going on throughout line and staff echelons.

How effectively compunications might assist these hierarchies in decision making obviously depends on what technology in principle can and cannot do. It also depends on the human needs and institutional contexts which determine how the new tools of technology are selected, integrated into organizations, and used in practice. I shall therefore explore the powers and limitations of the technology, look at the people and institutions that will use the tools to meet their needs for information, and sketch how the tools fit those needs.

Compunications and Knowledge

The essential power of compunications is to compress time and space to an extent and with an ease that falter appreciably only as far away as Mars. Within that radius anyone can instantaneously store or retrieve voluminous data in computer files anywhere within reach of the communications network. Widely scattered individuals can have face-to-face teleconferences with instantaneous interactions. How might such systems best be harnessed to meet an official's need for knowledge?

Knowledge is in the mind of the beholder; *data* are the raw materials from which he fashions his knowledge of the world with the *theories* at his disposal. Since either pure raw data or theories without factual foundations can give the appearance of knowledge, both are all too often confused with knowledge. Without data, the physicist's differential equations, the economist's input-output models, the social scientist's definitions of social indicators, and the statesman's political philosophies are all examples of pure theory. Reports of observed orbital velocities, freight-car loadings, riots in the cities, or body counts are in themselves pure data. Knowledge results only if there are theories to fit the facts and vice versa.

These terms are in widespread colloquial use and a wealth of professional jargon ascribes specialized and sometimes conflicting technical meanings to them, adding to the age-old epistemological confusion about the relations among data, theories, and knowledge. We sometimes speak of electronic data processing and information processing interchangeably, and we sometimes with more than a dash of wishful thinking equate "information" with "knowledge." To professionals in the intelligence field, "intelligence" means roughly what I mean by "knowledge" and "information" what I mean by "data."[4] The confusion is further compounded by qualitative questions about the precision of data or about the interpretative abilities of individuals. Let us use the terms as I have implicitly defined them and look at what roles compunications can play in the selections, collations, and interpretations that combine data and theories to produce knowledge.

Scope and Limitations of Compunications

The pure communications systems of the past were less troublesome to analyze than those which now combine computers and communications. The telephone and telegraph are *passive*, merely storing data as received and passing them on essentially unaltered. The voice at a distance or the face on a tube, to be sure, are not the same as the man across a table, and we cannot yet be as comfortable (or edgy!) in a conference by television as face-to-face around a table.

Pure communications systems do not actively combine data and theories, as compunications systems can be made to do. Under the control of a program embodying theories held by its human designers (whether explicitly formulated or not), a computer system can actively select, collate, interpret, and store data. The sources of data may be anywhere within reach of a communications network, as may the destinations of the resulting products. Some of the possible physical realizations of such systems have been sketched by John Kemeny.[5]

Some computer research is spurred by the hope that computers may someday embody an artificial intelligence as effective as human intelligence in some realms, or even more so. The theories embodied in computer programs range from the tried and true, as in the arithmetic of payroll programs, to the highly speculative, as in attempts to make computers "understand" written texts.

The only programs within this wide range suitable for service in action-oriented settings are those embodying well-tested theories. These fall in the following categories, which bracket the useful range of compunications systems in decision making:
1. physical theories, mainly quantitative in formulation, such as those that underlie the aforementioned heating system, continuous-flow process-control systems, and airplane or missile guidance systems;

2. models reflecting those limited aspects of economics and other social sciences which can be reliably and realistically quantified, such as inventory control systems, date-matching systems, systems for analyzing polls or samples as in the prediction of election outcomes, and macroeconomic models of national economies;
3. arbitrary but generally accepted conventions for the manipulation of either quantitative or nonnumeric data, such as payroll and other accounting and administrative systems, airline reservation systems, directories, file or library indexing, storage and retrieval systems, and systems like PERT and PPBS in their administrative control and retrospective accounting aspects.[6]

Systems based on physical theories are, in general, not so much aids to decision making as aids to implementing decisions and, as such, are not central to our theme. Modeling systems (like human decision makers) are consumers of raw data, and their practical value depends ultimately on the quality and quantity of data at their disposal. Systems based on arbitrary but generally accepted conventions are today's bread and butter. They are indispensable repositories of the accounting data that custom calls essential. They can help accumulate snapshots of tomorrow morning's passenger lists good enough to run an airline by or snapshots of the real world good enough to run a country by. They are barely beginning to do rudimentary data selection, collation, and interpretation. We must match them better to the information needs of decision makers and hierarchical institutions.

The Old Ways of Hierarchies

The ways in which a President keeps himself informed are both informal and formal, both private and public. Roosevelt persistently relied on "a myriad of private, informal, and unorthodox channels and espionage networks" and cross-checked his information by fomenting intense competition among his sources.[7] Eisenhower "preferred to let subordinates proceed upon the lowest common denominators of agreement than to have their quarrels—and issues and details—pushed up to him."[8] Kennedy used the various news media extensively.

My main concern here is not with informal or private sources of information but with the formal organs of the executive branch seen as a composite of many hierarchies, each topped by a department head with specialized interests (such as a member of the Cabinet) and each fanning downward through many levels of delegated authority and responsibility. Every level gets data from the outside and (except for the lowest level) also from subordinates in the hierarchy. In the formal hierarchical concept, the flow is wholly vertical—data upward and requests downward—with direct communication only between adjacent levels of the hierarchy. Data from each level of the hierarchy become grist for the next higher level's selections, collations, and interpretations, yielding *knowledge* in the minds of the men or in the drawers of the file cabinets at that level. Some of this knowledge is passed on as *data* for the same processes at the next higher level. Every man plays dual roles; he is both an Indian to his chief and a chief to his Indians; he is both a seeker of knowledge and a source of data.

One man's knowledge is thus another man's data. Relativizing the definition of data implies an ordering of data by rawness, from the rawest uninterpreted data (like a report of a million-dollar budget overrun) to highly interpretative data (like memoranda giving reasons for the overrun and suggesting appropriate action). The apparent simplicity of compunications systems based on convention is therefore deceptive. If they deal only with the rawest and most picayune data, the usefulness of such systems would be confined primarily to the lowest echelons of a hierarchy. But highly interpretative data based on the selections, collations, and interpretations of lower echelons are still data, and they serve the highest echelons.

How such systems function in practice is influenced by the mix of two equally vital but opposing tendencies (figure 2). The head of a level might at one extreme personally select, collate, and interpret the rawest data collected at all levels below him. This minimizes the filtering of data by others but maximizes communications requirements and information overload. At the other extreme he might rely entirely on the data furnished by his immediate subordinates and on the interpretations made by his staff and advisers, thus minimizing communications and information overload but maximizing filtering. Neither extreme is workable. None but the lowest echelons of a hierarchy can possibly achieve total command at all times of all potentially relevant data. As Herbert Simon noted, the attention of recipients is the scarcest commodity in information-processing systems.[9] Yet absolute reliance on subordinates and staff makes *informed* personal choices impossible and amounts to a total abdication of responsibility.

MIX I	Selection, Collation, and Interpretation of Data		
	done personally by chief from the rawest data collected at all levels below him	- - - - -	delegated to staff and advisers with data furnished by immediate subordinates only
Filtering	Minimum	Intermediate Options	Maximum
Information Overload	Maximum		Minimum
Communications Requirements	Maximum	- - - - -	Minimum
MIX II	Hierarchy - - - Intermediate Options - - - Anarchy		

Figure 2. Mixes of delegation and organization of data gathering

The mix of another related set of opposing tendencies is also important. Although the world obstinately refuses to be so neat, the pure hierarchical concept sees it as divisible into mutually exclusive dominions, which deprives everyone but the top man of data in someone else's dominion that may be relevant to his job. Significant collations and interpretations are at best delayed until all relevant data meet at a high enough level, and at worst they are never made at all, since data judged insignificant by itself may not be passed upward. A total absence of hierarchical partitioning, on the other hand, is quite impractical in an enterprise of the size and scope of the United States government. A vague partitioning can produce far too many reviews of the same data, and when responsibility is diffuse everyone passes the buck.

The hierarchy defined in the organization chart is indeed only a conventional abstraction in most healthy organizations. Varying degrees of horizontal communication, multiple allegiances, and other devices give liveliness to organizations that look dead on paper. Like the secondary blood vessels which gradually take over vital functions following failure of a main coronary vessel, these shifting organizational jumpers, frequently invisible to the casual eye, are often the key to understanding the balance between hierarchy and anarchy in organization.[10]

What Decision Makers Are Thought to Lack

Modern Presidents and their subordinates have lacked for neither reading matter nor willing advisers. Admiral William F. Raborn, shortly before stepping down as director of the Central Intelligence Agency, said: "We disseminate finished intelligence in an infinite variety of formats, tailored to specific purposes."[11] This tailoring recognizes the scarcity of attention and the need that Simon describes to organize the manager's environment of information so as to reduce the amount of time he must devote to receiving it.

Yet the present mix settings are unsatisfactory, and the dangers of tailoring or filtering are a major concern. In commenting on his brother's experience in the Cuban missile crisis, Robert Kennedy wrote that he frequently saw advisers adapt their opinions to what they believed President Kennedy and, later, President Johnson wished to hear.[12] Townsend Hoopes reports the following colloquy between Lyndon Johnson and Dean Acheson over Vietnam: " 'With all due respect, Mr. President, the Joint Chiefs of Staff don't know what they are talking about.' The President said that was a shocking statement. Acheson replied that, if such it was, then perhaps the President ought to be shocked. The President said he wanted Acheson's considered judgment; Acheson replied he could give this only if he were free to make his own inquiry into the facts so that he would not be dependent on 'canned briefings' from the JCS, Rostow, and the CIA."[13]

Similar situations lower in the hierarchy directly and forcefully influence the options of superiors as the effects pass through the endless chain. A Congressional subcommittee report on the U.S.S. *Pueblo* and EC-121 plane incidents states: "If nothing else the inquiry reveals the existence of a vast and complex military structure capable of acquiring almost infinite amounts of information but with a demonstrated inability, in these two instances, to relay this information in a timely and comprehensible fashion to those charged with the responsibility for making decisions."[14] A weak link in the endless chain weakens the whole chain. Chiefs at every level need Indians with knowledge and initiative in direct proportion to the chiefs' need to husband their own scarce attention.

It cannot be taken for granted that there are knowledgeable people at lower levels or that they will relay data in a timely and comprehensible fashion. As Harold Wilensky put it, "In reporting at every level, hierarchy is conducive to concealment and misrepresentation."[15] Harry H. Ransom took note eleven years ago that "as the specialization of the intelligence community's compartments deepens, it becomes a Herculean task to fit together into a coherent pattern the information so independently developed; . . . the endless compartmented accumulation of facts tends to be identified as the essence of knowledge."[16]

Solutions to the problems of compartmentation are often sought through such mechanisms as coordinating committees. But committee processes sacrifice timeliness and are likely to reduce information to a lowest common denominator of agreement, "so screened and selected before submission to the White House that it is scarcely indicative of 'problems and progress' in any real sense of the word—certainly not in any complete sense of the word."[17] As Robert Kennedy put it, "there is an important element missing when there is unanimity of viewpoint."

Compartmentation is deeply ingrained in the hierarchy of the executive branch, which is to some extent a hierarchy in appearance only. As Neustadt writes: "The men who share in governing this country frequently appear to act as though they were in business for themselves. So, in a real though not entire sense, they are and have to be" by the Constitutional and statutory definitions of separate institutions and shared powers within the executive and by the President's delegation of decisive tasks. Although responsible to the President, federal administrators "*also* are responsible to Congress, to their clients, to their staffs, and to themselves." Since "only after all of those do they owe any loyalty to each other," they tend to be competitors and they are not readily brought to meaningful consensus.

Shared power and competition in the framework of partitioned hierarchies, more than personal incompetence, are likely to account for sluggish and uninformative *institutional* responses to requests for data. Many office holders have "almost unlimited reserves of the enormous power which consists of sitting still." When Truman asked his Secretary of Commerce to sign wage orders and price requests during the seizure of the steel industry in 1952, although the Secretary "did not refuse to act, he managed to immerse himself in preparations."[18]

Technology and the Hierarchies

By virtue of compressing time and space, compunications technology offers perhaps our only hope for organizing the manager's environment of information while still minimizing his information overload and the necessary filtering and delays. This hope cannot be realized without institutional change. Indeed, without institutional change, compunications systems might just produce a more efficient and impregnable entrenchment of the old ways, a more comfortable exercise of the enormous power of sitting still.

Ransom reported in 1958 that, "although no published details are available, the Central Intelligence Agency employs modern systems and devices for processing and handling data."[19] In the new preface to the 1965 edition of *Strategic Intelligence*, Sherman Kent writes that "computers . . . are already becoming the indispensable tools for solving the intelligence analysts' problems of information storage and retrieval" and that "the computer has also had its dramatic impact on analysis." "The activity of intelligence research has deepened and broadened," he adds, "but thanks to the new uses of electronics it can move with a speed commensurate at least with the speed of the world's rate of change."[20] Many other parts of the executive branch now also use computers in various phases of their operations.

Yet the *Pueblo* subcommittee in 1969, granting that "the technical ability of military units involved in both the U.S.S. *Pueblo* and EC-121 incidents to transmit messages to other commands appeared, for the most part, to have been satisfactory," concluded that "the advantages of speedy, modern, and sophisticated communications equipment were often more than offset by the indecisive and inefficient handling of these communications by the various commands involved." Sufficient cause can be found in the persistent organizational problems of the executive branch as a partitioned hierarchy with shared powers and internal competition.

My conclusion is that the possession of technological devices is not sufficient impetus for change. The salesmen of technology are only too eager to "modernize" existing processes through the obvious and thoughtless expedient of pouring the old ways, essentially unchanged, into more expensive (to the government), more profitable (to the salesmen), and more dazzling (to the user) systems that often leave the results unimproved in any discernible way. However valuable in principle, new technology will not be valuable in practice unless its introduction is accompanied by appropriate institutional modifications.

The Case for Flexibility

Flexibility is vital in a compunications system used for both routine crises and an occasional extraordinary crisis. A chief's routine reliance on data furnished by immediate subordinates and on interpretations of these data by staff and advisers can serve appropriately to minimize his information overload. Facts endlessly accumulated in the various compartments of the hierarchies can be fitted into a coherent pattern as they percolate upward and eventually meet, using a "normal" setting between the extremes of the two mixes described in figure 2. But a system set at normal must promptly adapt itself to a change in what is meant by "coherent pattern" and must be immediately responsive to the sudden extraordinary crisis.

These requirements put a high premium on having knowledgeable people at all levels. At the present stage of development of computer technology it may take months to change computer hardware or software in response to accidental or rapid changes in their action setting. Knowledgeable people can adapt relatively quickly and intelligently. The requirements also place a high premium on having open communication channels capable of putting knowledgeable people face to face quickly wherever they might be in space or in the hierarchies. They put a high premium on having computer systems based on arbitrary conventions, whose modest but vital role is to put data of the appropriate level of generality in the hands of the people at all levels who need them, when they need them. By virtue of their very simplicity, such systems can adapt better than modeling systems to rapid shifts in focus from the general to the picayune as well as to rapid shifts in subjects of interest.

This hardly implies the absurd vision proposed by some overenthusiastic advocates of management information systems of the President of the United States or some other manager pecking away at a teletypewriter to retrieve high-level memoranda or the last known coordinates of the EC-121 from a computer file. Many executives a hundred years after the first telephone do not waste time dialing their own calls. Others do, and in time many people at all levels of hierarchies will think nothing of helping themselves directly to computer files or of putting data directly into them.

What is more likely to happen now is what Johnson did when Acheson asked for freedom (meaning authority) to make his own inquiry into the facts. "The President agreed he should have the necessary resources for an independent study. Acheson thereupon assembled a small group of knowledgeable people at the second and third levels and worked with them over a two-week period, holding meetings at his home where he cross-examined them at length."[21] One can readily imagine these people levying data from people several levels below them, thereby reproducing many times situations homologous to what took place in the President's office.

In extraordinary crises, when as Neustadt noted "a President . . . is virtually compelled to . . . seek control over details of operation deep inside executive departments," a President's staff (if not the President himself) may well find it necessary to gain direct access to data from the most general to the most picayune and to confer with knowledgeable people at levels from the second to the lowest, by-passing hierarchical levels and breaking through partitions. For less extraordinary crises, similar situations arise for chiefs everywhere in the hierarchies.

To be useful, compunications systems must be flexible enough for the settings of the two mixes in figure 2 to be changed promptly to fit the occasion. To minimize information overload, the systems must assist the regular flow of data upward step by step from subordinate to superior. To minimize filtering, they must also permit instantaneous leaps to detailed data or knowledgeable people across an arbitrary number of levels and partitions.

These systems must be planned to legitimize and reinforce horizontal jumpers, the informal channels that make knowledgeable people knowledgeable. These jumpers enhance individual initiative in normal crises, and by decentralizing and diffusing routine decision making throughout organizations they prevent catastrophic information overload of superiors. In extraordinary crises, they guarantee that knowledgeable people at all levels —who are so necessary at such times—will be not only knowledgeable but also intelligible.

A man confined to a narrow compartment of the hierarchy will be ignorant of the context of his work and thereby less knowledgeable and effective than he might be. Whether he is a historian, lawyer, soldier, or scientist, he will often fail to understand a question put to him when it comes from outside his accustomed channels. If he does understand the question, he will reply in unintelligible jargon either because he cannot help himself or because opaqueness is yet another guise of the enormous power of sitting still. By opening horizontal lines of communication, jumpers have a broadening and civilizing influence. A man with well-connected jumpers is better equipped to distill knowledge from the data his subordinates give him and to supply timely and comprehensible data to his superiors.

Compunications for Chiefs and for Indians

Flexibility in setting both of the mixes of figure 2 can be greatly increased by applying compunications technology effectively. The institutional changes necessary are implicit in the following two significant new principles governing all compunications systems in the executive branch:
1. the chief's principle: direct access to and control and supervision of all systems;
2. the Indian's principle: unfettered access by all hierarchies to all systems.

Both principles apply with equal force at all of the homologous levels of the hierarchy. They complement but do not supplant partitioned hierarchies and their conventional mix-setting mechanisms. The first principle applies especially to the Presidency.

Reorganization that alters the partitioning of hierarchies to adapt to new world views, such as creating new departments or shuffling bureaus, shifts the settings of the two mixes and may change competitive patterns within and among the hierarchies. Granted their well-known shortcomings, it would nonetheless be quixotic to suggest radical departures from partitioned hierarchies in the executive branch. Because these structures are vital links in the endless chain, they should not be wantonly tampered with; enshrined in statutes and traditions, they are hard to change. The enormous scope and diversity of modern executive routine requires the specific delegations of authority and responsibility inherent in hierarchy and the division of labor inherent in partitioning.

What makes these principles new and significant? Either principle could have been stated at any point in history. Both have always been practiced by governments of the tribal type. Without compunications technology, however, neither could be put into practice in the modern United States, given the wide separation in space and time of the people and files within the hierarchies and outside. Marshall McLuhan has spoken of "retribalization of the modern world" and the "new electric culture" which "provides our lives again with a tribal base."[22] In terms more specific to our purpose, Simon speaks of a shift in emphasis from the storage or physical possession of information to its access or use.

The first principle increases the practical ability of a President and other chiefs to choose what information to receive themselves and what information to have their subordinates receive. It allows them to zoom at the most knowledgeable people and the most relevant data wherever in the hierarchy or world they may be. It complements and thereby preserves rather than supplants or dismantles the normal selection, collation, and interpretation functions of the partitioned hierarchies, yet gives a President the ability to change at will the mix settings in all and only those areas that interest him.

The second principle puts analysts and experts in constant touch and interchange with people and data elsewhere in their own and other hierarchies, without altering their responsibility and the focus of their attention. They are given unlimited peripheral vision and the means to avail themselves of relevant expertise or data irrespective of the location. As Indians they are therefore better prepared to volunteer significant data or respond to requests in more timely and intelligible fashion. As chiefs they are better prepared to make decisions within the scope of their authority, and they can expect the same from *their* Indians.

It is still true that if a President does not ask, he may never know. But the filter settings are now in his hands and his subordinates are more knowledgeable. His ability to ask anyone in any department "the pregnant questions and not be put off by the sterile answers"[23] has been increased, as has been the likelihood that he will get timely and intelligible information from subordinates.

A fiction of the data-processing profession has it that decisions are dramatic discrete positive acts, while in reality the decision process is diffused throughout hierarchies, spread out over time, and bathed in a constant flux of change. Because of this fiction the conventional emphasis on information systems for chiefs, reflected in the first principle, is generally not balanced by an equally important concern for the Indians. The dependence of effective Indians on their jumpers, stressed in the second principle, is usually neglected.

Both principles invite practical objections and objections in principle. My assertion that these principles complement the hierarchies without supplanting or dismantling them is most vulnerable. I think there is no real issue, however, since I am concerned with the flow of *information* to a President and to other chiefs in a hierarchy, not with the exercise of authority.

The widespread confusing of access to information with exercise of authority unfortunately beclouds the issue. This confusion is commonly expressed through the aphorism that knowledge is power. But, as I have said elsewhere: "Clearly, the opening of information lines up, down and across would legitimize a leaping over organizational boundaries that, while essential for real accomplishment, is done nowadays only at official risk and peril. Organization lines reflect lines of authority, but while knowledge is power, the gathering of information is not the exercise of authority. It therefore seems perfectly proper for a manager to leap several levels down in search of answers, or for a subordinate to leap across organizational lines and occasionally over his boss' head *so long as decisions and orders travel by normal channels.*"[24] Since a President or other chief can rarely carry out his decisions and orders himself, however well informed he is, the distinction between the access to people and data and the exercise of authority is indeed a distinction *with* a difference.

Both principles must be asserted by the exercise of the full influence of the President, if he is to retain the vital decisions the Constitution says are his. Applying traditional leverage over twenty-five years has not set the mixes in his favor. Compunications technology is still a pliable infant, however, largely unbound by precedent and with its main period of growth and diffusion still ahead.

The President has an unparalleled opportunity for assuring flexible mixes by molding the diffusion of this technology throughout the executive branch. The opportunity will never be his again if the old ways get embalmed in the products of compunications technology. But there is reason for hope. Both principles are significant at every level of the hierarchy, given the dual roles people play at every level. Thinking only as a chief, one might accept the first principle but reject the second. Thinking only as an Indian, he might resent the first but welcome the second. Thinking as both an Indian and a chief, he might persuade himself that he stands to gain, as would all other competing Indians and chiefs, by accepting both principles in the national interest.

The Case for Practicality

Months before his trip to Moscow as Vice President, Nixon "talked for hours with every person [he] could find in Washington who had met and knew Khrushchev" and he "gathered up and tried to absorb every bit of personal information about him which was available."[25] Knowledge of personalities is important at all levels of the hierarchies. Sherman Kent has written: "Acquiring knowledge of personalities is one of the most important jobs of an intelligence organization. It is also an enormous job. . . . There must be a wide range of data because there are so many pertinent questions always being asked about people. The perfect biographical note must include a large amount of cold factual information and a large amount of critical appraisal."[26] The use of compunications technology to handle biographical files of various kinds is already widespread both in the government and in the private sector. For purposes of simple illustration, I shall consider only files assumed to contain biographies of foreign public figures such as de Gaulle.

The technical handling of biographical files by compunications systems can be largely a passive activity, storing data essentially as received and passing them on essentially unaltered—critical appraisals, in particular, which must remain the work of knowledgeable people. Some of Kent's "cold factual information" might be processed actively, with rudiments of automatic selection and collation. Such processing can be treated as amenable to arbitrary conventions more than as analytic and requiring an extensive theoretical basis.

Some might object to or fear the centralization of files that seems implied in the two principles, but this again confuses access to information with exercise of authority. Under the old ways, physical possession of experts or files by an organization meant that it could and usually did exercise negative authority by keeping everyone else away from them. But modern compunications technology provides the means—and the two principles provide the will—to give both Indians and chiefs free access to experts or files wherever they might be located. There being only one de Gaulle, it is logical that all the information about him be in one place for any inquirer.

It is of no more concern to an inquirer to know who physically possesses the files from *A* to *E*, *F* to *N*, and *O* to *Z* than to know where the files are physically situated. With access and dialogue by compunications, it does not matter whether a response originates next door or thousands of miles away. Nor does it matter where a new file entry is physically stored. Most people today are scarcely aware that phone calls to an airline in Boston might be answered by a clerk in New York or that Enterprise and area code 800 calls are not answered locally. They need care even less.

A chief can therefore delegate the physical possession and maintenance of fragments of biographical files on the basis of the budget or the prestige of those to whom this matters. Compunications technology evaporates the traditional fierce arguments about the centralization or decentralization of experts and files and permits independent determination of who should update or query the files and who should exercise authority. Whatever the hierarchical partitioning of authority and responsibility, it can be complemented by physical centralization or decentralization of expertise and files of any degree whatsoever. Changes in formal organizational patterns are neither demanded nor precluded by technological considerations.

Some people fear that dumping everything in one common file would result in a mechanical mangling and homogenization that would obscure the origin and credibility of cold factual information or authorship of critical appraisals. Some of this fear reflects genuine concern over enforced anonymity and loss of credit for personal contributions. But the fears are groundless in a well-designed compunications system. Computer files lend themselves admirably to exquisitely detailed annotations of sources and authors; the pedigree of every last bit of data in a file entry can be traced to the nth ancestral generation. Only the budget need limit the detail of pedigrees.

Suppose that a summary critical appraisal of some personality comes to the attention of the President and he suspects that it has been reduced to a lowest common denominator of agreement by the conventional coordinating machinery. The compunications system gives him the option of zooming almost instantaneously to underlying critical appraisals made by different departments and even to the original authors of these appraisals. He can zoom personally, if he puts a high premium on no filtering whatever, or he can ask one or more of his staff to do it for him. The availability of such comparisons can help other chiefs and Indians make useful jumpers to the authors of particularly informative or perceptive appraisals. In critical cases, the President or his staff can evaluate disagreements by zooming to original raw data to distinguish quickly between differing professional assessments of data with the same pedigree or assessments based on different raw data. Line or staff could use access to the raw data to think through arguments for an opposing point of view, thereby sharpening their thinking or preparing a defense of their position.

A compunications system can keep track not only of the pedigree of every entry in a file but also of every inquiry to every entry. Routine filing of inquiries addressed to a biographical entry or its ancestors enables zooming to more than one individual, department, and point of view. Someone who makes inquiries to the same source as you may have kindred interests and be a valuable source of correlative expertise and data, particularly if he turns out to be an analyst deep in the hierarchy who makes it his business to keep track of the biographee's relation to his analytical specialty. Such a person is likely to be overlooked under the old ways.

A big chief may well wish to delegate the details of zooming to others, but the option is entirely his under the two principles. In routine crises, any chief's information overload is minimized by the normal settings of the mixes, with reliance on data and interpretations filtered by line and staff as they rise upward from the lower compartments. In extraordinary crises, the zooming facilities provide the flexibility necessary to find and use data as general or as picayune as needed and the people capable of assisting with timely and intelligible interpretations.

The fact that compunications technology still faces its main period of growth and diffusion gives a President the opportunity to tailor the secrecy of a new system to accord with his needs, the separation of powers among the three branches of government, and public rights to information. The application of the two principles to new compunications systems in the executive branch is essential if the abuse of secrecy and the endless compartmented accumulation of facts is to give way to a more responsive and timely system. Hierarchies will otherwise find it easy to let the secrecy patterns of new systems simply reflect the old ways. Compunications systems can lend themselves as easily to stifling knowledge as to encouraging its sharing.

The tailoring of secrecy need not mean the condoning of indiscretions. The gargantuan clerical prowess of communications systems even now permits the screening of inquirers according to the time-worn criteria of need to know, affiliation, or rank, thus tending to reinforce the old ways. We must start from the premise that the refusal of access and not the right of access is what requires administrative or legislative justification. Then we can tailor screening techniques for new systems to guard against indiscretions without permitting the old ways to throttle the new principles in their cradle.

Filing practices throughout government and industry now differ from one office to another. It is safe to assume that no two biographical files within the executive branch have identical formats or updating rules. Reconciling such differences is a formidable task under the old ways. Seemingly petty matters like the use of index cards of different sizes that will not fit in the same file drawer, the use of thirty columns of a punched card to record a name when the card reader expects twenty-five, the transliteration as Tchaikovsky rather than Chajkovskij (where is it in the file?), are just a few of the current difficulties.

Most of these difficulties disappear with modern compunications technology. The index is inside a computer, not on file cards; the computer need not care how many columns are assigned to a name; it can be made to translate from one transliteration scheme to another; and with the help of occasional human intervention, it can assure that J. J. Smith and J. Jacob Smith are equated but distinguished from J. J. Smyth. A comical residue of interminable squabbles on such petty subjects can be observed in most organizations, but it is a deadly serious manifestation of the immersion in preparations which Neustadt has recognized as an effective substitute for an overt refusal to act.

In the Beginning . . .

Biographical files offer but one example of how compunications systems can give new flexibility to decision makers, given the institutional changes implicit in the two principles. Biographical files and similar systems based on arbitrary but generally accepted conventions lack the glamour of modeling systems. It can be argued with some justification that decision makers need macroeconomic models or budget control and prediction mechanisms more than they need electronic file cabinets.

Biographical files are as important to chiefs as to Indians, whereas other systems based on arbitrary conventions may assist little Indians more directly than big chiefs, at least initially. But what helps make a little Indian more knowledgeable also helps the big chief in the same endless chain, especially if the Indian is accessible to the chief through modern communications facilities, as he can be right now.

Modeling systems are consumers of raw data. Their practical value depends on the quality and quantity of data that can be put at their disposal. While beginning with systems like biographical files has the intrinsic merit of providing some assistance for decision makers at all levels here and now, it also is an absolutely necessary step toward modeling systems useful in the real world.

The wild claims and promises of technicians and salesmen are the old ways' best friends. By promising the blue sky and demeaning the practical first step, they cloak the immense power of sitting still with the appearance of strenuous striving. What they automate is immersion in preparation. Delays to protect the old ways can no longer be tolerated. Neustadt's conclusion that "as a matter . . . of preserving the essentials in our democratic order, a President these days is virtually compelled to reach for information and to seek control over details of operations deep inside executive departments" seems as valid today as ever.

Limitations of time, space, and hierarchy curtail the President's access to information under the old ways and induce unwanted delegations of his Constitutional responsibilities. The effective use of compunications systems offers a new way, likely the only way, to preserve this aspect of the essentials in our democratic order.

PANEL DISCUSSION

PACKARD. Oettinger's paper is exceedingly interesting to me in view of my experience in Washington during the last year and a half. Had I read the paper a year and a half ago, I would not have appreciated much of it. But now I can see case after case and example after example of the kind of problem it addresses.

The problem of filtering, for instance, is a real one. A prime example of a filter in an information system is a military briefing, and I have learned very quickly to take every military briefing with a grain of salt.

I was in Thailand last year, for example, at the base of a Thai military unit. I went into a little building open on the side and a Thai general stood up in front of me and went through the pattern of a standard American military briefing—charts, a description of the threat, his forces, and the terrain. His men had just attacked a little insurgency unit up in the hills. He described the attack in detail and said it was highly successful. When he was through, I asked him how many of the enemy he had killed or captured. Without changing his expression, he answered that he had not caught any of them, since they knew the territory and could run faster than his men. This is an example of what you can get through some of these information filters.

Ithiel de Sola Pool will now comment on Oettinger's paper. Dr. Pool's field is political science, public opinion, and communications.

POOL. Oettinger's paper is both sound and important. It strikes me as sound because I agree with it. It strikes me as important because many other people do not.

Oettinger is not advocating motherhood. On the contrary, what he has said is highly controversial. Most members of the national policy and intelligence community would disagree with him. Many would wax apoplectic at his suggestion to provide general access to raw data and permit identification of the sources of material in evaluated intelligence analyses. The generally accepted objective of intelligence analysis is to produce an agreed-upon, anonymous intelligence estimate. If it is not anonymous, it is passed on under the fraudulent signature of the head of the organization.

The basic principle in an embassy, for example, is that all reports home are from the ambassador himself. Other members of the mission are supposedly aides helping him prepare documents which he signs. It has not really worked that way since the time a hundred and fifty years ago when an ambassador was a plenipotentiary who sent letters home via sailboat and had a staff consisting of a cook, valet, coachman, and footman. Today a U.S. embassy in a major capital is a substantial bureaucracy with staff from AID, USIA, intelligence, the military, and various other agencies, all in contact with their agencies at home by cable, radio, and airmail. They correspond about economics, weather, visas, visitors, vacations, rotation, and personnel matters, as well as politics. For priority communication there is secure global telephonic contact with Washington. Nonetheless, in principle, all reporting home is by the ambassador and every report is supposed to be vetted by him. In practice, the deputy chief of mission clears every official report except when a post gets mammoth (as is London, Paris, or Saigon), and then the fiction of a single source finally gives way; but political reporting continues to be over the signature of the ambassador.

I once discussed this system with a former ambassador who had been thrown out of the country where he was posted after an anti-American coup suspended normal relations. He asserted that only rarely did he have to censor or disapprove things his staff wrote. I asked him what kinds of things he occasionally did censor. "Oh," he replied, "alarmist reports." One wonders whether Washington needed to be protected from the staff's alarm about the coming coup.

Professionals greet with alarm and consternation any suggestion that the State Department should be able to by-pass the ambassador and probe the varied views of all its personnel abroad, or that a President should be able to find out who contributed some assertion to a national intelligence estimate. They worry that the Secretary or President may be misled by some unevaluated random fact. Subordinate authorities always want to reserve to themselves the data base on which they rest their recommendations and pass on only their conclusions. President Kennedy's insistence ten years ago on knowing this country's contingency war plans met virulent resistance in the military. There are innumerable controversial research reports done under contract that a sponsoring agency has chosen not to release because of doubt about the validity of the results. The official who commissioned a study has an assumed responsibility to judge its merit before allowing its distribution.

If this bureaucratic principle of control is wrong for information distribution in general, as it is, it is doubly absurd in a computerized environment. The *interrogator*, not the *producer* of information should control how much of the raw data is brought to his attention. The new capability of the consumer to control the flow, format, and scope of information he receives is a significant result of the arrival of the computer and it reverses a hundred-year trend of increasing use of mass, standardized, nonindividualized communication.

Before the growth of mass media most communication was pairwise between persons, either in conversation or by exchange of letters, with both the information source and the interrogator influencing the content of the information flow. The printing press, radio, movies, and television changed that by providing the same message cheaply to many diverse receivers, putting the burden of selectivity on the originator. This feature of the popular mass media is found to a substantial extent in bureaucratic communication inside government. To learn about a person in the old days we sought out a mutual acquaintance. Now we can look the person up in *Who's Who* or in a printed biographical summary that serves many users cheaply.

The triumph of mass media is their economy. The marginal cost of informing one additional person by producing an added copy of the identical message is merely pennies, whereas rising labor costs continually increase the already high expense of hand-tooled information designed to meet individual inquiries.

Computers, xerography, and telecommunications are reversing the hundred-year trend toward mass media dissemination of information by making it less exorbitantly expensive to provide the consumer with individualized output from data bases. A good information-retrieval system permits access to just the wanted biographic information about a particular individual and provides a single copy at reasonable cost. One effect, as Oettinger suggests, is likely to be decentralization of decision making. Others besides the top brass can now hope to command all the necessary information. In principle, the same pinpointed information can be made available at any level and at any location of an organization.

The usual image of a Big Brother computer as a centralizing instrument is wrong. Conservative Soviet economists seeking arguments to show that a centrally planned economy could work despite the evidence of its years of inefficiency latched onto the computer as an answer to those liberal economists like Liberman who argued for a market economy. They fantasied a computer-managed economy with the computer knowing what each factory needed as inputs in every part of the country, what each was producing, and what the consumers required. No existing computer can do a thousandth of that job, and even if it could, the information could be made available to people throughout the system, not just to the planner at the top.

The capability of the computer to be a democratizing and decentralizing force, as Oettinger points out, depends upon the achievement of social changes. To achieve that result in our government, we must change both our national intelligence process and how we configure its computer systems. Our present image of the intelligence process is absurd. People view the Central Intelligence Agency as a cloak-and-dagger operation. The conservative is likely to visualize it as a romantic James Bond operation, pitting good against evil, while the liberal is likely to visualize it as a wicked conspiracy overthrowing democratic governments around the world and running military puppets. Neither picture has any relation to reality or pays any attention to the plain meaning of the word "intelligence."

Intelligence is knowledge. It is scholarship. It is research. It is an attempt to bring the benefits of facts and enlightenment to bear on public matters. I believe the scholar, journalist, and intelligence operative are all in substantially the same kind of business, the business of enlightenment. The intelligence operative may be a captive scholar working for a single sponsor, while the university scientist publishes his results for all to read, but that distinction is far less clear-cut than the usual polar contrast of plotters versus scholars.

One reason for the intense prejudices against intelligence is that intelligence responsibility has in many instances been given to cops instead of scholars because one part of the data governments want can be obtained only by clandestine sleuthing. An extreme example is the intelligence system of the Soviet Union. A police state quite naturally conceives of intelligence as a secret-police function rather than as social research. It would be in the best interests of the United States and world peace for the Soviet Union to have a superb intelligence system—a group of able scholars dedicated to giving the Soviet leaders an accurate and realistic picture of the outside world. Instead the Soviet leaders have been sadly and dangerously misinformed by their terrorist secret-police organizations. Oettinger has referred to how badly Stalin misinterpreted the many evidences of impending German attack in 1940. That is the subject of a forthcoming definitive book by Barton Whaley entitled *Operation Barbarossa*.[27] Whaley shows that the only Soviet intelligence organization that performed creditably was Army Intelligence, also the only one that was not a secret-police organization.

The primary job of the Central Intelligence Agency is to keep the President informed about the state of affairs in the outside world. If this job of enlightenment is to be done well, it should use the best research techniques of the social and information sciences and be subject to critical scientific criteria, including adversary proceedings, documentation of sources, and rigorous hypothesis testing. Yet our intellectual community, instead of recognizing the intelligence function as an attempt to bring the life of the mind into politics, shares in the general confusion of intelligence with the police function and wants nothing to do with it. That attitude has to change before information science and social science can be effectively put at the service of government decision makers.

Another necessary change is in the area of software. Present computer systems are not designed for economical information management. Oettinger distinguished *passive* from *active* systems and stated that for the present most useful systems will be passive. But most computer systems with their large instruction sets and powerful central processors are designed for active computation. Bulk memories and modest computing power would be sufficient for passive purposes and far more economical.

The active-passive distinction is perhaps misleading, however. It suggests that the act of storing data essentially as received and passing it along on request essentially unaltered is easy. It is indeed easy for any one file, but it becomes complex when millions of disparate bits of information are organized into thousands of overlapping files of different formats. To update, purge, collate, and retrieve subsets of this data requires complex software, different from what is needed for mathematical computations or modeling. To be efficient, such a system should not be blind to the contents or meaning of the data, a usual defect of data systems which we have tried to remedy in our ADMINS Mark V system at MIT.[28]

Are economies important? Some people argue that cost is the last consideration for a Presidential information system. I cannot agree. Presidential decision making should not be isolated from the whole system, as Oettinger has made clear. There is grave danger when it is. At moments of crisis and on highly sensitive decisions—such as the Cuban missile crisis or a major policy question on Vietnam—there is a tendency to draw the decision into a closed circle of top advisers. The more critical the event, the smaller and more elite the circle and the fewer experts consulted; for experts on any substantive problem are little men far down the bureaucratic hierarchy. Isolated Presidential decision making is a pathology to which the system is prone. The healthy situation is when top decision makers can and do constantly reach down for their answers to the levels at which detailed expert knowledge exists.

Thus a computerized information system of highly digested material for top management is not enough. The President should be able to obtain at will during the middle of the Cuban missile crisis information about the percent of U.S. missile sites, the number of planes, or the communications centers within x miles of Cuba. When talking about Vietnam he should be able to have retrieved immediately the best raw field reports on how peasants feel about the recent village elections. This kind of capability requires that the entire government information system be automated, which is why cost is critical. Only when automation regularly saves money, a rare event today, will the reforms now becoming technically possible (and for which Oettinger pleads so eloquently) begin to be implemented widely.

Since economics holds the key to the diffusion of modernized information management, we must develop systems with modest central processing units, cheap bulk storage, and operating programs optimized for file management and conscious of data contents.

In closing let me comment on the social implications of Oettinger's vision. He is clearly saying that computers and communications permit a great democratization of decision making and that partitioned bureaucratic hierarchies are no longer the best way to process information. In the Soviet Union communications are set up on elitist principles. The "key" telephone system (so-called because of the key needed for the phone) allows some two hundred members of the top elite to call each other freely. In at least one Eastern European copy of this system those selected people can dial a number and get a tape recording of the uncensored candid version of the day's news.

While person-to-person conversations are inevitably limited to small numbers, interrogation of computer information bases need not be so limited in a democracy. The full gamut of available information can be made available to everyone. For the first time in history inputs from all parts of an institution or society are available both to a decision maker and to all his subordinates and staff. The computer makes possible the replacement of bureaucratic by participatory decision processes. Whether it is used that way is up to us.

PACKARD. Again I find these observations interesting in terms of my own experiences. I have intelligence reports on my desk every morning from both the Central Intelligence Agency and the Defense Intelligence Agency. When I began to be concerned about certain things, I found that it was very helpful to go back and double check some of the raw data. This capability does exist, and it is being used.

The next discussant has made a great contribution to the Department of Defense over the last few years. The systems-analysis function that he developed has been a very important step forward in the management of the department. He was right in the middle of some extremely important decisions in government. He is now in industry, and he probably finds this a little less hectic. I had the reverse experience. Before I came to Washington, I had perhaps one or two crises a year and maybe one or two extraordinary crises in the history of my company. In Washington we seem to have several of each every day!

ENTHOVEN. Computer and communications technology has tremendous implications for many activities in our society, such as the automation of clerical work, the control of industrial processes, military tactical command and control, space flight, and certain aspects of medical practice. But I do not believe it has the potential to contribute much to the *national* decision-making process. The main deficiencies in the flow of information to decision makers at the national policy level are caused by people and particularly by persistent organizational factors. Computer and communications technology is not going to solve these problems on its own. Oettinger is basically right in suggesting that improvements will require institutional changes.

Decisions on national policy should be based on both judgment and analysis. Unaided judgment is a very poor substitute for analysis. Analysis should be the servant of judgment, not a substitute for it. It should supply the relevant information and alternatives and describe the key relationships between assumptions, choices, and consequences. More than 95 percent of the useful effort in most good analyses at the national policy level is taken up asking the right questions, formulating the problem, getting the basic facts roughly right, and deciding on good assumptions.[29] Computer and communications technology helps mostly with the other 5 percent and by creating unrealistic expectations creates some new problems of its own.

Management information systems might help Cabinet officers obtain needed information, but these systems are inevitably designed to answer questions that have already been asked and precisely defined. Most of the really important questions at the national policy level have not been precisely defined. Once the facts are well enough known to be codified in a management information system, the questions they answer have often moved from center stage. Management information systems also presuppose a supply of valid data. They have not and cannot help much with basic decision making on U.S. policy for Vietnam, as one example, when valid, meaningful information is conspicuously lacking.

Decision making interacts with the process of analysis that supports it, and analysis interacts in turn with the information flow that supports *it*. The judgments of decision makers and the analyses of their staffs determine the relevance of information and clarify the concepts whose counterparts are being measured. Information comes into existence in answer to questions. Nothing very useful can be said about the storage, processing, and communication of information at the national policy level that is independent of the analysis and decision processes it supports.

The main problems in the flow of information to national policy makers are caused by people, not by equipment or its lack. The information received at the top depends on the questions asked by people up and down the line (including the top), and these questions depend on what the people consider important. The answers they obtain are inevitably colored by the answers they want. That depends on what their interests are or how they are organized. The main problems are institutional, not technological.

Getting the basic facts roughly right is an extremely difficult and much neglected problem in many questions of national policy. Officials have exaggerated the size of the Warsaw Pact armies facing NATO for years, for example, in the sincere but incorrect belief that exaggerated estimates would scare NATO governments into providing more forces.[30] Writers on strategy have filled thousands of pages arguing about the best strategy to meet the huge threat, proceeding from the totally inaccurate premise that we were hopelessly outnumbered in conventional forces. The various bureaucracies reacted with outright hostility to presentations of clear-cut evidence that the Soviet forces were not as great as supposed.

I encountered an old friend in 1961 who had spent a number of years working in the military division of the Bureau of the Budget. I asked him what he had learned from the experience. "Alain," he replied, "I learned that a fact is not a fact." One day I was having lunch with Secretary McNamara after a particularly trying struggle to get at the basic facts underlying a problem; we had been given much conflicting and inaccurate information. I related the story of my friend's experience. McNamara laughed and said, "Now I appreciate the meaning of the expression 'a true fact.' "

The President and his advisers need sources of information in each significant policy area that reach to the basic facts of the problem independently of the vested interests (bureaucratic and otherwise). These sources can serve as a check on the often biased information obtained through the official hierarchies. An organization proposing a new technical development is likely to underestimate the costs, for example, and an operating organization will often overstate the significance of its achievements. The President and his advisers need a "loyal opposition" that has independent channels of information; they need access to people who get their points by disproving the "official" information.

The National Security Act recognized this principle in creating the Central Intelligence Agency as a separate organization independent of the State and Defense Departments. The independence of the CIA, although sometimes less than complete, has been very valuable. But in the provision of other kinds of information this principle has not been recognized. (The President does not have his own inspector general or General Accounting Office.) I believe the President and Secretary of Defense were most successful in the 1960's in those areas of defense policy where they had sources of information that were independent of the official hierarchies (such as in strategic nuclear weapons) and least successful in those areas where they lacked such independent sources (such as in Vietnam).

The President and his advisers do not get their knowledge straight from the computer or teletype. They must rely on staff analyses that focus the available information on the issues. As much as possible, these analyses should be, as I have said, "open and explicit. That is, each analysis should be spelled out explicitly and clearly and made available to all interested parties so that they can see what assumptions were used and so they can retrace the steps leading to the conclusions. Open and explicit analysis is our best protection against persistence in error and reaching conclusions on the basis of hidden assumptions. It helps to build confidence in the results. All calculations, assumptions, empirical data, and judgments should be described in the analysis in such a way that they can be subjected to checking, testing, criticism, debate, discussion, and possible refutation. And the analyses should be tested, checked and debated by all interested parties."[31]

Since we found the principle of open and explicit analysis to be of very great practical value in the Department of Defense, I react favorably to Oettinger's "Indian's principle of unfettered access by all hierarchies" to all compunications systems in the executive branch. But I think access to the analyses is more important than access to the compunications system, and I believe access must be limited to those who "need to know" the information.

The problems of communication and storage of information at the national decision-making level are insignificant compared to the problems of sorting out the relevant information and testing it for validity. Debate is a valuable and necessary tool for sorting and testing. I do not mean the kind of point-scoring debate some British parliamentarians learn in the Oxford Union and practice for the entertainment of large audiences. I mean constructive, convergent, disciplined debate in which the opponents seek to define precisely the points of agreement and disagreement and meet evidence head-on with evidence.

To illustrate, let me describe an important debate that took place several years ago in the Defense Department.[32] The Secretary of the Army and the Joint Chiefs of Staff recommended to the Secretary of Defense in 1966 that he approve full-scale deployment of an antiballistic-missile [ABM] defense of our cities against Soviet attack. (This proposal is different from the more recently proposed Sentinel and Safeguard systems intended to protect our intercontinental ballistic missile sites from Soviet attack and our cities from a comparatively simple Chinese attack.) The initial cost estimates were around ten to twenty billion dollars, but there was good reason to believe that the eventual costs would reach forty billion. But the decisive issue was whether a full-scale antiballistic-missile defense system deployed together with complementary fallout shelters and air defenses really would save millions of lives in a nuclear war.

This is an exceedingly complex issue. It involves assumptions and judgments about hundreds of technical factors, including offensive and defensive tactics, and thousands of calculations. The system-effectiveness estimates must be based not only on test results (about which we can be fairly confident) but also on guesses of future enemy technical developments. In the face of this complexity and uncertainty, how could the Secretary of Defense evaluate estimates of the effectiveness of the system?

Secretary McNamara noticed that the Army's estimates were much more optimistic than the estimates of the Systems Analysis Office. This was not too surprising since the Army was the main proponent of the ABM system, while I saw my job as Assistant Secretary of Defense for Systems Analysis in part to be the Secretary's prosecutor or interrogator. If a case was to be made against the system, it was my responsibility to make it. Mr. McNamara asked the Secretary of the Army and me to sit down together and prepare a memorandum for him stating points of agreement and disagreement precisely and explaining in laymen's language the reasons for the disagreements. The reasons could not be that we added differently or used different computers. Mr. McNamara wanted to be able to judge the reasons for himself.

The Secretary of the Army and I met with our experts and explained the exercise to them. They were to lay out all the calculations, compare them step by step, identify differences, and bring them to our attention so we could discuss them. They did just that and discovered some minor errors in the process, not unusual in such a complex problem involving so many computations, although each staff seemed much more zealous and effective in discovering mistakes in the other's calculations than it did in its own!

The staffs ironed out the errors and minor technical discrepancies and brought us perhaps a dozen differences in assumptions and methods they considered significant. The Secretary of the Army and I then met to discuss these points. In some cases one of us thought the other staff's approach was as good as or better than our own and we conceded the point. In some cases we debated the difference and subjected it to the test of common sense with the help of calculations that gave the outcome each way, holding everything else the same. Sometimes the calculations showed that an assumption someone thought very important really did not make much difference at all.

By this process we finally identified that the single most decisive factor was how the Russians would react to a major United States ABM deployment. On the Army's implicit assumption that they would continue to deploy their currently projected offensive forces, the ABM system would be very effective. Secretary McNamara himself first saw the significance of the assumption about Soviet reaction. It was on his suggestion that the Systems Analysis Office had made calculations based on the alternate assumption that the Soviet Union (like the United States) would react by deploying more missiles or more payload and multiple warheads and other devices to overcome the opposing defenses. These calculations showed that the ABM would not be effective in protecting our cities from Soviet attack.

The Secretary of the Army and I agreed on a set of calculations showing ABM effectiveness with and without Soviet reaction.[33] These calculations allowed the Secretary of Defense, the President, and other officials to focus on the key issue of Soviet reaction to ABM deployment. Once they made the judgment that the Russians almost certainly would react to offset the effectiveness of our ABM system, our calculations became the foundation of Secretary McNamara's case against deployment of a full-scale ABM defense of our cities.

This adversary proceeding between opponents each of whom had a serious interest in proving his point allowed the Secretary of Defense to evaluate the conflicting calculations. If the Army and Systems Analysis agreed, given their high competence and opposing motivations, then the calculations were likely to be as reliable as human minds could make them. This did not guarantee that they were right. Both sides probably accepted assumptions that later would turn out to be incorrect. Nobody can predict the future accurately. But if mistakes were made, it was because of inevitable limits on human knowledge about the uncertain future, not because of ignorance of what was going on inside the computer.

Accompanied by an adversary proceeding, computer-assisted analysis was a most important aid to judgment. It helped the officials discover which factors were especially important and where to focus their judgment. In a problem as complex as this one, the calculations would not have been reproducible as a practical matter without the computer. There would have been too many pieces of paper floating around.

The President and his advisers must have adequate staffs in order for there to be such adversary proceedings. Too many members of the executive branch represent the interests of particular constituencies to the President and too few help him discover the national interest and represent it to the various constituencies. The President and his advisers will not be able to supervise and control or even have access to all of their computer and communications systems unless they are supported by strong, effective staffs who can reach down and get the needed information. The quality of these staffs and the effectiveness of the organizational arrangements in promoting informed constructive debate are much more important than technology in providing a flow of valid relevant information to the President and his advisers.

PACKARD. I might point out that Alain Enthoven's contributions to the Department of Defense did not win him any popularity contests with the military services! But we are continuing to use the systems-analysis capability he developed. It is just as important for the Secretaries of the Army, Navy, and Air Force to get their facts straight as it is for the Secretary of Defense. We are trying to encourage the services themselves to use more systems analysis so they can do the job right in the first place.

I think we should now give Anthony Oettinger an opportunity to respond to the points raised about his paper.

OETTINGER. Enthoven, Pool, and I seem to agree on an essential quality of information handling. Enthoven argues for open and explicit analyses clearly spelled out and made available to all interested parties so they can see what assumptions were used and retrace the steps leading to the conclusions. Pool points to the need for adversary proceedings, documentation of sources, and rigorous hypothesis testing. But although Enthoven agrees with my Indian's principle, he finds it necessary to remark that access to the analyses is more important than access to the communications system, as if I had argued to the contrary. I stress again that new communications technology is important precisely because it can give better access to analyses and also to analysts at all levels than anything now available.

Enthoven cautions us about limiting access to those who "need to know." I clearly recognize the need to guard against indiscretions but believe we must start from the premise that the refusal of access and not the right of access is what requires administrative or legislative justification if we are not to permit the old ways to throttle the new principles in their cradle.

Enthoven tackles folk tales when he says that management information systems are *inevitably* designed to answer questions already asked and precisely defined. His quarrel can be neither with me nor with Pool, who spoke of the ability of the consumer to control the flow, format, and scope of the information he gets as a very significant new capability of the computer. I explicitly denounce those who speak glibly of *management* information systems and neglect the twin opportunities for decentralization and for central-management zoom that Pool and I clearly see resulting from the new technology. The effect is as if I had pinned on Enthoven and on Charles Hitch themselves the sins for which I blame their "witless disciples" in the chapter of my book *Run, Computer, Run* concerned with the myths of systems analysis in educational technology.

In concluding his critique with the statement that the quality of the staffs and the effectiveness of the organizational arrangements are much more important than technology, Enthoven obscures our strong agreement on this essential point. Compunications technology is vital precisely because it can remove physical impediments to effective organizational arrangements for high-quality staffs.

Pool clearly recognizes the importance of zooming but concludes that only when automation regularly saves money, a rare event today, will the kind of reforms I advocate begin to be implemented widely. This "top down" view is an unfortunate consequence of the prevalence of thinking about *management* information systems, neglecting the *Indians*.

If we do think of the *Indians*, and if we think of communications first and only then of computers, we can begin *now*. Let no manager at any level heed only the siren call to sexy front-office systems promising pleasure for him so long as his Indians are not given so much as a peek. The wily tactics of salesmen and technicians merely cloak the immense power of sitting still with the appearance of strenuous striving. We must build also from the bottom up if chiefs are ever to find more than empty promises under the attractive skins.

I have in the past made a careful distinction between a kind of information I call "bull," meaning context and frames of reference unembellished by facts, and a complementary notion I call "cow," meaning facts and data unleavened by context, frames of reference, or evaluation of their truth. When Pool talks of having systems that are not blind to the content or meaning of data, he is talking about systems that can bull, and the only systems I know capable of good bull are people. All that computers can do now is cow.

The problem of getting computers to bull with anything resembling the finesse of people is a long-range research and development problem, not an operational problem.

ENTHOVEN. I have heard the expression "bull" many times, but never before as a technical term! I really did not mean to disagree with Oettingers' points but merely to amplify a few of them with bits of pragmatic wisdom. I was often struck in the Pentagon with the tremendous effort that went into building computerized management information systems. After the systems were built, somebody would ask, "What does a B-52 cost?" or "What does an aircraft carrier cost?" There were cost factors stored in the system, but they were based on certain assumptions about what the rest of the forces were doing and where the B-52 was flying. You must formulate such questions with great precision and specify your assumptions. "What will it cost on the assumption that I replace something else with it, or do this, that, or the other thing?" The Air Force argued for the new B-1 bomber on the grounds that it would save money (by permitting phase-out of the B-52's). Many assumptions go into a cost estimate like that.

The data in a management information system must be answers to questions that are clearly defined. There just is no such thing as information independent of the precisely formulated questions it is supposed to answer.

As far as the "need to know," it does strike me as a bit utopian to start with the idea that the burden is on each agency to prove that information should not be made generally available. That is an awfully long way from where we are now, and although today's state of affairs has disadvantages, there is a great deal of information that I would not like to see freely moved around Washington on everybody's compunications system.

PACKARD. It is time for Dr. Greenberger to present questions from the audience.

GREENBERGER. There are some very good ones, most having to do with *compunications*, the term Oettinger has coined. I would like to take a poll. How many in the audience are *for* the word "compunications" as an addition to our vocabulary? [*Showing of hands*] How many are opposed to it? [*Showing of hands*]

OETTINGER. May I point out that the word is already in the *Congressional Record*!

GREENBERGER. We are too late!

ENTHOVEN. What was the score?

GREENBERGER [*faking a count*]. The score was 72 to 37 against compunications!

OETTINGER. A true fact!

GREENBERGER. But I did not for a minute think we would have any influence on the speaker.

The first set of questions has to do with the technical side of compunications systems. First, John M. Richardson, director of the Office of Telecommunications, United States Department of Commerce, asks about the growth curve for Oettinger's compunications system. How fast would it grow?

Second, Charles Joyce of the National Security Council states that compunications makes it possible for a chief at a high level to access directly incredibly large volumes of information. This capability requires a usable taxonomy or theoretical structure to organize the information. Does such a taxonomy or structure exist for national security or can we somehow function without one?

Finally, Mrs. Helen Brownson, who works in the intelligence community, asks whether it is now feasible to provide access through a computer-based biographic file to sizable quantities of narrative analyses and impressions, and not just selected elements of data. If the information given to Nixon about Khrushchev had been recorded, for example, would you put it in a computerized file?

OETTINGER. I believe the limitations on the growth curve of compunications systems are first and foremost administrative, political, and budgetary, and only secondarily technological. There now exists far more computer and communications potential within government and private industry than is being used effectively.

On the incredibly large amounts of information conceivably accessible to the chief executive, most of the detailed, raw information that we can now handle with computers is best suited to the needs of the Indians. The way the chief gets informed at this stage is by access to knowledgeable people. God help us if we depend on a taxonomy! This business of information systems for *management* is a snare and a delusion. Management gets better informed by having better-informed Indians.

As for biographic files, there is no technological problem now in storing and making available passively by computer narrative information prepared by people. It is simply a matter of cost. The question revolves around the comparative economics of storing large narratives in a computer file versus storing them in a filing cabinet and making them available by pointing a TV camera at a printed page or by teleprinting. Content analysis of the kind that Pool suggests, on the other hand, requires long-range research and development.

POOL. It is obvious that Oettinger and I do not completely agree about the matter of cost and the usefulness of systems that are extremely limited or totally passive. I still think that things will not move rapidly in the direction that Oettinger foresees until some of the capabilities he describes as active are available economically.

PACKARD. The computer and communications expenditure in the Department of Defense has grown over the last several years at about three times the rate of the entire defense budget. Under current financial constraints, we are working very hard to see whether we can maintain a continued growth in effective utilization without continued growth in cost. The utilization of our facilities is by no means as efficient as it should be. I hope we shall be able to make some significant changes in the way people use the system, and we shall probably get more benefit from this than from additions to hardware.

GREENBERGER. The last two questions we shall consider deal with some of the practical implications of compunications systems. J. Phillip London, a lieutenant commander with the Naval Materiel Command, United States Navy, asks Oettinger how his idealized compunications system by-passes the natural tendencies of large organizations to develop power pockets by emitting propaganda advocating their own political position.

W. Lester McGreer, staff assistant for data automation policy in the office of the deputy assistant secretary of defense for information systems, asks whether compunications could provide information to the mass media and the public generally in order to reduce the polarization apparent in segments of our youth-oriented intellectual society.

OETTINGER. I think the by-passing of power pockets is exactly what compunications systems make physically possible. There is no longer a physical need and possibility for control as when there is separation in time and space. My two principles go to the heart of the power question.

As far as information to the mass media is concerned, I think that if we start from the notion of unfettered access, we can begin to make reasonable judgments on what limitations are in the best interests of what portions of society. But if we start from where we are now (and I agree with Enthoven that we are pretty far in the other direction), then we are in grave difficulties with respect to the outside as well as the inside.

ENTHOVEN. At Harvard some administrative files were opened up to the younger generation and communicated to the mass media. My impression in reading about this from the other end of the country was that it did not have the effect of reducing polarization!

OETTINGER. The files were not opened up *to* the students. They were, as the language of the faculty resolution put it, "forcibly opened" *by* the students.

ENTHOVEN. You mean they did not have unfettered access? In other words, when your own ox is being gored, limitations become important!

OETTINGER. I was very careful to state my recommendations as principles, not as operating realities. The last thing a professor can afford to be accused of these days is hypocrisy!

POOL. A tremendously important problem that we have not discussed is where to draw the line between privacy and the extension of knowledge. It is not crucial to Oettinger's paper, since he is addressing the problem that most information not available today is lost somewhere in the vast maw of the system. Once that problem is alleviated, however, we come up against this other problem. Once we succeed in getting the information we need, we face the critical responsibility of deciding whether it can be disseminated.

DINNER DISCUSSION

GREENBERGER. Arthur Okun, you were in a key policy position in the last administration as chairman of the Council of Economic Advisers. Can you relate your experiences to the earlier discussion?

OKUN. I question how much of the problem in decision making at the national level is a compunications problem in the Oettinger sense and how much is simply a need for better access to and organization of data. I think Oettinger's recommendations are constructive but suspect that some of the most important problems lie elsewhere.

Enthoven's anecdote reminds me of my own experiences. The estimates of crop yields by the Agriculture Department, which were the underpinning of budgeted amounts for agricultural support programs, were lower every year than our estimates in the council and those of the Budget Bureau. This is the problem again of getting "true facts" as opposed to just "facts."

The main communications requirement in many economic policy areas is to put things in a way that is comprehensible to decision makers not familiar with the professional jargon. Young expert Ph.D. economists typically cannot communicate with the President because of the technical way they tend to think and formulate concepts. Half of my time in the council was spent as rewrite man trying to translate good staff material about slopes and elasticities into a form that was meaningful to the President, as well as to the White House staff and agency heads, for the decisions they

---

Participants: S. Douglass Cater, Academy for Educational Development (formerly Special Assistant to President Lyndon B. Johnson); Alain C. Enthoven, Litton Industries; Michael J. Flynn, The Johns Hopkins University; Henry S. Forrest, Control Data Corporation; Walter W. Haase, Bureau of the Budget; Hubert Heffner, Office of Science and Technology; Nicholas Johnson, Federal Communications Commission; Anthony G. Oettinger, Harvard University; Arthur M. Okun, The Brookings Institution (formerly Chairman of the Council of Economic Advisers); Ithiel de Sola Pool, Massachusetts Institute of Technology; David J. Rose, Oak Ridge National Laboratory; Andrew Rouse, President's Advisory Council on Executive Organization; Dael Wolfle, University of Washington; Martin Greenberger, chairman, The Johns Hopkins University.

had to make. I do not know how much the President would have been able to get from talking with the technical experts directly.

GREENBERGER. You seem to be saying that a direct line from the chief at a high level to an expert at a lower level may not be too productive because they do not speak the same language.

OETTINGER. Granted. This is why I emphasized the need for lateral communication and jumpers. Jumpers help lower-level staff to understand other areas of the hierarchy and consequently to improve their ability to explain themselves. This is a motivating force behind the Indian's principle. Technology can be enormously useful if it is put in the proper administrative and social context; but if it is not, it can be counterproductive. Any computer-communications system that tends to freeze compartmentation and hierarchical lines and thereby obstruct rather than promote lateral communication is worse than none.

CATER. I am troubled by the implication of the Indian's principle that all Indians have free and equal access. I remember graphically Carl Albert's dilemma while presiding at the 1968 Democratic national convention. Trouble broke out in one of the delegations, the TV cameras and walkie-talkies moved in, and the whole nation, along with most of the convention floor, which had its own TV system, knew immediately what was happening. But Carl Albert did not have a TV monitor. We witnessed the spectacle of floundering leadership caused by a communications gap.

This typifies one of the problems of leadership today. Its communications system is not able to give it adequate time to think through decisions before execution. The President looks down on government and sees not only Indians, but many warring tribes. He knows that intelligence made available to a tribe is immediately used to its advantage. The instinct of the President and his aides is to hoard intelligence until they decide what to do with it. This is where I have trouble with the Indian's principle.

ENTHOVEN. This story reminds me of an experience I had in the Pentagon. In the early 1960's we pushed hard for the build-up of the country's nonnuclear capabilities. We thought we had the problem under control when one day a newspaper headline appeared announcing a bomb shortage in Vietnam. Secretary McNamara knew nothing of the matter before reading the newspaper account and immediately called me in along with Paul Ignatius, assistant secretary for logistics, to find out what was going on.

We had nothing in our files to substantiate the report. McNamara was determined not to have a bomb shortage at that point in the war and had us drop everything to fly to Hawaii for a meeting with the commander in chief of all United States military forces in the Pacific, the commander in chief of the United States Air Force in the Pacific, the commander in chief of the United States Air Force in Vietnam, the group commander, and their subordinates. We started interrogating the man at the bottom who was closest to the problem and quickly verified that there were plenty of bombs there. The problem was that the Air Force had sent the bodies of the bombs to one base, the fins to another base, and the fuses to another, and there was a mismatch. As soon as we established this fact, the brigadier general asked the colonel why he had not been informed, the same question was asked of the brigadier general by the major general, and so on up the line like falling dominoes. (General Westmoreland assured us, by the way, that no needed sorties had been missed.)

With modern communications the average citizen can almost watch the war as it progresses and is better informed at times than the Secretary of Defense, as in this instance. I think it would be better for the country if the Secretary of Defense (or the President) had a chance to find out what was really going on, figure it out, and take a position before the general public learned the bad news.

HEFFNER. You have just made a very persuasive argument for a free press.

ENTHOVEN. I believe in a free press, but it would have helped if the press had taken the trouble to ascertain more of the facts before printing the headline.

POOL. The real problem was that three parts of the system had gone to three different places. This problem of lateral communication at the lowest level is where Oettinger's case is strongest. The problem might never have arisen if there had been rapid and easy lateral communication between the people with the bodies, those with the fuses, and those with the fins.

OETTINGER. The story also illustrates the need for a zoom capability to gain information other than by flying to Hawaii. Available technology certainly can provide chiefs with reaction times comparable to that of the press.

The problem of warring tribes is actually a motivation for the chief's principle. Computer and telecommunications technology can be used with extreme effectiveness to reinforce compartmentation and divisiveness unless the chief controls the information systems under him. If he does not, the warring tribes can use new technology as a powerful weapon against him, and he may find himself disconnected and at the mercy of his competing subordinates.

WOLFLE. How does the chief regulate not only the specific material but also the timing of what the warring factions make available? They can exercise control not only over *what* they put in the information system but also *when* they put it in.

OETTINGER. This is a reason for my argument against *management* information systems, systems addressed solely to the top. If the only purpose of the system is to inform the superior, then the tendency is to fudge and leave things out. It is only by attending to the lower-echelon needs that a system can assure some measure of reliability. If the fellow who enters information depends on it for his own operations, his incentive for timeliness and accuracy is greater. The information will be more current and reliable by virtue of its being a normal part of day-to-day operations.

CATER. My concern with protecting Presidential leadership has a second aspect. The President can never construct a perfect scanning system which will allow him and his aides to follow information flow in a radar-like way. If it were known that he had a powerful computer-communications system available to him that he did not use successfully in a given instance, his leadership would be compromised politically. This consideration may make him suspicious and allergic to such a system, particularly if he is uncertain of how tight his control over it is.

The U-2 incident illustrates how things are now. None of us knew until recently just how much Eisenhower knew about that episode. Maybe we are moving into a new age of total cognizance which will create a new kind of leadership, but it certainly has not yet emerged.

POOL. This is part of the reason why I differ with Oettinger on the value of passive versus active systems. Passive systems that enormously increase the amount of information available without helping the receiver digest it are going to create vast problems of overload. The crucial need is for active systems that provide sorting, guidance, and other processing services beyond simply producing information on demand.

OETTINGER. My point is that the only things we know how to do really well right now in computer technology are simple-minded passive systems for assimilating and massaging detailed data. A passive system can be useful to anyone in the hierarchy in his capacity as an Indian; it is less useful to him in his capacity as a chief. The creation of active systems with the kind of analytical capability Pool desires still presents important research and development problems which will someday be either solved or abandoned. At the present time, the higher one goes in the hierarchy the more important the communications aspect of compunications, and the lower one goes the more important the computer aspect. A solid passive data base is an essential prerequisite for useful active systems.

GREENBERGER. One of the other speakers, Herbert Simon, was emphatic about the need for active as opposed to passive systems and seems to believe their realization is nearer than Oettinger does.

I am now going to sound out those yet to express an opinion. Nicholas Johnson is the first on the silent queue.

JOHNSON. I think control of information plays an ever more important role than we have acknowledged. The fellow at the FCC who had the table of FM station assignments for the United States in his upper desk drawer did not want this information put into a computer where it would be available to me, let alone to his colleagues, and least of all to the public. Control of this information gave him power, whereas putting it on a computer would diminish him in the eyes of others and might eliminate his function altogether.

There is a multimillion-dollar industry that gets information from the FCC for clients for a fee before it is generally available to the public. I would far prefer to have reporters sit in on our executive meetings and get what I say first-hand, but I have yet to convince anyone of the merit of this idea.

Cater's convention story neatly illustrates the problem. Authority is represented by the man who chairs the meeting and holds the gavel. Yet it can be totally undermined by a television camera wandering the floor with access to fifty million Americans. The fight in this country over who can put his message on that little TV screen should be clearly recognized in discussing the use of technology to distribute information. This is where the battle may be won or lost.

OETTINGER. You are quite right. Use of the technology does affect the distribution of power, and there is indeed a power struggle at issue.

ROSE. At Oak Ridge we are in the very difficult business of trying to find consequences and alternatives to present to decision makers in the environmental area. How do you use computer and communication facilities to see what can be done for the rivers of the country, when this depends on salary trends in the lumbering industry, which has to do with the cost of wood, which has to do with upland fertilization, which affects downstream pollution? The problems are so complex that we cannot readily see through all the pieces. We need a scheme for searching and association, a taxonomy of some kind.

FORREST. As a representative of a systems manufacturer, I believe that the user must be told what he can expect from a system and what it will cost him. We have a responsibility to define the bounds of a system that will do some of the things Oettinger suggests.

FLYNN. I have doubts about the volume of data that the technology will allow us to store. A computer tape stores twelve million characters. A book of approximately the same size stores two million characters. If the problem is one of sheer volume of data, the technology to solve it is not just around the corner.

The most successful information-retrieval systems are ones where the volume of data is limited, the format fixed, the context well defined, and the data volatile. The airline reservation system is a good example. I agree with Oettinger that this is a system which the Indians have used extensively in their own operations.

ROUSE. Oettinger seems to be implying a monumental change in our social system and the way organizations behave. Is he just advocating compunications or is he saying that technological imperatives will bring it to pass no matter what we do?

OETTINGER. In some form the pressures toward increased use of computers and communications are well nigh irresistible. My point is that there remains now (but not for long) a choice on how we use the technology. Unless groups like the President's Advisory Council on Executive Organization pay attention to the problem, the technology will be used by default simply to freeze the old ways.

ROUSE. If you are saying that compunications is what we are going to get anyway and we have relatively little time to prepare, then your paper is not primarily about compunications but about a social system of nonhierarchical organizations controlled from above with information generally accessible below. How do you achieve this nonhierarchical mode?

OETTINGER. I explicitly did *not* discard the hierarchical mode of organization. One-level anarchy cannot run anything larger than a family or a tribe. We do need hierarchies, compartments, and the splitting of responsibilities. My point is that we can complement the hierarchical mode and make up for its shortcomings while still capitalizing on its undeniable and necessary assets by taking judicious advantage of the potential that technology offers for strengthening jumpers, providing the ability to zoom, and so on.

HEFFNER. I believe Oettinger is thinking of an ideal system, and if there is one thing I have learned in my few months in Washington it is that the present system of government is not an ideal, rational system. It sometimes seems that in Washington everybody can say "no" and no one can say "yes." The notion of a hierarchy of chiefs with the top chief making the final decision and individual chiefs at lower levels making subordinate decisions is a fiction.

No amount of data will substitute for the human process of asking the right question. What the chief needs is an expert to interpret the data. He normally does not want to go down deeply into the data himself, although David Packard may do this because there is certain data that he can evaluate from his own experience. The chief without experience in a given field wants an expert whose judgment he can trust, who is not part of the system, and who does not have a special ax to grind.

OETTINGER. We have no disagreement about the absolute importance of people in the system, except that I believe the zoom capability offered by technology can help a chief find the expert he needs.

HAASE. Oettinger has suggested that the President have an information system capable of zooming in on detailed operational information used by lower levels of management. Since I have responsibility for developing an information system for various elements of the executive office, I would be interested in Oettinger's views on how to develop such a capability.

I agree with Forrest that we must put bounds on what we undertake. We should not make excessive promises or oversell, and we need logical building blocks by which to proceed. The behavioral questions raised by Johnson are key. Information equals power, and visibility to some extent equals vulnerability. The concept of a relatively free flow of information on performance certainly brings up many organizational and individual behavioral problems and the basic question of power. It suggests the need for a whole new set of relationships between successive levels of management and a new kind of management philosophy.

Oettinger suggests building a system that serves the Indian so that it will have credibility and be useful to higher management. I agree with this notion and would be interested in Oettinger's ideas on how to create a system that the lower-level people will consider also in their best interest.

OETTINGER. This is the point of my observation that every man in the hierarchy is both a chief and an Indian. The fundamental power problem is that the demands of a chief and the demands of an Indian are incompatible. We are touching on one of the most delicate and sensitive issues in any organization. Technology is secondary. If there is any hope of making a beginning, it is through the realization that everyone in a hierarchy plays the dual role of chief and Indian; that what he gives up as a chief, he gains as an Indian, and vice versa. Even that much may be utopian. But without this realization there is no hope at all.

This indeed implies new relationships. We are abysmally ignorant on these matters, and it is high time that they were studied carefully. Relatively few people are studying the dynamics of organizations in a scholarly way, certainly far fewer than their counterparts in technology.

FLYNN. I want to support the notion of the importance of organizational matters over technological issues. The Federal Aviation Agency is in the process of spending several hundred million dollars to build a radar-computer-communications system to control air traffic. At the same time the country is spending several billion dollars for a much more powerful duplicate of this system for the ABM program. One of the reasons the ABM system must be so powerful is to filter out ordinary flights. The fact that the two systems cannot be integrated to avoid the enormous duplication is strictly organizational.

JOHNSON. There is a substantial body of opinion that the most efficient information retrieval system is the "ask a man" system (which I name after the counsel of my father, Wendell Johnson, who told me that if I ever was lost, not to fear, just "ask a man"). If you really want to find something out, six telephone calls will normally find you the person who knows. Maybe we should let the fellow keep the table of FM assignments in his top drawer. Then if we do not understand his first answer, we can always ask him a second question. I am playing devil's advocate.

CATER. I have a feeling we are shooting at a disappearing target, although I still cannot envisage a computerized system storing important biographical information about Khrushchev along with sources (many secret) of this information and the evaluation of those sources. Nor can I envisage a computer system giving Indians (other than those directly concerned) access to early-warning information that something is going seriously wrong with foreign policy, such as the enemy's installing missiles in Cuba or a new weapon's being developed. The main requirement is to move such information forward on a straight line to the top chief as fast as possible.

HEFFNER. I think we have all argued with Oettinger as critics by foisting on him a more extreme view than he has adopted. He is not offering panaceas. There is a great deal of merit in his two principles and in his way of looking at the individual as both a chief and an Indian.

REFERENCES

1. Richard M. Nixon, "Statement by the President on the Establishment of a National Goals Research Staff," Office of the White House Press Secretary, for release July 13, 1969, p. 2.
2. Art Buchwald, "Why Not Elect a Computer to Lead Us?" *Boston Globe*, March 20, 1969, p. 19.
3. Richard E. Neustadt, *Presidential Power*, New American Library, Mentor Books, 1964.
4. Harry Howe Ransom, *Central Intelligence and National Security*, Harvard University Press, 1958, p. 7.
5. John G. Kemeny, "Large Time-Sharing Networks," this volume.
6. Anthony G. Oettinger, "A Bull's Eye View of Management and Engineering Information Systems," *Proceedings of the 19th ACM National Conference*, Association for Computing Machinery, 1964. Reprinted in *Information Technology in a Democracy*, ed. Alan Westin, Harvard University Press (in press). Also, Anthony G. Oettinger, *Run, Computer, Run: The Mythology of Educational Innovation*, Harvard University Press, 1969.
7. Arthur M. Schlesinger, Jr., *The Coming of the New Deal*, Houghton Mifflin, 1959, p. 523.
8. Neustadt, *Presidential Power*, p. 161.
9. Herbert Simon, "Designing Organizations for an Information-Rich World," this volume.
10. Harold L. Wilensky, *Organizational Intelligence*, Basic Books, 1967, p. 47.
11. "Interview with Admiral William F. Raborn, Retiring Head of America's Most Secret Agency," *U.S. News and World Report*, July 18, 1966, p. 78.
12. Robert F. Kennedy, *Thirteen Days*, New American Library, Signet Books, 1969, pp. 111–12.
13. Townsend Hoopes, "The Fight for the President's Mind," *Atlantic*, October 1969, pp. 106–7.
14. *Inquiry into the U.S.S. Pueblo and EC-121 Plane Incidents,* Report of the Special Subcommittee on the U.S.S. *Pueblo* of the Committee on Armed Services, House of Representatives, 91st Cong., 1st sess., July 28, 1969, p. 1619.
15. Wilensky, *Organizational Intelligence*, p. 43.
16. Ransom, *Central Intelligence*, pp. 213–14.

17. Chester L. Guthrie and Thomas R. Kennedy, "Informing the Nation's President," *Advanced Management Journal*, vol. 34, no. 1 (January 1969): 29.
18. Neustadt, *Presidential Power*, p. 23.
19. Ransom, *Central Intelligence*, p. 35.
20. Sherman Kent, *Strategic Intelligence*, Archon Books, 1965, p. xv.
21. Hoopes, "President's Mind," p. 107.
22. Marshall McLuhan, *The Gutenberg Galaxy*, University of Toronto Press, 1962, pp. 7, 32.
23. Arthur M. Schlesinger, Jr., *A Thousand Days*, Houghton Mifflin, 1965, p. 422.
24. Oettinger, "Bull's Eye View."
25. Richard M. Nixon, *Six Crises*, Pyramid, 1968, p. 254.
26. Kent, *Strategic Intelligence*, pp. 140–41.
27. MIT Press (in press).
28. Stuart D. McIntosh and David M. Griffel, "Large Disparate Data Bases," and "The Requirements for a Computer-Based Information System (CBIS)," reports of the Center for International Studies, Massachusetts Institute of Technology, 1968.
29. Alain C. Enthoven and K. Wayne Smith, *How Much Is Enough?*, Harper & Row, 1971, chap. 2.
30. Alain C. Enthoven, "Arms and Men: The Military Balance in Europe," *Interplay*, May 1969, pp. 11–14; also Alain C. Enthoven and K. Wayne Smith, "What Forces for NATO? And from Whom?", *Foreign Affairs*, October 1969, pp. 80–96.
31. Alain C. Enthoven, "The Planning, Programming, and Budgeting System in the Department of Defense: Some Lessons from Experience," *The Analysis and Evaluation of Public Expenditures: The PPB System*, U.S. Congress, Joint Economic Committee, Government Printing Office, 1969, p. 903.
32. Previously described in Alain C. Enthoven, "Analysis, Judgment, and Computers," *Business Horizons*, August 1969, pp. 31–34.
33. "Statement by Secretary of Defense Robert S. McNamara on the Fiscal Year 1969–73 Defense Program and the 1969 Defense Budget," U.S. Department of Defense, January 1968, p. 64.

EDUCATION IN MODERN SOCIETY

Speaker JAMES S. COLEMAN
             Professor of Social Relations
             The Johns Hopkins University

Discussants EUGENE G. FUBINI
             Private Consultant

            PATRICK SUPPES
             Professor of Philosophy, Statistics
              and Education
             Stanford University

Moderator DAEL WOLFLE
             Professor of Public Affairs
             University of Washington
             (formerly Executive Officer of
             The American Association for the
             Advancement of Science)

WOLFLE. James Coleman was principal author of the massive study of the equality of educational opportunity commonly referred to as the Coleman report. Its major conclusions are provocative, controversial, and often quoted these days. In that study Coleman examined certain outcomes of education in sensitive areas, a difficult problem at best, and it is no wonder that he stimulated controversy in the process. Coleman is now going to take up another aspect of education, from the viewpoint of our changing society and the modern equipment and techniques available to us.

COLEMAN. The communication structure of society can affect education in two quite different ways. One is through application of new communications technology in schools: the use of closed-circuit television, computer consoles in the classroom, visual-aid equipment, and a wide range of other new possibilities. Some of these applications, potential and actual, promise to create sharp changes in the schools. It is these effects on education that technological changes in communication ordinarily bring to mind. But it has been characteristic of these applications that their promise precedes their reality by some years and that when the reality comes it never quite seems to match the expectation.

The second kind of effect that the communication structure of society has on education is very different. It is through changes in communication structure *outside* educational institutions, powerful and pervasive changes that have unplanned and unanticipated effects on schools. These effects are often not recognized until after they have wrought their changes. The reality precedes the promise and is more powerful than the expectation.

These indirect effects are by-products of technological change in the communication structure of society. As such, one might expect them to be less important than the effects of direct, planned introduction of new communication technology in education. This, I believe, is not so today. The indirect impact of changes in the communication structure of society has been and will be so great that the technological changes in the schools themselves must take place within the new frame that these developments create.

Information Richness and Vicarious Experience

The first attribute of change in society's communication structure as it affects education is the information richness to which Herbert Simon referred.[1] Not many years ago a child obtained most of his information from direct experience. It was information restricted largely to his family, neighborhood, and community. It was supplemented by a few windows to the outside world opened by reading material at home or in school. This reading material provided vicarious experience which extended a child's horizons beyond his direct experience. It gave him a broader base from which to act, a base that drew upon others' experiences as well as his own.

Throughout their history, schools have been the community's gateway for information. Schools have been a source of, and guide to, books, and books constituted the principal door to the world beyond one's own experience. To create for myself the flavor of that experience, I recently read an autobiography of a man born in 1870 and raised in a rural backwater, Dry Fork, in the area of southern Illinois known as Little Egypt. On books, he wrote:

Our books were an ancient, musty-smelling Bible, originally bound in black leather but with one of its covers missing, and a book about the great plains, called *The Buffalo Land*. Later we secured two more books from somewhere, a *History of Andersonville Prison* and *Robinson Crusoe*. We borrowed the county newspaper when we could and read it, usually three weeks late.

And about his school, he wrote:

There were four months of school in winter and two in summer. After the summer term in Hardscrabble, we moved into Ward school district; but the process was the same there, and everywhere, so far as I know. Our textbooks were not uniform; we took what we had and the teacher somehow managed to get along. . . . With what help the teacher could give, pupils gathered from this array of books the learning available in rural areas at that time. . . . One teacher in Ward School told us in a moment of pause that he had been on a train that "traveled sixty miles an hour." We sat open-mouthed and incredulous at that.[2]

In a society with this much poverty of information, the ratio of a child's vicarious to direct experience was very low. The vicarious experience gained through reading was a supplement to direct personal experience. But because reading was, and is, not a universal hobby, vicarious experiences were very unevenly distributed throughout the population of children. And because reading is a slow procedure for assimilating information, vicarious experiences grew only slowly as a child grew and read more widely.

Thus the vicarious experience gained through reading was a supplement to direct personal experience. For those who read widely, the ratio of vicarious experience to direct experience grew as their range of reading increased; but the rate of shift was limited by the rate and frequency of reading, which for most persons was not high.

The emergence of electronic methods of communication such as television has radically increased the absolute amount of vicarious experience. It has freed vicarious experience from the limitations of differential reading habits, slowly developing reading skills, and the intrinsically slow rate of assimilation that reading allows. It has shifted the balance between direct and vicarious experience toward vicarious experience for all of us, and it has done so most strongly for the young. Instead of information poverty they now experience information richness. Schools as they now exist were designed for an information-poor society, in part to provide a child with vicarious experience from books and contact with a teacher. Obviously that function is radically altered by television, radio, and other media outside the school. Vicarious experience is no longer a slowly developing supplement to direct experience, but an early and large component of the child's total experience. The adventure of discovering the world, the many simple but exciting facts, the amazement at hearing of a train that could travel sixty miles an hour are mostly gone from a child's experience in school.

The vast increase in children's vicarious experience loads their cognition with attributes characterizing vicarious experience. Vicarious experience obtained through communication differs from direct experience in those ways that research has shown rumors to differ from reality. In rumor transmission (and more generally in any information transmission), the content is sharpened: complexities of reality are lost, the selectivity of the camera or pen imposes an artificial unity of action, the intensity of action is increased, and the participants are polarized into heroes and villains.

Vicarious experience is not a full substitute for direct experience in another way as well. In vicarious experience, whether obtained through books or television, one is an observer outside the action, with no responsibility for affecting what goes on and no power to do so. One becomes a spectator at a wide variety of events rather than a participant in a few.

Social scientists do not yet know the consequences of these changes in the source of a child's cognitive world. The changes may lead to a more passive personality, a sense of frustration or powerlessness, a world viewed in more moralistic and less strategic terms, or all of these things. It is not known whether the mass of information from vicarious experience overwhelms one's capacity based on direct experience to assimilate it; but obviously some effects of this sort exist.

Until we know these consequences more clearly, we cannot determine how the school's function in providing information should be modified. Whatever else can be said, the school is confronted with a situation precisely opposite to that which it faced when the child's environment was information poor. The school finds itself with children who are products of the mass media, children whose vicarious experience, obtained outside school, has provided a flood of information which may or may not be useful as a guide to action.

Today's information richness and the pictorial medium through which information is transmitted have greatly changed the cognitive world of the child in very specific ways. In so doing, they have abundantly fulfilled (or overfulfilled) a major function of schools when words and books were the medium of transmission and a child's cognitive world was built largely from his own experiences.

Information Pluralism and the Shaping of Values

A second element of change in our society's communication structure is related to the information richness but is not a necessary consequence of it. This is a greatly increased pluralism in sources of information available to the young. When the child lived in a poverty of information, the family and school shaped the child's cognitive world by the selectivity of information they imposed. As the environment has become information rich, the child's cognitive world has begun to be shaped by neither family nor school, but by comic books, television, paperbacks, and the broad spectrum of newspapers and magazines that abound, from the *Chicago Tribune* to the *Berkeley Barb* and from *Reader's Digest* to *Ramparts*. A less open society, which attempts to exercise totalitarian control of the mass media, can and does reduce this pluralism of information sources but probably only delays the force of technology.

In the information-poor societies of the past, the school's relative monopoly of the child's nonexperiential information had a very powerful effect on his values. This influence did not arise so much from courses on civics, United States history, and state history, or in other activities overtly oriented to public affairs and politics; students are characteristically bored with courses explicitly designed to teach them values and virtues such as good citizenship. The effect rather came from what the school excluded. It arose from the selectivity the school exerted on visions of the outside world, through the alternative definitions of events it did not present. The school's shaping of values may have been good or bad, but it did so through the absence of competing sources of information.

The information pluralism to which children in modern society are exposed removes the school's shaping of values through selectivity. This function cannot be recovered in the old way. If it can be recovered at all, it must be through socializing experiences in the school that are strong enough to be effective in the presence of information from sources with diverse interests and ideologies.

In summary, two aspects of the communication structure of information-rich open societies are destroying two classical functions of the school. Information richness removes the function of the school in extending the child's horizons through vicarious experience; and information pluralism removes the function of the school in shaping the child's values through selectivity.

Information Richness and the Learning of Skills

The information richness of the society challenges another function of the school: its teaching of cognitive skills. Communities were once poor in the knowledge necessary to teach such skills as reading, spelling, mathematics, and languages. Now, many individuals and organizations can justifiably claim that they teach these skills better than schools. Educational television and the great number of books, toys, and games designed to help children learn to read or count provide many new learning devices for teaching skills *outside* schools. In Texarkana, Arkansas, as one example, an educational firm recently contracted with the federal government to increase achievement levels of children in reading and mathematics outside schools for a charge based upon increments in achievement.

These external resources are not collected in a central locus, a school, but are dispersed among bookstores, toy stores, reading institutes, foreign language centers, and educational divisions of large business firms like Westinghouse and Lockheed. They present a continuous and increasing challenge to the skill-teaching functions of a school, challenging the very assumption on which classical schools were based: namely, that the informational resources necessary to teach cognitive skills to the young were scarce and best provided by grouping children in a school around a teacher presumed to have such resources.

This does not mean that cognitive skills will automatically be absorbed by children from the environment. Disciplined effort, under the guidance of some agent, remains a prerequisite to learning. But the number of alternative agents outside schools, ranging from educated parents to reading institutes, is now greatly increased.

Information Processing

The classical function of schools in teaching cognitive skills is also likely to be affected directly by computers. It is now possible, through telephone lines and time sharing, to bring the information-processing capabilities of computers into the classroom or home. With a teletypewriter in my home, I can communicate directly with any of five different computers. I can play simple games with the computer and be taught by it. The computer can interact with my responses, correct them, and indicate where and how I am wrong. This capability on the other end of a telephone line is not as great as that of Mark Hopkins at the other end of a log; but it is greater than that of a teacher who must deal simultaneously with thirty students making different kinds of errors, progressing at different rates of speed, and needing different kinds of help.

There are, to be sure, still many deficiencies in the use of information-processing machines as learning devices. But it is only a matter of time, programming sophistication, and cost reduction before the computer will be competitive with certain instructional functions of the teacher. The work carried out by Suppes and others shows that many children enjoy computer-interactive drills and exercises more than ordinary drills in the classroom and learn more from them per unit of time spent. There are inherent limitations on the interactive capability of a computer; but so are there on the interactive capability of a teacher due to divided attention, incomplete or incorrect knowledge, and personality defects that obstruct the interaction. The limitations of the teacher in the classroom appear to present at least as many impediments to learning as the inherent limitations of the computer.

The capability of computers for teaching skills goes far beyond simple exercises and drills. Computers can be programmed to simulate a particular physical or social environment and respond to a student who probes that environment. A student may learn efficient means of sampling the environment and analyzing the data to infer properties. These capabilities simply have not been available in schools before except in laboratories in a few subjects.

A new kind of communication system is developing in the United States, a system which John Kemeny described and which his work greatly stimulated.[3] This is a long-range communication system between individuals with time-shared computers as intermediaries. The growth of commercial time-sharing systems into nationwide computer-communication systems has been phenomenal and shows no signs of slowing.

The implications of this new capability for education lie in a further loosening of the physical constraints of location, which has necessitated grouping children together into single buildings with teachers. This does not mean an abandonment of the school, but it does make possible organizational arrangements that were impossible under the communication structures of past societies. In the short run, simulation games can be played between classrooms equipped with computer terminals; one classroom can set a problem and another solve it; new exercises and teaching programs can be made immediately available to all those connected to the system. In the longer run, the very concept of the classroom or school is challenged. A school was necessary to economize on a teacher's time. When money permitted, some children were individually tutored without need of a school. For many classical skills, the tutoring capability of a computer makes a school equally unnecessary. There is no inherent reason for a student and computer terminal to be in a classroom with other students and terminals.

Another implication of this new capability lies in increasing equality of educational opportunity. I recently carried out with others a large study of equality of educational opportunity by race in the United States.[4] We expected to find major inequalities in the resources of schools attended by Negroes and whites in the form of different curricula, physical plant, textbooks, libraries, laboratories, and equipment. We found some of these inequalities; but we also found that the inequalities with the greatest effect on learning were the child's *social* environment (in particular, the educational backgrounds of other children in the school) and the verbal skills of the teacher. The development of a child's vocabulary appeared to be more a function of the size of his classmates' and his teacher's vocabularies than one of the resources put into the school by the school board.

In short, the principal source of educational inequality for lower-class Negroes lies in their confinement to a homogeneous environment poor in information or cognitive skills. This confinement has been relaxed as society has become urban and as mass communications have grown. In the past, in depressed rural areas, the confinement was almost total. Many intellectual differences are remnants of that past.

The capabilities of computers to teach and thereby to remove physical constraints of location have clear implications in this context. Computers can confront a child with a different environment and impose demands on him that his local environment does not. They can provide a cognitive environment that, although not as powerful as a human environment of classmates, is not restricted by the location of the school.

There is, however, an important defect in the computer's ability to substitute for the teacher. This defect lies in its inability to impose demands and motivate the student to meet them. The computer can pose a problem and aid the student in finding a solution, but it cannot cause him to approach the problem in the first place. Computer-aided instruction can generate motivation once the interaction is indicated, but it cannot help lead the student into the interaction. The computer terminal may merely sit in his home unless it can help him in some of the everyday problems he faces. It differs in this respect from the television set.

I have described four environmental changes in society that have profound implications for the schools: information richness, which expands a child's horizons through vicarious experience; information pluralism, which exposes the child to a diverse array of perspectives on the world; widespread cognitive capabilities outside the school, which expand the ability to teach cognitive skills; and information-processing machines, which can take over much of the teaching of cognitive skills now performed by teachers.

These changes permit resources once concentrated in the school to be brought into the nonschool environment, thus undermining the very rationale upon which the school was founded. It would appear that they should cause a "withering away of the school," a reduction in its importance. Yet the reverse seems to be true. School days and years in school have both become longer. These increases in schooling are often attributed to the growing importance of reading, mathematics, and other academic curricula in modern society. Yet one can suspect that there are other functions of the school for which the new capabilities of the environment are not useful and that the need for these has increased in recent years. Indeed, one can suspect that there are changes in the external environment that reduce its capability to provide its classical functions in the socialization of children.

The Action Poverty of Society for the Child

As our society has become information rich, it has also become action poor. It has become poor in the necessity and possibility for struggle against the environment. In the past, this struggle took the form of children actively involved in productive action in the household or supporting themselves from an early age. In the same autobiography that described Hardscrabble School at Dry Fork in Little Egypt, the author describes his activities as a twelve-year-old:

> On arrival in Geff our mother reported promptly to Mrs. Rapp and hired me out to her as chore boy about the store; it was the capsheaf of my ambition. I was to have four dollars the first month and then, in the winter, my board during the school months. I was twelve then and have never been out of a job since. Actually my pay was raised to five dollars a month the next spring and I stayed on there through three full years. . . . There was a garden back of the store; and back of the garden an orchard; this area, three town lots in all, with barn and pigpen, was my domain. . . . My experience with that yard was almost a duplicate of that related by Booker T. Washington in his *Working with the Hands*. I, too, had an uncompromising overseer; I, too, must work with a blunt-edged sickle; I, too, had to hack away hour after hour at the long tough grass to get it even. . . . When I had finished it the first time, Mrs. Rapp came out for inspection. She made no criticism or suggestion but praised me mildly. And, to quote the words of Booker T. Washington, "When I saw that all this change and improvement was a creation of my own hands, my whole nature began to change. I felt a self-respect, an encouragement and a satisfaction that I had never before enjoyed or thought possible."[5]

In other cases, this struggle against the environment took the form of a more primitive struggle for survival, a struggle that still exists in the slums of central cities. Claude Brown in his autobiography describes himself as a twelve-year-old.

> My friends were all daring like me, tough like me, dirty like me, ragged like me, cursed like me, and had a great love for trouble like me. We took pride in being able to hitch rides on trolleys, buses, taxicabs and in knowing how to steal and fight. We knew that we were the only kids in the neighborhood who usually had more than ten dollars in their pockets. There were other people who knew this too, and that was often a problem for us. Somebody was always trying to shake us down or rob us. This was usually done by the older hustlers in the neighborhood or by storekeepers or cops. At other times, older fellows would shake us down, con us, or Murphy us out of our loot. We accepted this as the ways of life. Everybody was stealing from everybody else. And sometimes we would shake down newsboys and shoeshine boys. So we really had no complaints coming. Although none of my sidekicks was over twelve years of age, we didn't think of ourselves as kids.[6]

What is striking about both of these descriptions, different though they are, is that the twelve-year-olds were no longer "kids." Twelve-year-olds, and indeed twenty-year-olds, in our present affluent society *are* still kids.

Neither the struggle in a rural backwater nor the struggle in an urban slum has a parallel in the society of affluence.

As affluence has increased, the child's environment has become impoverished in opportunities for responsible and productive action, or any action that tests and develops him. He is not needed at home, and there is little place there for him during the day. Many middle-class mothers who can afford it, even those not working, place their children in nursery schools as soon as they reach eligible age. Some upper-middle-class suburban school districts run a full summer program to occupy children. Schools in Beverly Hills are in full swing in July.

Because the child's productive activities are no longer necessary to the family, the school has become an important repository for him. The school has accepted this role without providing the child with opportunities for action. Except for offering "extracurricular" activities such as athletics and drama, the school has clung to its classical functions. The very character of the school, with the child in the role of student waiting to be taught, having no responsibility other than to learn, militates against departing from them. Organization of the school around learning provides no collective or joint endeavor in which students can take responsible, interdependent action.

This is the setting which the emerging structure of society is creating for education. The environment outside the school is now capable of taking over many of the school's classical functions, while educational functions traditionally carried on outside the school are now largely missing. The situation is peculiarly reversed from that of earlier times: in those intellective elements in which the society was once poor, it is now rich; in those action elements in which it was once rich, it is now poor.

In the past, one of the child's roles was that of student in a school setting directed toward his self-improvement. His task was to learn, and a teacher had authority to make him learn. This student role has always been a curious one, because it has no goal directed toward the environment, only the goal of self-improvement. The child also had other important roles involving productive activity: helping with child care; working at home, in the store, on the farm, at the shop; or merely surviving in a hostile environment. These were roles in which he was not a student but a young person with responsibilities affecting other people's welfare. And they were probably more important to his development than his student role.

These activities, however, have largely disappeared as the child's world has become information rich and action poor. The external environment can now take over many of the classical functions of the school, but there is nothing to take over the classical functions of the nonschool environment.

The external environment provided by society is deficient in another way because of the very wealth of information confronting the child. Nothing ensures that the child will be able to assimilate or make use of the flood of information. A young child watching an on-the-scene news report or a television drama or touring a foreign country is like a foreigner watching an American football game; the action is exciting but meaningless.

Although the school is no longer necessary to *provide* information, it is more important than ever in developing skills for the *management* of information. This requires a close interdependence with the environment, using the flood of information it provides rather than ignoring it or merely attempting to supplement it. Herbert Simon described the different strategies necessary in an information-rich society, strategies for using the information capabilities of the environment. These strategies do not arise automatically from the environment but must be developed, and the school is the principal locus within which they can be developed.

All of this leads to an inescapable conclusion. The school of the future must focus on those activities that in the past have largely been accomplished outside school: first, productive action with responsibilities that affect the welfare of others, to develop the child's ability to function as a responsible and productive adult; and second, the development of strategies for making use of the information richness and information-processing capabilities of the environment. The activities that have been central to the school's functioning, such as expansion of students' factual knowledge and cognitive skills, must come to play an ancillary role.

It is not clear just what the shape of future educational institutions will be under these changed conditions, but they must not have as their primary goal the teaching of children. Anomalous as this principle may seem, it is the key to successful educational institutions of the future. The failure to recognize this principle is a major source of malaise in present schools.

Only if the new educational institutions resist the temptation to direct themselves principally to teaching the child can they fruitfully redirect their goals. One of these goals must be the development of strategies for coping with an information-rich and institutionally complex society; another must be the use of external activities where children are not students but contributors to a larger enterprise. Working with others under the discipline imposed by a common task and purpose is incompatible with the wholly individualistic goal of learning around which current schools are organized. And it is such involvement that is necessary to provide both a direction to life and the motivation to learn how to implement it.

This principle does not mean that new educational institutions should neglect the child's learning. It means rather that a much broader conception of learning is necessary: a conception in which the roles, constraints, demands, and responsibilities of adulthood in a complex society are central; a conception in which experience once again becomes important; a conception that includes general strategies of how to make use of the environment to accomplish one's goals.

Policies for Educational Institutions of the Future

We are living in a society that contains residues of the past as well as intimations of the future. Many of our current educational problems, such as those in the central city and lower-class ghettoes, are legacies of the past. They are legacies of poverty and a rural society with slavery and servitude. Policies to resolve these problems must direct resources both within and outside public education to the classical functions of education: teaching children to read, write, and use the tools of mathematics. I will not discuss these policies except to indicate how the information richness of modern society can be best utilized.

A major difference between our present affluent, information-rich society, with its pockets of economic and information poverty, and past societies, with their general economic and information poverty, is the richness of educational resources lying outside schools. These resources can be brought to bear on basic educational problems by allowing part of the ghetto child's education to take place outside the public schools, drawing upon everything from women's clubs to military industries.

These resources could be applied by giving educational vouchers directly to the child's family. With a voucher to cover a portion of his education, a child's family could choose from among the educational resources that would flow into the open market to augment the public schools. Other courses exist; but I see no means by which information-rich resources outside the educational system can be brought *into* the system as currently constituted. It seems futile to me to attempt to change the educational system in time to affect the lives of this generation of students. The solution, then, is a structural one: to give resources to the families themselves and leave to the resulting market the innovations and intensity of effort necessary to bring basic educational skills to children in the ghetto.

An important complementary action—which depends upon information-processing capability—is to calculate and publish on a regular basis the average test scores and increments to test scores of public schools as well as those of the reading centers, auxiliary schools, and mathematics centers that would develop. A number of cities under pressure from community groups have begun to publish school-by-school test scores. This information, as it becomes more capable of identifying effective institutions, can become an important aid to children and parents in making their educational selections.

These policies are directed to solving educational problems posed by poverty and the past. But the problems I described earlier are problems of the future. They are less simple because they require changes not merely in the means by which formal education takes place but also in the very goals of the institutions. It would be incorrect for educational policy to ignore current pressing educational problems from the rural past; it would be equally incorrect to assume that the problems of the future will be merely extensions of those of the past. Educational policies must be designed to cope with the full range of historical strata that exist in our society.

In attacking the problems of modern society, the most critical step is to reduce the school's dependence on its classical functions so that it can take on new ones. This involves at least three kinds of policies. The first is a simple one: sufficient research investment to hasten the application of information-processing technology to learning. This technology is now close to the point of widespread application. The effect of funds employed in this development can be measured in the years by which application will be speeded, and thus by the number of children for whom these tools will be available.

The second set of policies are those that explicitly move the classical activities out of the school. The most efficacious way is through the use of what might be termed *skill-specific vouchers* from the federal government. A reading voucher, for example, could be paid to any approved agency teaching reading at a level of skill appropriate for the child. The use of such vouchers relieves the central educational institutions of classical functions. Once these functions move out of the school into a competitive arena in which new communications technology is properly used, the learning of cognitive skills (over which the school now stumbles) can be readily accomplished outside school.

A third set of changes is also necessary to free schools from their historic functions: removal of the "Carnegie unit" system of high-school course credits as the basis for entrance to college. This seems trivial, but until it occurs, secondary schools are bound to a rigid system of *courses* in particular *subjects*. The correct criterion is not what a person has *had*, but what he can *do*. These changes are already well under way, as colleges depend increasingly on standardized test performance. But they need to be accelerated so that children's outside learning can fully substitute for their learning in school.

As the learning of cognitive skills is moved outside the school through vouchers or similar means, the shifting of school goals becomes possible. This shift should be in two directions: (1) toward the learning of strategies for learning and managing information resources of the environment; and (2) toward the integration of the young into functional roles in the community, moving them into adulthood.

To accomplish the latter goal requires fundamental changes in the relation of the young to the community. Practices currently barring young people from productive activity in many areas must be relaxed. The school must be integrated with service organizations, such as those providing medical services, so that the young can help in them. Since the school's function will no longer be to protect the child from society but rather to move him into it, the school must be integrated with other organizations and not insulated from them.

There are several possible forms that new educational institutions might assume. I will mention two. Perhaps the simplest form of reorganization would be one which leaves the school relatively intact but changes its goals. The school from the upper elementary grades on would become a productive community in which the young would carry out responsible productive activities in the larger community. The teaching would center on general strategies for learning, especially how to employ the information resources of the complex social environment. But the principal orientation of the school would be toward external productive activity, similar to the aim of a summer work camp incorporating learning activities. The intent of the school-community would be far broader than that of present schools; namely, to make responsible, productive human beings who can lead in a task or follow and who are able to live with the consequences of their actions. Such socialization requires only a shift of attention away from the narcissistic goal of self-improvement, imposed on the young by making them students, toward joint constructive activities. The school-communities could be residential, but they need not be any more than factories or offices need be. Their essential property would be their focus on the outside, with learning as a by-product of the productive activities of their members.

A second, more radical reorganization would be to modify workplaces to incorporate the young. Older children would be partly integrated into work activities, with some time reserved for learning and some for productive work. The separation between economic and educational institutions would vanish; a workplace would also be an educational institution. This reorganization has implications for adults as well. The conception of full-time education up to a given age, followed by full-time work, would be replaced by a continuing mix beginning at an early age and running through adulthood.

A related conception of continuing and recurrent education has been expressed by Olof Palme, the former Minister of Education for Sweden, who is now Prime Minister. He focuses on postsecondary education:

I think that the best way for me to illustrate the question at issue is to assume . . . that all post-secondary education is organised on a recurring basis, that all people, after completing upper secondary education, go out into a job, that after some time at work they take another period of education, then return to a job again, pass through another period of education, and so on. . . . For the individual, recurrent education ought to have several advantages. We all have a need for variety, whatever our occupation is. The student with educational neurosis and the person in working life with symptoms of stress would both perhaps get to grips with their problems if they were given the opportunity of a change of activity for a time. Leisure time would be used by many in a more valuable way than now and the individual would have a better opportunity to get to know his aptitudes. Absolute individual failures would be less common, as everybody would have a repeated second chance.[7]

This conception of recurrent education envisions the young and older adult moving back and forth between school and economic institutions. It is different from what I described, yet both designs have a common thesis: a less sharp and complete separation between economic and educational activities in the future.

Whatever the particular form of new educational institutions, if educational changes are to come about in an orderly way without social convulsions it is necessary, first, to remove many of the classical school functions from their central place, and second, to replace them with functions currently not performed outside school. Three policies are necessary to accomplish the first of these tasks: an increased rate of development of technological aids for learning cognitive skills, use of vouchers or other means to bring about the learning of cognitive skills outside school, and substitution of achievement tests for course requirements. To accomplish the second task, the school must teach general strategies for use of the environment, but above all it must integrate children into the productive activities of the community.

What I have described is no less than a revolution in the concept and practice of educational institutions in modern society. As society has changed, and particularly as its communication structure has changed, the surroundings of the school have undergone a quiet revolution. The role of school must undergo an equal revolution if the school is to continue to aid society in its critical socializing function.

PANEL DISCUSSION

FUBINI. Among the many fascinating concepts Coleman has considered, let me single out one: future schools will teach students how to utilize outside educational resources by teaching strategies for learning rather than traditional material.

My point of view is closely related: information devices will have more effect on what must be taught than on methods for teaching. If information devices will modify our lives, as they will, changes will be needed in the subjects. Throughout the history of mankind, subjects taught in one period have disappeared in the next. If anyone needing to make a particular computation in the future has a calculator or terminal at his disposal, why should the school teach the procedure?

Coleman says that schools will not need to teach cognitive skills but only how to learn from other sources. In my view, there are many skills that will not need to be taught at all. While we can really never see the full impact of great discoveries, in the case of the computer we can dimly see an important consequence. People need not know how to do many of the things computers do, but they do need to be able to write the general rule or algorithm that establishes the procedure for an action they want to take.

There is a fundamental difference between doing something and writing a general rule for doing it. The latter requires a higher degree of skill. Can you define in words the procedure followed in driving a car along a winding road or staying upright on a bicycle? You will soon find how different doing is from knowing *how* to do. I predict a steady decrease in the need to teach students how to do things that machines will do in their place and a steady increase in the need to write general rules to do these things.

From doing, to writing the algorithm for doing—what is the next step? We can get a clue from what happened when machines took the place of muscular activities. The first machines to replace people required people to control them. Sometimes the control was direct, sometimes indirect, as with the cards of the Jacquard loom. About thirty years ago, a major change occurred when servomechanisms were built. Machines were told not what to do, but what the goal was (for example, to have an airplane go straight and level to a given place). How machines reached the goal was not important, only whether the goal was in fact reached.

I visualize a future where we shall need neither to do certain things nor to learn the basic rules to do these things. That is, in some areas the need for programming will change. We will only need to define the goal and teach machines how to learn. Initially this will be possible, of course, only in a restricted set of uses. A current example is an optical character-reading program where a machine is taught the rules that govern reading and shown a wide variety of characters of one or two fonts until it learns to read with a minimum of errors. Ten years ago, A. L. Samuel taught a 704 computer to play championship checkers not by giving the rules of good checker playing but by teaching the computer to improve its performance by playing a number of games.[8] This way of software writing will become more general but not universal, just as servomechanisms have not displaced looms.

The third step of setting goals and teaching machines to learn by repeated experience may be followed by a fourth step, which has no analogy in mechanisms. Machines may become so fast that it will be possible in a restricted but significant set of cases to set a goal and try all possible solutions. With machines available in the seventies, it will be possible to try one billion possible solutions of sixty instructions each every minute. In Forrester's model of a city,[9] for example, we could try all possible combinations of legal limitations and subsidies until we found the best solution.

I am at the end of the progression: from learning to do, to learning the general rules of doing, to setting a goal and teaching machines to learn, finally to setting the goal and letting machines find the answer. I believe we will follow this progression at different rates in different fields, and this will have a profound impact on what we teach.

I have seen concepts fade away in my lifetime. When I was young, mathematicians always tried to find solutions in closed form, thus reducing the problem to one based on functions already numerically computed. This concept is now obsolete, and present college courses are beginning to reflect the fact. Today even a sine or cosine is computed anew each time it is needed. The computer has altered the purpose of solution and the very meaning of the word "solve."

One thing no machine can do is set a goal. We will always need to learn to set the goals. This is the most difficult thing to teach and learn. In Forrester's model of a city, what is the *best* solution? One that minimizes population density, increases the uniformity of racial distribution, maximizes real estate values, or reduces the range between maximum and minimum income? Information-processing devices will move the school's purpose from teaching goal-achieving procedures, to teaching (as Coleman stated) how to learn, to learning how to set goals.

Let me now say something about the use of technology in the teaching process. I am opposed to using the new technologies mainly as direct substitutes for old methods. We characteristically do this in the first stage. We use a new discovery to do something we already do, but better. We think of an overhead projector in place of a blackboard, a time-sharing system in place of a teacher in a tutorial or Socratic mode, a video tape in place of a lecturer, a telephone in place of direct voice, and a computer in place of a skilled classroom administrator.

All important discoveries go through two stages beyond this first one. The second stage is when we employ the discovery to do something new in a new way; the third is when we modify our life pattern to take the discovery into account. I will not pretend to be able to foresee the third stage, but I think I can predict a piece of the second.

A computer can simulate a phenomenon, then present to the student the result of the simulation and allow him to study the phenomenon by changing its characteristics. This has been done for many problems. I have seen a simulation of a skyscraper bent by the wind, with a study of the effect of changing wind force and direction or the disposition and size of a member. I have seen a simulation of a manufacturing plant influenced by the introduction of a different process or new machine. I have seen a simulation of liquids of varying viscosity poured from a spout, from straight down like water to around the spout like molasses. And I have seen a dynamic simulation of social structures, where a population distributes according to racial feelings and social rejection.

But perhaps the most moving and impressive show I have seen is a simulation of the universe, and it is still in my eyes. A random population of uniform bodies obeying Newton's law was injected in a simulated space. Then in a few seconds, right in front of me, the moving bodies in apparently random motion acquired shape. It was thrilling to see spiral, nebular, globular galaxies appear in completely unexpected fashion. I did not truly realize that the shape of the universe was defined in its gross morphology by Newton's law alone. The ability to simulate physical and sociological structures and to examine in detail the effects of changes is one of the most powerful pedagogical tools I have seen. It can be used to teach in concrete and immediate form the ultimate consequences of a law or set of relations, and it can be used to teach a student to find the relations himself.

This example of a second-stage use of technology will look ridiculously unimaginative ten years from now. I know we will find new uses of computers to achieve new purposes and new things to teach. I am only sorry that my imagination is insufficient to do justice to the possibilities.

SUPPES. I am in fundamental agreement with the ideas expressed by Coleman. But his time scale worries me. Will his predictions take a decade, a half-century, or a century to be realized? In my own judgment, the predictions are too radical if they are interpreted as holding within the next twenty to thirty years. For example, I would predict that in the year 2001 almost all teaching of reading and elementary mathematics will still be in the schools. There will be many technical aids to this teaching, but the bulk of it will occur in the school in a setting not too different from the present one.

There is one force that may bring Coleman's predictions about sooner than I anticipate—the fantastic economic pressure building up in education. Since the tax burden as it is now structured is about maximal, new ways of financing and, perhaps more importantly, organizing education must be found. The most rapid and radical changes in the structure of education may occur at the level of the community college. The new movement toward open universities, street academies, and instructional television may be able to change in a few years the structure of at least the first two years of college. But I would doubt that we shall see radical changes in the bulk of elementary and secondary schooling within the next two decades.

I think the changes Coleman forecasts in the role of schools are too simple, since they will be accompanied by massive changes in the structure of society. Changes over the next fifty years in the structure of the family, in employment, and in the patterns of leisure activity will radically impinge on the structure and nature of education. Coleman's predictions are too dependent on the major variables elsewhere in society staying put, and I doubt that they will. The problems of pollution, birth control, and economic stability will have a major impact on education that is difficult to forecast.

I detect a paradox between the justly renowned Coleman report[10] and the present Coleman paper. The Coleman report indicates that deprived students and especially black students are more affected by their peer and general social environment than by the quality of the school curriculum and educational structure. The Coleman paper argues that the strong vicarious experience of television and mass communication provides an environment rich in information and examples of cognitive processes. Although the bulk of black students studied in the Coleman report had television in their homes, they were found to be below ordinary levels of achievement because of the homogeneity and limitations of their environment. The central thrust of the Coleman paper is the importance of information richness in our society, but this does not seem to be borne out for lower-class black students as analyzed in the Coleman report.

The theme of action, motivation, and values running through the Coleman paper is in the tradition of John Dewey. I would like to comment on it in this vein, not to be critical so much as to provide historical perspective and to remark on how the schools may deal with motivation and values more constructively.

It seems to me that Coleman's examples harkening back to the nineteenth century are looking at the problem from a mistaken viewpoint. I do not think we can solve the problems he raises by introducing a kind of playwork for students, and I see no reason why we cannot use instead a theme of serious intrinsic work. If sixth-graders are to manage a portion of the garden surrounding their school, for example, why not ask them to do it in a way that makes use of the best information available about plants, fertilizers, growth patterns, and principles of design and layout?

The schools could stress active student involvement in scientific research and artistic creation as well as the more passive endeavors of learning scientific knowledge and aesthetic appreciation. Schools already are exposing students to science curricula that educate them to think like young scientists, and an emphasis on active creative work is traditional in teaching art and music. The student need not produce something publishable or ready to exhibit. What is important is that the attitudes and skills characteristic of research and artistic creative activity be made a central part of the program of educational development.

Coleman's concept of strategy for information management seems vague. It may lead to something either like the classical curriculum, or like current courses in teaching methodology with all their weaknesses. The need it addresses is several removes from the main business of schools, since we still lack a good solution to the problem of producing well-informed citizens. Opinion polls show the average citizen to be surprisingly ill-informed on politics and economics. I would place ahead of Coleman's concept of strategy for information management the concept of strategy for informed citizenship.

I believe the same problem arises in Fubini's discussion of learning how to learn. There is as yet no serious literature on learning how to learn mathematics. There is not a single substantial scientific paper on how students learn any portion of advanced mathematics or the advanced portion of any other systematic science. It is certainly a matter of first-order scientific research to understand these matters better before we turn to a second-order strategy for education.

I want to express twofold skepticism about the voucher idea discussed by Coleman. The voucher idea originated with economists convinced of the efficiency and efficacy of the free-market mechanism, often independently of any empirical data. What is missing in discussions of the voucher idea by Coleman and these economists is any empirical critique of the commercial schools that operate in competition with public schools. There is no serious analysis of input and output, no discussion of production functions, nor any attempt to estimate rates of return for commercial schools in detail. Before we plunge into yet another major experiment in American education we should carefully examine evidence bearing on the advantages and disadvantages of the change.

There is actually considerable historical experience on privately run schools. Before 1850, the bulk of schooling in the Western world probably was private. I am not well versed in these matters, but I know that the abuses to which the private schools were subject are abuses to which mankind as a whole is susceptible, and the voucher idea might well invite such abuses. The schools it produced, for example, might disfavor the poor and disadvantaged, just as many private businesses do now in selling refrigerators and television sets.

In this connection, I cannot refrain from forecasting a revival of what was called the "monitorial" school in England at the beginning of the nineteenth century. One monitorial system was developed by Joseph Lancaster as a school of about five hundred pupils, with Lancaster as the only teacher. He organized the school through a large number of monitors chosen from among the pupils. Older pupils instructed younger ones; brighter pupils instructed slower ones. Think of the possible economic efficiency and rate of return of a school run on the basis of one instructor for five hundred students, with no technological aids nor serious investment in books.

Over the past decade I have had considerable contact with industry as it became interested in various parts of education. Based on this experience, I strongly doubt that industry has the proper experience and wisdom to run schools as effectively as they are now run. One reason for the apparent failure of schools today is that they are performing new functions. We are changing our conception of their job. It is natural that difficulties have arisen. I see little serious evidence that a voucher system of private schools will perform as well as the present system.

Let me close with some historical perspective. It is too easy to forget that the present organization of schools is a transient in Western civilization. Universal elementary education has gained widespread support only in the last hundred years. Much of the world's population still lacks it. Brazil, the second largest country of the Western Hemisphere, still has only a 50 percent literacy rate. The present structure of schools could undergo radical changes relatively soon, since it is not deeply built into our culture and has been changing continuously in many ways during the last hundred years.

One of the most significant developments of the last fifty years in the United States has been the consolidated high school offering a wide and varied curriculum. It would be easy to dissolve these large high schools, with their accompanying major social problems, into smaller, more comfortable, more intimate units of a hundred to two hundred students each. The technology that Coleman discusses will provide the means for doing this, given the necessary social decisions. But it is not easy to change the administrative and governmental structure. This will take at least two decades.

My own forecast is aimed at a substantial time scale. In historical perspective, the twentieth century may be known as the anomalous century with respect to education and service. This is the only century in the history of Western civilization when educated people have not had an abundance of personal service considered essential by them since the time of Aristotle. (A Cambridge don has deplored the havoc wreaked on academic enterprise by the disappearance of servants.) It is also the only century in which we have made a serious attempt to educate the bulk of the population. The anomaly of this century will be twofold. Service for the educated (which will mean everybody in the future) will reappear in the form of electronic and mechanical devices. Education in large schools will disappear, and schools will be dissolved into smaller units. Citizens a hundred years from now will wonder how we could have stood the crowded atmosphere, noise, and congestion of a modern high school or state university.

The vision Coleman has put before us could well come to be sometime in the latter half of the twenty-first century.

COLEMAN. I agree with Suppes that the time scale is missing from my discussion, but I do not agree that my analysis of education is too simple and neglects changes that will occur in society. In fact, a major conclusion of mine was that changes in the function and role of schools will result from extremely radical changes in the structure and function of the family. There already have been significant changes in the family in the past fifty to one hundred years, and there will be many more during our lifetimes.

I think that evacuation of certain functions by the family imposes needs on other institutions. The school may not be the institution to fulfill the needed functions, but in the absence of the family (and that is essentially what I am suggesting) there will have to be some institution performing a socialization function for the young.

It is true that there appears to be a disparity between the finding that black children are below white children in performance and the fact that all live in an information-rich society. But let me cite one other result from the report on the equality of educational opportunity. Black children in the rural South are just about as far behind black children in the urban North as black children in the urban North are behind white children in the urban North. In other words, black children in the urban North may be in a transitional stage. They are freed from some of the information poverty that still characterizes black children in the South but are not yet at the level of information richness that characterizes affluent middle classes and many white children. This result reduces, I believe, the apparent inconsistency if we recognize that it takes time for information richness to have its effect.

Suppes suggests that my proposals are similar to those of John Dewey. I believe there is a difference. Dewey attempted to develop within schools a kind of community far more characteristic of the past than of the society in which children were currently living. In that society outside school there was a wealth of written communication with organizations, rather than the face-to-face communication with other individuals characteristic of small, close communities. When children left these small communities they were not equipped to function in a large, complex, diverse, segmented society.

Dewey was seeking a model for learning by experience, and the model he chose was the model of a community-based society already fading. I may be guilty of the same fault, although the model I am using is not the same as Dewey's.

I am not convinced by the kinds of action goals that Suppes proposes. I think they can be quite powerful goals for some persons, but it seems to me a very long leap into the future or into conjecture to suggest that the goals of scientific research and artistic creativity can be central to the action of everyone in society. I see these goals as germane to only a small, although perhaps growing, segment of society. I find it hard to envision them as being a central activity either inside or outside of schools.

SUPPES. In referring to scientific research and artistic creation, I have in mind a wide spectrum of activities, including, for example, preparing a serious report on pollution. I think that students right now have widespread interest in music. That already exists. The opportunity is to deepen their participation in such activities.

WOLFLE. I now call on Martin Greenberger, who has been studying the questions passed to him.

GREENBERGER. The first question touches on the subject of computer-aided instruction. B. O. Evans, president of the IBM Systems Development Division, cites Suppes' reference to time scale and asks him for some calibration of the present status and immediate outlook of computers in education.

SUPPES. There are a number of forecasts, and Anthony Oettinger gives a somewhat different forecast than I do.[11] I think it is very unclear what will happen in the next ten years. It is especially unclear because of uncertainty in the federal sector. Computers will be used not because everyone is happy with them, but because there is no other feasible way to handle the severe problems of growing numbers of new students and rising costs. The cost and demand projections in New York City alone are absolutely staggering.

GREENBERGER. Helga B. Fagg, a Ph.D. candidate at George Washington University, observes that Coleman has shown how society has changed from being information poor and action rich to information rich and action poor. Further recognizing that adulthood is nowadays postponed and the necessity for action virtually eliminated within the family, Mrs. Fagg asks if the school's role in the future might be to provide action by offering challenging projects in art, theater, social work, and more varied athletics; in so doing, to provide a challenge to expand the student's consciousness; and to provide a better, or at least wider, arena in which to learn and practice social interchange and cooperation.

COLEMAN. I think this probably *will* come to be the school's role. The New York City projections which Suppes cited invite two kinds of conjectures: (1) we will find new ways to teach the same children the same things in the same institutions (which I think Suppes believes); (2) we will not have the same children learning the same things in the same institutions (which I believe).

I am distressed at the kinds of revolutions occurring in universities today because I think the classic function of the universities as arenas of scholarly and scientific endeavor must be preserved. At the same time, I think the rebellion of the white middle-class students is caused by the poverty of action that characterizes their lives. I believe the problems posed by the staggering projections will not be solved by having students learning the same things from machines that they presently learn from human teachers.

SUPPES. I did not mean to imply that computer-assisted instruction is going to be the only way to meet the crisis. It is an important way, but I think what Coleman is suggesting will be another way. Inevitably, however, I think we *shall* have to provide some educational structure (whether we should or not) simply for political reasons.

GREENBERGER. Here are two questions relating to each other and to the present discussion. The first one, by Neale Obedin, a teacher in Fairfax County, asks how we can make vocational and work-study programs more accepted and widely used by school systems in view of the increasing social emphasis on intellectual activities. The second question, by William T. Loring, a petroleum engineer with the Federal Power Commission, asks whether research and artistic creation in the future will effectively compete with the economic need of the past as a motivating force.

COLEMAN. I will comment on the first question. It relates to the issue of how future educational institutions will be structured. One possibility that I find quite attractive is to reintegrate economic and productive institutions with educational institutions. This is essentially an integration of the functions of elementary and secondary schools into the economic institutions of society, thereby partly transforming these economic institutions. It then would be quite feasible for young people to learn a variety of functional skills as well as cognitive skills.

FUBINI. Let me try to answer the second question. I contend the question does not recognize that the strong economic factors of the past had a masking effect on other valuable and very useful tendencies toward intellectual achievement, research activity, and artistic expression. The fact that economic needs may have decreased brings the others to the fore. I am confident they will induce as much effort and educational aspiration in the future as economic factors have in the past.

GREENBERGER. One might ask why society's relative affluence has not already produced a flowering of the artistic and creative.

SUPPES. There is some very interesting research about attitudes in various countries. In Denmark, for example, individual expectations have risen faster than economic results. People are generally not happier with their economic situation under greater affluence, contradicting the thesis of John Kenneth Galbraith's *The Affluent Society* that it will be easy to saturate economic needs. Everyone can aspire to having the personal income of a Rockefeller with no difficulty whatsoever. I do not see a near future where economic motivation is not a strong part of total motivation. I am not saying the world should be that way; it *is* that way.

GREENBERGER. The final question is from Joseph Cromlish, innovation-studies manager at the National Bureau of Standards. He suggests that there are shades of Parkinson in Coleman's description of the schools. At a time when more money and people are in education, the schools are least effective and gradually becoming obsolete. He wonders whether taxpayers should not try to reverse the trend, and how they can do it.

COLEMAN. I agree very much with this and know exactly how to do it. I would give money in the form of education vouchers to individuals instead of to schools. The best mechanism for promoting innovation and efficiency is the market mechanism. It has never functioned in education because education is effectively a public monopoly for all but a small portion of the population. I would like to do away with this public monopoly as quickly as possible without doing away with public schools.

Skill-specific vouchers issued by the federal government would allow students to learn reading outside the school. The school could come to be a kind of home base. The student goes to it, and it in some fashion manages his education, but much of his education is carried on outside the school through his use of vouchers in the open market.

Now, Mr. Cromlish, I would like to make a proposal to you. The National Bureau of Standards has been derelict for a very long time. There are a great many tests used in education to which great significance is attached. Institutions are themselves coming to be evaluated by these tests. They are supposedly standardized, but often in very odd ways, and they have other problems. I would like to recommend that the National Bureau of Standards develop truly effective standards for these so-called standardized tests.

DINNER DISCUSSION

GREENBERGER. I would like to ask Keith Glennan to begin the discussion.

GLENNAN. I was interested in one aspect of Coleman's paper and a question it prompted from a member of the audience. I did not consider the answers given completely responsive. When you change the locus of education, relying less on the classroom, how do you replace the motivation to learn and advance provided by the economic-deprivation incentives of my generation? Once you separate students from the competition of the classroom, which tended to reinforce personal drive, how do you get them to stay with it?

COLEMAN. I think this serious and fundamental problem occurs largely because of affluence. It is not easily handled, although some past instances are instructive. The British public schools, for example, gave the students a Spartan existence in a confined environment, while the upper-class adult generation continued to live at a high level of affluence. The problem of

Participants: Don D. Aufenkamp, The National Science Foundation; James S. Coleman, The Johns Hopkins University; Robert T. Filep, Institute for Educational Development; Eugene G. Fubini, Private Consultant; Bruce Gilchrist, American Federation of Information Processing Societies; Keith Glennan, Aerospace Corporation; Lincoln Gordon, The Johns Hopkins University; Caryl Haskins, The Carnegie Institution; William Huggins, The Johns Hopkins University; Winton H. Manning, Educational Testing Service; Sidney Marland, Institute for Educational Development; John Mays, Office of Science and Technology; Anthony G. Oettinger, Harvard University; Harold Orlans, The Brookings Institution; Martin Shubik, Yale University; Patrick Suppes, Stanford University; Dael Wolfle, University of Washington; Martin Greenberger, chairman, The Johns Hopkins University.

the British upper classes was to maintain the system as it existed. They solved their problem in a way which might be of considerable relevance to middle classes in the United States today.

OETTINGER. But whom are you talking about? Those who made it? Probably 80 to 90 percent of our population still have economic aspirations.

ORLANS. Our discussion sounds a little like a session of the Commission on the Year 2000 in which I participated.[12] Wassily Leontief at one point said that we shall surely still have economic and resource-allocation problems in the year 2000. His viewpoint did not prevail, unfortunately, and a dream world of affluence was spun.

FUBINI. I think well-to-do classes today pursue education with at least as much drive and desire as those with greater economic need. Who says economic motivation is the prime motivation?

GLENNAN. I thought in Coleman's model the schools might be dispersed, with students learning in their homes. That is the model I tend to quarrel with, because I wonder what the motivation would be.

GORDON. They could not be learning in their homes, because Coleman foresees the disappearance of the family, too. If the company in Texarkana can upgrade a student's reading and arithmetic skills using better ways of teaching these elementary but nevertheless indispensable cognitive skills, why not transfer their techniques to schools? The school environment has many advantages.

COLEMAN. The Office of Education has been giving Title 1 funds, amounting to about one hundred forty dollars per pupil affected, to local school districts for the last few years. It could have been giving them instead directly to families in the form of skill-specific educational vouchers for the children to use outside of school. The impact would certainly have been greater.

SUPPES. Some economists who are not wont to look at data seriously and do not know much about schools have made proposals concerning private education that include the voucher idea. We do have specific data to examine, and it is possible to make recommendations based on serious analysis rather than casual suggestions. What I find abominable in the discussion of vouchers is the lack of analysis of existing commercial typing and shorthand schools, for example, with a study of rates of return and production functions. The great tradition in education is to make changes on the basis of prejudice and opinion, without serious data analysis. I am very negative on the voucher idea in its present state.

MARLAND. We have had a voucher system for at least a hundred years in the parochial schools. Choices were made and discretion was exercised by the family and the child. It is not a new idea, and there is no evidence that the discretionary power it provides produces a system superior to the public schools.

MANNING. There is nothing inherently wrong with an educational voucher. The problem comes in defining the product for which the voucher should be exchanged. When a child learns to read or add a column of figures, he is involved in something more than learning that subject alone. He is learning how to go about learning, and he is also learning how to become an adult, through imitation of the role provided by the teacher as model. This kind of learning has implications that go far beyond the particular subject studied in a classroom. I am concerned that the voucher might tend to be exchanged for the most narrowly defined product without giving adequate recognition to the multidimensional character of the educational transaction.

OETTINGER. There are plenty of areas where private enterprise can provide a specialized educational product that conventional schools are unable or unwilling to provide. A current example is the commercial data-processing course. I believe the place to begin the voucher system is in the narrowly defined skills, such as parts of reading and arithmetic, where the product can indeed be measured. Getting this type of instruction out of the schools, where amateurs are doing a terrible job, would free the schools for active roles, for broadening the student, and for being sympathetic.

The voucher idea actually has knobs, as Coleman pointed out in another paper.[13] To promote integration, for example, the value of a voucher can be discounted if brought by a black student to a predominantly black school. Or it can be assigned a premium if brought to a school with few black students. The voucher can be a subtle and wide-ranging mechanism.

FILEP. These ideas cannot be considered alternatives until there are performance specifications against which they can be measured. For instance, the state of California has recently passed legislation requiring the school districts to spell out their goals and performance objectives. Plans call for a program-planning-budgeting system to assess how effectively these goals are being reached. A better concept of *payoff* is needed before we can judge the possible merits of computer aids to education, subcontracting instruction to private sources, and so on.

Paul Briggs, the superintendent of schools in Cleveland, recently was discussing the noninstitutional reinforcers causing black children to do better. First, the Negro mayor gives them an image toward which to work. School makes sense now; there is a reason for participating. Second, the work-study program has real payoff. The children in their ninth year can get out into the industrial situation and see that indeed they do have to learn how to read and write. They can see the payoff on the job.

SHUBIK. Most of the discussion has been concerned with motivating the students. I am of the opinion that it would not be a bad idea to try to motivate a few high-school teachers. I do not believe the present high school rewards the good teacher with anything near his social value. This is why I would like to see a marketplace opened.

GORDON. If the economic motivation of teachers was the only problem, it would be relatively easy to solve within the current system. I find some paradox in Coleman's image of our affluent society in which all economic motivations will disappear joined with his proposal to apply an economic market system to the educational process.

Medical education in this country, until it was reformed by The Johns Hopkins University, was done on a voucher basis, and the results were absolutely appalling. The medical schools were proprietary and sold their M.D. degrees for fees. The economic incentives worked in perverse fashion.

COLEMAN. I am suggesting that public education become more like higher education, with everyone getting scholarships for use anywhere. Part of the evidence Suppes desires is in the very existence of secretarial training and commercial schools. They have innovated in areas where the public educational system has not.

FILEP. Take driver education, for example. A person pays the driving school a hundred dollars, and the criterion measure is passing the driver's-license examination. If the person does not pass, the school must continue to train him at its own expense. If these schools were not doing something worthwhile, they would be out of business.

AUFENKAMP. How does the youngster make sense of the maze of opportunities produced under the voucher system?

COLEMAN. It is incumbent on whatever agency institutes a voucher system to establish public information measures of a sort that schools have been very reluctant to release on their own performance in the past.

HASKINS. Is not the voucher system a completely different proposition in the elementary school from the high school, and even more different beyond the high school?

COLEMAN. Yes, I think so. The voucher system is most advantageous at the elementary school level, at present, since existing commercial institutions currently are devoting themselves primarily to reading and arithmetic.

OETTINGER. In higher education we already have a voucher system. The vouchers are called National Merit Scholarships, National Science Foundation Fellowships, and New York State Scholarships. Some are regional, some national.

GORDON. But Coleman is referring to elementary and secondary schools, not colleges. I understood that each family or child was to be equipped with a book of vouchers. One would be for reading, one for arithmetic, one for civic studies, or whatever.

COLEMAN. There are different proposals.[14] I think the wisest is one where the student can still attend his public school as home base, rather than having vouchers and private schools substitute for the entire public school system.

GILCHRIST. I am very pessimistic about the public school system. I think it has to change, either peacefully (which I doubt) or by revolution. Our discussion seems to be off in the future without addressing how we get there.

COLEMAN. One way would be to use Title 1 funds for vouchers in a selected set of communities. One of the major virtues of a mechanism that does not force the adoption of a new technique by a large school system is that innovations developed outside the system can be introduced more naturally into the system than is possible now.

GILCHRIST. Do you think the voucher system could be introduced peacefully in New York City with all the entrenched interests?

COLEMAN. Yes, very much so. In fact, it may be the only way out of the morass in New York City. It may be the only way to resolve the current battle for control of buildings between the local community and the city. Instead of thinking about education in terms of schools and buildings, it would help to vest control in parents themselves.

FUBINI. I am relatively uninformed on this subject, but you men appear to have no data. I suggest you try an experiment in one locale. You need facts.

MARLAND. I think we are better off than you think. Having questioned Coleman's hypothesis, let me now defend it as a school administrator. I find the idea of the voucher system very attractive. We have had a voucher system of sorts in the public schools for many years. The schools give a family a voucher from public funds to place a student in an institution for mental health at a cost of eight thousand dollars per year against five hundred dollars for the typical tuition. Eye and ear care for deprived children is also provided by vouchers, with money given to the student to see a doctor and get glasses. Coleman is extending this concept to enable the private sector to come to the aid of the cities. Cities are desperately trying to find solutions to their educational problems, and Coleman's suggestion might be one.

I agree with Suppes and Fubini that the validity of the idea must be shown by means of some models. The Texarkana project is not a good model for numerous reasons. But take the street academies in New York. What is the mystique that makes the street academy a place where a high-school dropout can begin to learn and then go on to college successfully? Within the next two years, New York City will very likely incorporate the street academy into the public school enterprise, preserving its mystique—whatever it is that makes the street academies different. This is a voucher system, with the Negro ghetto leader receiving one thousand dollars per student, and it has been in existence for three years. If you take it as your evidence, along with other models (including some at the elementary level), you will find boards of education, school administrators, and central staffs in big cities willing and ready, if only through fear and desperation.

MAYS. The Nixon Administration has proposed a program of experimental schools to Congress that would provide money for just the sorts of experiments being proposed here. These experiments would produce the data that Suppes and Fubini desire.

OETTINGER. Without knowing who is to administer such a program and how, it is hard to tell whether to cheer or cry.

WOLFLE. Suppes suggested that all students become either researchers or creative artists as a substitute for the kind of work in which youngsters used to engage. That work had a variety of effects, in addition to its economic aspect. It helped define individual relationships in an adult rather than an academic or child community. It gave the students nonacademic standards against which to measure themselves. It gave them productive and responsible action roles. Are these virtues outdated, or can they be achieved with research and creative art?

COLEMAN. I would like to add an example before Suppes replies. I read a very interesting paper recently by the director of education of the Israeli Army. He describes the way in which the Israeli Army performs its educational function, particularly with regard to Eastern Jews. For a recruit's first six months in the army, no education is attempted at all. Instead, there is physical activity and training directed at the recruit's rising above private. It is considered very important for the recruit to get a sense of his or her abilities in other than cognitive directions before being taught in specific cognitive skills.

SUPPES. In referring to scientific research and artistic creation, I may have done a disservice to what I wanted to say. Take Coleman's example of the boy who had responsibility for maintaining three lots in back of a building. I think this would be an inappropriate task for a school of the future. What *would* be appropriate is for the sixth grade to couple maintenance of the school's gardens with an analytical attempt to understand the growth processes involved, plus study of information on how things grow and how to care for them. This gives the activity a depth that goes beyond a simple work orientation; this depth is needed for the kind of world we are creating. Everyone will not be a Ph.D. in science or an accomplished artist. But increasingly we shall expect of everyone the exercise of analytic intelligence in the performance of tasks.

SHUBIK. We are about to reinvent the apprentice system.

MARLAND. We could not do any better.

GREENBERGER. Just fifteen years ago, computer programming was considered analytic and creative. On the mass level, it is now mostly pedestrian and routine. The future may hold the same fate for a number of other intellectual activities that we regard today as creative.

MARLAND. We have been speaking a great deal about cognitive and vocational skills, but very little about values. I find reassuring Coleman's opinion that the youngster should still have his home base in an institution of some kind. I believe very deeply that the schools have much more to do with values and how civilized people relate to one another than with cognitive and vocational skills. If the home is indeed dissolving, if the church has dissolved, and if other institutions have abdicated in one way or another, then we shall be in a terrible state if schools do not help humanize youngsters.

COLEMAN. When I described our society as action poor, I had in mind children's becoming not only productive human beings but also responsible human beings with a sense of life and where they are going. It seems to me that filling this need is the principal future function of the schools.

GREENBERGER. Is the school the only candidate for performing the critical role that the family is dropping?

ORLANS. Coleman is dismembering everything else. He is dismembering the family and the technical function of the school; and he is rendering the free-enterprise system supreme. Surely it is the free-enterprise system and the excessive emphasis on personal as opposed to communal values that has led as much as anything to the crisis of our time.

OETTINGER. You are setting up a straw man. All we are talking about is humanizing the schools by removing from them some of their most mechanical rote functions, which can be done better with machines and mass production.

ORLANS. But you are stripping schools of their genuine work function of teaching something practical. You leave them with nothing but play. You have to invent artificial functions and you delude yourself into believing that suddenly a community will emerge from thin air. The way people get to know one another best is to work together. The discussion has concentrated so much on the technical overt function of schools that it has utterly neglected the emotional, covert function of together learning the practical thing.

COLEMAN. This is one of the most serious and unfortunate aspects of the way education takes place in schools today. The learning of cognitive skills is not a coordinated task; it is an individualistic task. Students do not develop joint products. What I am suggesting is that schools come to have much more of a role in providing coordinated productive activities.

GORDON. My impression is that what happens in a good classroom *does* involve considerable learning through interaction of the students.

COLEMAN. Saying this happens in a *good* classroom makes it true by definition. It is like saying that what happens in a *good* family is that children are brought up well. This is true, but not all families are *good* families. I am saying that the structure of activities in the classroom makes it difficult for the classroom to be *good* in this fashion. The roles are excessively individualistic and do not generalize to the whole society.

SUPPES. What constitutes a good classroom and how we deal with the affective side of education are subtle issues, not easily characterized. I will give an example. We recently instituted a program in an inner-city high school in San Francisco. I had previously visited some classes in the school and had found the passivity and lack of interaction and vitality depressing. The students were 80 percent black; all eight counselors were white and the teaching staff was 60 to 70 percent white. We instituted a program of computer-assisted instruction in computer programming. The program still needs improvement, but what is interesting is the way it has stimulated activity. The students are still working individually, but there is more interaction now with the teacher and other students. There are clusters of students, a high level of noise, and a feeling of activity. I do not propose this as a model, but we should not jump to conclusions about what constitutes interaction. Even though this program is aimed at individual learning, it produces more interaction than the typical verbal classroom.

FILEP. Computer technology has a high valence in our society and in the marketplace. Also, children can see immediate payoff on a computer in even the most minimal demonstration of their skills. I believe these factors have much to do with the students' excitement about using computers.

GREENBERGER. The computer is very concrete. It is real, something students can get their hands on and see the effects of directly. It is a refreshing change from abstract discussion in the classroom.

HUGGINS. Students today, at least at the college level, live in a completely symbolic world: a world of symbols, mathematics, and words. They do not get the hands-on, active experiences that give symbols meaning and physical definition and produce intuitions that I find missing. I am bothered by Coleman's suggestion to use simulation games on a computer, because simulated interactions still deal with symbols.

FILEP. The widespread preoccupation in schools with mathematical and verbal symbols is one of the fallouts of our technological civilization, along with increased specialization. Who are the adult models that children see in schools? Over 80 percent of the elementary and secondary school teachers have gone from their own school experience into college and perhaps one year of a graduate program back into the classroom with no real work experience. They are reinforcing the manipulation of mathematical and verbal symbols as the major high-payoff activities.

GREENBERGER. There is time for one last topic.

MARLAND. Let me try. The discussion has concentrated on the United States. Within the next ten years international responsibilities will be impinging very heavily on our nation. The illiteracy of the world is increasing by six million people a year. Of the two hundred fifty million school-age children, one hundred fifty million are not in school. Can computer-communication technology help us discharge our international responsibilities, albeit we are still not fulfilling our national responsibilities?

FUBINI. There is one thing technology has given us that we do not fully appreciate yet. For the first time in the history of mankind, we can talk to one-third of the entire world at the same time at relatively low cost. The National Aeronautics and Space Administration will soon be putting up a satellite to transmit television programs to one-third of the earth at a total cost per distributing station of about a thousand dollars. This completely new approach will be tested first in India.

MARLAND. It is possible that breakthroughs are easier to make abroad, where views are not as firmly fixed as in our country. We may be able to find ways in India and Africa to solve the illiteracy problem, and then bring the solutions back home.

SUPPES. I have been involved in some of the initial planning on the NASA project. It is not at all clear that we can use the technology effectively, but it will be tried because of the feeling of pessimism and hopelessness for other possible routes. Brazil may be one of the first countries to try spreading large-scale education by satellite. Despite all the money spent on educational television and some experience in teaching by radio, we really do not have a very good basis for predicting the outcome. There is a radio experiment in Kenya that has had some success. Sweden has used radio successfully in rural schools to teach English, but this is very different from Brazil or Africa. I am uneasy about the ability to generalize successes into areas of massive populations, and wonder if failures might not generalize better.

It is much easier to talk about technology than about human issues. There is no shortage of engineers, but there are precious few people deeply cognizant of the human problems at the receiving end. Whether it is in India, Brazil, or Ghana, the problem is primarily educational, not technological.

REFERENCES

1. Herbert A. Simon, "Designing Organizations for an Information-Rich World," this volume.
2. S. S. Lappin, *Run, Sammy, Run*, Bethany Press, 1958, pp. 35, 58–59.
3. John G. Kemeny, "Large Time-Sharing Networks," this volume.
4. James S. Coleman et al., *Equality of Educational Opportunity*, U.S. Government Printing Office, 1966.
5. Lappin, *Run, Sammy, Run*, pp. 75, 77.
6. Claude Brown, *Manchild in the Promised Land*, Macmillan, 1965, p. 21.

7. Olof Palme, speech to the Sixth Conference of European Ministers of Education, Versailles, May 1969.
8. Arthur L. Samuel, "Some Studies in Machine Learning Using the Game of Checkers," *Computers and Thought*, ed. Edward A. Feigenbaum and Julian Feldman, McGraw-Hill, 1963.
9. Jay W. Forrester, *Urban Dynamics*, MIT Press, 1969.
10. Coleman et al, *Equality*.
11. Anthony G. Oettinger, *Run, Computer, Run: The Mythology of Educational Innovation*, Harvard University Press, 1969.
12. "Toward the Year 2000: Work in Progress," *Daedalus*, Summer 1967.
13. James S. Coleman, "Toward Open Schools," *Public Interest*, no. 9 (Fall 1967).
14. James S. Coleman, "Incentives in American Education," *Educate*, vol. 2, no. 4 (September 1969): 1824.

CIVIL LIBERTIES
AND COMPUTERIZED
DATA SYSTEMS

Speaker ALAN F. WESTIN

*Professor of Public Law and Government
Columbia University*

Discussants CHARLES L. SCHULTZE

*The Brookings Institution
(formerly Director of the Bureau
of the Budget)*

RALPH NADER

*Lawyer
Washington, D.C.*

Moderator DAVID L. BAZELON

*Chief Judge of the U.S. Court of Appeals
Washington, D.C. Circuit*

BAZELON. We all have things about ourselves that we want either no one or just a few selected people to know. These are our secret vices and our secret virtues. But privacy is much more than this. Arthur Goldberg once described private things as matters we do not mind others knowing, so long as they do not remember them too well. We carry on many activities in public without feeling we have sacrificed our privacy. But if we were to find someone recording our every public activity, we would be profoundly troubled.

Why is this? I think it is for two reasons. Each one of our public activities taken by itself may be of little import, but together they can reveal things we truly desire to keep private. We consequently expand the concept of "privacy" to create a buffer zone around the core area we seek to maintain inviolate.

Privacy also serves a second function. Many of us who make no secret of our political views would be aghast if we were asked in a civil service job application how we voted last year. Civil service is based on the principle that an employee's politics has no bearing on his job qualifications. We can tell the hiring officer not to take the applicant's politics into account; but decision makers do not always follow the prescribed guidelines. So we seek to prevent a decision from being made on the wrong grounds by not providing the grounds to the decision maker at all, again applying the concept of privacy.

Privacy in this sense is not an end in itself, but a device that serves as the first line of defense against the unallowable exercise of discretion. With increasing frequency, public and private agencies are making decisions about us that may profoundly affect our lives, and we are vitally concerned that such decisions are made within what we consider proper guidelines. The concept of privacy can play an important role in assuring this.

Although privacy supports the integrity of the decision-making process, it is only part of the answer. For even if the right standards are applied, a decision may be wrong if the information upon which it is based is inadequate, untrue, or only partly true. As data banks are used increasingly to provide information for decisions about us, we must be ever more concerned that the data they contain are adequate. We can provide some safeguards by, for example, allowing an individual to examine his file and challenge information that appears to him incorrect or incomplete. But review, whether judicial or administrative, can operate successfully only if most decisions to be reviewed are correct in the first instance. To be sure, the mere availability of review will to some extent bolster the integrity of the process in its earlier stages; but review can never do the whole job. We must concentrate our attention on the data-gathering process itself, seeking not review but structural reform, so that review is necessary only in the rarest of cases.

There is something incongruous about being called upon to introduce the speaker at a discussion concerning invasions of privacy. In many ways the function of an introduction is to invade the privacy of the speaker and present him not only in his public cloak but as an individual human being as well. Alan Westin's interests are broad. He has written on such varied matters as civil rights, the federal judiciary, and politics in America, Europe, and the Soviet Union. But for almost two decades one of his central concerns has been the matter of individual privacy. His first published work on wiretapping appeared in 1952, and he has since become our foremost authority on privacy. Privacy is a right often undervalued, and Alan Westin's concern has been not simply with the protection of privacy but also with its functions and values. He has brought relief to a critical and often beleaguered citadel and helped us take an important step on the road to self-understanding.

WESTIN. A business executive sitting in an elegant office stares angrily at a note he has just opened in the morning mail. It reads:
"Would you like your wife, Mary, to receive a print-out of your travel data-bank itinerary for last weekend? If not, send fifty dollars in small bills to Friends of Privacy, care of General Delivery...."
This nervous humor from a recent cartoon is typical of the worried literature about data banks that arose during the 1960's. As we now enter the 1970's, are there any trends that indicate what the privacy and databanks issue will be like during the next fifteen years?
To develop the proper perspective, I shall consider not merely data banks, but all information systems arising from the use of computer and communications technology. I shall treat due process as an issue distinct from privacy in the protection of civil liberties in computerized data systems. My discussion will be in the context of government data systems, though many of the issues also arise in the data systems of large private organizations.

Are Traditional Liberties Relevant in an Electronic Age?

Are the traditional civil liberties of American constitutionalism relevant to the new technological milieu of American society? If privacy and due process are outmoded concepts for a data-rich civilization, then the only problem we face is to adjust as gracefully as possible to this latest stage in social evolution.
Some thoughtful commentators have argued for this position in recent years. They suggest that civil-liberty concepts developed in the loose, prescientific, limited-government eras of early America should not be retained in the coming age of better information and more objective decision making. They believe that systems of high disclosure will minimize the shame-guilt culture and increase social toleration, leading to healthier personality

development. They also expect more complete information to render obsolete many of our present adversary procedures for judging guilt or innocence. And they feel the average man will opt enthusiastically for the material benefits that he will acquire from better information handling, leaving the anxieties over civil liberties to the elites that have been their real advocates for so long in a mass democracy.

This case cannot be dismissed out of hand, but my conclusions are very different.[1] I believe that humanism and democratic participation have been and remain core goals of our society and that privacy and due process are vital elements for pursuing these goals regardless of technological level. Let me sketch my reasons in outline form.

Privacy is the right to determine what information about oneself to share with others. It is crucial to a free society because: (1) it nurtures the development of self-reliance and self-realization in the individual citizen; (2) it protects the innovative and critical role of private organizations, especially in a pluralistic culture; and (3) it shields valuable areas of social and political life from supervision by authority, thus working against the rise of totalitarianism.

Due process is the right to have rules of conduct specified in advance; a fair hearing to defend oneself against punitive action; and an appeal to higher authority for review. It also is central to a free society. Its procedures, including confrontation, counsel, and cross-examination, are vital to the exposure of error and bias in adjudications; the privilege it affords against self-incrimination affirms the dignity of the individual, even when he stands accused of misconduct against society; and its guarantees of habeas corpus and jury trial are essential protections against the exercise of arbitrary power by the state.

These rights are not outmoded in the electronic age. The basic problems of human nature and social institutions will not be swept away by any new technology. Whether information is scarce or abundant, delivered late or instantly, there will still be conflicts between underclasses and elites, science and humanism, local cultures and central authorities. Political power will still corrupt unless limited, and there will be no end to ideology. Men will still believe at times that they have been judged unfairly and will want redress, and they will continue to feel it vital to their personal integrity to withhold certain information about themselves.

Thus we will need rights to privacy and due process to help us deal with old problems in new circuits. But we should not attempt a literal transfer of rules that were framed for a vanished environment. We must redefine guarantees of civil liberties to make them relevant in an electronic age, just as our fathers and grandfathers redefined these guarantees when industrialization and urbanization altered the agricultural society in which these rights were first enunciated in the American Constitution.

I conclude that civil liberties will continue to be a relevant concern in the coming decades despite the rise of information technology.

CIVIL LIBERTIES AND COMPUTERIZED DATA SYSTEMS   153

Of Records and Liberty: The Trail from Hammurabi to the Computer

Did the computer create the issue of record surveillance that troubled the American public in the 1960's, or was a conflict between civil liberties and government record systems already arising in the era of file cabinets?

If we trace back this question to ancient civilizations, we see the shift from oral traditions to written records as necessary for commercial and intellectual development, but also as threatening individual freedom through bureaucratic controls. Yet written codes of law and the recording of private and public transactions also protected individuals (especially the poor) against arbitrary actions by judges, priests, and the rich, as the story of Hammurabi's code illustrates. Records have always been a two-edged sword.

From the time that written records began to emerge in the agricultural civilizations of antiquity until the nineteenth century, most records about individuals were collected and kept by local authorities. The few central records that were compiled were the *administrative surveys* developed by the Egyptians, Persians, Hebrews, and Greeks for the purposes of collecting taxes and conscripting soldiers more effectively. "Take a census of all the congregation of the people of Israel," the Lord told Moses after the flight from Egypt, "by families, by fathers' houses, according to the number of names, every male, head by head, and from twenty years old and upward, all in Israel who are able to go forth to war." The Old Testament also relates that Moses took a census to tax each Israelite "half a shekel a head" to furnish the new Tabernacle.

The more urban societies of antiquity made even greater uses of these administrative surveys. In Rome, from the sixth century B.C. through the imperial period, special magistrates conducted a regular inspection of each household to apportion taxes and note vacancies to be filled in the aristocratic orders. The magistrates also judged each citizen's performance of civic duties and his fidelity to public morals, with power to revoke his citizenship or place a *nota censoria* alongside his name on the roll of citizens.

Central record keeping fell into decay in Europe during the early Middle Ages, but rose again in 1086 when William the Conqueror conducted the famous "Domesday Book" survey of property holdings in his new English realm. This was done primarily to fix feudal obligations for military service on the conquered Saxon population. Similar administrative surveys were taken by Phillip II of Spain in 1577 to inventory his North American resources; by Virginia and other American colonies in the seventeenth century; and in the Swiss cantons, German cities, and Scandinavian states during the sixteenth through eighteenth centuries.

A second type of information collection developed from antiquity to the nineteenth century was the *intelligence system*. The Spartan secret police, the *frumentarii* of imperial Rome, the agents of the Spanish Inquisition, and the royal regimes of the early nation-state all conducted surreptitious surveillance of suspected enemies of the regime or disturbers of the peace, usually holding the information in close secrecy. During the two centuries from Sir Francis Walsingham's appointment as Queen Elizabeth's Principal Secretary of State (in the late sixteenth century) to the career of Napoleon's infamous Minister of Police, Joseph Fouché, the modern intelligence *dossier* made its appearance.

As the name implies, this was usually a bundle of letters and reports on an individual by informers and paid agents. Sometimes the intelligence records were centralized, as with the register kept by Elizabeth's Privy Council on suspected papists; but more commonly they were locked in the desk or cabinet of the police ministry to be made available to the ruler in the form of confidential summaries or to be used as evidence in state political trials. By the nineteenth century, intelligence dossiers were routine in most European governments.

The third and final major record keeping developed by the nineteenth century was the *statistical system*. It resulted from the institutionalized separation of administrative from statistical functions in the nineteenth century. Rules were set against using census information to regulate or prosecute individuals in keeping with the laissez-faire and limited-state ideology of that era. Statistical records were compiled by compulsory reporting to agents of the central government to aid socioeconomic understanding and lay the basis for wise governance of "enlightened nations." Individuals were assured of confidentiality in return for their disclosures.

There have been two competing traditions in the history of government records in the West. The authoritarian tradition, exemplified by Sparta, the Roman Empire, the autocracies of Europe in the seventeenth through nineteenth centuries, and the modern totalitarian state, regards close surveillance of individual and group activity as a legitimate function of the "moral state." These societies have sanctioned extensive collection of personal information through administrative and intelligence records, circulation of dossiers among government agencies, and an absence of meaningful due process to challenge the accuracy and fairness of collected information.

In contrast, the libertarian tradition, typified by Periclean Athens, the Roman Republic, parliamentary England, the Swiss and Scandinavian systems, and the American Republic, places social and legal limits on the power of authorities to keep individuals and groups under close surveillance. Citizens have rights under the law to contest official records collected on them. The United States from the start rejected population registers and internal passports in the European continental manner. During the eighteenth and nineteenth centuries, it had few local police dossiers and almost no national police dossiers in peacetime. Any use made of an individual's records impinging on civil rights was closely supervised by the courts. The statistical census was given full confidential status by the mid-nineteenth century. The citizen could secure access to information on him in most government files, appealing to the courts or involving legislative committee pressures if necessary. Finally, it was an article of republican faith that much information about the citizen was none of the government's business. James Madison assured the First Congress that there would be no question on religion in the national census, and a leading Supreme Court decision in 1881 prohibited Congressional investigations from inquiring into "the private affairs of individuals."

Thus, the libertarian tradition applied to government record systems produced three cardinal principles by the late nineteenth century:

1. government should extract only limited personal information from its citizens; religious preferences, voting choices, and confidences with legal advisers, for example, are strictly private;

2. information on the citizen used by government in administrative or judicial proceedings should be subject to the tests of due process;

3. administrative, intelligence, and statistical records on the individual should be treated separately, either by separate storage or by output formats reflecting the different principles of civil liberties involved in each system.

If the computer had arrived in 1880, the possibility of consolidated data systems through computerization would have been seen as a clear departure from the liberal tradition in government record handling. But several fundamental developments in government and society occurred before the computer arrived. Social welfare programs led to giant administrative record systems for identifying, qualifying, and monitoring individual participants. The growth of revolutionary movements during two hot wars and a cold war expanded the use of intelligence dossiers for a variety of loyalty-security programs under conditions of less than full due process. Mass educational programs created kindergarten-to-college record systems. The increased mobility of working forces led employers to compile detailed personnel records, sometimes including elaborate personality tests. A whole industry of private intelligence collectors grew up to supply data to employers, credit grantors, and insurance companies, exchanging information freely with government investigators. Social scientists began to collect vast amounts of behavioral data about individuals and groups, presumably useful for formulating and evaluating public policies, and this led to increasing use of social-science data analysis by government agencies.

The nineteenth-century rules of privacy and due process were not abandoned during this period, but collection of personal information rose steadily, access to files by the citizen became more difficult, and information began to seep through the walls between administrative, intelligence, and statistical systems.

The principal characteristics of government record keeping concerning individuals on the eve of computerization are summarized in the following table.

TABLE 1. GOVERNMENT RECORD KEEPING BEFORE COMPUTERIZATION

	Administrative	Statistical	Intelligence
How was information collected?	Compulsory self-reporting by individuals; open inspection by government employees.	Compulsory self-reporting by individuals.	Secret surveillance and reporting by informants.
How was it stored within the system?	Individuals identified.	Individuals identified.	Individuals identified.
Were individual records shared within government?	Yes, with limited exceptions.	No.	Only with other intelligence agencies.
How was the information made available to the public?	On an individual basis and as statistical data.	As statistical data.	Only as evidence in criminal trials.

This was the situation in the early 1960's. At that time of major new social programs, several diverse groups in the United States began to chafe under the government's expanding record policies. Militant blacks objected to the intrusive inspections and information collection in welfare and housing programs. Political radicals alienated by the Vietnam War and the continuation of racial discrimination opposed any increased rationalization of Establishment programs. Hippies and liberated students wanted government to keep its information-collecting hands off personal behavior. Liberals, remembering the blacklists and dossiers of the McCarran-McCarthy era, worried about possible government reaction to the new dissenters. Businessmen spending excessive money and time to comply with the reporting requirements of state and national agencies asked Congress to take drastic action against the federal paperwork jungle.

These groups had a common feeling that there was too much insensitive zeal for efficiency in the way government was demanding information from the citizen. Then, Congressional hearings and popular discussions in the early 1960's took up wiretapping, personality tests, polygraphs, and credit bureaus. These began to be viewed as pieces of a larger problem— "invasion of privacy." What was being contested was the product of fifty years of momentum by rational government, accelerated in the 1960's.

Thus the public debate depended in no sense on the arrival of the computer. What the computer did contribute, however, was a profound sense of urgency. The privacy campaign had to take a powerful stand on record surveillance before the situation moved from an atomic bomb to a hydrogen bomb-ICBM level of threat. The computer also gave the campaign a handle with which to grasp an otherwise slippery issue; the magic and menace of the Big Brother machine provided ready drama for legislators and the popular press.

Computer Capabilities and the Civil Liberties Tradition

Moving from the political to the technological-organizational issue, we now examine whether computer data systems represent a fundamentally new stage of information collection with drastically new risks and benefits to citizen rights. Compared to manual files, computers offer greater storage capacity for data; greater speed of processing; lower processing cost per item of information; greater capacity for complex logical operation; simultaneous access to multiple records; ability to link data on the same person, place, or thing from different files; remote access to central facilities for input and output; and the ability to exchange information with other computer systems. In each of these categories, the improvement has grown steadily with every new computer generation, and it will continue to increase in the coming decades.

These capabilities offer government a virtually irresistible psychological temptation to launch a total information attack on the pressing problems of our society. Rational government has as an article of faith that what is missing from the policy-making process is better information about social processes, social problems, the actual effects of existing programs, and the possible effects of new programs. Many observers (myself included) are not certain of this and believe that more often than an information shortage it is a failure of political skills and public wills that impedes better decisions. Nevertheless, the article of faith spurs the creation of more and more advanced types of computerized information systems with two basic principles at their core: full *consolidation* of relevant data and full *circulation* of this data to all appropriate agencies. Not to consolidate and circulate data would be to deny the essential logic and thrust of the technology. Such self-denial has often occurred in the very early stages of a new technology (for example, using the automobile as a horseless carriage), but is not usually continued once the essence of the new technology has been realized.

This logic of computerized data systems produces psychological effects on the citizen. He sees uncontrolled consolidation and circulation of information as threatening the basic principles of civil liberties in record systems. He views with alarm the more personal information collected and shared by agencies to provide a richer information base for social analysis and policy making. He despairs at the increasing difficulty in knowing how information about him is being used and in verifying or challenging it. Computerized data systems captivate the public administrator and alarm the citizen in ways that *do* represent a new stage in the records-versus-liberty dilemma.

Whether computerized data systems *will* have these potential effects, however, is a question of social policy, not technology. It depends on how computer usage is shaped by the American political culture. A look at the past fifteen years of computerization will help us see what patterns of use and control have been developing.

Three Stages of Computerized Data Systems: 1955–1970

It has become fashionable lately for public agencies to call almost any new collection of information they plan to create and maintain a data bank. Perhaps in our private enterprise system the term "bank" is expected to create an image of probity, efficiency, and even accruing interest. No doubt it is also meant to suggest a community of users depositing and withdrawing information, with a computer serving as "banker."

For clear analysis, we need to go beyond the term "data bank" and classify computerized data systems into stages according to the degree to which they link and integrate information. Between 1955 and 1970, there have been three stages of development. (This analysis uses data collected in a project on information technology in government decision making, conducted under the auspices of the Harvard Program on Technology and Society. A first book on that study is in press.)[2]

1. *Computerization of Files.* During the late 1950's and early 1960's, some agencies and departments made their files machine-readable and used computers to facilitate linkage, retrieval, and manipulation of the data. Examples are the United States Internal Revenue Service, the California Department of Motor Vehicles, and the Chicago Police Department. Their systems are essentially automated card files, with information on each subject consolidated under a unique name or number.

2. *The Data Bank.* During the early and middle 1960's, certain public agencies put machine-readable data from various sources within a particular field or governmental jurisdiction into common computer systems, making the data available to a variety of users. Three main types of data banks resulted: (a) collections of one-time surveys or reports stored in archival fashion; (b) collections of information on people, places, or things, updated periodically; and (c) similar collections updated immediately by real-time events recorded at remote on-line terminals. Examples are the Detroit Social Data Bank, which collects trend data on social health and decay in local neighborhoods; the Washington, D.C. Real Property Data Bank, which records transactions on land parcels; and the New York State Identification and Intelligence System, which collects summary criminal history data from thirty-six hundred agencies within the state.

3. *The Centralized Computer Service, With Data Bank.* During the

middle and late 1960's, some government jurisdictions created computer service centers to process both archival and real-time information from various line activities such as police, welfare agencies, hospitals, and schools. The data were put into central computer storage, where each agency could continue to use its own information for operational purposes, while cross-agency master files and trend studies were also possible. Similar centers might serve a group of agencies in different political jurisdictions within the same geographic area, such as twenty metropolitan police departments. So far, these centers have been primarily at the county level, as the service centers in the California counties of Alameda and Santa Clara illustrate.

Within these three stages, one trend is for the essential separation of information into statistical, administrative, and intelligence compartments to continue after computerization. Statistical agencies such as the U.S. Bureau of the Census and the Bureau of Labor Statistics have computerized their files, but they continue to hold data under rules of statistical aggregation and confidentiality and have not connected to larger governmental data pools. Statistical data banks for policy analysis and program planning are producing information on aggregate trends and indicators, such as rates of truancy, venereal disease, crime, and new job starts; they do not produce individual dossiers. Examples include the Detroit Social Data Bank; the San Francisco Bay Area Transportation Study; the Tri-State (New York, Connecticut, and New Jersey) Transportation Commission Data Bank; and the San Gabriel Valley (California) Municipal Data System.

Many administrative agencies have essentially continued their regular operations after computerization. Typical computer applications include the regionally established Job Bank System of the U.S. Department of Labor for matching unemployed persons to available jobs; the pupil and employee personnel data bank of the Palo Alto, California, School District; the Management Information System of the U.S. Office of Economic Opportunity; the Automated Management Information System of the California Department of Motor Vehicles; administrative operations of the Las Vegas, Nevada, Sheriff's Department and the New York State Police; the National Crime Information Center of the Federal Bureau of Investigation; and the National Driver Register Service for revoked license registration. A long list of tax departments, welfare, health, and educational agencies, and similar bodies have also installed computerized systems. These systems generally reflect preexisting statutory and administrative policies regarding the confidentiality or openness of individual records. Social Security data are not being distributed to other government agencies or the public any more widely since computerization than before, and the automated system of the California Motor Vehicle Department still has the disclosure policy the department followed in its days of manual files.

Intelligence systems also seem to be following policies that were standard before computerization. The systems include a data bank on persons liable to harm the President or other federal officials protected by the Secret Service, an Organized Crime Information System of the Department of Justice, and the computer systems of the National Agency Check Center and the Defense Central Index of Investigations, both located at Fort Holabird, Maryland.

A second trend has been the emergence of data-unifying systems in which statistical, administrative, and intelligence functions have begun to be amalgamated through computerization. A typical pattern is for data from agencies either within one government jurisdiction or at different levels of government to be linked and distributed to contributing agencies.

One small example is the National Accident Injury Analysis Center, an information pool being developed on individual driver records by the National Highway Safety Board of the Department of Transportation. This center links local, state, and federal data sources to help agencies decide when to withdraw driving privileges and to formulate and evaluate safety programs.

A second example is the New York State Identification and Intelligence System. Created in 1965 by legislative act, its users are police, sheriffs, district attorneys, courts, and probation, correction, and parole offices, at municipal, county, and state levels. Remote terminals located systematically throughout the state collect, coordinate, store, process, retrieve, and disseminate summary histories of convicted individuals and other information "relevant to the investigation and prosecution of crime and the administration of criminal justice." The system is connected to the FBI's National Crime Information Center for purposes of circulating information on wanted persons and stolen property, and it has interfaces with criminal justice information systems in a growing number of other states and regions.

A third example of a data-unifying system, the computer service center with data bank, is illustrated by the LOGIC system of Santa Clara County, California. The welfare, medical, juvenile probation, adult probation, and health departments presently store personal identification and welfare-history information on 180,000 individuals to help participating departments respond to requests for county aid or services. A similar system in Alameda County, California, has two basic subsystems: a Police Information Network (PIN) providing all police agencies in the San Francisco Bay area with data on wanted persons and stolen property, and a cooperative system for the county departments of health, welfare, probations, and institutions.

The growth of such data systems has been stimulated greatly by federal grants-in-aid to state and local governments to develop computerized information systems. Four states were funded in 1970 by the Department of Health, Education, and Welfare under the Social Security Act to develop social information systems for administering individual welfare and Medicare assistance. The United States Office of Education has sponsored development of a model total management information system for individual school districts, as well as a national data bank for educational records on 300,000 migrant children. The Department of Justice under the Law Enforcement Assistance Act has financed ten states to computerize a uniform summary file of criminal histories. Similarly, the Department of Housing and Urban Development funded an experiment with two comprehensive municipal information systems and four municipal data bank subsystems in public safety, public finance, human resources, and physical development.

The distinctive feature of these data-unifying systems is that administrative, intelligence, and statistical information is in common storage under central management control. So far these systems have been operating primarily under rules for data sharing and information disclosure that were carried over from precomputer eras or by new administrative regulations promulgated by system managers. Very little in the way of new statutory rules or new court decisions has been applied to define citizen rights in these systems.

Three Civil Liberties Phases of Computerized Data Systems, 1956–1970

Between 1956 and 1970, while computers moved to their third generation, there were three phases in the development of civil-liberties issues. Up to 1966, system developers and government officials concentrated on moving from automated bookkeeping and filing to new ways of organizing and using data. Studies of local and state governments' data needs by J. A. Postley, H. H. Isaacs, E. F. R. Hearle, and R. J. Mason led to a flurry of early pilot projects and first-phase developmental programs. These included the Los Angeles Municipal Information System, the five-city Metropolitan Data Center Project, the real property data bank in Washington, D.C., the Alexandria, Virginia data bank, the Alameda and Santa Clara County computer centers, and the New York State Identification and Intelligence System. Only a few professionals spoke publicly about issues of privacy or due process during these years, with primary attention focused on how to get the systems to work at bearable costs.

The second stage came in 1966 and 1967, with public debate over the proposed national data center. Several advisory panels and the Bureau of the Budget suggested placing data from numerous federal agencies into a national center for statistical purposes. Hearings were held by two Congressional committees, and witnesses from the proponents and executive agencies were asked about the possible creation of master dossiers on virtually all adults in the nation. Their testimony indicated that identifying names would have to be attached to the data to allow consolidation and updating of the data, making intelligence uses possible if someone in or out of government were able to get access to the center. Social scientists speaking for the national data center did not provide convincing proof that they had considered the problems of privacy sufficiently or that they had a well-formulated program to contain the risks. Congressional and public opinion solidified against the proposal, and it was shelved.

Many beleaguered social scientists say that the real enemies of privacy are wiretappers and polygraph operators and that if any computerized data systems need investigation it is the law-enforcement and intelligence data banks, not the statistical systems. But the statistical systems with their excellent record of protecting confidentiality became a convenient target for latent fears over the power of the computer industry and associated industrial and military interests. To understand this deeper dimension of the debate, we should recall that 1966–67 was not the hopeful, romantic period of 1962–64, when new programs in education, antipoverty, and civil rights were attracting the energies of most progressive men and women. It was the era of Newark and Watts, the deepening morass of Vietnam, and a President believed by many critics ready to seize every possible lever of power to defend his embattled policies. It was not a time for giving government the benefit of the doubt.

In the third period from 1967 to 1970, computerized data systems have been springing up within individual agencies, in regional and cooperative information-sharing systems, and as computer service centers for whole jurisdictions. What has been taking place regarding privacy and due-process safeguards?

First, there have been informative federal and state legislative hearings and a continued discussion of the issues raised in 1966 and 1967. As of mid-1970 there still is no state or federal legislation defining civil liberties specifically in computerized data systems. As in the legislation creating the New York State Identification and Intelligence System, the practice has been to incorporate precomputer confidentiality rules and delegate the power to make new regulations to the director of the system.

Second, there have been no significant judicial decisions on individual rights in computerized data systems. The fields of common law and Constitutional law are still unplanted, although test cases now in the lower courts may provide the seeds.

Third, no significant role has been played by state and federal regulatory agencies, despite a question about the possible need for government action to protect privacy in the inquiry on computers and communications conducted by the Federal Communications Commission. Nor have interagency coordinating committees been very influential as yet. Some interesting efforts that may bear fruit include a privacy-oriented subcommittee of the California State Intergovernmental Board on Automatic Data Processing and a recently created committee of representatives from various federal agencies concerned with data systems.

Finally, while the administrators of data systems have begun to speak seriously about protecting civil liberties, often they are confused in their thinking and attend to the wrong issues. Their primary focus has been on hardware and software measures, resulting in some valuable theoretical papers by systems experts, some off-the-shelf packages by hardware manufacturers and software houses, and a few elaborate combinations of working measures to safeguard the movement of information from collection through storage and processing to distribution.

Some of these efforts contain a basic confusion between security and privacy. A system for security clearances or psychiatric records may be enormously secure yet thoroughly intrusive to individual privacy and lacking in minimum rights of due process. The key questions relating to privacy are: What personal information about an individual should be put into the system? To what extent should information from different sources or collected for different purposes be merged to give a more unified view of an individual? Who should be entitled to use the information, and for what purposes? These questions are *not* answered by scrambling data as it goes over the wires, using password keys, or taking other measures crucial for holding information securely.

Similarly, the key questions relating to due process are: Should an individual be entitled to know that information about him has been put into a government data system? Should he be entitled to know part or all of its contents, including the sources? Should he be entitled to challenge the presence, accuracy, and completeness of his file, and if so, before what agency or tribunal, and based upon what standards of accuracy and completeness?

The basic questions are *political,* not technical. They are matters of social policy to be worked out by balancing the value of civil liberties against efficiency and secrecy in government operations. Technological possibilities and their costs can be considered once these balances are defined and set, *not* before.

In reviewing the past fifteen years, I conclude that society has been made well aware of the civil-liberties issues at stake and that a few managers of data systems have begun to fashion the new rules, procedures, and safeguards required. But far more needs to be done, especially considering the advanced stages of computerization coming in the next fifteen years.

The Stages of Computerization in 1970–1985: Greater Integration, Greater Risks

I mentioned computerized files, data banks, and central computer services with data banks as the first three stages of information integration in government records. Based on the technological literature and plans already drawn up by consulting firms and computer specialists, as well as on the data needs of government as portrayed by official planning groups, I think the following are realistic predictions of the next three stages:

4. *Integrated (or Total) Management Information Systems.* Data-reporting systems within a governmental jurisdiction (a city, county, or regional system) will be restructured to provide on-line updating and use by agencies needing to know. Only essential information for decision making will be included rather than all data traditionally collected. Examples of early efforts to design such a system include projects in Los Angeles, California, Dade County, Florida, and New Haven, Connecticut, among others. The efforts of municipalities to experiment with such systems have been aided considerably by grants-in-aid from the Department of Housing and Urban Development. If the pilot programs are successful, there could be considerable adoption by other government jurisdictions in the late 1970's.

5. *Regional Federated Information Systems.* The *federated* information system was conceived by Lockheed in 1965 in a study of state information-processing needs in California. The idea is to link diverse computerized files, data banks, computer services, and management information systems into a state data network, with an *information central* facility or facilities serving to index information and switch inquiries to the proper location. Both California and Alaska hope to develop such a federated system under five-year plans, and a related effort has been outlined in the state of Washington. A system may come into operation in the middle or late 1970's on an experimental basis.

6. *National Information Systems.* It has been estimated that a national statistical data center collecting selected information from various agencies at the federal level could become technologically feasible before 1980. A bigger step would be a national comprehensive information system, both by subject matter and regional jurisdiction, resembling an enlarged civilian version of the military defense system for North America. In the United States, such a system would require reorganization of political boundaries and functional agency divisions. Descriptions of this concept can be found in the projection of a Japanese national information system and Robert MacBride's portrayal of an American version in *The Automated State*. Writers assume that it will be the early 1980's before either the technology or political interest will be ready for serious consideration of the idea.

Continued consolidation and circulation of information in larger and larger units of government are the projected trends for the next fifteen years, whether it be in one of the six stages depicted or in some other form. Meanwhile, existing computerized data systems are still in shakedown phases, so that civil-liberties safeguards can indeed be installed if society insists this be done. Thus the first half of the 1970's may well be the most important period in the next fifteen years.

CIVIL LIBERTIES AND COMPUTERIZED DATA SYSTEMS   165

Policy Approaches for the 1970's

To summarize, I have argued that the basic issues of privacy and due process in record systems are seriously aggravated by computerization but are not caused by it. What the computer is doing, in effect, is sharpening to a razor edge the existing problems of bureaucracy, social control, and government-citizen relations created by extensive record keeping in a complex society. Computers give us an important new technical tool for working out desirable political judgments as well as a new physical setting for record management.

I do not see any value in trying to outlaw computerized information systems as noxious per se. Some particular data systems may indeed be too large, intrusive, or vulnerable to misuse to permit their initiation at this point in our technological and social development. The California National Guard, for example, recently applied for a federal grant under the Crime Control and Safe Streets Act to create a data bank on "unlawful antigovernment activities" and "projected activities of the militants and revolutionaries that cause disturbances." This plan was opposed not only by the State Attorney General but by Governor Ronald Reagan. Another disturbing plan is the one of army intelligence to computerize its national data-collection network and manual file system on civilian political activity as a way of dealing with future insurrections and civil disorders. If there are social costs in collecting too much information, however, there are also serious social costs in not collecting enough for informed judgments, sensible planning, and decent program evaluation. In our concern for individual liberties, moreover, we must not create such islands of protected data within government that the press and responsible parties are excluded. We also must not encourage elements in government loath to publish for reasons of administrative convenience or self-protection.

No single public policy can, or should, be applied to every collection of information by government. Different functions are served by administrative, intelligence, and statistical systems, and each requires its own set of rules and procedures. I believe that keeping the three types separated inside computerized data systems (as can be done technologically) and in the output of these systems is still the best primary measure for protecting civil liberties.

We must also distinguish clearly between situations where we want to forbid the collection of information and those where we want to change the legal or social consequences of an act. Perhaps we need to change our judgments, for example, about the significance of previous arrests of ghetto residents applying for government employment rather than insisting that arrest records not be stored for administrative or intelligence purposes.

If we are to use the next five years wisely, here are some things I think we must do:

1. We must define the core elements of individual privacy and due process that deserve protection in computerized information systems by drafting model statutes in particular advanced areas, such as criminal-justice information systems; enacting legislative standards for new computerized data systems in sensitive fields, such as health information systems (the Proxmire-Sullivan bills to protect individual rights in credit, insurance, and preemployment reporting offer excellent examples of what is needed); developing ethical guidelines and project codes whenever federal agencies give grants-in-aid to finance local and state computerized data systems; and specifying privacy and due-process rights for individuals whenever called for by some special relationship to government, such as the Ervin bill to guarantee rights of privacy for federal employees.

As a basic premise, when the information sought is personal and creates feelings of intrusion in reasonable men, the burden of justifying the need for such information should be on the agency that seeks to collect it. When personal data is collected for one governmental purpose, further use of it should require fresh consent by the individual in most instances. A citizen should be able to see the information held on him in the files of government agencies or private organizations, with some exceptions made for intelligence files or cases involving the privacy of other persons. Mechanisms for contesting and correcting information in such files are vital to the citizen's rights of due process in our information-rich society.

2. We may need some new regulatory institutions. A new telecommunications agency might have jurisdiction to ensure the general rights of citizens in computer-communication systems, and federal and state legislation could create regulatory mechanisms for particular fields. Interagency and intergovernmental coordinating committees could also play an important role not only in the evolving of standards but in the sharing of concrete experiences. Special offices created to supervise long-range plans for state information systems, as in California, should give civil-liberties issues high priority.

Within each computerized data system maintained by government, a public review committee of outside appointees should be created to conduct an annual civil-liberties audit of the system's general operations and hear specific complaints about violation of individual rights. This can be thought of as a combination of the visiting committee that inspects educational institutions and the public review board created by labor unions such as the United Auto Workers to hear complaints by union members of improper action by union leadership. The public review body could be made up of representatives from legal, professional, and occupational groups as well as persons experienced in the subject field of the data system.

A final possibility for a new institution is an independent registry and rule-making commission on computerized data systems, as proposed recently in the Canadian and English Parliaments. Whenever a government agency decides to computerize its operations, it would have to register its intent with the commission. The commission would conduct hearings to examine system design, needs for confidentiality and disclosure of data, and proposed rules and procedures for ensuring individual rights. Like license hearings, they would be open to representatives of the regulated groups, the public, and other interested parties. The commission would receive and publish standards and procedures of operating systems, have power to promulgate rules for particular types of systems, conduct regular inspections and audits, and approve the significant expansion of a system.

3. We badly need national studies of where computerization of personal records stands right now and how systems are actually operating at each governmental level in the American political system as well as by different subject-matter agencies (such as law-enforcement, welfare, and education). These studies should compare developments within government with actual systems in the private sector, since many basic trends flow from private organizations to the government. The studies might be conducted by Congressional and state legislative committees, which have supervisory and subpoena powers to compel disclosures that executive agencies may be reluctant to make voluntarily, and by interdisciplinary teams of lawyers, engineers, public administrators, and social scientists.[3]

4. A recent lower court decision in New Jersey ordered a local police department to stop collecting detailed information on individuals involved in public demonstrations for a manual data bank maintained by the State Police. This ruling was reversed by the New Jersey Supreme Court in 1970 on the ground that no concrete injury to freedom of speech and association had been proved by the complaining parties. Future test cases, however, are likely to lead courts to set boundary lines between proper and improper "surveillance data banks," whether manual or computerized. This underscores the critical point that much of our problem is socio-political rather than technological. If we do not find ways to deal more effectively with issues of racial conflict, poverty, education, ecology, and peace keeping, computer data banks may become in many minds powerful tools for maintenance of an intolerable status quo. "Off the data banks" will join "off the pigs" as a protest slogan. If, on the other hand, we develop responsive and effective social policies and reconstruct the social consensus that was rent so badly during the 1960's, computerized data banks might yet realize their potential usefulness, and questions of the proper scope and necessary safeguards in their operation could be dealt with directly.

In concluding, I am reminded of a social-studies unit widely used in American secondary schools called "From Subject to Citizen." It traces for high-school students the gradual change of man's status in Western societies from subject of the ruler to citizen of a constitutional state. Today, we face a possibility that this process could be reversed not by deliberate tyrannical actions but by such increases in compulsory inquiry that citizens would be made to feel like *subjects* again.

During the development of citizenship in English history, one of the major weapons for liberty was the writ of habeas corpus. The Great Writ was a command from the courts to the Crown to produce the body of a named person from whatever recesses of the executive realm in which he was being kept and to justify publicly his continued imprisonment. Perhaps what we need in the electronic age is a modern counterpart, installed by statute or judicial decision: a writ of *habeas data*, commanding government to produce and justify the use of information it has stored in the recesses of a computerized data system on which it is basing judgments about the individual. The Great Writ of English constitutional history helped bring kings under the rule of law; perhaps a new Great Writ will help us do the same with uses of computers.

PANEL DISCUSSION

BAZELON. Proposals for a national data bank center came as the result of a feasibility study commissioned by the Bureau of the Budget and completed in 1965. Wide publicity and much flak attended this report and two subsequent reports commissioned by the bureau.[4] Charles Schultze, as Director of the Bureau of the Budget from 1965 to 1968 and Assistant Director the three previous years, was at the center of the storm over the data-bank proposals. Like a storm center, he has always remained calm, no matter how heated the discussion around him!

SCHULTZE. I propose to concentrate on one particular aspect of the issue Westin raises—namely, the problem of civil liberties associated with statistical data systems used for social-science research. Westin distinguishes three kinds of data collections: statistical, administrative, and intelligence. For my purposes I would like to categorize by *use* of the data rather than by nature of the data collection.

First, data may be used to gain knowledge about specific individuals or institutions. I call this *personal* use. Administrative files of the Social Security Administration and intelligence files of the National Agency Check Center and the Defense Central Index of Investigations are collected primarily for personal use, as are the mushrooming private credit files.

Second, data may be used to gain knowledge not about particular persons but about *classes* of individuals and institutions and socioeconomic interrelations. I call this *statistical* use. How many families earn between $6,000 and $7,000 per year? How many of these families are black; how many are white? How many have a high-school education; how many do not? The data files needed to answer these questions must contain information about particular individuals or organizations, but this personal information is not legitimately the concern of the ultimate statistical user.

Administrative data files are often a rich source of information for statistical purposes, Social Security and Internal Revenue files being a case in point. Much of our national income accounts are based on administrative data files. Conversely, some statistical files, such as the Census Bureau's files on specific business firms, contain data whose confidentiality could be abused if they were made available, for example, to the Antitrust Division of the Justice Department. Herein arises a civil-liberties problem in connection with statistical files. Ironically, this problem has been receiving far more attention than the growth of public and private intelligence dossiers, which is the principal threat to civil liberties at the present time.

A central statistical data bank whose data are put only to legitimate *statistical* use poses no privacy threat. But the fear is that such a system would be used to gain knowledge about individuals per se. I shall first explain why I think there is a pressing need for improved statistical data on individuals and organizations and then suggest some safeguards which could ensure that such data are used only for statistical purposes.

Two kinds of information needs are most pressing. First, we need better measures of the social performance of various kinds of individuals and families. What is the distribution of educational attainment by age, race, sex, income, and family background? What is the health status of different income groups, by geographic area, family background, and race? What is the probability of high-school graduation of a black child from a low-income family in the inner city compared with the white suburban child? How are these comparative probabilities changing? We need to be able to sort out and arrange in systematic form demographic information classified by various social characteristics. Our current measures of social performance are still far too aggregate to give us vitally needed information on the incidence and distribution of social problems.

Second, we desperately need more reliable information on social production functions. What educational inputs produce what outputs? What effects do various income-maintenance programs have on work incentives? What is the impact of alternative manpower-training programs on subsequent employment and earnings? As a nation we have embarked on ambitious social programs, but all too often without the foggiest idea of how to achieve our objectives. We stumble from one unevaluated new program to another. We pay for ignorance by having inefficient programs followed by pessimistic backlash and resigned quietism.

Three kinds of data improvements are needed, and each directly raises the privacy problem. First, *matching data on individuals (and organizations) from different surveys and administrative files* are required to construct measures of social performance by various population groups. Social Security and Internal Revenue data must be matched with each other and with census data. Special surveys, as on health status, must be matched with Census Bureau files. Matching program data with demographic data already on file may be the only way to avoid expensive, repetitive, and irritating special surveys for each program analysis.

Second, *longitudinal data files* on individuals extending over a series of successive time periods are required to evaluate manpower-training and educational programs and to measure changes in social performance. We need to know the probability of a group's moving from one social state, such as a particular level of income or educational attainment, to another. Data covering more than one time period are essential.

Third, we must provide the research analyst with *individual file data as opposed to summary classifications*. Statistical systems still reflect the tendency of precomputer days to publish only summary classifications. Using them as raw input for analytical models sharply reduces the power of analysis and generates what the statisticians call collinearity problems.

Let me give an example. Educational performance is strongly affected by the family background of both a student and his fellow students. But these two characteristics tend to go together. A poor child is likely to live in a poor neighborhood and have poor fellow students. Data based on school averages usually cannot disentangle these two factors. But within many schools there is enough individual variation so that data about *individuals* can be used to separate the two effects.

Publishing only summary classifications represents a major waste of statistical information. Analysts should also have available samples drawn from original data files. Modern computers make this possible.

Organizing the federal statistical effort to meet these principal data needs of policy analysis runs headlong into the problem of privacy. The major conflict has arisen over proposals for a federal data center. Congressmen and witnesses concerned with invasion of privacy have imagined a huge data "dump" or master tape combining all survey and administrative files (including security information and criminal records). It was feared that its code could some day be broken by unscrupulous persons seeking power or personal gain.

Can privacy be protected while meeting current statistical needs? It can if safeguards are erected around the relatively small number of people who collect and maintain files for statistical purposes. It is technically possible for user computers to manipulate raw file data through on-line connection to a data center while being barred from displaying the raw data itself.

Intelligence data need form no part of a statistical file for analytic users. Whatever the very real problems raised by dossier types of data, this is not a relevant part of the statistical controversy.

For practically all purposes, legitimate statistical analysis can be satisfied with *sample* data. The matching of individual information from different files is urgently needed, but a sample is enough. Sample files do not lend themselves to illegitimate use. A one-in-twenty sample containing no material from intelligence dossiers is hardly an attractive target for an attorney general seeking information for a security case. Were he to try to use it, he should be fired more for his stupidity and lack of imagination than his faulty ethics.

Therefore a comprehensive central data dump is neither needed nor intended. What are required are some very carefully specified improvements over the current system. I recommend that:

1. A highly competent statistical staff in a central statistical development agency should be established under Census Bureau confidentiality rules; the bureau has an unblemished record on the protection of data confidentiality.

2. Matched sample files should be constructed containing demographic and social-status information. Complete population coverage in the matched files is not necessary, and dossier types of information from legal and judicial files should be excluded.

3. Where sampling characteristics permit, individual file data should be made available to users when feasible without individual identification. When this is not feasible, computer techniques should be developed to allow user computers to manipulate the original data file and provide result-oriented measures to users without revealing the file data itself.

4. The central agency should cooperate with users to construct model files that could be manipulated by users. Joseph Pechman at Brookings, for example, has a sample of 100,000 tax returns, which permits analysis impossible from summary published data. To calculate the impact of a specific change in the tax laws, the computer recomputes the tax liability of each unit in the sample. To estimate the income elasticity of existing or proposed tax systems, the analyst feeds in a series of assumptions on income and income distribution, and the computer recomputes tax liabilities at alternative income levels. Such models could be developed in other areas and made available.

5. The central agency should help analysts match special survey data with central data files, manipulate the matched data, and prepare the combined results in appropriate summary form. For confidential information like juvenile delinquency and parole records, the system should see that core memory is erased and that the individual matched files are never displayed.

Excessive generality has plagued proposals for a national data center. What is needed now is a detailed specification of the powers, functions, and responsibilities of the center. It would not be a data dump; it would deal primarily in sample populations; and it would have the census type of confidentiality standards, tighter than those used by most administrative agencies.

My recommendations reflect some minor disagreement with Westin. My view is that it is not really fruitful in discussions of privacy to distinguish statistical from administrative files. Many statistical data systems rely heavily on data from administrative files. It is the *statistical* versus the *personal* use of data that is basically at issue. It is impossible to maintain a strict, universal compartmentalization between statistical and administrative files. They need to be merged for many purposes, though I stress again, only on a sample basis.

BAZELON. Some associate Ralph Nader primarily with automobiles, foodstuffs, and the Federal Trade Commission and may wonder why he is involved in a discussion of privacy and data banks. There is a very good reason. All too often the structures of the law have been designed or have developed almost entirely as a mediator between powerful interests. When these interests begin to impinge upon individuals (as is increasingly the case today), the individual may have no recourse. For if the relative power of two adversaries is grossly unequal, the weaker one may be effectively foreclosed from use of the legal process; not because the substantive rules are against him but rather because the process for decision assumes the opposing parties are of comparable strength. When this assumption fails, the process can fail with it.

Throughout his career, Ralph Nader has been concerned with precisely this weakness in the legal system. As a student at the Harvard Law School studying automobile negligence law, he discovered to his amazement that the law took almost no notice of matters regarding safety in the design of automobiles and highways, and also that there was almost no information available on the subject. His well-known book *Unsafe at Any Speed* resulted from this concern. As he turned his attention to similar matters in other fields, he began increasingly to ask not merely what was missing but why it was missing, to ask not only what rules the law should follow but also why these rules either had never been set down or else had been set down and disregarded.

These questions have led him down many roads. He has examined the legislative process both in the states and in the federal government; he has studied the federal regulatory agencies to find how they can be led to weigh public as well as private interests in regulation; he has been instrumental in developing a new concept of the lawyer serving not only the paying or nonpaying client but the public interest as a whole; he has sought to make legal education more sensitive to problems often obscured by doctrines of deceptive simplicity; and he has jousted with many of the huge private concerns that often have as profound an impact upon our lives as does the government itself.

Central to all of his work has been a concern with the public interest as something more than just the sum of the interests that have the power to make themselves heard. This is one of the most serious problems we are treating, and Ralph Nader is superbly equipped to discuss it.

NADER. Westin reviewed in ample detail the many elements of cost and benefit in the extremely bewildering problem of privacy. A large amount of brainpower has been applied to making many valid (and some specious) distinctions in discussions of privacy; but many of these distinctions have been too abstract, without the discipline which comes from adequate rooting in empirical case studies.

The Russians have a tendency to call this kind of problem a "zato, zato" (on-the-one-hand, on-the-other-hand) problem. Almost every argument on why information is so critically needed by government for the progress of social policy or the accuracy of prognosis has a counterargument on the cost to the individual's freedom, independence, and ability to dissent. Discussions of this kind tend to spiral upward and onward into almost metaphysical terrain. I found myself listening to Westin and Schultze for over an hour, scarcely disagreeing with a thing they said—which troubles me.

One of the questions I have yet to answer for myself in a very reasonable way is, what is privacy? What are the elements that come under the word "privacy"? Frankly, I do not like the term at all, since I think it connotes too luxurious a number of very fundamental and critical rights.

The Bill of Rights covers some rights of privacy quite clearly, such as restrictions against illegal search and seizure. I am glad we never called them "rights of privacy." I recommend that forces on both sides of the fence get together and abolish the term. It may have originated in a *Harvard Law Review* article by Brandeis and Warren in the 1890's, when it was considered pioneering;[5] but today it is an extremely strong impediment to communicating the seriousness of the problem to millions of people who have not given it much thought.

The seriousness of the problem is not new to us. One argument against collecting data on race or religion, for example, has been that it will lead to the kind of silent language and unexaminable evaluation standard that many of us consider invidious and irrelevant.

Does privacy have any absolute boundaries? In a list of fifty potential pieces of data affecting individuals, can we say that the first ten items are clearly private and require protection? Or is it situational, so that a particular personal fact about individual *A* is considered subject to protection because of *A*'s status but is not for individual *B*?

Our courts (in another dimension) have recognized this principle with the degree of criticism that a so-called public figure must now receive without having counteracting rights. The so-called Sullivan case (along with other cases) says in effect that a public or controversial figure is deemed to assume a hard armor. He must endure libel and slander (so long as they are without malice) with no right to claim damages or other remedies.

Another question concerns the relative control over information enjoyed by different institutions. There are some very specific and detailed files in Washington, for example, on members of Congress. I am sure we can all guess in which institution they reside. Does the inaccessibility of these files to the Congress constitute an abuse of and deterrent to members of Congress?

Then there are questions, raised by Westin, about the purposes for which information is being obtained. About five years ago, the U.S. Air Force advertised in a procurement journal for bids to develop an automatic system for storing and retrieving derogatory information; this was exactly the way it was phrased. The Public Health Service keeps extensive dossiers on people who speak out against fluoridation, whom it characterized decades ago as official "nuts." The dossiers contain data far removed from the issue at hand.

There is also the question of who receives protection and to what degree. I have been told by the senior partner of a large law firm in Washington that his firm has a right of privacy from inquiry or investigation. We must consider the difference between elected and appointed representatives and between citizens in corporate frameworks and citizens simply standing on their own.

I do not believe we are ever going to get functionally applicable answers to such questions as these unless we root our concepts and distinctions in empirical case studies about the liberties and tyrannies found in different situations. Such inquiries, incidentally, might help resolve the tremendous tension between the two points of view and maximize the massive benefits that proficient information systems can produce for health, safety, allocation of resources, and social welfare.

I might add, in reference to Westin's comment on the history of totalitarian and democratic states, that I suspect our democracy collects a tremendously greater amount of personal information about its citizens than any totalitarian system. I think there is a greater amount of information about citizens available to industry, unions, and government agencies in this country than, for example, in the Soviet Union. Granting that the dossiers of certain individuals may be very much fuller in totalitarian systems, there are just so many decentralized and diverse systems of collecting information in this country that in the aggregate we must be far ahead of any other country. Of course, our unparalleled credit economy is a great spur to this. One credit bureau in Atlanta, Georgia, for example (the largest in the country, to be sure), has files on over 48 million Americans. And it tends not to close its door to other companies or agencies who want to lunch off this information.

I would now like to suggest four defensive or anticipatory mechanisms or safeguards. First, as Westin discussed, we need to look upon a proposal to establish a new data system (whether by a government department, the government as a whole, or a large private institution—which can exercise just as arbitrary authority over people) as something like a rule-making procedure in government or specification of a new safety or public-health standard. We should bring any such proposal by a government agency within the safeguards of the Administrative Procedure Act and allow submission of materials by interested parties, including any citizen. We must do this at the beginning, before the die is cast and subsequent remedies can be only minimally effective.

Second, we need what might be called *shredding standards*. Many of the extreme alarms that are sounded about invasions of the rights of privacy might be attenuated by a system wherein information is shredded from its linkage to the particular individual. This is the critical linkage that has raised so much concern. Again, we can discuss this at the general level to a point, but we vitally need empirical information in which to root the discussion.

A third mechanism of defense is to develop the rights of access and reply, discussed by Westin. I would just add a caveat. The rights of access and reply may not redound entirely to the benefit of the individual, since they may legitimize the file for broader use. At present there are inherent restrictions on the use of a file because of its blatant partisanship. I do not raise this possiblity as decisive but as an element to be taken into account.

The fourth mechanism is to develop a variegated array of sanctions based on how a violation occurs, who commits it (public or private institution), its gravity, the number of people involved, and so on. In the great discussion of the development of law to meet new challenges and new tensions, very little attention is normally given to the study of sanctions. No subject of comparable importance in the entire legal literature has been so little studied. Much recent consumer legislation, for example, has floundered principally because it is sanctionless or because its sanctions are extremely narrow and almost unworkable.

There is opportunity for great intellectual creativity in developing an extremely sophisticated array of sanctions covering illegal transfer of information between data systems, illegal uses of data, and indiscriminate users. We know that credit bureaus in the near future will probably be routinely sued for damages, but it is more difficult to see what kinds of sanctions can be designed for an administrative agency. The sanctions must be applied to the responsible officials to produce the maximum deterrent effect.

Let me end on this note. As I talk with and write to professional specialists and corporations about consumer and environmental issues, I never cease to be astonished at the tremendous variety of subtle pressures and inhibitions that operate but do not surface. I may go through a whole panorama of reasoning with someone on why a certain course of action should be taken, and we may agree; but then something holds him back.

Observers of corporate behavior know that companies systematically collect files of personal information on key employees for contingency purposes. They know that an employee who has a strong desire to speak out on a matter of great professional conscience can be deterred by a piece of information of relative insignificance to most people but of great significance to him. Nobody knows to what extent this occurs. But there is enough reliable evidence to be sure that this is indeed a practice and one that can be explained in a functionally protective way by those who want the company to continue on an undisturbed path.

There is also a practice occurring in some corporations of implicating procurement officers of government or business customers in certain personal activities involving the oldest profession and other inducements. This is not so much to increase the pleasure of their visit as it is to generate a do-it-yourself personal-privacy file for whatever restraints may be needed in the future.

Those who have studied the permutations of tyranny over the ages must recognize that today the largest problems and threats are clearly not visible chains; they are invisible chains. With society's activities becoming extremely interconnected and complex, the probability of more and more of these invisible chains being forged is increased. As Westin suggested, these new forms of tyranny require new forms of law, administrative actions, judicial decisions, and legislation.

We must shed our persistent, outdated psychological concept of tyranny and recognize today's much more complex and hardly describable forms. We must understand that violence now comes in many more sophisticated shapes than a hundred or two hundred years ago. And we must bring up to date our psychological antennae to perceive the gravity of these incursions. Otherwise we will not be able to foresee and forestall the onrush of violations of personal dignity, civil rights, and civil liberties, many of which are rights of privacy.

WESTIN. The speaker's right of reply is normally an opportunity for him to explain that he is really not wounded or that his commentators do not understand all his subtlety and wisdom. But in the present instance I feel we have had two additional statements.

Charles Schultze has given a persuasive case for how to build and protect a large statistical data system. We differ in terminology. Schultze draws his distinction between statistical use and personal use, whereas I draw mine among administrative, statistical, and intelligence types of files. The difference is one of focus. Schultze is focusing on output, while I am emphasizing the amalgamation taking place inside the system.

The reason for my emphasis is that the keepers of an amalgamated data system will be under more pressure for disclosure than ever before. We need to create a network of legal, administrative, and practical boundaries around some group whose probity is so strong that we will feel confident that pressure on it can be defied. It is not unknown in our history for a President to have an interest in penetrating Internal Revenue files or other semisecure data systems. We must recognize that the problem is greater when statistical, administrative, and intelligence files are amalgamated in a unified data system, even though the intended output of the system is only statistical.

I agree with Ralph Nader that "privacy" is an unsatisfactory term. And yet after having looked through literally hundreds of articles, books, and works by everybody from poets to anthropologists to lawyers I cannot find a more effective term. We can refer to personal dignity, and we can break the concept into component parts, such as immunity from illegal search and seizure or the right to refrain from giving self-incriminating testimony. This is often useful, but there is still something larger called "privacy" that we must identify and safeguard.

Unsatisfactory as it may be at times, men live by labels. They need some way of expressing a whole thrust of ideas, a whole welter of aspirations. Until somebody comes along with a better term, I think we will have to try to make the term "privacy" operational.

BAZELON. We now have some questions from the floor, which Martin Greenberger will present.

GREENBERGER. The first question is from Richard Barry, director of the Education Institute at the Computer Command and Control Company. It is directed to Ralph Nader. Mr. Barry asks whether in our zeal to keep government information secure we endanger our ability to make it accessible to the public. Would a privacy act destroy the intent of the Freedom of Information Act?

NADER. No. In my own experience, the information I have wanted from government never invaded the personal privacy of individuals. Nor do the types of information that come under the Freedom of Information Act involve personal privacy.

GREENBERGER. Phil Hirsch, Washington editor of Datamation, asks two questions. First, does the increased ability of the computer to manipulate aggregated data create a need to limit the use of, and access to, this data? In this context, are special census tabulations for business firms a threat to privacy?

Second, with regard to Westin's distinction between data security and data privacy, is it not so that the amount of security available is closely related to what the user is willing or able to spend, which is often not enough?

WESTIN. I agree that security protection costs money and also can slow down an operation. Privacy protection, however, is more complicated from a cost-benefit standpoint. To ensure privacy may entail a cost of separating data and, more often than not, a cost in loss of efficiency and reduced performance. If a certain body of data is not included because it is too sensitive, the price may be that the system is not able to answer certain questions and run certain programs. If the criminal-justice information system protects the individual's right to privacy, for example, by not including grand-jury minutes, wiretapped information, or personality tests, it thereby limits the questions that can be asked. The balancing process involved in deciding how much to pay for security by scrambling messages and using passwords is very different from the one involved in deciding how much to pay for privacy by not collecting certain information, not associating it with other information, or not making it available to users.

SCHULTZE. Let me see if I understand Mr. Hirsch's first question. If he means that through the manipulation of aggregate data one can discover that the steel industry is rigging prices, then I do not see this as a threat to privacy. In my view, the gathering and use of information which identifies particular individuals and/or particular organizations is at issue, not the fact that clever analysts can discover things about social interrelationships which might be embarrassing to groups. Far from being a problem, this seems to me a hopeful sign.

I think the privacy problem of individuals is different enough from that of business firms to be considered separately. My general impression is that the major privacy guarantees now in the law and in practice for business information are not based on civil liberties. I think a different purpose is served in safeguarding institutional versus individual information.

GREENBERGER. The next question is from Oliver Bryk, a consulting scientist at Exotech, Inc. He asks, where can the citizen turn to find out who has data about him? How can he force disclosure, and could there be a single target? The question might be asked in the future as well as the present tense.

WESTIN. The law could require, as pending legislation provides, that he be given official notice automatically when he is denied credit, insurance, or employment. Given the context of the citizen's concern, what is still needed is a way of pointing him to the relevant system. The registry idea proposed in Canada and England would serve this function. It would be a registry of all data banks operating in the governmental sector. In an ultimate sense, there might be a button the citizen could push someday to produce for his own inspection and verification a grand print-out of all the information about him held by government.

Suppose that unified information systems become operational by sometime in the 1980's. Suppose there is a total management information system at the city or county level in which all of the information held on John Doe in the welfare file, police file, tax file, property file, and so forth, is consolidated. Then John Doe should enjoy the same increase in capacity to find out what information about him is in the system as the government has through consolidation. If the government has the right to consolidate, then the citizen should have the equal right to check, see, and challenge the unified file.

SCHULTZE. Much of the opposition to the idea of a federal data center resulted from the fear that an unscrupulous insider in government would lay his hands on the information; bringing the information together would make it that much easier for him. If giving people the right of appeal requires a central registry describing where all the data is, this seems to raise far more questions than it answers. Quite apart from whether it is a good idea or not, it would be opposed by precisely those who oppose the much more modest objective of bringing together sample data.

GREENBERGER. Good point. The next question, by Bruce Lilienthal, bureau counsel at the Civil Aeronautics Board, is directed to Alan Westin. It refers to the idea of a writ of habeas data with which Westin concluded his paper, so perhaps it is appropriate (as well as necessary) to make it the final question. Mr. Lilienthal asks how in the writ of habeas data you differentiate between raw data and "work product" produced through the use of the data?

WESTIN. That is a very serious problem. A piece of information comes into an agency; it is associated with other pieces of information collected from other sources; the agency analyzes it, works it up, shifts it around, and creates a presentation, an idea, or a conception, which Mr. Lilienthal calls a work product. In an intelligence agency, an intelligence estimate of a piece of data might be very different from the data itself. In an administrative agency, the conclusions drawn by a case worker about the psychological disposition of a welfare applicant might be very different from the information about the individual that went into the file for purposes of deciding qualifications.

I think the traditional right of an agency to temporary privacy for its work products ought to be preserved. The judgments of the agency which have not been published nor issued to the public should be private to it, except when they have been used for decision making about individuals, in which case the individuals' right of access should be honored.

In my book *Privacy and Freedom* I suggested that groups and agencies of government have an interest in privacy, too. To force disclosure of the private memos and work products of a government agency would not be in the public interest. Agencies could not function under this kind of total visibility. There has to be some privacy for the interior working process of an agency or organization, generally on a temporary basis, just as there has to be privacy for the individual.

DINNER DISCUSSION

GREENBERGER. Westin's writ of habeas data would require the government to deliver up information it was using in evidence against an individual. Suppose this information was private to someone else? Robert Fano is concerned lest protecting one person's privacy might mean intruding on another's. He wonders if a third-party mechanism could get around the problem.

WESTIN. The problem takes other forms. A professor makes written comments on a student's performance with the clear expectation they will be read only for purposes of recommendation by colleagues and potential employers. If he knew the student himself might have access to the comments, he would write them differently.

By a third-party mechanism, I believe Fano has in mind an ombudsman of the system who looks at the data in place of the individual himself. I am afraid the individual might not find this sufficiently reassuring.

FANO. The point of my question is that information pertaining to mutual relationships can be *joint* property. Furthermore, information can be the property of entities rather than individuals. Family information is the property of unborn children, for example, in the sense that it will someday affect them. The conflicts of privacy inherent to the jointness of information must be resolved. I raised the third-party mechanism as one possible solution without having any particular enthusiasm for it.

I always liked the definition of privacy that Westin emphasized in his book. It is the right to decide personally when and to whom to disclose information about oneself. But when information pertains to more than one individual, two personal decisions may be in conflict. What do you do?

HOWARD. This is a frontier kind of question in that it extends the subject of privacy beyond the individual psyche. Privacy relating to groups may be more interesting and more important. The only comparable situation treated by the legal system I know of was in the 1940's when the Supreme

---

Participants: David L. Bazelon, U.S. Court of Appeals, Washington, D.C. Circuit; Edgar S. Dunn, Resources for the Future; Joel Elkes, The Johns Hopkins University and Hospital; Robert M. Fano, Massachusetts Institute of Technology; Stuart Fergusson, private consultant; Alvin H. Hansen, Harvard Professor of Economics, Emeritus; Lance J. Hoffman, Stanford University graduate student; Charles C. Holt, The Urban Institute; J. Woodford Howard, The Johns Hopkins University; Ralph Nader, lawyer; Anthony G. Oettinger, Harvard University; Emanuel R. Piore, International Business Machines Corporation; Walter S. Salant, The Brookings Institution; Richard M. Scammon, Governmental Affairs Institute (formerly Director of the Census); Charles L. Schultze, The Brookings Institution; Alan F. Westin, Columbia University; Martin Greenberger, chairman, The Johns Hopkins University.

Court declined to protect a third party's rights in the wiretapping of a conversation.[6]

PIORE. I am shocked at the morality of a teacher who is not willing to tell a student point-blank what he thinks of him, yet would write it on a form!

SCHULTZE. I disagree. Civilization is built on white lies. People do not tell each other what they think of them. Human nature being what it is, I do not believe a system in which all recommendations must be made public would survive.

GREENBERGER. Your premise is that people cannot stand to know the truth about themselves because of human nature. If it were rather because of social training and a product of the culture, a system that brought more candor to interpersonal dealings might be good therapy for society.

ELKES. What is privacy? Is it something enclosed in one's own skin, private to a person and to a person alone? People are solitary, but also social. They are alone, and they have to share. They are caught in a paradox. Is privacy shared with friends still privacy, or is it communication in the public domain? It depends then on what one wants to preserve and why one wants to preserve it and with whom. We protect ourselves against invasions of privacy as we do against viruses and other assaults from the outside. What is the biological function of privacy? Is it related or essential to personal growth? There must be good reason why we preserve it so assiduously.

There is a reverse and reciprocal relationship between privacy and trust. Trust is not God-given or immutable. It can be engendered in childhood and even in adult life. The rules of trust by which we live in our society are changing rapidly: between parents and children, between teachers and students, between colleagues. Large corporations are spending a great deal of money teaching people how to trust each other so as to improve the working climate. Is this real or an artifice? Something may be evolving, with or without the benefit of computers, which will make it much more possible for people to be comfortable sharing their privacy with one another in limited groups.

I was in the civil service for seven years and was very impressed with the practice there of reviewing a subordinate's record with him to his face. I think Schultze underestimates the strength of people to view themselves, provided they have trust in the evaluator.

GREENBERGER. Holt has posed a question for Westin which may reopen Pandora's box. Would the type of statistical data center outlined by Schultze constitute a threat to privacy and civil liberties?

WESTIN. I do not think it would, so long as the limitation of data collection, transformation stages, and security measures Schultze outlined were followed. Incidentally, some of those who objected publicly to the original designs for a national data center were technical specialists who had done work for the intelligence and defense communities. They were thinking of the most sinister threats to security and saw the proposed system as wide open to these threats.

PIORE. Security has meaning only at a certain point in time. There is nothing absolute about it. Intelligence security officers treat it this way. They want security for twenty-four hours, forty-eight hours, or six months; they do not want it forever.

SCAMMON. A black man who crosses to white does not want this known twenty-four hours from now or ten years from now. I am against the concept of a national data center because I do not believe it could achieve the necessary security. When I was Director of the Census, a county in South Carolina wanted the names of people not counted in the Census of 1960 to prosecute a case of payroll padding. We did not provide the names, of course, but no data-bank system that I know of could be certain to withstand this kind of pressure.

OETTINGER. Piore is perfectly right about the time aspect of security, except that the times can sometimes get very long, running into multiples of human lifetimes. When the Nazis used municipal files to check on people's Jewishness, they went back generations.

SCHULTZE. The proposal for the national data center is not primarily to collect new data but to combine certain existing data and facilitate manipulation of it for analytic purposes. The real question is whether this makes the data more accessible to illegitimate users than it is now. I think history shows that data is much more secure when handled by a statistical agency than when handled by an administrative or intelligence agency.

SCAMMON. I do not believe you can apply to the data bank the same protection that now exists in the census (which many scholars seek to have the census remove, by the way). The Census Bureau is concerned not only with its responsibility to the citizen but also with the validity of its data and, most important of all, with what the *average* citizen thinks is being done with this data. One letter I received as Director of the Census was scribbled in pencil. "Your Current Population Survey agents have been here. My wife and I are so worried we are going to move out of this town so your agents cannot get us." This kind of alienation is very personal and real. The nightmare of the citizen is that the computer will come lurching off its pedestal and pursue him through the halls of time. Though it sounds paranoid, it is troubling and cannot be disregarded.

If Schultze can design a data bank in which the average citizen feels that his input is controlled by him or is not related to his name, then no one would have any objection. I have not yet heard of a scheme for a data bank that can meet either of these requirements.

WESTIN. In one very interesting job-bank program, the system separates the identity of its clients, the job applicants, from the description of their qualifications. The employers' requirements are circulated among the clients, and only when a client requests it is his file or identity given to an employer.

DUNN. An operating statistical system containing longitudinal information must have some way of updating the records, requiring identifiers for individuals. The identifiers would not be needed for output purposes, only for file maintenance and updating, which could take place periodically using a code jointly supervised by a member of the Supreme Court, the Vice President of the United States, and a member of Congress.

NADER. Westin's job-bank example is a heavily service, nonconflict system. Trust is more meaningfully considered in an adversary situation. It is interesting to note how certain companies keep their critical trade secrets secure. The formula for Coca-Cola is in the hands of about four Coca-Cola executives. They use trust, and it has succeeded. It behooves us to look at places where trust has worked and ask what are the motivations and sanctions that make it work. We may be able to develop a process where critical information is held by a very small number of people who are publicly identified and in a special status.

ELKES. I am glad the subject of trust is coming up again. Westin used a key word: "client." I like to think of the citizen as a client who gives information and receives something in return. He must be convinced that he is indeed receiving something. This is much harder to achieve in a global system than in a *regional* system (such as the one we are currently developing in the new city of Columbia, Maryland, for example). The Resource Council of Columbia is currently asking what information should the citizenry of Columbia be asked to supply to central statistical services for planning further beneficial developments in the city. Once the citizen becomes aware of the future benefits to him as client of this system, he may be willing to provide the information.

WESTIN. This assumes he believes in his government and its policies, which is not true for many subgroups of the population. The problem is more complex.

NADER. Instead of expecting people to trust the government, the system might rather ask them to trust identifiable people in the government.

FANO. Placing a screen of properly cleared people around a system to make it secure reduces the number of individuals who can have access to the information and the type of information to which they can have access. Since having knowledge is power, this can create a power gap in society.

DUNN. Our democratic society is confronted with an acceleratingly complex social process. We need better information for social management, without which our concerns about personal privacy will be meaningless. We must design and implement systems addressed to key social problems. We shall never solve our problems so long as people talk past each other at an abstract level, with a naive image in their minds of a massive data dump containing everything. We must build on a piece-by-piece, subsystem-by-subsystem basis.

PIORE. You can relax. No one in the world at the moment knows how to put together a universal data bank.

SCAMMON. I question how much the tremendous amount of data already in the census is being used by those making public policy in humanistic areas.

Dunn before used the phrase "updating the records." What does this mean? It means John Jones, born in 1926, is assigned a number; then subsequently the system is told how much he is making in 1938, 1948, 1958; when he crossed the color line; who his fourth wife and third illegitimate child are; and when he had a hernia operation for which he claimed insurance five years later, *twice*. You say these are not matters of intelligence, but can you convince the citizen of this?

HOLT. When we put money in the bank, we do not worry about exactly how the money is to be protected, because of the security built into the banking system. *Absolute* security is never possible and it is unreasonable to insist on it in a data center. A very high level of security certainly can be built into the organization and computer system of a data center with adequate legal safeguards. I do not think very many people spend time worrying about whether the Census Bureau is going to abuse the data it collects on them.

PIORE. We could have two tapes—a working tape without any names on it and a master tape that is sent to the White House. Let Mr. Nixon sleep on it.

OETTINGER. You are making untenable assumptions. It might be agreeable to the middle-class white American to have the master tape under Richard Nixon's pillow, but how about the Black Panther? Or, how about thirty years ago under Adolf Hitler's pillow?

SALANT. I have two points. On trust, trust is just one of several reasons why people may be willing to give information. Another reason, which Elkes mentioned, is that they may believe they will benefit from use of the information. It is appropriate for an economist to suggest still another reason—that they may be paid for the information. From this point of view, trust is a tactic. If the notion of privacy centers on a person's willingness to give information about himself, then making him willing by inducing trust, by appealing to his interest in the use of the information, or by paying him overcomes invasion of privacy.

My second point is rather a question for a realistic political scientist. Economists like Schultze and myself tend to think that a policy problem is more rationally approached when the situation is analyzed properly than when the facts are unknown. Our assumption is that there are benefits in having the facts, and the present discussion has been concerned primarily with the costs of these benefits. But is the policy decision really better when the facts are known?

I am reminded of the county agent who told the farmer that he had some new information to help him farm better. The farmer said, "No thanks; I don't farm half as well as I know how to already." It may be worth asking whether, and by how much, social policy would be improved by more facts, when there are so many things we now do not do as well as we know how.

HOWARD. I believe there *is* a point of diminishing utility for information, but it varies with the kind of information. Going back to beginnings, I am not sure it is correct to relate privacy to what the citizen is willing to reveal. Does the consent principle really apply to privacy, or are there certain questions no legitimate government ought to ask?

WESTIN. I think there are, and I would include this in the definition of privacy. A society has the right to exclude certain kinds of questions, which is what the Bill of Rights is all about.

SALANT. Do you mean to say a person should not be allowed to give some information about himself when he is willing to?

BAZELON. Yes; a wife ordinarily cannot testify against her husband even if she wants to.

WESTIN. Who are the people most affected by data collection? Most of the time it is the dependent sectors of the population. They are often against the system, because they can say quite objectively, "I am not getting mine. I am not getting a fair shake from the system." I recently examined the data processing system for welfare of a county in California. Many social case workers feel that computerizing the welfare decision interferes with the client–case worker relationship. When I began to do some interviewing, however, I found hearty approval of the system among the black citizens of the area. Why? It gets them payment faster, and the nosy case worker cannot get between the objective standards and the welfare check. This is one of the realities.

NADER. Walter Salant's two points on the willingness to give information and the value of additional information have an interesting relationship. More study should be given to the psychological and biological functions of preserving privacy. Lowering certain barriers could conceivably produce social chaos. If people enter the courtroom with knowledge of the judge's private life, this could absolutely destroy the whole credibility of the judicial system. Maybe the quest for preservation of privacy is one of the functional prerequisites of a social existence.

Consider a senator who has two things he wants to keep private: one is that he has a mistress, and the other is that he indulges in what the lawyers call "animal contacts." Which one would he most desperately want to keep private, and why? And what has this to do with his being a senator? The individual has two roles: his very private role and his professional or public role. The former can literally destroy the latter. Perhaps this helps explain the enormous intensity of personal interest in privacy protection.

Who knows it best? The mass media and the writers of the pulp magazines. What is it that grabs everyone's interest, no matter how sophisticated? The private life of celebrities. Understanding why this is so might give us a better idea of the potentially devastating effect on public society of lowering privacy barriers.

SCHULTZE. I agree with Scammon that we must distinguish between trust in the system, based on the kind of data that is collected, and the objective threat to privacy. They are not the same, and they require different provisions. I failed to make this distinction in my own thinking about the problem.

Let me make very clear, if I have not already, that I think there *is* a terrible and growing threat to privacy in this country. But it is primarily in the intelligence files that are maintained; the increasing use being made of them by the Federal Bureau of Investigation, the Justice Department, the Internal Revenue, and other agencies; the implicit threats to the Congress; leaks of wiretapped information to national magazines; and so on. I am not saying there are no problems of privacy relating to improvements in statistical data systems, but so much emphasis has been concentrated on this issue that we are in danger of neglecting the real threat to privacy.

BAZELON. I am reminded of my twenty years of experience with the problem of the faceless informer. We have this problem as much today as in the McCarthy era; in fact, it is getting worse, not better. The data-bank problem may follow the same road.

Just the other day in California, a psychiatrist refused to testify in civil litigation involving his patient's sanity. This was despite the fact that the law grants no privilege in this instance and the patient had given his waiver. The psychiatrist's position was that the confidentiality of his relationship with the patient was so important that no waiver could be meaningful. This may or may not be going too far. I do not know.

We have always had to make these hard choices. Do we accept the testimony of a faceless informer or risk having the source dry up? Most of us would give up the benefits of the information rather than have a faceless informer.

WESTIN. I agree with Schultze that we have spent a disproportionate amount of time on the problems of the statistical data system and that people must pay more attention to developments in the intelligence area. Let me give an example. Army Intelligence maintains a far-flung network collecting information on civilian political activity and people who might encourage insurrection and civil disorder. It includes reports, for example, on Minister X who gave a sermon at church opposing the war in Vietnam, and on Stokely Carmichael, who was here last night and said these things. The network is now a manual teletype system, but there are plans to transform it into a computerized system. The system already raises very serious questions about the proper function of Army Intelligence in the civilian area, yet its operation would be broadly expanded if and when computerized.

These things are happening today. It is absolutely right that they need more attention by the public, even though it may be simpler to focus on the specter of a national data center. Whether potentially dangerous systems indeed turn out to be dangerous, or whether their potential usefulness is realized without the peril, will depend on the guidance given the managers of these systems by legislators, public opinion, judges, and others, so that they do not just do the easy thing. The easy thing is to make a pious statement about confidentiality without establishing the necessary hardware and software provisions, rules for personnel, and restrictions on what goes into the system. This is a sure formula for ending up with a fundamentally dangerous system.

REFERENCES

Because of space limitations, an extensive set of references and footnotes originally contained in the main paper has been omitted here. These references and notes will be incorporated in the monograph mentioned in reference 3.

1. Alan F. Westin, *Privacy and Freedom*, Atheneum, 1967.
2. Alan F. Westin, *Information Technology in a Democracy*, Harvard University Press, 1971.
3. *Editor's note*: Not long after Westin presented his lecture, the National Academy of Sciences announced the formation of a research project on civil liberties issues raised by computerized data banks. Funded by the Russell Sage Foundation, this study is being conducted under the aegis of the Academy's Computer Science and Engineering Board. Professor Westin, director of the study, plans to have a report ready on it by the spring of 1971, with a monograph to follow.
4. Richard Ruggles et al., *Report of the Committee on the Preservation and Use of Economic Data*, Social Science Research Council, 1965; Edgar Dunn, *Review of a Proposal for a National Databank Center*, Hearings on The Computer and Invasion of Privacy before the Committee on Government Operations, House of Representatives, 89th Cong., 2d sess., July 26–28, 1966; Carl Kaysen et al., *Report of the Task Force on the Storage of and Access to Government Statistics*, U.S. Bureau of the Budget, 1966.
5. Samuel D. Warren and Louis D. Brandeis, "The Right to Privacy," *Harvard Law Review*, vol. 4, no. 5 (1890), pp. 193–220.
6. Goldstein v. U.S., 316 U.S. 114 (1942).

# PROPERTY RIGHTS UNDER THE NEW TECHNOLOGY

Speaker   RALPH S. BROWN, JR.
          Simeon E. Baldwin Professor of Law
          Yale University

Discussants   BENJAMIN KAPLAN
              Royall Professor of Law
              Harvard University

              DAN LACY
              Senior Vice President
              McGraw-Hill Book Company

Moderator   CARYL P. HASKINS
            President
            The Carnegie Institution

HASKINS. The protection of property rights is perhaps the hottest subject addressed in this series both because of its many controversial features and particularly because of its deep significance for society. It is a very technical subject with a series of dichotomies: hardware versus software, copyrights versus patents, and profit enterprises versus nonprofit enterprises. The deeper issues of the subject, however, are how to safeguard and promote the propagation and dissemination of knowledge in our society and how to coordinate or mesh the rights of individuals with the rights of groups.

I am reminded of two pithy Grooks by the Danish sculptor and linguist Piet Hein which seem to me to epitomize our subject in many ways. The first one is called "On Problems."

>   Our choicest plans
>   have fallen through,
>   our airiest castles
>   tumbled over,
>   because of lines
>   we neatly drew
>   and later neatly
>   stumbled over.

The second one is on "The Double Door Effect."

>   Double doors are justified
>   because they're comfortably wide.
>   Therefore you only half undo'em;
>   and therefore nothing can get through 'em.[1]

I think aspects of these two Grooks apply to our subject.

BROWN. Since our subject is property, let us recall a few elementary propositions about it. Both in law and in economics, property can be best viewed as the right and power to exclude others from the various incidents of possession and use. Possession and use of what? The simple and classic cases are a piece of land or a bench. If I sit on my bench or till my land, and the law helps me repel trespassers, I have property.

A manufacturer combines materials to produce a machine, which is similar to the bench if we only view the rudimentary capacity to keep others from using or stealing it. But the creation and use of the machine may involve intellectual processes of considerable complexity. Machines called computers process information. Information can now be multiplied, manipulated, and disseminated with fantastic ease. It is becoming increasingly difficult for private persons and entities to monopolize information and correspondingly difficult to make it the subject of property. As soon as men begin to make claims to property rights in information, in ways of dealing with information, and in the knowledge that can be distilled from information, important consequences emerge that are different from the consequences of property in the land, the bench, or the inert machine.

How is it possible to maintain exclusive rights in ideas and their expressions? They can be kept secret, but this is often antithetical to their use. The legal systems of industrial society (and to some extent of primitive societies) have devised ways of permitting people to publish and exploit their intellectual creations while giving them limited powers to exclude others. We call these arrangements patents and copyrights. They can be and are being used in the new technologies. The great question is, to what extent should we permit and encourage such exclusive rights?

The overwhelming presumption in our society favors the freest possible dissemination and exploitation of information and knowledge. I take this as axiomatic. At the same time, two substantial interests pull against full and free exploitation. First is the personal interest of a writer, a teacher, or a researcher in preserving the identity and integrity of his work and its attribution to him. Property rights are one way of protecting these psychic or moral rights, although they can be handled just as well (and perhaps better) in other ways.

The second substantial pull is society's desire to have new information and knowledge. The Constitution establishes the power of Congress to recognize exclusive rights in the writings and discoveries of authors and inventors "to promote the Progress of Science and useful Arts." The efficacy of the patent and copyright systems in stimulating new ideas and their application is for some an article of faith, for others an object of considerable skepticism. By conferring rights to exclude, the twin systems create economic inducements, but the inducements are those of a partial monopoly. They result in a higher price and lower output for a given innovation than would prevail if it could be exploited without any restraints on competition.

These assertions are not intended to stigmatize by using the language and analysis of monopoly. After all, it is the means enshrined in the Constitution. The question is *how much* intellectual and industrial property (the power to affect price and output by excluding others) is necessary to direct the optimum commitment of resources to innovative activity.

Most economists would agree that the problem is highly indeterminate. Machlup puts the issue vigorously:

The absence of any empirical evidence for either the claim or its denial that the patent system is an effective promoter of inventive research—and thus of the production of socially new technological knowledge—is most frustrating. The doubting Thomases are usually timid and reserved lest they invite the wrath of the faithful. . . . Advocates of patent protection have for centuries propounded the faith in this institution, and their statements admit of not an iota of doubt. They may well have the truth—but faith alone, not evidence supports it.[2]

I proceed from a presumption that any change in the existing equilibrium toward increased protection has to be justified. In considering whether property rights should be created or extended, we must ask "why?" rather than "why not?" Economists ask "why?" about any monopoly extension. It is imperative that we ask "why?" when we are trenching upon freedom of communication.

There are ways of stimulating innovation other than by conferral of property rights, notably by private and public awards to innovators and by public subsidies, either open or concealed. But in the absence of any developed system for supplanting patents and copyrights with prizes and other subventions, the computer and communications industries are not likely candidates for these forms of stimulation.

The New Technology

We have in computers and communications two huge industries, one new, one old; both with dominant firms, IBM and AT&T. I shall say nothing about the communications industry. It is a textbook case of the exclusive territorial franchise as a form of property but does not offer us much on issues of intellectual property. I shall also bypass the importance of patents in computer hardware and focus on the subject of computer programs or software.

Among the producers and users of software are the agile giant IBM, rival manufacturers of computer equipment, manufacturers of peripheral equipment, service bureaus, time-sharing companies, leasing companies, hundreds of software houses, and every conceivable combination of these enterprises. All are concerned with the property rights of themselves or others. We have a spectrum of vertically integrated firms, ranging from hardware manufacturers offering a full spread of software systems and applications to specialized software producers whose entire business consists of the creation of programs.

The question is whether sufficient business incentives and profit opportunities exist to provide the mix of software and hardware necessary to produce the magic optimal rate of advance for the computer industry. To sell or lease his machines, the manufacturer of hardware must see to it that they are workable and useful. He must provide systems software as a basic extension of the design of his machine, and he must offer applications software for customers who do not wish to create their programs themselves. In the developing stages of the industry, a good deal of downward vertical integration was to be expected.

Consider now the would-be seller of services and programs or of programs alone. He argues that investment in innovation will be too risky unless he has property rights in what he introduces. Otherwise the big manufacturers will adopt his innovation and make it part of their sales package. The independent software supplier has found it hard to break into the market, especially when prospective customers act like credulous housewives and believe they are getting software "free!" from the hardware manufacturers.

Comes now "unbundling," the introduction of separate pricing by IBM (and some of its rivals) under antitrust pressure. Unbundling opens new markets and sets up price targets that may be encouraging to independents, and these new opportunities increase the clamor for protection. The position of the software firms is not entirely self-centered. With programming skills in short supply, resources are best used by developing proprietary programs adaptable to many customers. These programs can and presumably will be sold at prices below what it would cost to develop them individually for each user. But without some form of protection against copying, such investment might be excessively hazardous.

To assess whether the industry or any part of it needs additional incentives to invest in innovation, we look first at rates of growth and profit. What we see is so dazzling compared with the economy as a whole or with other growth industries that one is tempted to suspend further discussion. If the growth of the industry has been accomplished with only modest recognition of property rights in software, why do we need any more? One rejoinder is that the more open market will be tougher for nonintegrated software firms without protection.

Even if this argument has merit (and there are simply not enough facts publicly available to verify it), it encounters a difficulty. No one so far as I know has devised a form of legal protection that will help only the sectors of the industry that need protection. Patents are readily available to those with deep pockets and are most effectively defended by them in the expensive game of litigation. We should be dubious about any extension of property rights that might increase market control by billion-dollar firms proportionally as much as by little multimillion-dollar enterprises, nor can we rely entirely on antitrust enforcement to keep the giants in check. Still, there may be a case for a limited zone of protection for investment in proprietary programs, and I shall return to this issue in its legal setting.

The next group whose property rights are seriously affected by the new technologies are authors and publishers producing and marketing information in traditional forms. The interests of authors and publishers are obviously not identical, nor do authors form a coherent group within themselves. Some academic authors are pulled both ways on some of the issues before us. The publishers are the spokesmen, since their pocketbooks are most crucially affected. Aspects of the new technologies that make it cheap and easy to multiply copies of their products are most threatening to them. Today the enemy is the ubiquitous copying machine. Tomorrow it will be the computer, when the problems of getting printed works cheaply into and out of a computer are resolved.

A classic form of property protection available to publishers of the printed word is copyright. But copyright at the moment cannot be effectively enforced against users of the new technologies. Any attempt to control the output of the office copying machine seems doomed to failure. It may be, as Freed has suggested, that "we will have to suffer through with the present system until fully computerized libraries are in use. Then complete enjoyment of copyright protection will come into flower."[3] Assuming for the moment that copyright protection can be made effective, the question again is, should it be? Now we are talking about preserving property rights that have long been recognized, not about creating new ones. Copyright property, as one way of rewarding authors, has not led to conspicuous misallocation of resources. In time the new technologies may substantially expand the market for the writings of authors, and syntheses will doubtless emerge between the large demands on authors to produce the desired supply of new material and the rewards needed to evoke that supply. The immediate problem is to find some way out of the impasse that has developed between publishers and prospective computer users.

One should note, however, that the appearance of clear conflict between old-line publishers and newfangled computer industries is deceptive. Publishing and computing firms have gone through a burst of integration. When RCA acquired Random House, General Sarnoff is reported to have said, "they have the software and we have the hardware." Indeed, it may be that if this trend continues, the lines will not be drawn between publishing and computing firms but, as Perle has predicted, "between the private and the public sector; between those who create and market intellectual property—the authors and publishers—and those who wish freely to use that property—the educators, the academic world, and the world of nonprofit science and research; in brief, between the profit and the nonprofit." [4]

The users who will be left out of the network of profit-seeking relationships are those who are predominantly customers: universities, schools, and libraries. They can with more force than others raise principled objections to prices increased by monopoly powers created by public agencies. They can (and some of their spokesmen do) argue that the extension of even old property rights into new media is not self-evident or self-enforcing. The state gives these rights; the state can withhold them. It should at least keep them to a minimum when those who pay are such deserving and undernourished institutions.

Pertinently, we observe that a monopolist can discriminate and (within profit-maximizing limits) force some of his customers to pay more than others. By the same token, he perhaps can be required to allow some of his more deserving customers to pay less than others. On the other hand, principles of welfare economics argue for every user to pay his own way, with any required subsidies brought out into the open.

These are large, difficult, sometimes emotional issues. Without attempting to settle them at large, we can observe that vigorous claims will be made on behalf of nonprofit consumers of information through old and new technologies, and it may be politic to recognize them when we turn to the adjustment of particular property rights.

The Spheres of Patent and Copyright

The author and inventor, although joined together by the framers in the Constitutional matrix for copyright and patent, have to a remarkable degree been put asunder in life and in law. Until the emergence of the problems we are discussing here, conflict or overlap between copyright and patent was an occasional curiosity. There was a generally tacit understanding of their respective spheres, distinguished in the kind of protection they gave. Whatever an author wrote could be protected by copyright, but only against copying. In Judge Learned Hand's illuminating example, if an author had never heard of Keats, he could compose anew an "Ode on a Grecian Urn" and have a copyright on it. But he (or Keats) would have protection only for the "expression," not for the "idea," of his ode.

The inventor, on the other hand, had to do more than record his own thoughts; he had to make enough of an advance over everything that had gone before to be credited with an invention. If he succeeded, the patent during its life let him exclude all others from making, selling, or using his invention, even if they arrived at it independently. He would be protected not only for his expression of the telegraph but for the idea of the telegraph however expressed, if the courts confirmed that he had invented it.

Another major distinction between patents and copyrights lies in their duration: for a patent, seventeen years; for a copyright, fifty-six. There is more than a little incongruity in applying statutory grants of seventeen years (to say nothing of fifty-six) to fast-moving computer technology, especially in view of the typical interval of several years between invention and the grant of a patent.

Patents for Computer Programs

With these very general propositions in mind, let us consider the appropriateness of patents as a means of establishing property rights in computer programs. The question has had a rapid and dramatic history. Less than ten years ago the first polemical journal articles on it began to appear. The President's Commission on the Patent System made a weighty recommendation in 1966 that Congress bar such patents. Then in August 1969 came the decision (after a rehearing) in the *Prater and Wei* case.[5] It was far from conclusive, but it clearly tended toward the patentability of programs, and in November 1969 the Patent Appeals Court came down with another decision that solidified the implications of *Prater and Wei*.

Let us look at this more recent case, *Bernhart and Fetter*. There the applicants disclosed equations for programming a computer to work out a plot of two-dimensional representations of three-dimensional objects. "These claims recite," said the court, "and can be infringed only by a digital computer set in a certain physical condition, i.e. electromechanically set or programmed to carry out the recited routine." The court went on to rebut the Patent Office contention that the computer was unchanged by the program:

To this question we say that if a machine is programmed in a certain new and unobvious way, it is physically different from the machine without that program; its memory elements are differently arranged. The fact that these physical changes are invisible to the eye should not tempt us to conclude that the machine has not been changed. If a new machine has not been invented, certainly a "new and useful improvement" of the unprogrammed machine has been, and Congress has said that such improvements are statutory subject matter for a patent.[6]

While noting the court's admonition that "it may well be that the vast majority of newly programmed machines are obvious to those skilled in the art and hence unpatentable," we nevertheless now have a legal proposition of great simplicity and force. Every general-purpose computer becomes an improved machine by the application of a new and useful program, and the algorithm of that program can be patented. Indeed, in *Prater* and in *Bernhart* the disclosure seems to have been expressed at the even more abstract level of mathematical formulas. Unless I misunderstand the claims, the algorithm was not even presented; we were simply told that the invention could be programmed.

That the inventions could be disclosed and accepted in such an abstract form seems to me a fatal flaw in these cases. They are simply not in the traditional statutory scope of patents; and it is almost a fiction to say that they become statutory because the inventions are executed by an electronic machine. My objection is not that the idea is expressed in words and symbols; any invention must be. It is that the symbols *are* the invention. Patentable inventions must deal with things, or, if this sounds too simple-minded, with "physical quanta."[7] An algorithm is a way of solving a problem that is separate from the machine, whose electrical operation most programmers need not (and do not) understand.

The arguments admittedly depend on analogy and characterization. The court in *Bernhart* conceded that Congress "meant to exclude principles or laws of nature and mathematics, of which equations are an example, from even temporary monopolization by patent."[8] But the opinion took a specious escape by saying that the patent would not "prohibit *all* uses" of the equations found in the application. (No, only the uses of any consequence.) Then it went on to its main premise that the applicants had invented a new machine and should not be prevented from explaining their machine by way of an equation.

None of this reasoning, whether one agrees or disagrees with it, is conclusive on the more important question of whether algorithms *should* be patentable. To address this question we must look to the health of the industry and projections of the pace of its future development. The sector of the industry that needs patent protection, we are told, is that occupied by independent software producers. If they falter, society will be the poorer. We shall have to depend on massive monopolists who will exert less initiative at higher prices.

What sort of property protection is needed? Enough so that the investment required to develop a marketable program will not be discouraged by the threat of having competitors copy it or users use it without payment. If the ratio of perspiration to inspiration in developing a usable program is as high as it is said to be, what is needed is something to prevent the appropriation of the developed program. This can be done without excluding others from use of the algorithm.

Copyrights for Computer Programs

If the real need is to protect the expression or developed program rather than the idea or algorithm, we might rather look to copyright. Is copyright a proper vehicle for the creation of limited property rights in programs?

The Copyright Office has been accepting programs for registration since 1964, but fewer than two hundred programs have been registered, so the experience is inconclusive. There are several likely reasons why resort to copyright has been held back. First is the uncertainty about the eligibility of programs for copyright under the present statute. Second is the dearth of authoritative opinion on what would constitute an infringing copy, especially if copying occurred on magnetic tape or in some other form that was only machine-readable. Third, and probably foremost, is doubt about the scope of copyright protection of a program. The firm selling or licensing a program wants to control its *use,* not simply the illicit making of copies by a competitor. Patent confers an exclusive right to use; copyright does not.

Lawyers' discussion on this point always starts from and returns to a venerable Supreme Court case, *Baker* v. *Selden,* of 1879. There the Court rejected the plaintiff's claim of copyright in a system of bookkeeping while conceding his right to copyright a book about bookkeeping. It said that:

whilst no one has a right to print or publish his book or any material part thereof, as a book intended to convey instruction in the art, any person may practise and use the art itself which he has described and illustrated therein. The use of the art is a totally different thing from a publication of the book explaining it.[9]

I think we must accept this distinction between protected expression and unprotected use until we receive fresh guidance from Congress or the Court. Does this mean that copyright is worthless? Certainly not. Programs are appropriate subjects for copyright, in my opinion, and substantial copying by a competitor could be enjoined. This should reassure a considerable number of would-be producers of proprietary programs. But if a prospective customer came lawfully into possession of the text of the program, it does seem unlikely that he could be prevented from using it. This remains a severe constraint on the practical utility of copyright.

The merit of copyright is that there is supposed to be built into it a narrow range of protection confined to the particular manner of exposition. Since ideas and expressions do not come neatly tagged in a play or a novel, courts sometimes have difficulty in maintaining the proposition that ideas are not subject to copyright. But the distance between an algorithm and a completed source program seems to mark an idea-expression divide that can be recognized. Copyright protection of the expression defines a price others will pay for the expression if the price is less than their cost of developing it independently. The algorithm is free to be improved or to inspire other algorithms or more effective modes of expression in a variant program. The art remains open, while the investment can be protected—so long as the application of the program can be effectively licensed. For this purpose I suggest a new statutory right of exclusive application of a developed program.

An Application Right for Programs

If the firm that develops a program at considerable cost or trouble deserves some protected head start, we should consider a limited broadening of copyright to exclude unauthorized use, especially commercial use. Let us label this an *application right*. The present statute and the proposed revision both create rights that go beyond strictly copying, for example, the right to exclude others from performing musical works. A musical copyright would not be worth much nowadays if it only protected revenue from copies of sheet music!

An exclusive right to application of a developed program could be delimited by specific provisions for fair use and by admonitions that no idea, plan, or scheme embodied in the program was covered. It seems intuitively apparent that the application right should be of short duration—say five years. The ever-lengthening term of copyright reflects solicitude for the individual author, who counts on royalties for his old age, a consideration that does not apply to corporate undertakings in a fast-changing field.

To sum up, we have been considering whether copyright is appropriate as a means of creating exclusive rights in developed programs. I take the position that programs in a form intelligible to human readers are statutory "writings of an author." If a telephone directory is eligible for copyright (and it is), surely a computer program is, too. The difficult question is how to make copyright effective in protecting the investment and industry of the programmer without shutting off the free flow of new ideas in the field. Copyright meets this test; but it may not be of much commercial advantage to software producers unless the law confers upon them a limited right to control the application of developed programs by users.

Secrecy

Before moving on, we should touch upon what is doubtless the most prevalent mode of protecting programs—secrecy. Keeping programs from competitors and confining their use and dissemination today are accomplished partly by common-law copyright and more extensively by the law's regard for confidential relationships, buttressed by contracts not to disclose information accepted on a confidential basis.

Secrecy is socially the least satisfactory form of protection. It leads to a wasteful expenditure of talent and skill on solving problems already solved and writing programs already written. Markets for ideas and their expression are made gravely imperfect when information is suppressed. But the "cesspool of secrecy," as Edwin Land once called it, is to some extent self-cleansing. Maintaining secrecy requires silencing people, a hard thing to do in view of our simian propensity to chatter. At a sinister level, resort to secrecy is countered by resort to industrial espionage. More wholesomely, things simply leak. Basic ways of solving problems are in people's heads, and with the continuing scarcity of engineers and programmers there is great mobility. People take ideas with them, and restrictions on the use of their knowledge and skills vis-à-vis their former employers are properly limited. It is possible (we really do not know) that secrecy protection may give an adequate head start to the innovator without unduly locking up the field.

But the Supreme Court has put trade secrets under a very dark cloud. In the case of *Lear v. Adkins,* decided in June 1969, the Court gave a long-delayed "decent burial" to the proposition that a licensee of a patent may not attack the patent's validity. Justice Harlan also raised the "question whether, and to what extent, the States may protect the owners of *unpatented* inventions who are willing to disclose their ideas to manufacturers only upon payment of royalties." The Court "concluded after much consideration that even though an important question of federal law underlies this phase of the controversy, we should not now attempt to define in even a limited way the extent, if any, to which the States may properly act to enforce the contractual rights of inventors of unpatented secret ideas."[10]

The most ominous phrase in *Lear v. Adkins* is clearly "if any." In what the Court said there and in the *Sears-Compco* cases[11] there are propositions, not fully articulated, about the reach of the patent system and its preemption of remedies under state law. If, as I have argued, program algorithms are not within the statutory definitions of patentable inventions, should we conclude that Congress (and maybe the Constitution) intend them to be (1) incapable of any protection? (2) protected by copyright? or (3) protectable by state law (in the guise of unfair competition, breach of confidence, or contract)? If, as I have further argued, copyright no more than patent law protects algorithms *as such,* it would seem incongruous to give them untrammeled protection through common-law doctrines. Such an outcome would tend to set at naught the supremacy of the federal copyright-patent scheme.

Next, if we take a developed program, which I argue *is* within the scope of copyright, the logic of *Lear* v. *Adkins* still urges what the Court seems to be saying about ideas and patents: one must either take the benefits and burdens of the national scheme or do without protection unless Congress in shaping the national scheme explicitly permits the protection of state law to continue.

The present copyright statute does have such an escape hatch, and a big one, as follows: "Nothing in this title shall be construed to annul or limit the right of the author or proprietor of an unpublished work, at common law or in equity, to prevent the copying, publication, or use of such unpublished work without his consent, and to obtain damages therefor."[12] This leaves to common law and equity (that is, to the states) claims of infringement through the *use* of an unpublished work (just what the national scheme denies). But it does not say that the states must afford such protection, and it applies only to unpublished work.

There is not likely to be an immediate resolution of the future scope of trade-secret protection, nor need there be a total solution. That is, the Court may not entirely demolish state protection of material in the ambit of patent or copyright. The *Sears-Compco* cases, which had to do with imitation of industrial design, left room for state protection against deceptive labeling. Similarly, leeway may be left for protection against deceptive business dealings. What remains of state law on trade secrets will be influenced by the kinds of protection made available or deliberately withheld by federal statutes.

Copyright Works in Computers

We now turn to the other major intersection of copyright and computers: the ingestion by computers of textual material. Some of the labels may be the same as with copyrights for programs, but the issues are quite different. When a work protected by copyright is stored in a computer, at what point and for what uses must the property interests of the copyright owner be recognized? Few contend that copyright should be ignored; but there are claims for considerable exemption on behalf of science and education.

Controversy has arisen around the clear intention of the copyright revision bill to make unprivileged input an infringement. The latest draft of this buffeted legislation backs off and proposes to leave the law in its present state—whatever that is. Our concern is, what should it be?

Authors and publishers insist that the statute recognize copyright at the point of input. Computer users are equally insistent that this is unreasonable in that no meaningful copying occurs (if it ever does) until there is recognizable output that goes beyond the limits of what the courts consider fair use. Whether manipulations of the work within a machine might also be identifiable as copying is a possibility that most contestants prudently avoid. Having previously adhered to the infringement-on-output-only camp, I am now of the equivocal and therefore hazardous view that this may be a dispute between Big-endians and Little-endians (though I do not mean to characterize the disputants as Lilliputians).

What fears of the publishers drive them to insist on input control? In their view, outputs cannot be monitored and people will cheat, just as they now do with copying machines. But cannot a user just as surreptitiously introduce a copyrighted work into a computer? The detection problem, however, is only auxiliary to the basic fear of publishers that books will be supplanted by noncompensatory computer uses. An input charge must replace other lost revenue and pay for authorship and publishing. The reply is that income from a book depends on the volume of sales, the computer counterpart of which will be the volume of printouts or displays. But to this there is a neat rejoinder that a library pays the same price for a book whether no one reads it or hundreds read it.

Beneath these somewhat simple considerations lies a deeper concern. Once books are introduced into computer networks, they may never reappear as books. They will be extensively used and will displace the need for the published work. But the use will be selective and the output fragmentary, in segments and forms that may each look like a fair use and that will be impossible to meter. There must be a charge at input or nothing will be recovered.

What are the fears of potential computer users of copyrighted works? They suspect that many authors and publishers may simply refuse access or set prices prohibitively high. Works of esteemed authors are not readily substitutable, and those who hold valuable properties may prefer to exploit them in traditional ways. *Après nous, le déluge.*

Writings may not be as unique as their authors like to think they are, and if the author of one useful manual decides to go down with Gutenberg, someone else will write another for a computer. But it takes time for competition to rouse itself. The developing integration of publishers with computer interests may foreshadow networks built on major backlists, with copyrights used to beat off rivals desiring access to the same collections. This would bode ill for independent firms at all levels: nonintegrated publishers, software houses, and other emerging enterprises offering computerized information services to educational and business markets. Their profitability and survival will depend as much on cheap and ready access to inputs as on markets for outputs.

These are causes for concern in the middle-range future. It is hard to flesh them out, and they may be kept thin by antitrust purges.

For the short run, user hostility toward the threat of copyright controls on input arises from the cost and inefficiency of getting clearances. Anthony Oettinger's dismay, expressed at Senate hearings on the revision bill, is characteristic. Before he could experiment with new inputs, he said, he would have to:

> seek out the owner of a copyright, if any, make formal requests for permission to use the material, pay royalties if any are due, etc. All this before any material could actually be used, and, in fact, before I could find out whether or not the material was useful! The delays, the frustrations and the chaos inherent in such a process now seem so formidable that if the bill were passed in its present form I would be tempted to return to the safer occupation of copying out manuscripts with a goose quill pen.[13]

As things now stand, all participants are hindered by the absence of effective pricing and administrative arrangements. Since these arrangements are not developing spontaneously, the parties concerned must be put under some pressure to devise them. With computer uses of copyright publications still so undeveloped and machine costs of storage and retrieval of voluminous texts so high, the practicalities and uncertainties on both sides seem to me to require some kind of clearance at input.

But if at the input end of the process the law bestows on the author-publisher an extensive right to withhold everything, and if bargaining channels are clogged (as they are), progress will be slow. A considerable effort has been made by users to avoid input rights. There has been no comparable effort to find solutions to problems of clearances and payments. The immediate need is for a bargaining procedure that will facilitate development of beneficent computer networks and information banks. While I am in favor of further study, I believe the pressure of unsatisfied wants on *both* sides might produce results.

Compulsory Licensing?

Accordingly, while I think that copyright is the main way we will continue to encourage and support authorship and publication and that copyright should include considerable control over computer storage and retrieval, I also think we should recognize the need for relatively untrammeled research and development in computer use. This leads me to consider a privilege to copy at a reasonable royalty—a compulsory license, in lawyer's parlance.

Compulsory licenses have frequently been used as a remedy for alleged abuses of patents; and there are similar instances in the copyright field of rights of access to protected works. The most familiar case, created by the present copyright law in 1909, permits anyone to record a musical composition after the composer has authorized one record of it. The new version of the copyright revision bill adds others, notably for cable television.

The obvious difficulty about any scheme of privileged access for a price is in setting the price. What is a *reasonable* royalty? The existing and proposed statutory arrangements simply state a price. In the case of phonograph records, it is two cents a song. It has been so ever since 1909, and the only important change in the revision bill is to nudge it up to two and a half cents. This would be indefensible, except that it seems to work. But there is no basis whatever for setting a statutory rate for computer input. The utter uncertainty as to what fees are appropriate may be a major block to authorized computer use.

Another possibility for pricing is the traditional rate-setting or rate-supervising body, like a public utility commission. But it would be preposterous to create an elaborate structure of rates for general application at this stage of undevelopment.

A third and more plausible solution is to let the parties bargain, with a mechanism for compulsory arbitration if they cannot agree. A panel could be constructed in the Copyright Office in the usual tripartite form: one publisher, one user, and an impartial chairman.

One could envision combining in a statute a provision for a *temporary* five-year compulsory license and a three-year study commission, thus giving Congress two years to digest and act upon the commission's recommendations. One could expect that resort to the arbitration panel would be infrequent. Objections that the panel would be cumbersome and costly could be cheerfully acknowledged, with the response that we planned it that way—to stimulate voluntary agreements.

A compulsory license invoked simply by serving notice of the proposed use on a copyright owner would be strong medicine. What if the copyright holder did not want to get into computer uses on any terms? Such deep recalcitrance might have a variety of motives. Would it deserve to be respected? Would it be enough to follow the phonograph-record pattern part way, so that when (and only when) one computer use had been licensed, others could enter? This might scare off development, since copyright owners would hesitate to take the first step.

What kind of computer uses would be subject to compulsory licensing? Suppose that an enterprise combining computer and reprography techniques proposes to issue hard copies of books on demand. Should this directly competitive activity be able to demand a license from a publisher? I am doubtful.

In the end, the zone of friction requiring lubrication between copyright and computer may be so narrow as not to justify special legislative treatment. Still, the narrowness may be that of a cutting edge that does not cut. As long as we think and legislate in terms of total rights or total immunities, we encourage each contesting group to hope for total victory. We need instead to push everyone to the bargaining table and get on with the intricate job of shaping a modus vivendi.

Observations in Conclusion

Patent and copyright are where the action is, and we must be cursory about other forms of property and substitutes for property. One important possibility is implied by the idea of a computer utility. Functionally, this points to the development of time sharing, data banks, and information networks serving all comers. Technologically, it involves the interaction of computers and telecommunications, with one or a few carriers as necessary and convenient instruments. Economically, it raises questions of monopoly control such as the telephone companies have in voice communications. Legally, it suggests regulation, with the Federal Communications Commission possibly allocating exclusive rights.

This subject is discussed by Nicholas Johnson.[14] I only want to observe that regulation always imports the risk of extending and legitimizing monopolies that, enjoying the law's protection, are hard to dislodge. Justified on the grounds that competing services are unfeasible, they garner returns that might support investment in innovation but lack the spur of competition. Fortunately it is by no means certain or even likely that the computer utility will develop in this direction.

An assessment of the relative adequacy of research and development resources for the computer and communication stream of tomorrow shows no major alterations in incentives or property claims necessary for hardware (putting aside antitrust possibilities). Communications are lagging, but they may need, more than property incentives, a regulatory push toward as much competition as possible. Through and around these tangible technologies swirl the elusive constructs of software. As machines become cheaper, and *if* communications do, software may use up the largest slice of resources. Innovation and efficiency will need stimulation. How much and of what kind?

There is no occasion for public subsidy of computer technology in commercial applications, although subsidized work in universities has been widely beneficial because it has been open to all. Kemeny pleaded persuasively that the public sector may be relatively neglected here as elsewhere and that we may be missing out on the development of desirable noncommercial computer applications.[15] Some public assistance could be desirable.

For applications with a likelihood of profit, the property magnets of patent and copyright (because they are already here) exert the strongest pull. Patents, I have argued, are inappropriate for most software, especially at the level of abstraction of the Bernhart equations. I do not think the attempt to reify software inventions by finding inside every digital computer an infinity of special-purpose machines will survive the icy scrutiny of the Supreme Court when a proper case reaches it.

The copyright climate is warmer. Computer instructions, input, and output are expressed in words and symbols. These are the province of copyright, although the present shape of copyright is not well adapted to the computer world. Copyright, lodged in the Constitution for the "Progress of Science" (that is, of knowledge), has been molded to the needs of the entertainment industries. It will need some readaptation to yield the correct balance between protection of commercial investment and freedom and facility of access. The modest needs for software protection are impersonal, while the manifestations of modern copyright are highly personal. The song-and-dance man is always there, along with the words and music. The duration of copyright takes care of an author's middle-aged orphans, and it reaches from one medium to another in a way that suits the relationships of authors across publishing, films, and television but that seems excessive for the computer media. The revision bill includes a comprehensive right "to prepare derivative works based upon the copyrighted work," resting on a definition of "derivative work" that I have come to regard as pernicious.[16] It sweeps up "any other form in which a work may be recast, transformed, or adapted." This provision should not pass without further study of its implications for computer use. On the other hand, the latest version of the bill has an admirable new statement of the fundamental proposition that copyright does not extend to any "idea, plan, procedure, process, system, method of operation, concept, principle, or discovery."[17] With typical legal redundancy, this drives the wedge between idea and expression that I have been hammering.

We still do not know much about the relationship between copyright and computer. The proposal for a Commission on New Technological Uses of Copyrighted Works is too modest in being confined to copyright. We should also look at other proposals, including general-purpose devices such as the "petty patent"—easily obtained, short-lived, and narrow in scope— and special-purpose innovations like the IBM registration scheme, which is tailored to the partial protection of programs.[18]

My hunch is that it will be easier to adapt copyright than get a new statutory scheme. It is hard enough to change the copyright law. The general revision effort has been before the Congress since 1964, after lengthy preparation. But compare the attempt to pass a special statute for industrial designs, which now lodges clumsily in both patent and copyright. That reform has been before Congress since 1957. Old bottles will hold new wine. Why try to sell a distracted Congress new bottles as well?

PANEL DISCUSSION

KAPLAN. I start by agreeing with Brown on a fundamental: that the dominating purpose of copyright and patent is to provide just enough incentive to call forth optimal production and distribution of new works. Thus proposals to expand patent or copyright must justify themselves by reference to the quite unsentimental standard of whether additional incentive is needed.

Agreeing with Brown on the fundamental, I still have doubts or questions about his two main specifics. His first concerns property rights in computer programs. The computer industry has grown very rapidly with a great deal of free and easy exchange of information and no particular thought of patent or copyright protection. Would the industry have done better if further incentive had been laid on through a regime of legal protection? I doubt it very much. But some say that conditions are changing, and we are urged to reverse course one hundred eighty degrees and clamp protection on computer programs across the board. Where is the factual evidence to show that anything of this sort is needed? Brown's paper does not offer the evidence, as I am sure he would agree. Nor was adequate evidence tendered at the hearings on the copyright revision bill. Indeed, facts remain conspicuously in short supply all along the line.

But if a case can be made for some protection of programs, what form should it take? Brown is unhappy with patent. He thinks the recent decisions of the Court of Customs and Patent Appeals go too far when (in his reading) they interpret the current patent statute as allowing overarching protection of the abstractions that go by the name of algorithms. Brown would confine protection to developed programs as distinguished from algorithms, and the medium of protection would be copyright. Thus, says Brown, the programs themselves would be safeguarded against copying, but the algorithms would not be covered and would remain free.

This is an interesting proposal, but I doubt that it would work as just described. For if you prevent me from copying or simulating your program, you can shut out or seriously embarrass my using the algorithm. Consider the analogy of Selden's bookkeeping system in the great case of *Baker* v. *Selden*. Suppose Selden in his book exhibits forms either indispensable to or very convenient for working the system. Then if Selden can bar me from the forms or charge an exorbitant price for them, he impedes me in employing the system that in theory is supposed to be free. If the system is really to remain open to me, I must be allowed in the last resort to imitate the forms in order to employ the system, although not necessarily to go into competition with Selden in selling the forms to third persons. This reasoning seems to apply to the problem of computer programs: the developed program is comparable to Selden's forms and the algorithm is like Selden's bookkeeping system.

It has been intimated, however, that one who wants to avail himself of the algorithm can always do so safely by preparing his own developed program—that is, by making some more or less immaterial changes or twists in the copyrighted program. But the risk of infringement would be there; the courts very likely would not take the lighthearted view that plagiarism can be avoided by making only slight changes of the copyrighted program. Another difficulty is perceived by Anthony Oettinger (my oracle as well as Brown's): that a practice of varying programs in order to avoid infringement of copyright would amount to a kind of purposeful subversion of the standardization of programs. In that sense, says Oettinger, it would play "a very grim practical joke on every taxpayer."[19]

Later in his paper, Brown seems to change his stance. He suggests a superadded five-year application right—so that a man who simply acquired ownership of a copyrighted program might have to pay again to use it in the machine. Why the copyright owner could not use his control over the copying of the program in such a way as to control its subsequent use, thus rendering an application right superfluous, is not really explained. But I think Brown may be involved in a kind of Freudian slip. "Application" or "use" is redolent of patent. It may be that the cleaner way to protect developed programs is to forget about copyright and give such programs protection of a patent character at their level of concreteness. But in that case should you not require that they be *novel*—a significant advance over the prior art—rather than merely original? Novelty is a conventional requirement for patents. This question Brown avoids by presenting his analysis in terms of copyright and application right. No doubt many businessmen would like to have protection for original but nonnovel devices, procedures, and gimmicks, but we do not allow that in American law. Why should it make a difference that a procedure is carried out by computer?

My feeling is that if protection comes to be justified at all, it will be for certain kinds of programs in certain respects, not just for programs generally. There is already an almost infinite variety of computer programs —programs to run petroleum refineries, programs to overcome urban blight, programs to teach English to high school sophomores—and they were not necessarily created legally equal. Again we need facts: about types of programs, kinds and sizes of markets for the several types, and (a matter that needs intense examination) the transaction costs in terms not only of royalty payments but of the variegated expenses of search, negotiation, delay, and frustration that would be incident to a copyright-bound or patent-bound regime.

Brown's second specific relates to utilization of copyrighted works in computers. Here comes the input-or-output question. Brown suggests that the input itself should be held an infringement, and the most plausible argument for this view is that otherwise a work might be nibbled to death without compensation to the copyright owner. Imagine encyclopedia types of materials in the machine, repeatedly consulted. Each single utilization might look like a *de minimis* or "fair" use, but when the utilizations are aggregated it would appear that the materials have been heavily exploited. But this does not point inevitably to hitting the input; it may point instead to defining realistically which utilizations by the computer should amount to infringement. Furthermore, the input solution will not work where all the prospective computer utilizations of a copyrighted work are deliberately exempted by law from copyright liability. Under the copyright revision bill certain kinds of utilizations by nonprofit educational institutions would, in fact, be thus exempted.[20] If you make input an infringement here, you are indirectly undermining the exemptions.

I am prepared to assume that in practice it would be convenient in a great many cases for the copyright owner and the operator of the computer to make their deal before the copyrighted material was introduced into the computer. But that does not prove that it would be legally sound or convenient to enact as a universal proposition that input is an infringement unless authorized by the copyright owner. But I cannot imagine that the problem is a blockbuster. It will work itself out in due time. We are all agreed that in general the computer should respect copyrighted items; the particular point of incidence of liability seems a technical detail that experience or experimentation will solve. With respect to tricky situations we do well to remember that the computer itself has awesome powers to keep track of what it does from start to finish as a basis for calculating what is owed to copyright proprietors.

Much more important in the long run than the input-or-output question is ensuring that the law does not interfere with a possible goal of computer science—furnishing wide and speedy access to and virtuosic manipulation of complete stocks of information and intelligence, including copyrighted material, in vast quantities. The law gets in the way by requiring permission (clearance) from multitudinous copyright owners. Clearance procedures adequate to such demands have not yet come into sight. They should certainly be worked on, with attention to the nature of the different repertories of works, the demands likely to be made on them, and particularly the requirements of research. Brown sees the compulsory license as a temporary expedient, but in some form it may be needed even in permanent legislation.

This entire question of the utilization of copyrighted works in computers is not on the urgent list because computers cannot yet double as libraries in effectively absorbing large amounts of material. In fact, the future in this respect may lie mainly with ultramicrofiches or similar devices and only incidentally with computers. And reverting to Brown's first question, protection of computer programs, this, too, can hardly require an instant answer. Thus there is time for a national study commission, preferably with broader scope than is now proposed by the copyright revision bill. I should hope that here, finally, the facts will out. Permanent legislation can await the results of the study.

A third question—the reprography question symbolized by the Xerox machine—seems rather more urgent than the other two. Brown treats it briefly. The legal doctrine of fair use excuses copying to some extent, but in fact a considerable amount of the copying that is now going on exceeds the bounds of fair use as it is understood today and is illicit. The threat is not only to printed texts but to nearly every other kind of work. Sound recordings are threatened by the home tape recorder, and so on. Some large part of the lawless copying results from the absence of viable clearance procedures.

I have two observations. First, I think it would help practically as well as atmospherically to install a regulatory agency that could keep track of changing conditions and furnish guidelines from time to time as to what is and what is not fair use. In due course we might have settled practices and less bootlegging. But second, in the long view the publishers (using the word in the broad sense) must look to changes in their own technology that will beat the copiers at their own game. No amount of prohibitory legislation can immunize book publishers from the effects of ultramicrofiches.

Let me end by giving some short reactions to a few of Brown's remarks along the way.

About the duration of rights, he says he realizes intuitively that if there is to be an application right it should not run for more than a short time. What about the duration of regular copyright? The proposal in the revision bill is to extend the period from the present fifty-six years to roughly seventy-six years—surely a bad idea. If this drastic change is intended to increase incentives to produce, I doubt that it will succeed even in microscopic degree. And as to the casual benefits of the extension of the term to a minute number of lucky authors or publishers or their descendants, are these not outweighed by the burdens imposed on users during the couple of decades that would be added to all copyrights?

Brown is somewhat dubious about legislative preferences for nonprofit educational institutions as users of copyrighted works but seems prepared in the end to go along with such a policy for political reasons. Of course, preferred treatment of education can go too far, but moderate preferences are justified on principle. If education can be favored while still leaving adequate overall incentives for producers, it makes sense to give education the break.

The revision bill's strangely broad definition of "derivative work," considered as a measure of what may constitute an infringement, seems pernicious to Brown, and I agree with him. They say that praise is all right until you begin to inhale. The same applies to copyright. In respect to the derivative-work definition, as on the question of duration of copyright, the draftsmen of the bill have been inhaling.

Brown is sensitive to the problem of secrecy. His remarks are valuable. They encourage irreverent speculation. For example, should the law always demand that intellectual productions be disclosed to the public as a condition of enforcing claimed rights of ownership in them?

Finally, Brown's paper is alert to the fact that our subject is intimately connected with others and is bewilderingly broad. You cannot talk copyright or patent without getting involved in antitrust, freedom of speech, and other things. And "new technology" can cover everything from broadband cable to satellites. Too much for one symposium!

LACY. There are certain untrue or misused assumptions underlying many discussions of copyright and the new technology. One is that the only justifiable purpose of copyright is as an incentive for authors to write. The probably rhetorical definition of the purpose of copyright in the Constitution is far broader: "To promote the Progress of Science and useful Arts." The promotion of that progress requires not only the creation but also the dissemination of writings. Certainly to provide an incentive for investment in the publication of a book, the making of a film, or the staging of a drama is as legitimate an object of copyright as to provide an incentive for the original composition of the works. Moreover, creators should be rewarded for their labors and contributions to our well-being even though the hope of reward may not be an essential stimulus to their activities.

A second assumption often held is that a subsequent use of an author's work should require payment to him only if it replaces or injures the sale of his work in its original form. It is argued, for example, that the extensive use of an author's work in a computer may not demonstrably reduce the sales of the book in which it was originally embodied; or that the photoduplication of articles from a journal may not demonstrably reduce the circulation of the journal. But even so, an author still ought to be compensated for a new or additional use of his work. Making a film from a novel usually sharply increases the sale of the novel, as does its adoption by a major book club. Yet no one would suggest that the film company or book club has a right to use the author's work without compensation.

A third assumption is clearly set forth in the Perle statement quoted by Brown. Perle suggests that controversies over copyright will be "between the private and the public sector; between those who create and market intellectual property—the authors and publishers—and those who wish freely to use that property—the educators, the academic world, and the world of nonprofit science and research; in brief, between the profit and the nonprofit." This is an almost Alice-in-Wonderland reversal of the facts. It is rather "the academic world, and the world of nonprofit science and research," as well as federal, state, and local governments, that create most intellectual property, whereas profit-seeking corporations are rather consumers and secondary distributors. Many of us and our organizations are both creators and users of intellectual property, just as many of us are both earners and spenders, borrowers and lenders, performers and spectators, producers and consumers, owners and tenants, and buyers and sellers. There should be no Armageddon lining us up on opposite sides of a controversy or dividing us on a profit-versus-nonprofit basis. All of us have a common interest in finding a system that will stimulate both the creation and use of intellectual products and that will provide an equitable sharing of costs and rewards without imposing cumbersome or wasteful red tape.

Brown has addressed two problems:
1. rights in computer programs;
2. the copyright structure that should govern transformation or reproduction by the new technology of works initially copyrighted in more traditional forms.

I think there is a third problem that is even more important:
3. the copyright structure that should govern and provide incentives for the creation of works intended primarily for use through the new technology.

With respect to computer programs, Brown presents a thoughtful and judicious solution. Patents are too hard to get, and they protect too much; copyright, if it protects only the making of copies, protects too little. Since a computer program, like a song, a symphony, or a comedy, is a work created to be performed, an application right, analogous to a performance right, is clearly the solution. But I am not persuaded that a special five-year limit in the duration of the application right is necessary or wise. If the rapid obsolescence of programs makes longer protection useless, it also makes it harmless. So long as a program remains of value, why should its creator not continue to share in that value?

There is definitely a need for more incentive to produce programs. The development of hardware has far outrun the development of software. Until the unbundling decision, the incentive for producing computer programs was primarily for hardware manufacturers to make their machines more marketable and for users to meet their individual requirements. The economy and the technology need a stronger software-producing industry independent of the hardware companies. This is unlikely without greater protection for software.

With respect to using the new technology for copyrighted works originally published in traditional forms, assuming we all agree that the rights of the creator should be respected, there remain two questions: the input-or-output question, and whether some form of compulsory license is required. I do not feel that having output as the only point of copyright control can possibly protect the rights of the author. If computer displays were normally brief enough to come under the doctrine of fair use, and if input were exempted by statute, the user would completely escape payment. If, on the other hand, displays were normally or frequently to require permission of the creator, there would be an insuperable practical problem, since what a computer causes to be displayed at any moment is typically unpredictable. An advance agreement with the proprietor that printouts would be permitted within the generally specified functions of the system realistically can be made only at the point of input. Payment can still be based on the amount of printout, just as author royalties are on the basis of the number of books sold under a contract made *before* the book is published. I think it will be much simpler for proprietor and user alike to make copyright arrangements on blanket use at the point of input. To say that copyright control should be applied only at output is to say that there should be no copyright control at all.

The argument for a compulsory license rests on Oettinger's assumption, apparently shared by Brown and Kaplan, that proprietors may refuse to permit input or may charge unreasonable fees, or that it will otherwise be difficult to negotiate permissions. These problems exist only in anticipation and are, I believe, greatly exaggerated. Our publishing house owns perhaps the largest body of publisher-controlled materials likely to be of interest for computer input. Yet in the last few years we have probably received fewer than ten requests for permission to put copyrighted materials into computers. All have been promptly granted, save for one or two so vague or general that it was impossible to ascertain what rights were wanted for what uses of what materials. Most were requests for experimental use and were granted without charge.

Our company, far from resisting computer uses of materials for which it controls the copyright, has for a long time actively sought out opportunities to license materials for computer use. Two examples suggest that the problem of obtaining licenses can be far simpler and less cumbersome than inexperienced scholars may fear. University Microfilms has successfully obtained licenses to make photocopies of probably hundreds of thousands of titles without significant delays or difficulties or unreasonable costs. The Library of Congress has had similar success in its program to make available Braille or recorded editions of books for the blind.

I believe that books and computers organize and use information in inherently different ways. Computers will remain a very minor way of using the content of books, and books will remain a very minor source of the data ingested by computers. The computer will normally mediate between the raw data and the book text, not between the text and the user.

To set up a ponderous machinery of compulsory licensing to deal with what is likely to be a minor flow of business, and to do so in the absence of any persuasive evidence that it is needed and in the presence of a good deal that it is not, is surely unwise. Indeed, nothing would be more likely to delay working out the wrinkles in the normal flow of negotiated licenses than to embed it in such a context.

When a document is made available by photocopy, microfilm, microcard, or facsimile transmission, figures are often quoted that microcopies (for example, ultramicrofiche) are many orders of magnitude cheaper than producing the same text in the original form. A ten-dollar book may be compared with a twenty-cent microfiche. But this is false accounting. The true social cost of the microfiche includes *all* the costs incurred in producing the original edition up through the printing of the copy from which the microfiche is made. It also includes most of the marketing and distribution costs involved in making the original publication viable and getting it reviewed and listed in bibliographies. The *only* cost not involved in the creation of the microfiche is the printing, paper, and binding cost of the individual book, against which must be weighed the cost of filming the book, reducing the film to microform, and making a positive print. These two sets of costs are rather comparable and indeed may be nearly equal for relatively large editions.

Sound public policy requires that when any work is made available in more than one format, each must bear a fair share of the total cost common to all formats. This has long been recognized among the traditional media: live public performance for profit, broadcasts, record sales, and sheet-music sales all share the cost of creating a piece of music; cinema and stage versions, translations, British editions, abridgements, and book-club and paperbound versions all share the costs of creating a novel. The same principles should apply to uses of a work in the newer technologies.

An aspect of the problem only lightly dealt with by Brown may be, in the long run, the most important of all: to devise the copyright structure that best promotes the development of content materials (as distinguished from operational programs) designed from the beginning for computer use. Examples are data banks, including statistics assembled by the Bureau of the Census and other governmental agencies; vital statistics from local agencies throughout the country; standard reference data for chemical elements and compounds and for physical properties of materials, assembled and verified by the Bureau of Standards or other authoritative agencies; formulas in various areas of science and technology, which the computer can evaluate; and systems of computer-assisted instruction in which bodies of teaching materials are devised, created, and organized in such a way that a computer may select them and present them to a student in a sequence triggered by the student's responses.

Many of these bodies of input will be created or assembled by public authority. If the cost is provided from tax funds, it will not need to be met from payments by users. But if the material to be used in computers is not to be confined to what governmental agencies or foundations, directly or indirectly, choose to pay for, there must be a means of assuring the right of those who invest intellectually or financially in the creation of such materials to charge for their use. There simply will not be private funds for the very large investment required to organize data banks, to develop systems of computer-assisted instruction, or to carry forward the necessary experimental work unless there is a clear definition and protection of rights. Many publishing houses are now investing large sums in the development of computer-related instructional systems, investments that may in time produce results of great social value. Yet this investment would halt instantly in the absence of effective copyright protection.

There is a simple first step toward the solution of this complex problem. The input of materials into a computer must be regarded as the making of a copy, and the input of copyrighted material beyond the limits of fair use without the permission of the proprietor must be considered an infringement. This principle will provide a basis on which we can begin to negotiate clearance procedures, normal payments, standard forms of agreement, and equitable relationships like those in other areas of life where society encourages, uses, and rewards the investment of brains and funds to add to the sum of usable knowledge.

HASKINS. The speaker has indicated that because of the pressure of time he would like us to proceed directly to questions from the audience rather than replying at the moment to the discussants. So I will turn the podium over to Dr. Greenberger.

GREENBERGER. The first question is asked in three different ways: Judge Giles S. Rich of the U.S. Court of Customs and Patent Appeals asks Brown, since when has patent protection under the statutes been limited to *things*? Processes are not physical things.[21] Professor Irving Kayton of the George Washington University points out that the patent statute expressly provides for the patent protection of processes as well as machines. Is not a new and unobvious process carried out by a computer under the constraints of its program proper statutory matter meriting protection? Finally, Ronald Thurman, research fellow at the George Washington University asks why the process inherent within a program and symbolized by a flow chart should not be patentable even though the more abstract algorithm cannot be. Although the primary value of most programs is in their development, in some it is in their novel process (as in the *Bernhart* case). Should not both types of programs get protection?

BROWN. I am not an expert on the patent law, but I have tried to get a grasp of the particular issues here. Process patents involving chemical, physical, electrical, or mechanical operations do not, as I understand the important cases, go to the level of abstraction that is involved in the computer cases we have had so far. Under the concept propounded in the *Bernhart* case, a general-purpose computer is at one minute one invention and in another minute another invention. How do you detect the infringement of patents when these things come and go with the high speed at which a computer works? The notion that the same general-purpose computer can hypothetically in the course of an hour infringe a thousand different patents is too much for me!

Beyond this, the commercial interests that need to be protected are in the investment in developed programs. It is not until after a great deal of "debugging" that one knows whether an algorithm is any good, and by that time a substantial investment has been made. I would simply assert that the investment is reflected in the developed program, and this is what is entitled to some degree of protection, not the abstract proposition.

KAPLAN. My difficulty is in seeing why, as soon as you go from what you call an algorithm to something more concrete that you call an expression, you necessarily pass from the realm of patent to copyright. If you are going to protect developed programs, there is a real issue whether you should proceed on the basis of mere originality, which means that practically everything will secure protection, or proceed on the basis of novelty, a stiffer requirement.

GREENBERGER. The next question echoes Lacy's point on the need for input control. Curtis Benjamin, retired chairman of McGraw-Hill, asks Kaplan how and at what point he would offer protection of copyrighted materials inserted into a computer system and used only for computation or problem solving—materials that will not be copied within the system or printed out in any form for use by a subscriber to the service.

Mr. Benjamin states that Kaplan has in the past referred to "clearance at the source" as affording protection of copyrighted works used in computer-aided information systems, but apparently has some lingering doubt as to whether it is prudent to require permission at the input stage.[22] The question has special pertinence at this particular time because McGraw-Hill has just negotiated a contract under which the contents of as many as thirty of its copyrighted handbooks may be inserted and used in the manner described in an on-line, real-time computer service for engineering computations and analyses. The company and its contracting party, United Computing Systems, believe that effective protection against unauthorized usage of this kind can be secured *only* at the input stage.

KAPLAN. Curtis Benjamin has repeated in graphic form my example of a copyrighted work that is utilized by a computer but is not reproduced by it in the usual sense. I think he means to argue from this example that the law should declare all inputs of copyrighted works to be infringements; but that goes too far, as I tried to show. Indeed, input itself is not a significant utilization. The question of substance is which subsequent utilization shall be considered infringement and shall thus be compensable; the rest is a matter of convenient procedure. Protection, of course, is only infringement looked at in another way.

GREENBERGER. The next question is from Sigmund Timberg, an attorney in Washington. He asks if some form of copyright protection is not necessary for the small, nonintegrated software producer in an industry dominated by large, integrated hardware-software companies. A related question by William Knox, a vice president of McGraw-Hill, casts doubt on Brown's assessment of good health for the software industry. Knox surmises that all but six software firms operate at a loss. He asks Brown if he still finds little need for software protection and inquires about his reasons for believing that it will be simpler to stretch the copyright law to cover noncopying situations than to create a new statutory right.

BROWN. As to Sigmund Timberg's question, I did propose some limited rights in the interest of small firms, but any extension of rights will benefit IBM as well as the small firms except to the extent that IBM is constrained by antitrust considerations.

As to Knox's comment about most software firms not making a profit, I do not doubt it. But this is not generally known, which indicates what little information outsiders get and how hard it is for us to make a judgment. On the possibility of creating a new statutory right, my political hunch is to avoid tailor-made devices for one's own industry, such as IBM's proposal (which would fit nothing but the computer program industry and on reflection is a monstrosity). I admit we have tailor-made systems of protection already—for agriculture, shipping, and elsewhere—but since I do not like them, I want to believe that Congress does not like them either!

GREENBERGER. Let us conclude with two questions in the programming area. The first one is by our former student at The Johns Hopkins University, Brian Crissey, who is now with the Office of the Secretary of Defense. He asks what prevents a person from changing a few meaningless source-language statements to change the appearance of a copyrighted program but not its function, so as to circumvent the law?

The second question is from Lawrence Glassman, a patent attorney with the Army. He notes that another new area of technology is the use of numerical tapes to control manufacturing machinery to produce, for example, a replacement part. Does this type of software raise any different problems from those discussed?

BROWN. Yes, I do see a difference, and it is very hard to know where to draw the line when software is enmeshed in manufacturing operations. I realize there are many patents already granted and functioning for milling machines and the like.

On the first question, it is not right to assume that copyright infringement is avoided just by making a few trivial changes. Also, it takes time and energy to write around a program. On the other hand, the possibility of being able to write around a program keeps its price down and can be a very useful constraint.

KAPLAN. If you can simply fool around with a couple of steps in a program and avoid copyright infringement, the whole thing becomes very foolish. Those of us who are opposed to overly broad protection fear that the courts will themselves begin to "inhale" and deal with copyright in somewhat the way they deal with patents. They may begin to think of equivalents and all sorts of things that will make the supposedly harmless copyright as serious as an overarching patent. I am not saying that a patent is necessarily septic; but if we adopt a system of protection, we should do it with our eyes open. We should not assume that copyright protection means very little when in the end it may mean a great deal.

DINNER DISCUSSION

GREENBERGER. The proposed Commission on New Technological Uses of Copyrighted Material is embedded in the pending copyright revision bill. Herbert Koller wonders if it would not be desirable to establish the commission in a separate bill, since the present bill is unlikely to pass in this session of Congress and the commission could serve many useful functions.

KAPLAN. This is a political consideration. I do not know where it would fit in the whole cosmology of reform; but I am persuaded that we ought to have a study commission.

ZURKOWSKI. The commission was structured as part of the ongoing revision effort itself. There are important questions about the make-up of the

---

Participants: Donald Baker, Department of Justice; Joseph Becker, Becker and Hayes (formerly Vice President of EDUCOM); David Bender, The George Washington University; Stephen G. Breyer, Harvard Law School; Ralph S. Brown, Jr., Yale University Law School; Benjamin V. Cohen, retired Washington lawyer; Sheldon S. Cohen, private law practice (formerly Commissioner of Internal Revenue); Wallace C. Doud, International Business Machines Corporation; Morton David Goldberg, private law practice; Lincoln Gordon, The Johns Hopkins University; Caryl Haskins, The Carnegie Institution; Benjamin Kaplan, Harvard University; Irving Kayton, The George Washington University; Herbert Koller, American Society for Information Science; Dan Lacy, McGraw-Hill Book Company; W. Brown Morton, Jr., private law practice; Carl Overhage, Massachusetts Institute of Technology; Giles S. Rich, U.S. Court of Customs and Patent Appeals; Barbara A. Ringer, U.S. Copyright Office; Leonard Silk, New York Times (formerly at The Brookings Institution); Gerald Sophar, Institute for Scientific Information; Paul G. Zurkowski, Information Industry Association; Martin Greenberger, chairman, The Johns Hopkins University.

commission, its location, and its mandate in the event that the revision bill does not pass. Will it, for example, become the repository for all unresolved copyright issues? It also is not clear whether the zeal that has kept the bill alive will persist in the next Congress.

KOLLER. The point is that many provisions of the proposed bill have not been thought out sufficiently so that we can see their full implications. The commission could study their effects in advance if it was created before these provisions became law. The commission might also explore new implications for copyright law that will be identified only as the new information technology develops. The law and the technology influence each other. The fit of the present 1909 copyright law with 1970 technology is not very good, and a continuing commission could help us bring and keep the law up to date.

MORTON. The copyright revision effort was started before the computer really got going. It has completely valid reasons for existence that are entirely independent of the computer. Every time it is brought to the point of action, it gets bogged down by advancing technology and an insistence on solving everything at once. The 1909 act was bad in 1909. We need not worry about the revisions fitting 1970; if we could just get it to fit 1950, we would be doing fine!

RINGER. I agree that we should not be writing off copyright revision completely. It is in trouble, although the reason has to do not with computers but with cable television. If the package does not pass, a commission will probably be established to study the entire copyright law. This will not be any more productive than the study efforts of the last fifteen years, and to court this as a desirable goal is foolish.

BAKER. Copyright law does not get revised in accordance with the technical needs of society but in accordance with the political interests of a particular class of people, such as the television broadcasters. This is distressing from the point of view of meeting the needs of people who do not have great political clout.

KAYTON. This discussion of copyright law is largely inapposite. If we are going to have property rights protecting the innovator's contributions to this new technology, then we need a mechanism that will really protect. We do not have to develop it; it is the patent statute. It will not protect obvious contributions to the art, but it will protect investment in the creation of new and unobvious ideas.

There is an almost total misapprehension of the new technology and its industry by most of the copyright lawyers here. Nothing could be more specific and concrete than the mathematical equations in the Bernhart disclosure. They are the blueprint for the machine and the blueprint for the process.

I hope that the Supreme Court of the United States is not as untutored and myopic as Brown believes. I feel that the Supreme Court *will* realize the fundamental facts of the industry's growth (which Brown does not): that a technology in which millions of dollars were spent tooling up new plants and machines is now converted into a technology where the factory for tooling up is a general-purpose digital computer and that the engineers who design the new equipment are known as programmers and systems analysts. They feed their blueprints not to welders or lathe operators but to the computer. I think the Supreme Court is too sophisticated to penalize the new inventors because the new mode of setting down their invention is in the form of programming languages.

DOUD. Computers in the future are going to be easier to program; it will require less inventiveness to make them do your bidding, and only a fraction of the things people will want to do with computers will be truly inventive. I think there is a need to protect investments in computer programming other than by patents, since it is critical for our economy and the economy of the world that these investments be made by as many as possible. We must either clarify the copyright law or else find some new kind of protection. Patenting of computer programs on a large scale would cause nothing but chaos in the industry. We need some other way that is administratively feasible.

KOLLER. When IBM unbundled, it announced that application programs would be copyrighted. Has IBM started to file for registration?

DOUD. Yes, it has. We have two classes of programs: the *systems-control programs*, without which it would not be possible to use the computer, and *program products,* or application programs, which do specific jobs. It is the program products that we are copyrighting. We couple this with a contract in which our customers agree to certain conditions for using the program product.

GREENBERGER. Have you thought through the hazard of a customer's changing a few nominal instructions in the source program to make it his own? Or the related problem of his compiling your source program using his own compiler, resulting in a different-looking object code even though the basic program is unchanged?

DOUD. There are indeed many problems. Consider, for example, the problem of ensuring that when a product is printed out by a customer, it is marked properly so that we do not lose our copyright. We have transferred the not inconsequential problem of protecting our copyright to our customers, and this gives rise to a complex programming requirement. We have difficulty finding copyright attorneys who can give us the answers to these problems. We may be making copyright law as we go along.

KAYTON. It is noteworthy that IBM is not *opposed* to patent protection of programs but simply believes it to be inadequate. I seriously question whether as a matter of public policy we should protect anything that is not new and unobvious.

BENDER. The positions of Kayton and IBM, once antithetic, now seem to be coming together. The main difference appears to be over what percent of programs qualify for patent protection. Doud thinks many fewer qualify than Kayton.

With respect to programs that do not qualify, the protection they get, if any, must currently come from the law of copyrights or the law of trade secrets. The law of trade secrets has the advantage that we understand its scope of protection, but it has the unfortunate public policy aspect that there is no disclosure. Protection with disclosure would be better; but if we cannot get it, then perhaps we should settle for second-best: trade-secret protection.

In *Lear* v. *Adkins*, the Supreme Court raised some uncertainties about the future of trade-secret protection. But it is very much embedded in the law. Of the three justices who raised the question, one has already left the Court and the other two are likely to leave before long. This, plus our international agreements (in the form of the Pan American and Paris Conventions) to provide protection against unfair competition, plus the billions of dollars in investment being "protected" in this way, should ensure that trade-secret protection is with us for some time to come.

OVERHAGE. The computer revolution is just beginning. The things we have been considering are very early manifestations of a phenomenon that is going to sweep society during the next three decades in an even more spectacular way than most of us foresee. There is broad consensus that patents apply to those aspects of computer programs showing definite novelty. Whether or not protection is needed beyond this for the burgeoning software industry is still debatable.

The view taken in our discussion about books and book-like publications is too short-ranged. In the long term, information in which originators and authors have property rights will be stored, diffused, manipulated, distributed, copied, duplicated, and transferred in extremely fluid patterns. Compensation to the originator will have to be attached to the substance itself (the ideas and formulations) rather than to any particular mode of storage or transmission. It will be too easy to transfer information from one form to another.

GREENBERGER. Are not ideas (in other contexts) circulating all the time and being terribly useful to people without their authors' gaining remuneration?

OVERHAGE. This is one possible answer. People going down this track generally point out that originators of new ideas in certain academic pursuits are compensated by receiving recognition and promotion rather than patents and royalties.

I support Kaplan's suggestions that we need more experimentation in exploring new patterns of compensation and new ways of protecting legitimate property rights in this very fluid technology. If we had a commission making such experiments, we would be in a far better position at the end of five years than we are today to discuss the problems.

SOPHAR. I can put one concrete situation on the table. My corporation is proprietor of a data bank that was *not* created using government funds. We want to maintain our proprietary rights and market this data. We would like our compensation to relate to the value received from use of the data by our customers, but we are very uncertain what this value is. The data base, which is the Science Citation Index, was created as a by-product of a printed volume. Technology has turned things around so that the by-product (a tape file) has become the main product. How do we ensure that the customer's use of the file stays within the terms of the contract?

SHELDON COHEN. Internal Revenue has a similar by-product it is now selling to industry: a tax model showing the income distribution of taxpayers by zip code.

BREYER. The case for protection has not yet been made. The two observations that *have* been made are first, there is a big difference between the initial cost of producing a program and the cost of copying it; and second, a program is a writing. I believe this is just a beginning. There are a host of other questions we should ask. First, what harms might copyright cause? To what extent would it raise prices? To what extent do people currently benefit from users' groups that trade programs, and how extensively would a "permissions" requirement interfere? How easy would it be for someone to reach a publisher to get permission to copy? Might a publisher hold back permission for competitive reasons? Would people be forced to invent around a copyrighted program? How wasteful would that prove?

Second, we should ask how necessary it is to use copyright as a way of channeling money to the originators. To what extent are programs tailored to individual users? (To the extent they are, we need not worry about copyright.) Could not buyers' groups or time-sharing companies help in organizing customers so that copyright is not needed to secure protection? Would hardware manufacturers produce substantial software without protection, and is this good or bad? I think there are a series of such questions which could lead us somewhere toward tailoring a "right." Simply to point to the difference between production cost and copying cost does not get us very far.

SILK. From an economist's standpoint, the subject under discussion is really a very complex set of problems: the development of the new computer-services industry in relation to computer manufacturers and the communications industry, book publishing in relation to reprography and to computer services, developed countries versus underdeveloped countries, economic development, world interests, the poverty issue, cable versus broadcast TV, public education, diversity of services, and representation of minority interests. This is about as complicated a set of interrelated problems as I have ever encountered, particularly because the technology is changing, everything is very fluid, and there are no fixed characters in the drama. We need a sorting out and clarification of the types of problems and the economic, social, and political objectives.

I think the wisest thing Congress has done (perhaps for all the wrong reasons) is to fiddle around endlessly with these problems. In its infinite wisdom, it has decreed it premature to impose a solution while things are still evolving. Congress has been very sensitive to the bargaining that has been going on, to the interests that are affected, and to the strengths of these interests. It has been careful not to hurt or antagonize them. I think over time some of these interests will indeed find bargaining solutions. In the meantime, the existing situation is probably no worse than many conceivable alternatives. As a general principle, we want institutional arrangements that will facilitate bargaining.

LACY. Silk implies that the normal workings of the bargaining process can produce equitable agreements in copyright as in other matters. I agree with this and believe the economic distortions that occur come principally when the law permits consumption of real goods and services without payment, which can result in a misallocation of resources.

BAKER. I think the series of questions raised by Breyer suggests the best approach for resolving the policy problem of legal protection. I would like to ask Leonard Silk if it is possible for an economist to provide a *method* to resolve these questions—a means of quantifying the various gains and losses.

SILK. Let me reply by saying that Adam Smith was able to reach some important basic policy conclusions by a combination of logic and intuitive insight. Also, welfare theory in economics provides a structure for analysis of difficult problems of conflict between interested parties and may point the way toward optimizing the social interest. Incidentally, the protection of intellectual property safeguards a place in our society for the individual writer, scientist, engineer, and other creative persons. I hope that intellectuals in the future will not all have to work for IBM, General Motors, the Navy, and other large organizations.

GOLDBERG. The economic systems approach has much to offer, but legislative definitions of intellectual property rights should not be geared only to increasing productivity of intellectual goods. The primary resource is basic creativity, but important secondary resources include skills in dissemination and such limited resources as the broadcast spectrum. The goal is not merely to maximize productivity but also to enhance freedom of speech and press and the dignity of the person. I believe the realization of these goals requires a sound system of appropriate proprietary rights.

BROWN. We are all in favor of an author's having appropriate encouragement, but we should remember that authors need to be able to draw freely on all that comes before them.

RICH. A great deal of intellectual wealth is not accorded the status of intellectual property and therefore is in the public domain. For instance, the basic idea propounded in Adam Smith's *The Wealth of Nations* on division of labor was never anyone's private property.

As the only member of the judiciary here, I would like to point out that the concern of my job is not with what the law ought to be but with what it is. It may be that patents under the existing statutes are not the most appropriate form of protection for computer programs, but the courts have to apply the law as it exists. Whether we should have a different kind of law is a question for the legislature on which I have no opinion.

BENJAMIN COHEN. Before we are in a position to recommend what protection should be given to programmers, we should know more about the nature of their contribution, to what extent a typical program represents creativeness, or to what extent it could be produced by any programmer with a reasonable degree of competence.

KAPLAN. I agree. It seems very clear from Brown's paper and the whole tenor of the discussion that we do not yet know enough to legislate on the subject of protection of computer programs. Yet the latest text of the copyright revision bill appears to sweep all computer programs under the protective wing of copyright. This is folly. If the bill should ever pass in this form, it would become hopeless (as a practical matter) to change it later and withdraw any of the protection, even if the wisdom of doing so should become apparent. The question of computer programs should be submitted to the national study commission. In the meanwhile, it should remain in standstill status as provided in certain other cases by the moratorium section of the bill.

REFERENCES

For other references, as well as valuable original material, consult the student project, "New Technology and the Law of Copyright: Reprography and Computers," *UCLA Law Review*, 15 (1968), 939.
1. From *Grooks 1* (Doubleday & Co., New York, 1969) by Piet Hein; © 1966; reprinted by permission of the author.
2. Fritz Machlup, *The Production and Distribution of Knowledge in the United States*, Princeton University Press, 1962, p. 176.
3. Roy Freed, quoted in Crossland, *South Carolina Law Review*, 20 (1968): 242.

4. Edgar G. Perle, *Bulletin of Copyright Society of the U.S.A.*, 15 (October 1967), 5.
5. Prater and Wei, *Federal Reports*, 2d series, 415 (1969), 1378, 1393.
6. Bernhart and Fetter, *Federal Reports*, 2d series, 417 (1969), 1395, 1400.
7. A. W. Puckett, "The Limits of Copyright and Patent Protection for Computer Programs," 16th ASCAP Symposium, 1968, pp. 81, 115. Cf. David Bender, "Computer Programs: Should They Be Patentable?", *Columbia Law Review*, 68 (1968), 241.
8. *Federal Reports*, 2d series, 417 (1969), 1399.
9. *U.S. Reports*, 101: 99, 104.
10. Lear, Inc. v. Adkins, *U.S. Reports*, 395 (1969), 653, 674, 675.
11. *U.S. Reports*, 367: 225, 234.
12. *U.S. Code*, vol. 4, title 17, section 2.
13. U.S., Congress, Senate, *Copyright Law Revision*, Hearings before the Judiciary Committee, 90th Cong., 1st sess., 1967, part 2, p. 588.
14. Nicholas Johnson, "Developing National Policy for Computer Communications," this volume.
15. John G. Kemeny, "Large Time-Sharing Networks," this volume.
16. Senate Bill 543, 91st Cong., 1st sess., 1967, sections 101, 106(2).
17. *Ibid.*, section 102(b).
18. Wallace C. Doud, "The Business of Software and its Protection," *Proceedings of the Law of Software Conference*, George Washington University, 1969, pp. P-16, P-17.
19. Senate, *Copyright Law Revision*, part 2, p. 589.
20. Senate Bill 543, 91st Cong., 1st sess., section 110(2).
21. *U.S. Code*, 35: 101.
22. Benjamin Kaplan, *An Unhurried View of Copyright*, Columbia University Press, 1967, pp. 104, 122.

7

DEVELOPING NATIONAL POLICY FOR COMPUTERS AND COMMUNICATIONS

Speaker   NICHOLAS JOHNSON
Commissioner
Federal Communications Commission

Discussants   LEE C. WHITE
Former Chairman
Federal Power Commission

RICHARD POSNER
Professor of Law
University of Chicago

Moderator   KINGMAN BREWSTER, JR.
President
Yale University

BREWSTER. The objective of this series of analytical discussions has been to explore the dimensions of the problems and opportunities posed by the combined revolutions in communications and information technology. The purpose of the present discussion is to examine the instruments by which the public interest might be asserted in the face of these revolutions.

It has been many years since Congress passed the Communications Act of 1934 and created a new agency to carry out and develop regulatory policy for the communications industry. The Federal Communications Commission [FCC] was Congress' answer to the need it perceived for separating regulation of communications from regulation of transportation. The Interstate Commerce Commission was burdened with both responsibilities at the time. Its involvement in communications had little justification other than the fact that early telegraph services used the rights of way of railroads. Communications started out as an extension of transportation, but since the Communications Act of 1934 it has gone its separate way.

This is somewhat the reverse of the situation today concerning computers and communications. The computer industry has developed impressively in its own right during the past two decades. Only in the last few years has its impact upon communications become apparent. Once again an overworked regulatory agency, this time the FCC, has had to examine and deal with unpredictable policy problems.

Nicholas Johnson has been a commissioner at the FCC since 1966. During this period he has been actively involved in several key decisions in the area of computers and communications. He has often been an outspoken critic of the means used by the government to develop and implement regulatory policy. Hardly an anonymous public servant, he gives high visibility and sprightly presence to everything he undertakes.

My own interest in regulation goes back to my days as a professor of law. I welcome this opportunity to take a break from the cares and concerns of my office to hear Commissioner Johnson and the subsequent discussion. Commissioner Johnson's willingness to be the target for this discussion is in the spirit of the adversary process he knows so well.

JOHNSON. Soon half of all telephonic communications in this country will be between machines rather than people. During the last decade the computer population has grown fiftyfold; the average computer has become ten times smaller, a hundred times faster, and a thousand times less expensive to operate. Computers today can do thirty trillion computations every hour. Computers have risen exceedingly fast in their own right, and now they are getting an additional boost from communications. The union of these technologies has enormous potential impact for society, and the policy decisions they require will have important ramifications for years to come.

Who should make the decisions? Who should be permitted to influence the decision makers? To what extent should the decisions accommodate special interests? How should the public interest be represented? Should substantial new analyses of the issues be prepared by intellectually independent parties? Should decisions be in the form of integrated, long-term policy statements or in the form of case-by-case responses to applications and crises? Should the arguments presented to the decision makers and the reasons for their decisions be made public? Should it be possible for decisions to be appealed and reviewed?

Such questions are not concerned with the substantive part of the issues, nor do they depend on whether the decisions are made by corporate executives or government officials. They are strictly procedural questions, and I wish to address them here in their broadest sense.

As a commissioner of the Federal Communications Commission, I am a direct participant in the process of formulating policy on computers and communications. By a confluence of events, the FCC has been actively considering many of the most important policy issues affecting computers and communications. The procedures it uses to address these issues will have as much impact as any other single force on their ultimate resolution.

Why the Federal Communications Commission?

As computer technology continues to advance, it is not unusual for communications costs to become an increasingly significant share of the total cost of using computer systems. But communications poses more than a growing cost problem. The communications facilities desired are often not available at any price, either because communications common carriers follow outmoded or unnecessarily rigid practices or because the communications system was simply never designed for the new uses the computer industry is now demanding. These problems have led the computer industry to the FCC—the agency responsible for tariffs and systems expansion. The computer industry now finds itself facing a very unfamiliar kind of regulatory problem. As unpleasant and unnatural as it may seem, the industry is involved with the FCC by necessity—for its own growth and perhaps even survival.

As is well known, the FCC launched a formal public inquiry into computers and communications in late 1966, thus taking the rather unusual step of initiating an inquiry before a formal request by outside parties.[1] The problems presented by the convergence of computers and communications had been slowly growing since the early 1960's. The Business Equipment Manufacturers Association, in response to the notice of inquiry, estimated that the number of on-line computer systems using communications grew from thirty-one in 1960 to twenty-three hundred by 1966. This was only 7 percent of the computer systems but 14 percent of their total annual rental value.[2]

The *Bunker-Ramo* case offers one illustration of the emerging problems. In 1965 Bunker-Ramo sought to offer a communications and data-processing system to the stock brokerage industry. Bell Telephone and Western Union refused to provide the communications facilities Bunker-Ramo requested, citing tariff barriers on the resale or sharing of communications facilities. During informal negotiations, a compromise was evolved,[3] but it was obvious that no satisfactory resolution had been obtained.

Another illustration grew out of the Commission's investigation of the telegraph industry, begun in 1962, with the final report issued in 1966. In commenting on Western Union's diversification program, the report noted: "When the proposed modernization program [of Western Union] merges the public message and Telex systems into an integrated operation interconnected with public service computers in New York, Western Union will be in a position to offer a 'national information utility' service to firms that can serve their needs through shared-use systems and services."[4] Western Union's intention to establish a national data utility was becoming clear.

In late 1966 and early 1967 Western Union offered a new set of packaged data-processing and communications services called SICOM and INFO-COM. Segments of the data-processing industry felt that Western Union's services posed dangers of unfair competition and cross-subsidization, and they demanded comparable access to communications facilities. Over my objections, the FCC declined to block institution of the new services and evoked considerable criticism—much of which was justified.[5]

The FCC notice of inquiry was drafted by consultants and personnel of the Common Carrier Bureau who were aware of the growing regulatory problems and acted with initiative and foresight—unusual qualities for a regulatory agency. The action can scarcely be characterized as premature. But for it, the FCC would have had on its hands a communications crisis of substantial proportions.

While emphasizing the wide-ranging and somewhat informal nature of the inquiry,[6] the FCC rejected the Department of Justice's suggestion that the FCC permit respondents to request information from each other. The FCC promised to ask for additional information if warranted, but it never did despite the great unevenness in the quality of the responses. Adoption of the Justice Department's suggestion would have allowed for a limited "discovery" procedure and would have helped get all the cards on the table. Those who hold relevant but damaging information are naturally reluctant to volunteer it without some prodding.

Government and Technology

To understand the issues and aftermath of the inquiry in context, it is useful to examine how government makes scientific and technological decisions. No one would deny that government officials have made some colossal blunders about new technology; but businessmen have made their share, too. The Eastman Kodak Company failed to see the future in the Xerox process, videotape, and the Polaroid camera. The Ford Motor Company, not the Department of Defense, developed the Edsel. Even the highly esteemed computer industry was caught with its plants down when transistor technology first came upon the scene. The faults of the human race are not unknown outside of government. But government does play a tremendous role in affecting the growth of technology, often with less imagination and courage than could reasonably be expected.

C. P. Snow has told us that "we are letting technology ride us as if we had no judgment of our own." It is true. The United States becomes wealthier each year, with a gross national product approaching a trillion dollars. Our people live in the midst of more abundance than ever before. But our skies have filled with smoke and our rivers with waste. In giving us increased luxury, technology has polluted the necessities. How does a highly industrialized nation prevent the cancerous effects of a technology run wild? How can we encourage technological judgments that make sense socially, politically, and aesthetically, as well as economically?

In the problem C. P. Snow has characterized as "two cultures," scientists and engineers have difficulty communicating with lawyers, economists, and other decision makers. Decisions made without understanding all the ramifications of a new technology are likely to produce harmful and unforeseen effects. Automation has caused dislocation in employment. Airplanes that fly faster and carry more passengers have produced sonic boom, congestion in airport parking lots and baggage handling, and hazards to human life. Processed food has reduced nutritional values. The automobile has caused fifty thousand deaths a year from accidents, 80 percent of all air pollution, a paved nation with billboards, and the dehumanizing commuters' crush.

At the end of the last century, both England and the United States faced declines in shipping and tried to aid their shipping industries. The British decided to invest in research and development of steam-powered, steel-hulled ships; the Americans subsidized their once-competitive wooden-hulled sailing ships. Ship technology in Britain was given a new impetus, but in the United States it stagnated to a degree still felt today.

Government makes decisions on technology almost daily. Should it develop the SST? High-speed passenger trains? The ABM? Should it give tax advantages to firms with pollution-control equipment? Should it require safety equipment on cars, trains, and planes? Should the FCC encourage an AT&T-operated nationwide portable radio communications system? A competitive cable television [CATV] system? Is desalinization a fruitful source of fresh water? Government influences the development of modern technology in many ways: by determining rates and routes, awarding monopoly privileges such as television licenses, being a big consumer like the Department of Defense and the General Services Administration, writing matching-funds grants, awarding subsidies, setting standards and specifications, and funding research and development, policy studies, and pilot projects.

In dealing with technology, government has lacked adequate information and staff to do the hard analysis that decision making requires. A limited staff turns as a matter of necessity as well as political expediency to special-interest groups willing to provide information and opinion. Without these groups bureaucracies might not be able to function at all, but their heavy reliance on such groups leads to less-than-perfect public service.

The FCC and the New Technology

The FCC faces all of these problems and more when trying to evaluate new technology. It suffers from a lack of data, a lack of experienced, qualified staff, and a lack of communication between scientists and those who implement policy. Nowhere is this better demonstrated than in the inquiry on computers and communications. Some hard-working, dedicated, bright people have worked on these problems, but their number and influence have been very limited. The resources of the FCC in the common-carrier field have not increased in five years, although the problems have been growing enormously in complexity and scope.

As Charles Schultze, formerly Director of the Bureau of the Budget, has said:

The most frustrating aspect of public life is not the inability to convince others of the merits of a cherished project or policy. Rather, it is the endless hours spent on policy discussions in which the irrelevant issues have not been separated from the relevant, in which ascertainable facts and relationships have not been investigated but are the subject of heated debate, in which consideration of alternatives is impossible because only one proposal has been developed, and, above all, discussions in which nobility of aim is presumed to determine effectiveness of program.[7]

How well has the FCC handled technological policy questions? Here is my interpretation of a few examples.

Allocation of Frequencies. The FCC is charged by the Communications Act with responsibility for the efficient, equitable allocation of radio frequencies between competing users, from radio amateurs and taxicabs to television stations and microwave relay towers. It substitutes for the more usual free market in allocation of this natural resource. The decisions as to who gets what part of the spectrum have obvious effects on the design of equipment by users and have a multibillion-dollar influence on gross national product. (The telephone company's revenue is about fifteen billion dollars; homeowners have over twenty billion dollars invested in TV receivers; and mobile radio is estimated to contribute on the order of twenty billion dollars annually to the GNP.) Yet the FCC has failed to come forward with the data and analysis necessary to avoid waste and promote the most efficient and rational allocation of frequencies. Its failure is even more pronounced considering the possible social, political, and aesthetic consequences of its actions. The FCC does not have a rational policy statement for allocating between competing uses. It does not possess even the most fundamental data, such as the results of regular monitoring of channel occupancy or the location, height, and transmitter power of antennas.

Year by year studies accumulate asserting the need for a response to a growing national crisis.[8] And year by year the FCC continues in essentially the same regulatory mold. It perceives spectrum regulation as a technical engineering and legal exercise and has no economists at all to deal with the questions. The decision-making framework simply does not allow for rational choices among competing uses of the spectrum.

Cable Television. In the early 1950's the FCC's staff recommended that the Commission immediately recognize cable television as a significant new technology with serious policy implications and assess its role in the nation's total communications system. Ignoring this advice, from the late 1950's to the early 1960's the FCC consistently denied that it had jurisdiction over the growing industry, presumably in the hope that it would just go away. Broadcasters and the broadcast-oriented FCC saw CATV as a threat to over-the-air television, and broadcasters spent considerable energy and political coin trying to stifle its growth—almost as much as they later expended in a frantic scramble to buy up the systems. Now they have a substantial ownership interest in CATV, and the FCC has asserted virtually full regulatory authority over it in an effort to develop consistency with its other broadcast policies.

The FCC's change of direction began in December 1968, when it issued a notice of inquiry and rule making proposing an entirely different attitude toward the role of CATV.[9] It emphasized the positive contribution CATV technology could make to the total communications system and tried for a policy solution with primary reliance on the marketplace. The FCC never undertook anything approaching a systems analysis, policy-planning review, or study of the policy options. It seriously considered making a policy review prior to the 1968 rule making, to be funded under its fledgling research and policy studies program, but scrapped this as redundant when the notice of inquiry was issued in 1968. The Ford Foundation almost immediately announced a large contract with the RAND Corporation to do precisely the same thing, leading to a report by Leland Johnson in early 1970.[10]

Color TV. The FCC's difficulty in addressing policy issues springing from new technology is not of recent origin. In 1946, after some twenty years of development, the FCC denied a petition by the Columbia Broadcasting System to establish color TV standards for broadcast on frequencies other than those used for black-and-white TV. In 1950 the FCC reversed field and adopted the CBS noncompatible field sequential color system, rejecting the fervent urging of those who thought a compatible system was possible within a very short time. (A compatible system of color television transmission produces a black-and-white picture on a black-and-white receiving set, a political necessity in a country with a massive consumer investment in black-and-white receivers.) In 1953 the National Television System Committee, an industry engineering advisory group, made a presentation to the FCC on new compatible color standards which the Radio Corporation of America had developed after extensive testing and refinement of techniques. The FCC adopted this system the same year after having rejected it three years before. These standards are essentially the same as the ones that prevail today.[11]

UHF Television. In 1945 the FCC authorized the use of thirteen VHF (very high frequency) channels for commercial television with some provision for experimental broadcasts on UHF (ultrahigh frequencies). In 1948 it deleted channel 1 for use in nonbroadcast television service and froze further assignment of TV licenses (with substantial economic benefit to those already licensed) while interference problems were studied. Then in 1952 it granted most of the four-year backlog of VHF applications, thereby making America a VHF nation for the years that have followed. Subsequently realizing that twelve VHF channels were not sufficient, it assigned the seventy-two channels of UHF spectrum for broadcast television—a futile gesture. It previously had rejected the still valid argument that UHF could never develop equally unless all television was placed in the UHF band. (Japan recently decided to clear out its VHF band for land mobile radio and to move all television to UHF.)

Between 1953 and 1964 UHF spurted and floundered. Stations went on the air only to go bankrupt. Only a few UHF receiving sets were manufactured and hardly anyone could receive the UHF signals, a decided handicap in a business that worships ratings. Virtually all network affiliations went to VHF stations, leaving UHF with the added handicap of having no programming that people wanted to watch.

In 1964 "all channel" legislation was passed requiring that television sets be equipped to receive UHF. This was politically more acceptable to the powerful VHF stations than deintermixture (making communities all-UHF or all-VHF), since established stations were not forced to change channels. UHF will remain at a competitive disadvantage until all sets can be converted. About 60 percent of television sets in the United States can receive UHF in 1970, but UHF tuning is still not equivalent to VHF tuning. This, taken together with the lack of deintermixture, network affiliations, and the VHF viewing habit, makes it clear that the FCC has bungled any sincere effort to develop UHF.

As in other areas of FCC bumbling, this is a classic example of the proposition that the FCC is not even a good handmaiden to the industry it thinks it serves. It clearly did not serve the public interest well, as illustrated by its failure to spur development of meaningful local TV programming and competition in national networking and by the congestion in land-mobile-radio operations resulting from its holding back frequencies. But it even did a disservice to the highly protected and supposedly well-cared-for broadcasters, who lost billions of dollars in profits that could have come from two decades of viable UHF operations. Advertisers suffered from the lack of additional outlets and the inflated prices they had to pay oligopolist station owners and networks. Those in the TV programming business lost markets and struggled to serve a tightly controlled three-network economy. It is simply not true that industry benefits from weak and unimaginative government.

Domestic Satellites. A domestic communications satellite system has been a possibility for the United States since the early 1960's. The FCC had done little if anything to bring such a system into being or even to permit others to do so. As a result, the United States (which was first with the technology) will watch Russia, Canada, Japan, India, and other nations put domestic communications satellite systems into operation before it has one.

In 1965 the American Broadcasting Company proposed a domestic satellite system for television distribution, causing the FCC for the first time to open an inquiry into the entire domestic satellite question.[12] In 1966 the Ford Foundation proposed a satellite system which would funnel the savings from network programming distribution into educational broadcasting as a "people's dividend." General Electric proposed a complete domestic satellite system employing random-access techniques primarily aimed at the growing data industry. President Johnson established a Presidential Task Force on Telecommunications Policy to review the domestic-satellite issue, among others, and the FCC deferred action while the matter was studied. The report of the task force released in early 1969 recommended that a pilot system be undertaken by Comsat.[13] Then in the summer of 1969 the Nixon administration asked the FCC to delay once again while another White House review was undertaken. This review, completed in early 1970, recommended that free competitive entry be permitted in domestic satellites,[14] a position that varies significantly from what the FCC had in mind six months earlier. The FCC has now asked for applications on a competitive basis.[15]

What conclusions can be drawn from this random sampling of past FCC brushes with technological problems? The lack of policy planning is crucial. Policy planning at the FCC is essentially a part-time job for people whose main responsibilities are the line operations of trying cases and processing applications. It is the last activity to get going and the first to be dropped. As with the economic analysis of spectrum allocation, it is not that the FCC does it poorly, it does not do it at all. Policy planning simply cannot be a part-time operation in an agency like the FCC. In a very real sense, it is its *raison d'être*.

A second problem is the FCC's dependence on outside interested parties for information. There is almost no research done within the agency. The FCC does not even use its powers to extract additional information from the vested economic interests, despite the fact that the rapidly changing technology makes agreement on basic information and assumptions unlikely.

The FCC's inability to seize an issue and dispose of it usually works to the advantage of some party who promotes all the delay in his favor. Matters which the FCC should initiate and decide often are decided for it on the outside. Most commissioners actually seem to prefer it that way and encourage contending interests to reach an agreement that will eliminate the need for them to act. One wonders why the FCC was not long ago dubbed the Fumbling Communications Commission.

The FCC Inquiry Into Computers and Communications

The FCC's computer inquiry stands in marked contrast to its past inability to anticipate policy questions. The inquiry attempted to deal comprehensively with the issues presented by "the growing interdependence of computers and communications" and to take action in anticipation of regulatory problems rather than react to a crisis. It provided a forum and the opportunity for a desperately needed dialogue between the two affected industries.

The communications industry has traditionally been subjected to detailed federal regulation under public-utility principles. Regulation and monopoly are firmly established. The data industry, by contrast, has existed in a free-market environment. With the nexus of computers and communications, a whole series of unregulated, competitive enterprises is added to the picture in ways which infinitely complicate the policy decisions.

The computer inquiry consolidated and reformed a number of old issues, including foreign attachments and interconnection. Tom Carter had been waging the *Carterfone* battle with AT&T—a battle AT&T would come deeply to regret—for some time. He wished to interconnect to the Bell system the "foreign" (non-Bell) mobile radio-telephone coupler which he manufactured. The FCC set the *Carterfone* question for hearing on October 10, 1966 and began the computer inquiry on November 9, 1966. The overlap was obvious.

A second issue concerned specialized common carriers in competition with established ones. New carriers could provide the data industry with services either unavailable or too costly from established carriers. This issue was part of the larger question of the usefulness of the communications system to the data industry. The application from Microwave Communications Incorporated [MCI] for a private microwave system from Chicago to Saint Louis had been designated for hearing in February 1966. Both the *Carterfone* and *MCI* cases contained policy questions raised in the computer inquiry.

A third old issue was the danger of cross-subsidizing by a monopolist entering competitive markets. This was of particular concern to data processors, who feared unfair competition from communications common carriers offering data-processing services. The FCC had faced this problem on numerous earlier occasions without real success: the *Telpak* and private-line rate cases, the telegraph investigation, and the study of the Bell system's rate levels and structure. The questions also resembled those presented by telephone carriers offering CATV services to the public through subsidiaries that bought facilities from other subsidiaries. The FCC received numerous complaints from independent CATV operators and ordered a hearing.

A final old issue was the prohibition of the sharing of communications facilities by user groups. This issue also arose in considering the lawfulness of the Telpak tariffs, which the FCC set for hearing in mid-1967.

The fact that many of the issues in the computer inquiry were already before the FCC in other contexts illustrates the problems of decision making faced by a regulatory agency. Many of the issues could have been decided long ago. Cross-subsidization, foreign attachment, and interconnection had been before the agency for more than ten years, but the needs of the data industry dramatized these questions and forced their reconsideration. The necessary steps in decision making—accumulation of data, analysis, development of alternatives, and testing of hypotheses—take place at the FCC in a variety of adjudicative proceedings, rule makings, informal conferences, and oral arguments. This practically guarantees that the FCC will not bring a single focus to the policy questions involved without a central staff to plan and integrate disparate activities.

The computer inquiry also contained some relatively new issues. One question was whether a whole new communications system was needed for data communications, thus challenging the long-standing assumption that the telephone system was the best network for everything. (Many responses expressed the judgment that telephone carriers could not do the job.) A second question asked whether data users could buy communications to package in their products under the same conditions as common carriers that provided data services. A third question asked whether data processors should be allowed to offer communications services at all, or what limits (if any) should be attached to their offerings. The question of privacy was raised, and finally it was asked whether data processing using communications facilities should be regulated as a common carrier. The vision (or perhaps specter) of a monopoly information utility loomed more clearly in 1966 than it does today.

These were some of the important issues specified in the notice of inquiry. There were old issues which gained a new importance because of the entry of the computer industry into data communications, and then there were new issues raised especially by this development. With the filing of responses and the maturation of other proceedings the FCC began to address these issues.

Aftermath of the Inquiry

In June 1968 the FCC decided *Carterfone* by striking down certain tariffs prohibiting foreign attachment and interconnection.[16] In the two years since that decision some progress has been made, but all too slowly. The Department of Justice's recommendation that hearings be held on the new tariffs has been ignored, and informal conferences are being used to resolve the remaining differences, principally the problem of control over the dial mechanism or network signaling. In my judgment the FCC should set a firm deadline for the resolution of these questions and require that all private agreements be filed publicly with the agency, along with summaries of all attachment and interconnection controversies. Undue delay only works to the advantage of those surprised by the vigorous competition resulting from the *Carterfone* decision who are now scrambling to catch up.

In August 1969 the FCC decided *MCI*, a new specialized carrier service for data users unhappy with the restrictions of established communications facilities.[17] Bell responded by proposing a new Series 11,000 tariff and appealing the *MCI* decision with an argument on why the FCC should hold off the numerous additional competing applications that *MCI* encouraged, including proposals for a nationwide data-communications system separate from the established carriers.

The FCC now has under consideration a decision recommended by the Chief of the Common Carrier Bureau in April 1969 in the *Telpak* proceeding. This would hold that the present sharing provisions are unlawfully discriminatory and leave to the carriers the job of eliminating the discrimination. Unlimited sharing was the position recommended by William Melody of the Common Carrier Bureau when he testified in the case. Again the FCC has the opportunity and discomfiture of making basic policy decisions in the context of a specific proceeding.

Two other FCC decisions have a bearing on the computer inquiry. The FCC has held that telephone companies cannot supply CATV facilities to their affiliates for resale in an area where they provide telephone service. This touches on an issue raised in the computer inquiry of a monopoly supplier entering markets where it faces competition. According to the report of the Stanford Research Institute: "If the carriers are allowed to offer data processing services in competition with non-carriers, they may subsidize the data processing portion of their business from the proceeds of the monopoly portion of their business. This possibility exists whenever a regulated industry incurs competition in one segment of its business and has monopoly power in another that allows it to recoup any losses incurred in the competitive segment."[18]

The need for proper pricing guidelines for regulated carriers serving competitive markets also arises in CATV and telephone company relationships, domestic satellites with free entry and competition, the entry of specialized common carriers, private microwave systems and Telpak, and competition in supply of terminal equipment. It was the basis for my dissent in the FCC's decision of July 1969 that no pricing guidelines would be developed in the four-year investigation of the Bell system's rates.[19] The White House addressed the issue in its policy statement on domestic satellites, recommending evidentiary hearings on cross-subsidization. Without pricing guidelines there may be an inclination to exclude monopolists from competitive markets altogether.

In its first report in the computer inquiry issued on May 1, 1969, the FCC indicated that the interconnection and foreign-attachment questions would be handled in ongoing informal conferences, questions about privacy would be deferred, and a new proceeding would deal with carrier entry into data processing and data-processor entry into communications. This proceeding has not yet been initiated.

The commissioners have no policy-planning staff and on a matter as complex as the computer inquiry typically rely on a single bureau's presentation. This gives them only one developed option from which to choose, since the bureau does not forcefully present viewpoints with which it does not agree and the commissioners do not require it to do so. They are not equipped to challenge a bureau's presentation or elicit alternatives. They are almost wholly dependent upon outside information and only rarely and haphazardly evaluate this information critically or launch an independent inquiry.

On one occasion dubbed by the trade press as "the FCC's first experiment in thinking," the commissioners did take a direct hand in developing new policies. When it became clear in 1968 that CATV would have to be changed, we scheduled a two-day meeting at a remote conference center, without staff or prepared position papers but with six outside consultants generally knowledgeable in problems of regulation, communications technology, and industrial organization. We talked out the problem and later worked on it some more with our staff. From this grew a set of proposals in December 1968 for a complete change in CATV. This useful experience, with variations, could be an important regular component in the decision-making process.

On April 3, 1970, the FCC issued a notice of proposed rule making and a tentative decision in its computer inquiry in an effort to gain further comments and allow for an oral argument of the issues.[20] The decision suggested that the telephone carriers have been responsive in meeting many of the expressed needs of the data industry. Problems on interconnection and foreign attachment were again left to informal conferences and to a panel report by the National Academy of Sciences. Sharing of facilities or services by customers was left to other proceedings, and privacy matters were tabled altogether. On the question of new common-carrier facilities, the FCC concluded:

> It must be understood that the outstanding proposals for new common carrier services which are now pending before the Commission remain to be evaluated in accordance with applicable standards and regulatory policy. It is our view, however, that all the foregoing developments signify that since the inception of this Inquiry, major progress has been made and is continuing toward improved and more economical communications services for computer users. These developments also lead us to the conclusion that the questions relating to interconnection or to the need for other improved common-carrier service offerings, regulations, and practices to serve computer needs can best be handled through rate, tariff, and licensing proceedings that are now pending or that may be initiated in the future, rather than through a continuation of our Inquiry in this Docket.[21]

This somewhat optimistic view is not shared by everyone in the telecommunications field; one observer's reaction was that "the marriage between computers and communications is on the rocks."[22]

The tentative decision did propose some affirmative actions. Regulatory authority would not be asserted over data-processing services even when communications facilities are employed. Common carriers would be allowed to enter the data-processing field only when safeguards such as the establishment of separate subsidiaries existed to ensure fair competition. AT&T would continue to be barred from offering unregulated services under the 1956 Western Electric consent decree.[23] The FCC would not require tariff filings for data telecommunications services where "message-switching is offered as an integral part of and as an incidental feature of a package offering." Where message switching is the primary thrust of the service, tariff filings *would* be required, but there was no substantial elaboration on how the distinction was to be made.

Conclusion: Governmental Decision Making and Technology

The dramatization of the issues raised in the computer inquiry occurred principally because a strong and vocal industry appeared at the door of the FCC to challenge the telephone company. It is very difficult for a regulatory agency to move without strong impetus from the outside. But even a strong confrontation can only result in a stand-off unless the regulatory agency has the capacity to resolve conflicts—the ability to sort out conflicting claims and choose a course of action.

The FCC clearly needs substantial independent resources if it is to engage in information gathering, research, analysis, and advocacy. Its consultation with groups affected by decisions must be something more than occasional oral arguments and written briefs. It should include a critical evaluation of individual positions, information, biases, and analyses. The FCC should consider conducting a set of conferences on computer-communications problems, bringing the highest management and decision-making levels together with staff personnel responsible for back-up material and knowledgeable individuals whose only allegiance is to their own intellectual honesty.

The FCC needs a policy-planning activity in its central staff. Operating bureaus in the crush of their varied activities simply cannot perform this integrative function. Decision makers must have real alternatives from which to choose—alternatives from different sources, fully developed and critically reviewed—not just documents that say, "Here is what the staff thinks you should do."

The FCC's handling of the issues raised by the interdependence of computers and communications is a microcosm of regulatory decision making. In many ways it is the FCC at its best—anticipating problems, using limited resources as effectively as possible, employing outside help in imaginative ways, and generally trying to maintain a useful dialogue to encourage private response to changing needs. But is this enough? I leave it to you to decide.

PANEL DISCUSSION

WHITE. I share Commissioner Johnson's concern over the failure of regulatory agencies to secure adequate budgets. The Federal Power Commission [FPC] has fewer employees today than it had four years ago despite the increasing complexity of the issues it faces and the growth in demand for electric energy and natural gas. But I believe this choking off of essential staff is not so much a function of industry opposition as the inability of agency leaders, myself included, to persuade Congressional appropriations committees of the need for additional money.

I have a hard time accepting Johnson's suggestion that a policy-planning staff could solve many agency problems, since agency managers tend to use their best people in operating responsibilities. There is generally a very limited number of staff people with the ability to communicate with policy makers, to appreciate what can be accomplished in a real situation, and to analyze broad policy issues and alternatives. Agency heads are not likely to permit very many man-hours of such rare talent to focus on tomorrow when there are dozens of fires to put out today. I am not saying this is how it ought to be; it is how it is.

I believe a regulatory agency *can* in a general way be a forum for the identification and analysis of problems and the discussion of alternative approaches with the help of data supplied by a knowledgeable staff. Commissioner Johnson suggests that in part this has been the case in the FCC. He is his own example that not every commissioner is a babe in the woods uninterested in major policy issues. We had bright, imaginative, and well-grounded staff members at the FPC, and at least some of our commissioners were capable of creative, analytical effort themselves. (In fact, some of them were smart enough to be assistants to commissioners.)

The FPC response to the Northeast power blackout of November 1965 illustrates an agency working out a technological problem. Some elements of the power industry long ago adopted the practice of installing equipment which would automatically eliminate certain power loads in the event of a shortage of available power. The FPC, with practically no legislative authority but with great confidence in its chief engineer, pushed, shoved, and cajoled utilities to install and use this equipment. Most utilities now have it and consequently have avoided blackouts and total collapse of their systems. Rule making was not appropriate in this instance, but pressure had a beneficial impact.

The use of computer technology to design the optimum pipeline network for collecting gas from offshore wells in the Gulf of Mexico offers another illustration. Pipelines operating offshore had been seeking approval of various pipeline networks for a number of years, and company experts who had originated the designs would test their feasibility and efficiency using computer techniques. During the summer of 1968, the Office of Emergency Preparedness assembled a small team of young mathematicians from several colleges to analyze transportation and electrical network problems in the event of nuclear attack or other disaster. One of these bright young men happened to hear from the chief of the FPC's Bureau of Natural Gas about the problem of designing pipeline networks for gathering gas from numerous offshore wells for delivery to selected points onshore. The team got interested in the problem and was generously made available to the FPC by the OEP. It worked with FPC staff members for three months and developed a computer program that gave the computer's idea of the optimum method of meeting the requirements of a particular gathering and transmission problem. The beauty of the solution was that it was capable of being tested, examined, and analyzed like any other design. The industry had initial doubts, but its disbelief ultimately evaporated. Pipeline executives were concerned that the FPC would refuse to approve any application for a certificate of public convenience and necessity until the new computer approach had been perfected, but the FPC could not declare a moratorium on new construction for the delivery of gas, which is critical to the industry, particularly gas from rich offshore areas. Instead, my response was that we would instruct our staff to use any legitimate methods available to it, including the computer, to ensure that the commission met its responsibility to test applications against feasible alternatives.

In Johnson's color TV illustration, perhaps the nation could have waited while technology was catching up. If I understand his description, everything eventually worked out fine. I also wonder why Johnson believes that an FCC policy-planning staff would have produced a better and more useful study and series of recommendations on the very important problem of frequency allocation.

I agree with Commissioner Johnson that governmental decision makers need a far better information base and more capability for economic analysis of alternatives. I, too, was uncomfortable about having to rely on information available from the regulated industries. But governmental demands for information must be reasonable. There is a tendency to ask for more than is essential or can be satisfactorily digested.

Johnson implies that the adversary process has not proved effective before the FCC. I believe that, properly employed, the adversary process *can* produce the substantive content and critical analysis required for a sound result. I have supported, as I know Commissioner Johnson has, the concept of a people's or consumers' counsel to help ensure that decision makers have before them the broadest set of attitudes that effective advocacy can produce. The agency must do the balancing, but it is likely to do a better job if the consumers' interest or the interest of the public at large is presented in the most vigorous fashion—as an advocacy rather than as part of a consensus.

Commissioner Johnson fails to recognize the role of the Congress in formulating basic policy. Every regulatory body implementing a mandate given to it by the Congress has the obligation to refer back issues which the Congress is better equipped to decide. The Congress, after all, is the body in our society with the responsibility for formulating basic national policies. I do not believe that I was ever timid in finding legislative authority for the FPC to undertake its broad missions, but there were situations where I felt it appropriate to refer the issue to the Congress, together with the commissioners' recommendations. I do not know if the computer-communications problem before the FCC falls in that category, but at least the question should be asked.

The general impression Commissioner Johnson leaves is that with more money, more resources devoted to policy planning, abler staff members and commissioners, and a new resolve to face squarely the difficult and complex issues posed by the marriage of computers and communications, the FCC just might make a sound and timely decision. Although I happen to agree with many of the reforms recommended by Commissioner Johnson, they will be difficult to accomplish.

POSNER. Commissioner Johnson touches on many disparate topics in the regulation of the communications industry, and it is impossible to determine exactly what he conceives to be the public-policy issues raised by the burgeoning use of computers in conjunction with communications facilities. He sees a desperate need for better planning by government in this area but does not explain why or what it would consist of.

It would promote clarity to ask at the outset why the government should concern itself at all with developments in the computer industry. Why not leave the provision and pricing of computer services to the free market, as with most products? Would the market produce unacceptable results? I believe not, if we ignore for a moment the provision of communications-related computer services. Computers do not pollute. Nor does their manufacture, programming, or use appear to exhibit such large economies of scale as to make monopoly inevitable. In the absence of any specific source of market failure, such as natural monopoly or externalities, the decentralized incremental decision-making process of the market seems appropriate.

The adequacy of the market becomes more problematical, however, when we turn to communications-related computer services, since communications services are provided under monopoly conditions and are comprehensively regulated by state and federal agencies, principally the FCC. These circumstances alter the analysis, though not in the end the result.

The first question is whether the regulated communications carriers, primarily the Bell system and Western Union, should be permitted to offer computer services. A subquestion is, if so, should these services be regulated? In the case of an unregulated monopolist, it is sometimes argued that the monopolist will use its monopoly profits to finance below-cost pricing in competitive markets in order to obtain a monopoly of those markets. For reasons explained elsewhere, the argument is a weak one.[24] A policy of limiting firms to particular markets can also be quite costly. The integration of communications and computer services, for example, might lead to cost savings—a question, incidentally, that cannot be answered by analysis but only by experience.[25]

When the monopolist is regulated, the question is more complicated. Regulation, to the extent that it is effective in limiting the profits of the regulated firm, creates a situation where a firm can sell below cost in some markets with impunity.[26] The firm can recoup its losses in those markets simply by raising rates in its monopoly markets, all the while remaining within the profit constraint set by the regulatory agency. An unregulated firm cannot recoup its losses: it is already charging the monopoly price in its monopoly markets. Only the regulated firm can sell below cost in some markets without any diminution of profits. In addition, a regulated firm might enter a new industry simply to complicate the regulators' task by creating "separations" (accounting) problems.

My conclusion nevertheless is that regulated firms should be permitted to compete in unregulated markets without being subject to minimum-rate or other regulatory constraints. The private treble-damage suit enables a victim of predatory pricing to recover three times his business losses plus a large attorney's fee. This, along with other antitrust sanctions, should be adequate to deter predatory behavior. Regulation seems redundant, and as I have already mentioned, restricting the entry of communications carriers into the computer industry could prove costly.

A second policy question is whether computer companies should be permitted to offer services (such as certain kinds of switching) now provided only by regulated communications carriers. A subquestion is, if so, should the carriers be required to let these would-be competitors connect physically with their facilities? My answers are "yes" and "no." The danger in permitting competition with regulated companies arises from the fact that these companies frequently set rates that reflect the average cost of many different services and routes whose cost characteristics may be quite dissimilar. An example is the uniform charge for long-distance telephone calls. According to industry sources, the costs of two calls of the same distance and duration may vary by as much as a factor of ten; but the cost difference is not reflected in the charge.

Uniform rates create false signals for prospective entrants. A firm seeing the telephone company charging five times the apparent cost of a service may conclude that it can provide the service at lower cost than the telephone company. But the telephone company's cost may be only one-tenth of its price. It may be making up for stiff losses sustained elsewhere in the system. The problem of false signals would be only transitory if upon entry of the new firm the telephone company could immediately reduce its rate, terminating some of its losing services in other markets if necessary. But regulators, sensitive to the demands of consumers in those other markets and to the complaints of the new firm, may well forbid such a rate reduction. The result will be an inefficient pattern of service in the market where entry occurred, with too many firms operating at too high a cost.

Despite this problem, my conclusion is again that free entry should be permitted. It seems more likely than not that the result of free entry will be to jar the regulated firms and regulatory agencies into adopting more sensible rate policies. An agency that decided to permit entry would be compelled by logic to permit existing firms to compete with the new entrant. But perhaps I exaggerate the compulsion of logic.

The growth of competition in the communications industry would in all likelihood be accelerated by a rule requiring carriers to offer physical connections to any firm desiring to provide on-line computer services. This would enable a company to form a network without having to duplicate carrier facilities. The problem is to decide at what price a carrier *must* offer interconnection to a potential competitor, as opposed to the price at which it would happily offer it. What is sought by a mandatory connection rule is a lower price. The fixing of a proper price and decisions about related questions of technical compatibility seem to me such difficult undertakings for regulators that I would prefer no rules, even though this would postpone erosion of Bell's communications monopoly. I emphasize that if Bell is rational, it will consent to interconnection whenever the result is to lower the cost of communications service, for it is in a position to benefit from any cost reduction. This conclusion is merely a specific application of the general proposition that a vertically integrated enterprise, even a monopolist, will seek to purchase inputs at the lowest possible cost, even if that means buying from an independent supplier rather than from its own divisions: a reduction in a monopolist's costs will lead to an increase in its profits. (To be sure, this proposition presupposes a rational profit-maximizing enterprise; and regulation, to the extent it is effective, prevents a regulated firm from maximizing profit.)

My general conclusion is that no particular regulations, planning, or other governmental initiatives are clearly dictated by the growing interaction of the computer and communications industries. I cannot demonstrate this rigorously, but there is enough reason for doubt to justify the position that those who would benefit from regulation, whether carriers or computer companies, should bear the burden of establishing a convincing case for it —something they have failed to do.

Unlike Commissioner Johnson, therefore, I consider the FCC's computer inquiry, to the extent it really was self-generated, premature and very largely a waste of time. It would appear to illustrate not a commendable initiative in attacking problems before they have become serious, but the traditional anxiety of regulatory agencies toward unregulated activities that impinge upon the firms they regulate. The paltry results of the inquiry evidence its dubious utility. If, on the other hand, the inquiry was really just a response to pressures from the computer industry, the FCC can hardly be applauded for anticipating problems before they arise.

The fundamental problem with Commissioner Johnson's approach, as with the approach of most regulatory activity, is that it lacks a theory of the behavior of firms, in particular, firms that are monopolists, regulated, or both. I have tried to suggest that such a theory can help identify situations in which regulatory inaction might cause misallocation of resources or other harm. Lacking such a theory, Commissioner Johnson is reduced to upbraiding his colleagues for not having created a planning capability whose characteristics and functions he does not explain.

JOHNSON. Posner appears to believe that it is not really important if his theory is simplistic or inadequate. Well, I am sorry, but I think it *is* important, and I think his theory *is* simplistic and inadequate. His constructive and useful point of view is that there ought not to be any regulation, and he proceeds to test it in sensible and thorough ways, examining what would happen in the absence of regulatory agencies and concluding that more often than not we would be much better off. We would have lower prices, greater competition, more adequate services, greater responsiveness in the marketplace, and so forth.

By and large I think he is right. The problem is that we are not there yet. The question is how do we get there from here, not what would we do if we were there. Posner has been discussing why we should not have a Federal Communications Commission (a subject upon which he and I have a fairly high level of agreement), whereas I have been considering the fact that we *have* a Federal Communications Commission and have been asking how we can get it to perform more adequately.

I disagree with Posner's judgment about the anticompetitive and predatory practices of monopolistic firms. It amuses me that he can be so down on regulation in general but so enthusiastic about the regulation performed by the Antitrust Division, as if somehow the antitrust laws have all of the answers. He may think the FCC computer inquiry was premature, but there are many people in the computer business who do not think so and who feel there is a great need to restrict some clearly anticompetitive practices of the communication carriers.

The trouble with profit maximization as a theory is that it does not seem to work out in practice. It is different for different firms at different times, and it is different for monopolists than for others. Bell may have thought it was maximizing profit when it fought the *Carterfone* case. What it really was doing, however, was trying to minimize its risk, and the price it paid for this was actually *less* profits.

Bell's preference for equity as opposed to debt financing, as one example, has simultaneously produced higher charges to consumers and a lower rate of return to shareholders. For years Bell raised capital by selling stock rather than by borrowing money as the electric utilities have done to the benefit of their shareholders. Bell does not maximize profits. It reduces risk and does this very well.

With respect to predatory practices, I submit that the history of the FCC's inquiries into *Telpak,* private microwave, telegraph, private-line telephone, and CATV suggests that there is a problem here. A great many American businessmen certainly think so, and they come to the FCC for help. Throwing them all into open competition is not the solution.

POSNER. My position here is not to abolish the FCC. Nor am I suggesting that the FCC should cease regulating the telephone business or giving out television licenses. I am suggesting only that when a new business floats into the FCC's ken the Commission ought not to react automatically by extending its regulatory control. In the present case, what the FCC should have done is simply nothing. If computer companies wish to provide communication services or enter specialized communications markets, the FCC should permit them to do so. If the Bell system wants to lower its rates in order to meet the competition of these new firms, it should permit that, too. A policy of inaction when dealing with new firms pressing for a role in an industry is a good first step and has support in basic economic theory. The burden should be on the industry to make a convincing case for extension of regulation. It seems to me mischievous and a waste of time for the FCC, without being pressed by industry, to launch a massive "inquiry" that proceeds on the assumption that the FCC's powers should be extended to the legal limits, that it should take under its wing every new service as it emerges.

BREWSTER. Dr. Greenberger will now present questions submitted by the audience.

GREENBERGER. This first question bears directly on the issue that Posner has raised about the appropriateness of the FCC inquiry. It may give Lee White the opportunity to express his opinion. Richard A. Solomon, a lawyer, asks whether a general rule-making inquiry in which an agency asks a lot of difficult questions and then tries to analyze a mass of comments (which are more or less responsive) is an appropriate procedural device for establishing policy in an area in which the agency has no initial expertise and no advance position. Should not rule making be used instead only as a device for permitting public comment on a proposal fully or almost fully formulated?

WHITE. I think a rule-making inquiry *is* an effective way for an agency to smoke out a variety of viewpoints, including those of other government agencies such as the Department of Justice. But I think one first must address the critical question that Posner has raised of whether the agency should do anything at all. My own instinctive reaction is always to do something; even if it is wrong, I like to do something! Given that, I have no objection to conducting a rule-making inquiry, if only to demonstrate that there should be no rule, as frequently happened at the FPC. I think this is a valid role for a regulatory body to play.

GREENBERGER. I believe it is fair to say that the FCC's computer inquiry did leave the door wide open to the possibility that there should be no new rules.

JOHNSON. There is much in what Richard Solomon was trying to suggest by his question. Many things that the government does it does very badly and ought not to do at all. There are other things that it can do constructively and one of these things, in my judgment, is to present carefully considered white papers for discussion by the Congress, the industries involved, or the public at large. I think an appropriate procedure for the FCC to follow when it sees a new problem on the horizon is to address it on its own, using its own expertise plus conferences, retreats, and other personal involvement by the commissioners to arrive at a position which it then makes publicly available for comment.

I agree with Posner that often the best thing to do is nothing, except that I also agree with White that a public official with responsibility for an area must at the very least make an initial inquiry to determine if the proper course is indeed to do nothing; that is, to do nothing deliberately rather than by default. The FCC is very good at doing nothing. But there is a difference between doing nothing and doing nothing deliberately.

GREENBERGER. The next two questions are closely allied. Ethel Marden, assistant to the director of the Center for Computer Science and Technology at the National Bureau of Standards, asks if a new federal entity is required to resolve the complex policy and regulatory questions related to telecommunications and computers. Phil Hirsch, Washington editor of *Datamation*, asks if the proposed Office of Telecommunications Policy may provide the FCC with some of the research and analytic capability it now lacks, or is there a better way to obtain this capability?

JOHNSON. The FCC needs something more than what it now possesses, whatever resources are elsewhere. It must at least have the capacity to read the material that others prepare. That is a bare minimum below which we have already fallen and should not have. If the Office of Telecommunications Policy has thirty people producing theoretical studies, the FCC needs at least thirty people to read these studies and try to understand them. The current problem is illustrated by the FCC's contracting out to Stanford Research Institute the job of reading and digesting the filings in the computer inquiry.

The solution to the problem of an agency with inadequate resources is not simply to set up another agency to do its job. It is altogether appropriate and probably useful for the President to have a communications-policy resource near at hand, but we must also put more resources into the FCC. I think we need to do both.

POSNER. Shuffling organization charts is the cheap and ineffective way to deal with social problems. There is already an Office for Telecommunications Management; the proposal seems to consist of giving it a new name. I do not know of any organizational change in the past that has solved any difficult problem.

GREENBERGER. The last question is by Lawrence G. Roberts, director of information processing at the Advanced Research Projects Agency, Department of Defense. He asks what possibilities exist to unify data-communications service so as to avoid an extremely costly, incompatible proliferation of private computer networks. He feels that AT&T is ineligible because of antitrust, Western Union is inadequate for the task because of lack of resources, and a private overlay is impossible because common carriers are not permitted to resell communications. What then?

POSNER. AT&T is not barred by the antitrust laws or the 1956 consent decree from providing whatever data-communications service the data industry is willing to pay for. I do not understand talk I have heard about forcing a social decision to encourage construction of a huge data network. If there is a demand for communications-linked computer services, again assuming AT&T has some modicum of rationality, it will build whatever size system is necessary to meet that demand.

Western Union does not need resources. If it has a marketable idea, the resources will flow to it.

As to a private overlay, it may be true that without compulsory connection or sharing rules the growth of competing networks will be retarded. But to the extent that real cost savings are possible, I again would expect AT&T to permit development of private communications segments.

WHITE. Commissioner Johnson described the UHF debacle before, and this last question implies that perhaps we have a similar situation about to be thrust upon us in the area of communications networks. It makes sense for somebody like the FCC, not to halt everything, but to look at the problem and determine whether there should be some rules requiring compatibility. This strikes me as a very reasonable question and seems to be the sort of thing we ought to be looking at. Once we look at it, we may decide that the best thing to do is leave it alone and let everybody work out his own little system and talk to each other through some other linkage. But I think it is an important question to ask.

GREENBERGER. In the early history of public utilities, incompatibilities resulted from the fact that no central control was exerted and development was left to market forces. Would you care to comment on that example?

WHITE. Industry worked that one out without the benefit of the government!

DINNER DISCUSSION

GREENBERGER. Richard Posner, at one point in the earlier discussion it sounded as if you might be saying that there was no role for the FCC at all, but then you insisted that was not your meaning. Can you be more explicit on the kind of role you think the FCC should be playing?

Participants: Donald Baker, Antitrust Division, Department of Justice; Robert Bennett, Northwestern University Law School; Kingman Brewster, Jr., Yale University; John A. Carver, Federal Power Commission; Kermit Gordon, The Brookings Institution; Lincoln Gordon, The Johns Hopkins University; James Hoak, Federal Communications Commission; Leland L. Johnson, RAND Corporation; Nicholas Johnson, Federal Communications Commission; William A. Morrill, Bureau of the Budget; Richard A. Posner, University of Chicago; Lawrence G. Roberts, Advanced Research Projects Agency, Department of Defense; Bernard Strassburg, Federal Communications Commission; Donald F. Turner, Harvard Law School (formerly of the Antitrust Division, Department of Justice); Lee C. White, private law practice; Clay T. Whitehead, White House; Dael Wolfle, University of Washington; Martin Greenberger, chairman, The Johns Hopkins University.

POSNER. One can make a tolerable argument for the proposition that a service like telephone service provided under conditions of natural monopoly should be regulated in order to prevent misallocation of resources. One can also argue the other side, but I am willing to admit to a good case for regulating natural monopoly. The question is whether the regulators should extend their rate and entry controls to new industries that abut on the regulated monopoly. This question has arisen often in the history of regulation. When trucking became a significant competitor of regulated railroads, the railroad industry pressed for the extension of regulation to cover the new competitor. Today, when a regulated communications carrier like Western Union desires to provide computer services that are also provided by a new industry, there is a movement to make regulation follow Western Union into the new industry. And similarly when nonregulated companies in the new industry wish to provide a service provided by the regulated carriers, there is pressure to subject these companies to regulation. I see no persuasive reason why an agency established to regulate natural monopolists should concern itself with other markets and other firms, even though they do relate to the regulated services.

NICHOLAS JOHNSON. We must distinguish between "concern itself with" and "regulate." Is it your position that we should not even be studying these issues, or are you saying that you have already studied them and have concluded that we should do nothing about them?

POSNER. What I would like to see is a presumption by the FCC against extensions of regulatory control. When some firm comes in for a ruling, then the agency has an obligation to study the question in depth and come to a decision. But otherwise, why invite trouble?

STRASSBURG. I am surprised by Posner's characterization of the computer inquiry, since he worked with the Stanford Research Institute group that analyzed the responses. The inquiry was not a grasping for additional power by a regulatory agency that is already inundated with more jurisdictional responsibilities than it can effectively manage. It was an effort by the FCC to find out what was going on in the industry and why. There were complaints that the communications common carriers were not adequately responding to the needs of the burgeoning computer-services industry. There was concern that the carriers were moving into data processing in competition with nonregulated firms and would use monopoly profits to subsidize their entry. The purpose of the inquiry was to see whether such concerns were valid and whether any prophylactic action was called for and could be taken. It was to provide a forum to exchange views and expose the needs and concerns of parties on all sides. Jurisdictional questions were secondary, and it is unfortunate that Posner misrepresented the inquiry in the way he did.

NICHOLAS JOHNSON. I think Posner is trying to make too hard a case and is failing. If he made less of a case, he might succeed. He has recognized that there is reason for having an FCC to regulate a monopoly like AT&T, but he does not allow that the agency must then concern itself with charges of predatory practices that derive from the monopoly power and complaints by consumers that the monopoly is not responding to market demand as competition would.

POSNER. There are a number of grounds on which to object to monopoly, but the only one I find plausible and well based theoretically and empirically is that monopolists may charge excessively high prices and restrict output. The FCC should prevent exorbitant monopoly pricing, but it should not worry about the monopolist's trying to take over other markets. There is no basis for assuming that a monopolist will engage in predatory conduct or be unresponsive to consumer demand.

KERMIT GORDON. The case against a monopolist is *not* simply with respect to its price and output behavior. That is a narrow, microeconomic, Marshallian view. The real case is with respect to the strength of its incentive to engage in technological innovation. This is the essence of the problem of the tight monopoly. Hicks regarded the greatest of monopoly profits as "a quiet life," and you can read the same inflection into Schumpeter.

POSNER. Schumpeter's view was that monopoly is a necessary condition for technological progress (which seems false to me).

LELAND JOHNSON. Why did AT&T not offer its own device for connecting mobile radio to the telephone network rather than fighting the *Carterfone* case?

POSNER. AT&T does offer a mobile-radio service tied to its regular network.

LELAND JOHNSON. But it does not offer a service like the Carterfone whereby anyone with his own mobile radiotelephone can connect to the Bell network.

POSNER. I do not think one can solve these issues by asking rhetorical questions about the behavior of the Bell system. We do not have enough facts about the Bell system to form judgments about its technical efficiency. And since there is no competitive system in communications, we have nothing with which to compare Bell.

WHITEHEAD. I would like Posner to comment on the current filing with the FCC of the Datran Company, which is proposing to invest several hundred million dollars in building a data network on the grounds that the service is not available from AT&T.

POSNER. I would be delighted to see it. If someone wants to spend several hundred million dollars to build a data network, let him do it.

TURNER. I think Posner's faulting the computer inquiry is a phony issue. If the Bell system has not developed the facilities it should, there is no reason to suppose on any theoretical grounds that it must have developed those facilities. I feel as Posner does that certain kinds of claims are unlikely to prove out. But surely the FCC cannot say we are just not going to bother with those claims. The real issues are what the FCC does after the inquiry.

POSNER. I accept that, if as Strassburg says, the inquiry was just a procedural device for responding to pressures from industry. But Commissioner Johnson seemed to be claiming that for once the FCC had not waited to be pushed by industry—had rather instituted the inquiry in anticipation of problems arising. Since the problems seemed to me unlikely to be real problems, I felt such an initiative was misplaced.

GREENBERGER. Pressures certainly had been developing in the computer industry for some time before the inquiry, but the FCC still was demonstrating initiative.

KERMIT GORDON. At this moment the panelists are badly split, and since all of them are lawyers, it might be helpful if I were to restore unity to the group by uniting them against me. The legislation underlying the activities of the regulatory commissions grew out of a legal tradition. The laws were written by lawyers using nonoperational words like "fair," "equitable," "just," "reasonable," and "balanced." Words like these give little useful guidance. What is more important is the performance of the industries being regulated—what they do, what they accomplish, their services, progress, costs, and prices. But the law has nothing to say on these subjects.

LINCOLN GORDON. It talks about "public interest, convenience, and necessity."

KERMIT GORDON. Right! The regulatory process has been distorted by statutory standards that give more weight to the rights of the companies involved than to the quality of their performance.

NICHOLAS JOHNSON. I basically agree.

WHITE. If you say that the present criteria are amorphous and weak, you have a responsibility also to say what you would do instead.

KERMIT GORDON. I would prescribe the kinds of results desired. I would instruct the regulatory commission to conduct its affairs so as to produce desired results with respect to price, the rate of progress, quality of service, and so on.

WHITE. That would not be very helpful to a commissioner trying to decide whether a company should be allowed to get a 7 percent or a 7¼ percent rate of return.

BREWSTER. Kermit Gordon and I go back to a common ancestry when under Edward Mason's chairmanship we argued about these same matters. The lawyers were as skeptical of the economists as the economists were of the lawyers. So this is a nostalgic occasion for me and resurrects my old biases.

The economist sees the whole problem of the political economy in economic terms, whereas the principal moral burden on the commission is not how much the person who does business can make but who has the right to do business. The economist is so oriented to results, performance, costs, prices, and products that he leaves out of the equation the very real opportunity-rationing problem that any regulatory agency must face. This shows a blindness of the dismal science.

KERMIT GORDON. Spoken like a lawyer! Note that Nicholas Johnson's critique of the FCC ran almost entirely in terms of the results it has produced. Legal thinking tends to subordinate operating results to its concern with everyone's getting a "fair shake." I do not really understand what "fair shake" means in the context of the allocation of channels and other rights. Posner suggests an auction, and something along that line seems to me to have a good deal of merit.

TURNER. The problem is not basically one of lawyers or legal draftsmanship at all. Lawyers by and large write what Congressmen tell them to write. A major reason we have bad results, as Posner stresses, is that we are greatly overregulating. That is not the fault of lawyers. It is a political decision, and many economists have been critical of it. We cannot really write desired results into a regulatory statute with any degree of precision and expect them to be enforceable.

Another problem is that regulatory agencies are instructed to take into account totally incompatible interests. In the Interstate Commerce Act, the Congress decided that regulation should recognize the interests of workers, the postal service, national defense, and so on. I defy anyone to write a statute that satisfies all of these conflicting interests. The tendency is to throw all bargaining positions into the statute, and this makes it very difficult for the regulatory agency. But as bad as many of the statutes have been, the commissions could still have done a vastly better job, given their broad mandate and considerable latitude to write interstitial rules.

KERMIT GORDON. You administered a very different and much better set of laws. The link between statutory language and results was much clearer in antitrust.

TURNER. That is an oversimplified characterization, although I did have one enormous advantage in administering the antitrust laws. I was only supposed to protect competition, not balance competing interests. Because economic science is still not terribly informative, we did have to guess about the consequences of some kinds of business behavior; but at least I did not have to make value judgments.

KERMIT GORDON. Because you were oriented toward results.

BENNETT. How can a statute do other than speak in terms of results? The Communications Act states that broadcasting licenses are to be granted when they serve the public interest, convenience, and necessity. It says that telephone rates are to be just and reasonable. Perhaps these criteria are too vague, but they do refer to results.

KERMIT GORDON. Does the Congress consider diversity a desirable goal in television programming? The word "diversity" probably does not appear in any statute, and it is much more specific and precise than any of the words that do appear.

LINCOLN GORDON. Years ago the regulatory agencies were referred to as the headless fourth body of the federal government, implying that they were without policy guidance. The feeling was that these multifunctional, politically appointed, theoretically bipartisan bodies were really a very poor way of making and implementing public policy. The current problem of computers and communications suggests that the White House must think so, too, or it would not be establishing the new Office of Telecommunications Policy.

I would like to ask Whitehead if the new office will examine questions like those addressed by the FCC inquiry, leaving the FCC to handle applications to particular cases. In our kind of world it is often necessary to separate broad policy making from application to particular cases. Is the new office just a reshuffling of bureaucratic boxes as Posner suggests, or is there more to it?

WHITEHEAD. I recently had to explain a comment ascribed to me by the press to the effect that the White House had no qualms about influencing regulatory commissions. We certainly have no intention of influencing agencies in any of their quasi-judicial functions, but we do feel that we have a growing responsibility to be able to comment on the policy matters before them. That and the executive branch's own telecommunications problems are the primary purposes of this new office. We expect that when the office has something to say it will be listened to and in that sense will influence the FCC. But that is more in the nature of partnership than of trying to take over the policy function of the FCC.

LINCOLN GORDON. Do you think quasi-judicial functions should be combined with broad policy making? Why not have a policy-making body in the executive branch that studies the problems and makes recommendations to the Congress to guide the quasi-judicial agencies in applications to particular cases? In short, why *not* take over the policy function of the FCC?

WHITEHEAD. Because I do not think the executive branch or the Congress has the flexibility to set out policies that cover all particular cases. In the domestic satellite matter, we sent out about eight pages of policy comments. That leaves an awful lot of policy room for the FCC, even if it were to accept everything we said.

CARVER. I have held posts with the Department of the Interior and I now serve on a regulatory agency, so I have a pretty clear idea of the limitations on the decision-making process both in the *collegial* form of a commission and in the *directive* form of an executive department. I see no reason to suppose that the directive form will give better results or a better process for resource allocation, given the pluralist, diverse interests of our society. Also, however inefficient a statute, it does give a finality and set of rules on which people can base decisions and act. We are not as likely to get this without the formal structure of an agency. I do not think the decision of an executive department is likely to be any better than (and many times not as good as) a decision reached in the present rather cumbersome regulatory way.

WOLFLE. Regulatory agencies are expected to concentrate on the industries or activities they regulate. Can an executive body like the Office of Telecommunications Policy bring a larger range of factors into consideration or pay more attention to the often unrepresented consumer?

NICHOLAS JOHNSON. I think that institutions are strengthened by building into them the capacity for public disagreement. When we perceive the administrative process simply in terms of legal rights, we tend to look only to the parties who happen to be before us at the time. The adversary system goes on operating whether or not the appropriate adversaries appear, and the winner of those who do appear prevails. We conceived the cable-television problem at the FCC as one of broadcaster versus cable operator and concerned ourselves with the impact of innovations in the new technology on the rights of the broadcaster. Kermit Gordon says we ought to be looking at more than just legal rights. Lee White says that if the adversary process is going to work, other parties with an interest in this case must also appear before the FCC to argue their points of view and must have access to the resources they need to make their appearance effective and forceful. I agree that we should set up citizens' advocate centers and we should support people like Ralph Nader to make the advocacy system work better.

BAKER. Regulation is a quasi-legal framework for solving economic and policy problems. It embodies the courtroom process of adversary confrontations, expensive legal bills, and long and often complex and inconclusive briefs and memoranda written by lawyers. This approach is fine for traditional courtroom issues, such as "Was A negligent?" But it is inappropriate for the broader set of questions exemplified by the computer inquiry. Those questions are basically political. Similarly, the central question on CATV of how much fragmentation of media we want cannot be answered by citing an old case in the second circuit court or footnoting a speech by an assistant attorney general. It must be faced as a political question.

MORRILL. On Lincoln Gordon's question about how the new Office of Telecommunications Policy might function, at the very least it will provide a somewhat different viewpoint, perhaps indeed the viewpoint of the adversary not present in the proceedings. It could also take a hard look at the basic statutes underlying regulatory activity to determine what changes might be productive. It is not at all clear that a commission framework provides the best way to handle such problems as the scarcity of available frequencies, which are considerably more complex than *A* versus *B*. There may not be any really satisfactory definition of the boundary between the functions of the FCC and the proposed Office of Telecommunications Policy, but it is quite clear that the executive branch should be doing more in this area than it has been doing.

POSNER. Does anyone think there is a case for regulating communication-related computer services?

GREENBERGER. No brief submitted in the FCC inquiry to my knowledge advocated regulating services offered by computer firms.

STRASSBURG. Right, except that some did propose regulating the computer-service offerings of communications carriers to prevent predatory practices and protect the competitive environment for further technological development. The Department of Justice filed a brief urging that while the common carriers should not be disqualified from participating in the furnishing of computer services, they should be required to establish separate corporations for offering these services so as to avoid any commingling of activities or possibility of cross-subsidization.

ROBERTS. A case can be made for regulating the data service that interconnects computers. If this service is left free to proliferate, the result could be disastrous for the country and the economy. We need a single homogeneous service, and I do not see any way of getting it except by regulated monopoly. The FCC might invite competitive bids for data service in each area and then evaluate the proposals on the basis of merit rather than who is the fastest to file.

LELAND JOHNSON. But the interconnection of computer services throughout the country could be achieved by the enforcement of technical standards. That is quite different from a regulatory policy to ensure uniformity. Nothing would be more stifling of innovation than to insist that there be a homogeneous nationwide data service operated as a monopoly.

ROBERTS. At the present time the only data services available are what the carriers choose to offer: circuit-switched communication "pipes." I need a message service that will allow me to send messages to and receive messages from any other computer in the country. I do not like the idea of its being a regulated monopoly, but if we allow competition I will have to subscribe to ten different data services. Requiring interconnection of the different data services might achieve the same end, but it would be far more difficult and much less economic than having one regulated monopoly.

GREENBERGER. I think Roberts hopes that someday a person at a single computer terminal will be able to communicate using a single procedure with any data offering anywhere. He is afraid that if development of the interconnecting service is left to the open market without any central control overseeing it, there will be a multiplicity of systems about which each user will have to be informed.

LELAND JOHNSON. I still think the problem can be solved with a good set of technical standards covering operations among different terminals and lines owned by separate and competing entities.

ROBERTS. The single data service I am proposing would indeed use different lines from separate companies, such as AT&T, Western Union, and Comsat. The service, not the lines, is my concern. Why should we suppose that ten different companies will offer the same service, even if technical standards are enforced by the FCC?

POSNER. As I recall, the standard gauge for railroads in the nineteenth century was worked out by the railroads themselves, just as Lee White indicated that electric power standards were worked out by the power industry. There is an obvious mutuality of interest that leads industries such as these to adopt whatever level of compatibility is necessary. The communications industry is a curious case in that we do have a monopoly: the Bell system. I do not understand why Bell does not offer the service Roberts wants. The traditional criticism of Bell is that it is overly capital intensive, that it installs too much plant.

ROBERTS. It is not installing enough plant. My organization set up the data connection for a national network and asked Bell a year ago to take it over. Bell has not responded, presumably on the basis of antitrust considerations and the claim that the Justice Department considers data services as Western Union's domain.

GREENBERGER. This same problem came up in the discussion after the Kemeny session. Edward David from Bell Telephone Laboratories indicated that he felt AT&T ought to provide the service that Roberts now has to provide himself, but that then Western Union would complain to the FCC; to which Bernard Strassburg replied that the FCC does not hold a protective umbrella over Western Union.

BAKER. AT&T has not been knocking on the Justice Department's door to modify the 1956 consent decree so it could offer this kind of data service.

TURNER. Bell went to bed on that decree. It loves it.

STRASSBURG. One of the problems is that the Bell system has a voice orientation. Its current plant is primarily for analogue communication. It will gradually convert that plant, but the necessary investment is enormous and today Bell has all it can do to keep up with the requirements of its voice business.

WHITEHEAD. The Bell management, while exceedingly competent, has limited time and unlimited problems. It is unreasonable to expect it to respond overnight to the demands of the data industry. Bell is so large that its raising capital in the financial markets to expand the telephone plant can cause trouble for the financial markets as well as for itself.

MORRILL. For those of us who have sympathy for Posner's general proposition that there is too much regulation, an interesting operational question is how quickly the FCC should move toward less regulation. It has not been moving at all consistently in that general direction.

GREENBERGER. Before adjourning, I would like to ask Kingman Brewster for any final thoughts, particularly on how the topic of discussion relates to education.

BREWSTER. I worry over whether the representative democratic process in its present form is capable of dealing with the problems in this field any more than it is in the area of inflationary control. Whether the statutes are drawn by economists or lawyers, ultimately it is Congress that reconciles the interests. There is a real problem of how a representative as opposed to a parliamentary democracy can exert a public conscience which is more than the log rolling and pork barrel of competing political interests. We kid ourselves in thinking that there can be a purely administrative, judicial, rule-making, or delegated legislative solution. We should be more candid about the inadequacy of representative democracy in dealing with its problems.

On the educational side, I cannot help but think of the potential role of universities as resources for policy briefing and analysis in a society whose objective brain power is in very short supply and whose agency employees are underpaid and underrewarded in other ways. I wonder if those who dwell in the fragile sanctuary of academia could make a greater contribution than they now make. We may not have been imaginative enough about how to institutionalize academic input to public policy while still preserving the objectivity and sanctuary of academia. Universities cannot solve the problems, but they may be able to provide a useful input to the solutions.

GREENBERGER. Those two points go well together. A representative form of democracy poses special problems in the handling of regulatory issues affecting the public interest, but it perhaps also offers unique opportunities for obtaining the needed intellectual input from the academic world.

REFERENCES

1. U.S., Federal Communications Commission (FCC), *Official Reports*, 2d series, 7 (1966–67): 11, 19 (hereafter referred to in legal style).
2. Stanford Research Institute, *Report on F.C.C. Computer Inquiry*, no. 2, 1969, p. 116.
3. Manley Irwin, "The Computer Utility," *Yale Law Journal*, 76 (1967), 1306–7.
4. *Report of the Telephone and Telegraph Committees of the FCC*, April 29, 1966, p. 166.
5. Stuart L. Mathison and Philip M. Walker, *Computers and Telecommunications: Issues in Public Policy*, Prentice-Hall, 1970.
6. 7 FCC 2d 19 (1967).

7. Charles L. Schultze, *The Politics and Economics of Public Spending*, Brookings Institution, 1968, p. 75.
8. Joint Technical Advisory Committee (JTAC), *Radio Spectrum Conservation*, McGraw-Hill, 1952; idem., *Radio Spectrum Utilization*, Institute of Electrical and Electronic Engineers, 1964; U.S., Department of Commerce, Telecommunication Science Panel, *Electromagnetic Spectrum Utilization— The Silent Crisis*, Government Printing Office, 1966; U.S., FCC, *Report of the Advisory Committee for the Land Mobile Radio Services*, 1967; JTAC, *Spectrum Engineering—The Key to Progress*, Institute of Electrical and Electronic Engineers, 1968; President's Task Force on Communications Policy, *Final Report*, Government Printing Office, 1969, chap. 8; idem., *Staff Paper no. 7*, 1969.
9. 15 FCC 2d 417 (1968).
10. *The Future of Cable Television: Some Problems of Federal Regulation*, RAND Corp., 1970.
11. National Television System Committee, *Color Television Standards*, McGraw-Hill, 1955, pp. 1–41.
12. *Federal Regulations*, 31 (1966): 3507.
13. President's Task Force on Communications Policy, *Final Report*, chap. 5.
14. White House Memorandum on Domestic Satellite Policy, reprinted at 22 FCC 2d 125 (1970).
15. 22 FCC 2d 86 (1970).
16. 13 FCC 2d 420 (1968).
17. 18 FCC 2d 953 (1969).
18. Stanford Research Institute, *Report*, no. 1, p. 6.
19. 18 FCC 2d 761, 769 (1969).
20. *Federal Regulations*, 35 (1970): 5822.
21. *Ibid.* at par. 10.
22. *New York Times*, May 6, 1970, p. 65.
23. United States v. Western Electric Company and American Telephone and Telegraph Company, 1956 CCH 71, 134 (D.C. NS 1956).
24. Lester G. Telser, "Cutthroat Competition and the Long Purse," *Journal of Law and Economics*, 9 (1966): 259–277.
25. Caleb A. Smith, "Survey of the Empirical Evidence On Economies of Scale," in *Business Concentration and Price Policy*, National Bureau of Economic Research, 1955, pp. 213–30; Milton J. Friedman, Comment, *ibid.*, p. 230.
26. Richard Posner, "Natural Monopoly and Its Regulation," *Stanford Law Review*, 21 (1969): 548, 593–616.

MAN AND THE MACHINE: PROSPECTS FOR THE HUMAN ENTERPRISE

Speaker   GEORGE WALD

               Higgins Professor of Biology
               Harvard University

Discussants   DANIEL BELL

               Chairman of the Commission on the
               Year 2000 of the
               American Academy of Arts and Sciences

               HARVEY BROOKS

               Chairman of the Committee on Science
               and Public Policy of the National Academy
               of Sciences

Moderator   JAMES B. FISK

               President
               Bell Telephone Laboratories

FISK. Our purpose is to discuss how we may make best use of science and technology for the benefit of people. Most scientific effort today *is* directed toward this goal. Yet in some areas our very success has created social and environmental problems, some not expected and some anticipated but not thought to be seriously harmful.

Few scientists and engineers are unaware of or unconcerned about the effect of their work on people and the environment. They are hurt, even angered, by the sudden outcry of young people and the nontechnical sectors of society against them. Scientists and engineers were acclaimed ten years ago as heroes and even saviors of our way of life and nation. Today they are the villains. They are very sensitive about their role in society and more than a little confused about where their social responsibilities begin and end. But they must take into account the changing nature of the social climate in which they live and work.

The deep public involvement in social issues now current will continue into the 1970's and will probably grow in scope and intensity. Technically based organizations and individuals will be the particular focus of public scrutiny. Their success will depend largely on their ability to recognize, understand, and cope with this new public involvement. Young people will continue to participate heavily in social issues and will be a major factor in creating social change. Protection of the natural environment is the next great cause of young people; it is not a passing fad.

Scientists and engineers will bear much of the blame for creating what people find objectionable in the environment and lacking in our quality of living. As part of the establishment, they will be subject to growing anti-establishment attacks. As creators of modern technology, they will be targets for neo-Luddite movements. In order to survive and prosper, they will have to recognize the new interdependence between technology and social change. Social changes were once regarded as the outcome of courses of action in science and technology. Today it is often the reverse, as our program to put a man on the moon illustrates.

The needs of society and the wants of people may well become the *major* considerations in guiding scientific and engineering development. This has always been the case in my field, telecommunications. Future technological developments may be determined more by their social significance than by their technical feasibility.

George Wald's thesis has for some time been that science is for man, and he is most eloquent on the subject.

WALD. Man throughout his history has been engaged in an unceasing struggle to know. This is epitomized in science. Science represents a systematic attempt to understand all reality. Facts are only the raw material of understanding. The facts in themselves constitute only a catalogue. It is the web of relationships, the fabric, with which science is concerned.

As an attempt to know and understand, science is altogether good as our culture interprets the good. There can be no such thing as bad science. Any other view would be a plea for ignorance.

Technology

Technology, the application of science toward useful ends, is a very different type of enterprise. It is *not* altogether good. Technology is for use and should be constantly reviewed and judged in terms of the needs, goals, and aspirations of society.

Another dichotomy of equal importance is the distinction between *creation* and *production*. Creation again is altogether good as our culture interprets the good; but production is for use and like technology should be constantly adjusted in terms of the needs, goals, and aspirations of society.

Some years ago when in the company of scientists I tried now and then to raise the question of whether one should do everything one can. At that time it seemed a strange and somewhat upsetting question. People took it for granted that the answer was "yes"; one should do everything one can and as soon as one can. But people have now begun to recognize that the proper answer is "no"; among all the things that can be done, choices need to be made in terms of the needs, goals, and aspirations of society. My position is that one should know all one can but should do only those things that promise best to fulfill social needs and ends.

Who is to make such decisions? Currently they are being made almost wholly by producers—by persons who see in technology an opportunity for increased profit, power, or status. Those persons should have their say, but I think ultimately such decisions should be made not by them but by those who will live with the products.

Is this a utopian view? Do we have institutions and procedures for making such decisions? I think we do, if only we used them effectively.

The supersonic transport (SST) is a case in point. It represents a technological possibility that will be unpleasant to live with and may be impractical economically. The SST in any form yet proposed promises to be a major polluter of the air, and its sonic boom will spread a wide swath of auditory and mechanical shock along its path. To what end? Who in our society feels the need to travel that fast? Yet the decision to go ahead has already been made by business and government. Why? The answers are illuminating. We are told that having recently lost *our* dominant position in the world market in every field of civilian production excepting aircraft (and computers), we must at all costs retain *our* lead in aircraft. We are also told that the Soviet Union is building an SST.

The antiballistic missile [ABM] is another case in point. Scientists, including those most knowledgeable about weaponry and many with wide experience in government and defense problems, displayed an astonishing unanimity in opposing the ABM. They testified that it was not needed, that it would decrease rather than increase our national security, and that it very probably would not work. Every former Presidential science adviser came out flatly against the ABM program in all its forms. Yet the Nixon administration decided to go ahead.

This does not seem to have been a military decision, since we have been assured repeatedly by our military men that the Soviet Union's ring of ABM's around Moscow presents no serious obstacle to our nuclear missiles. Moreover, we are proceeding simultaneously with programs to develop weapons designed to circumvent ABM's, and the Soviet Union undoubtedly has comparable programs. If this was neither an engineering nor a military decision, what was it? The twelve billion dollars in defense contracts to build the ABM in the present thin Safeguard program and an estimated seventeen billion dollars to build new weapons clearly spoke more loudly than the needs, goals, and aspirations of society.

I speak of those needs, goals, and aspirations as though I knew what they were or people agreed about them. The need to formulate some commonly accepted sense of national meaning and purpose is surely one of the most pressing needs of our time, as is the formulation of a more commonly accepted sense of *human* meanings and goals—some wider concept of the nature of the human enterprise. We need proposals, however tentative, of how best to proceed with it. I am sure that science must make basic contributions to such a formulation. The too-rapid development of an unrestrained technology during the past century and a half has badly eroded both our ancient cultural traditions and our more recent national tradition. No society can long survive such losses and drift aimlessly as we have been doing for some time. We must bring technology under control, but we must also try to achieve a more conscious and widely accepted formulation of what we are and where we want to go.

Two Kinds of Design

All about us we see evidences of design. In an increasingly technological world we mistakenly assume that all is technological design. One asks of a car and of a refrigerator, "Who made it?"; and so it comes naturally to ask of man, "Who made him?"

In fact, we have to do with two entirely different processes of design: technological and organic. Technological design begins with specifications. One lists the specifications and then attempts to realize them as best one can.

Living organisms are the products of organic design, the process that Charles Darwin characterized a little over a century ago as *natural selection*. Its mechanisms are almost the reverse of those of technological design. It begins with an endless outpouring of variations together with a mechanism of inheritance. This can be ordinary biological or genetic inheritance, or it may be learned behavior, including in human societies cultural inheritance. Cultural inheritance can closely mimic genetic inheritance. There are few tasks so difficult in science as determining whether any given inheritance is by nature or nurture.

Natural selection also has a third component, a selective factor, an element of competition, which Darwin called the "struggle for existence." Every population of organisms expands automatically so as to utilize and eventually exceed its resources. Darwin called the outcome the "survival of the fittest." Those forms of anatomy and behavior that work a little better are permitted to go on, while those that do not work so well are eliminated.

Natural selection is almost the reverse of technological design. There are no specifications. It is a process not of authorship but of *editing*. The Great Author of our being might better be referred to as the Great Editor.

Compared with technological design, this process seems slow, wasteful, and inefficient. But we should think well of it, for it has given us all the living organisms we know; and the simplest of living organisms is more intricately designed, more adaptive in its responses, more closely integrated with its surroundings, more flexible in meeting new challenges, and—to cite a modern value—more highly miniaturized than the most complex of technological devices.

Natural Selection in the Social and Political Sphere

Darwin realized that natural selection is a universal principle. In his second book on evolution, *The Descent of Man*, he did not hesitate to apply it to a wide range of human and social situations—to ethics and aesthetics, to the development and competition of cultures, and to the wars of nations.

I should like to give an example of the distinction between organic and technological design operating in the social sphere. As is well known, there is no written English constitution. The founders of our own government in their insecurity and facing a wilderness did write a constitution. It has made a lot of trouble since. The great base of our legal tradition is the so-called common law. This *is* a genuinely organic development. It is a system of tradition and precedent, the outcome of centuries of social experience, of trying out an endless variety of procedures, retaining whatever worked well and discarding whatever worked less well. In contrast to the common law, we have such technological systems of codified law drawn to specification as the Roman law, the German law based upon the Roman law, and the Code Napoléon.

A second point: The most cogent expression of natural selection in the political sphere is democracy. The indispensable element in democracy is its open-endedness. Like the common law, it is potentially a system of endless social experimentation. If we can achieve some degree of democracy, I would take my chances on it, however slow and muddled it seems, in preference to such technological contructs as the planned societies drawn to specification that so captivated my generation in the period between the world wars, however brilliant the plan or benign its intention.

A third comment: Uniformity is the death of evolution. Evolution demands a constant outpouring of variations. This is the best argument I know for tolerance; but tolerance is only its negative aspect. We should do more than *tolerate* anatomical, behavioral, and political differences; we should *foster* them as the ultimate source of all further development.

A final observation: All my life I have been told that science is ethically neutral, that it is concerned only with what is, not with such value judgments as right and wrong, good and evil. Our ethical principles come to us generally in the form of categorical imperatives, as absolute and arbitrary affirmations, statements that have the quality of Martin Luther's "Here I stand; I cannot do otherwise." It is easiest to accept them in this form, sanctioned by ancient tradition, and needing neither challenge nor defense. Yet they are not wholly arbitrary. Any society lives by its basic affirmations; no society could long survive a choice of faulty affirmations.

Consider for example our Ten Commandments. The first four are tenets of the Judeo-Christian theology and in any other theology would be different. But not the next six. Try the experiment of inverting these six commandments to read: kill, commit adultery, steal, bear false witness, take from your neighbors their wives and belongings, and (one that rings strangely just now) have contempt for your parents. Such rules could hardly produce a society even remotely like ours. Hence, those six commandments are accepted almost universally, by Buddhists, Hindus, and Zoroastrians alike, not ultimately as supernatural commands but for social survival.

Having spoken so enthusiastically of variation as the source of further development, let me say a word for conservatism. Natural selection as a mechanism for evolution is highly conservative. During ages of selection among all the variations offered there runs a constant trend toward optimization. The optimal selections have already largely been made in any ancient stock; hence almost all mutations are deleterious in races of living organisms. There is nothing intrinsically wrong with mutation; but each race of organisms has usually long since tried and selected among the available mutations and incorporated the most advantageous into its normal structure.

To a degree, that is also the way with social and political traditions. They are distilled out of centuries, sometimes millenia, of human experience. They should be regarded with respect. One of the most important elements in biological evolution is the evolution of *dominance*. The most advantageous characters have tended to become dominant to almost all the sporadic mutations that arise. That is why we find most mutations not only deleterious but recessive to the normal characters. So it is also, and should be, with social and political innovations that are incompatible with basic social and political traditions. They must be regarded as tentative and on trial until they prove themselves in practice to be more advantageous, and then they may be incorporated into the basic tradition.

Novelty is not a value in itself, nor is change; novelty and change are good only to the degree that they promote *adaptation*, and hence the fitness of organisms to survive. There can also be overadaptation. Adaptation must not go so far as to surrender flexibility. An organism may become so closely adapted to a given set of conditions as to be unable to meet changed circumstances. Most biologists believe that such rigid overadaptations account for the extinction of past races of organisms.

It is the good fortune of man, while achieving a high degree of anatomical specialization in certain directions, to have remained a remarkably generalized animal. We still retain the primitive vertebrate pattern of four limbs, each ending in five digits. We can still walk, run, jump, and climb. Long ago we (together with the anthropoid apes) lost our prehensile tails; and now we are clearly losing our toes, which are already little more than ornamental. If we manage so poorly as to need again to take to the trees, those losses will be a great embarrassment.

Man as a Technological Product

We are what natural selection makes us. The only alternative view, deeply embedded in our religious tradition, presents man as a technological product designed and manufactured by God. It seems strange to me that this view should ever be regarded as giving man a nobler or more spiritual status than he is accorded by science.

I know of nothing remotely as awesome, moving, or beautiful—nothing that gives man as much dignity, and life as much sanctity—as our present scientific view of the place of man and life in space and time. The very substances of living organisms—the carbon, nitrogen, and oxygen that principally compose them—were generated in the deep interiors of earlier generations of dying stars. Spewed out into space, they were gathered up over billions of years to compose eventually the substance of our sun, our planets, and ourselves. It took three billion years of evolution on this planet to bring forth man. In a sense, man incorporates a large part of the history of the universe; it reaches a culmination and self-realization in him. Life is a great thing in the universe, and man is the noble, local culmination of life.

Yet in an increasingly technological world, an astonishing number of persons wish themselves to be technological products—not the work of God as in the older tradition, but products of human technology. Modern biology is developing techniques for controlling human heredity and hence designing human evolution. Such prospects arouse considerable enthusiasm in biologists eager to show what they can do and in their lay audiences. The prospects have all the blandishments of novelty and progress but in fact represent something very old, what Darwin called artificial as opposed to natural selection. This is how we bred pigs that are fat, cows that give a lot of milk, hens that lay many eggs, horses that are strong, sheep that bear a lot of wool, and all of them stupid—for a clever animal can make a lot of trouble. The essential process is to control heredity and so design animals to specification by selective breeding (or otherwise). The question before us is whether we are now to domesticate man. We might in this way produce a more uniform, more reliable, more useful creature than we have or are likely to get through natural selection. But reliable to whom? Useful to whom? Who is to set the specifications? And to what end? For end it would be, the end of man as the dominant experiment in the evolution of life on this planet, still evolving, capable of unfolding still unrecognized potentials in ages to come.

Every creature now alive represents a continuous line of life stretching back to the first living organism on this planet; for if that line had ever been broken, how could we be here? This is our stake in physical immortality—an unbroken line of life stretching back some three billion years. That is the status of our germ plasm, of human eggs and sperm, a potentially immortal line. Generation after generation, the germ plasm has made bodies, each discarded by death; but the line of germ plasm goes on. Think what this means. Some five hundred million years ago, our germ plasm made fishes; some time later, amphibia; still later, reptiles. Now it is making men; and if we only have the good sense and restraint to leave it alone, there is no knowing what it will make in ages to come.

Our greatest problem now is to see that it has that chance. We need to ensure not only that the line goes on but that it is guarded from technological interference. We need safeguards. I should like to see established in law a principle of the *inviolability of the human germ plasm*, much like our present principle of the inviolability of human life. Society at times will elect to violate the principle. There may come a time, for example, when we know how safely to introduce into congenital diabetics the gene that makes insulin. If that proves possible and demonstrably advantageous, we would want to do it. But the barrier to manipulation of human germ plasm should be high, and now is the time to erect it.

A Crisis of Crises

The human enterprise is threatened as never before. We have come into a period that John Platt characterizes as a "crisis of crises," with a series of largely interrelated and extraordinarily threatening developments coming to a head within the next fifteen to thirty years.[1]

Lewis Mumford has pointed out that men developed over the millenia a pattern of village life in which they lived in symbiosis with animals and plants to mutual advantage; the men, the animals, and the plants were all fostered by the association.[2] There were lapses, but this was the general pattern.

Suddenly and violently this ancient pattern of social existence was destroyed by the Industrial Revolution, which took hold and started its exponential development about a century and a half ago—recently enough to give us some hope of dealing with it. We are on a collision course. Curves representing many aspects of our present condition are rising exponentially toward an infinity that does not exist. All our resources are limited. Our per capita consumption of mineral resources and fossil fuels and our scientific output are growing exponentially. These curves must somehow be brought to level off, and certain of them even to turn downward.

Basic to the other developments is the way population is rising. By all present indications our world population, now at about three and a half billion, will have doubled by the end of this century. We expect famine on an unprecedented scale in many parts of the world long before that. But that prospect is not the heart of the problem. If it were, one might have some ground for optimism, since in the last decade the world production of food has increased somewhat faster than world population. The main object of the human enterprise should not be in seeing how many persons can be kept alive on the face of the earth. That would be an altogether bankrupt and meaningless end for humanity, since however well managed, space and resources must eventually become insufficient to meet the needs of an unrestricted increase in population. Man must go on to produce a more widely shared, richer, and more meaningful culture. He must go on with creation and not be degraded into a meaningless venture in production.

The point is not how many people can be fed on this planet, but what population can best fulfill human potentialities. We need to be concerned primarily with the quality of human life rather than the quantity. From that point of view the world is probably already overpopulated. China and India once were the seats of great cultures, enormously creative in the sciences, painting, sculpture, ceramics, and literature. They were the fountainheads of great world religions. Indian and Chinese culture declined centuries ago. It would take more courage and insight than I possess to attempt to account adequately for that decline; but I feel sure that overpopulation looms large among its causes.

The Western world is now becoming overcrowded, and there is erosion of our occidental culture. The quality of our production in the arts has declined markedly in the last century since the Industrial Revolution took hold and population began to explode. Novels, poetry, music, painting, and sculpture are no longer what they were. A new literature concedes this and pictures it as permanent. It tells us to recognize that our ages of creativity have passed and to stop struggling.[3]

This age is kinder to science than to the arts, but it is not kinder to the individual scientist than previous periods. His life is nothing like what it was a century ago, and his productivity has declined enormously. It would take a whole galaxy of the most productive living biologists to compete with the breadth, quality, and scale of Charles Darwin's accomplishment. One can say the same in reference to such physicists as James Clerk Maxwell or Hermann von Helmholtz. These earlier men had no labor-saving devices. They performed their own experiments and wrote their papers and books in longhand, without dictating machines, microfilm, or computerized information-retrieval systems. They did have privacy and quiet, clean air and water, and the chance to walk through green fields beside quiet rivers.

We have taken a wrong turn recently enough so that we need not accept it as permanent. We cannot allow so ancient and impressive a history to be degraded so quickly. In this overcrowded world in which many of us feel we are drowning in people, there is some relief in regarding oneself in time rather than space. If we take thirty years as a human generation, then only one hundred of our ancestors in line take us back to about 1000 B.C. That is not very many ancestors. One could have known that many persons intimately, valued their opinions, and hoped not to disappoint them.

Man in the Universe

The human enterprise needs saving. Any attempt to save it must be based upon some common understanding of its nature, of the place of life in the universe and man in life, of our cosmic history and our contribution to cosmic development. The heart of that contribution is in man's unique attributes—his capacity to know and create. He is the science-making and art-making animal.

We are not alone in the universe, neither in being living things nor probably in our aspects of humanity. Life is part of the order of nature. There are a hundred billion stars like the sun in our home galaxy, the Milky Way. It is conservatively estimated that at least 1 percent of those stars have planetary systems capable of supporting life, or a billion solar systems in the Milky Way. Since there are about a billion such galaxies within view of the most powerful telescopes, something like a billion billion places exist in the already observed universe that might support life. Enough time should have passed by now to bring forth life in many of those places.

Some such contemplative and technological creature as man seems also to be in the order of things. The primary rules of the game of organic evolution are to be possible and to be successful. Since we exist, we are obviously possible; and as the dominant species on earth we are so successful that we now have the power to extinguish virtually all living species, including our own. The probability is negligible that evolution has brought forth specifically man, *Homo sapiens*, anywhere else in the universe, since that would demand an almost exact replay of the whole course of human evolution in a different place and under different conditions. Yet in many places in the universe, including our own galaxy, something like man probably has occurred and, having occurred, has bred a technology. I consider that technology part of nature, since it is part of human nature and must be part of the nature of any comparable creature. There is only one universe of nature, and the machines are part of it.

Other Civilizations in Space

Technological civilizations that have developed far beyond our own may exist in many places in space. How far ahead of us may they be? It is hard for us to imagine what progress our own technology may make within the next hundred years (neglecting the possibility of disaster), and the thought of what it might become in another thousand years is staggering. One thousand years, however, is but a day in the life of the universe. Some civilization on some other planet in our galaxy might be not only a thousand years ahead of us, but a million, ten million, why not a billion?

Perhaps internal laws choke off such developments. This is a possibility that is beginning to interest us. There is more order in nature than we yet know. To the silly question, "Why is the solar system six billion years old?", I have heard the answer, "Because it took that long to get someone to find it out."

Enrico Fermi once objected in a conversation to the notion that there might be other civilizations in space. Fermi said, "Nonsense! Why aren't they here?" If there are technologically advanced creatures elsewhere in space, they should give us evidence of their presence; they should visit us. Of course some persons think they have, in the form of the unidentified flying objects (UFO's), a view now officially rejected.

But why *should* they be here rather than somewhere else? It is a little like saying that there cannot be a man named Swenson in Stockholm because if there is, why isn't he here? The trip is possible, but Swenson may choose to be somewhere else, perhaps to stay home. Of the three and a half billion persons on this planet only a few, fortunately, have chosen to be here. A billion of the hundred billion stars in our galaxy may have planets that support life. Granted even the widest capacities for space travel, why come here?

Unless we call them. It has lately been proposed that we attempt to establish radio communication with more highly advanced technological civilizations in outer space. A few years ago the National Radio Astronomy facility in Green Bank, West Virginia, began a project of this nature with the characteristically corny title, Ozma, after the Magician of Oz. The director of this project, Frank Drake, was quoted in the press as having said, "We'll have a lot of questions to ask those fellows. We'll ask them the cure for cancer and how to run a controlled thermonuclear reaction."

What a strange view of the human enterprise! I would be proud if we discovered cures for cancer, as one day I think we will; and only a little less proud when we learn to control thermonuclear reactions. But to attach humanity as by an umbilical cord to some superior civilization in outer space that would answer our questions and solve our problems, and indeed might be as far ahead of us in the arts as in technology, would be the end of the human enterprise. It would in effect fold our civilization and turn its future over to another. What dignity, pride, or meaning would remain to us as men? I think this dependence would be the ultimate disaster.

There is little danger of that happening. The nearest star to the sun that might possibly have a planet supporting life is thought to be almost eleven light-years away. The chance that it is the seat of a superior technological civilization is very small indeed. Even if it were and all other improbable conditions were fulfilled, it would take eleven years for a message from here to reach there and another eleven years for the answer to come back, hardly the basis for a scintillating conversation.

The prospects of our ever being visited from outside the solar system are similarly slim. Even if creatures elsewhere have developed ways to travel at the speed of radiation (and it is hard to imagine doing that without *being* radiation), the distances are so formidable and the incentives so problematical that there is little possibility of voyaging between stars.

The creatures who I believe exist elsewhere in space, who psychologically and technologically may resemble men, are not men. They are not our species or genus or even likely to be in any phylum of organisms we know. They almost surely represent an altogether alien development, presenting analogies but no homologies with life on earth. There is little reason for us to feel a sense of kinship with them or to assume they would feel benign toward us.

Conclusion

During the past half-century our cosmic horizon has expanded far beyond all earlier imagining. I think the time has come to contract it in its human aspects. Our home in space now and in any conceivable future is the solar system. Thermodynamically it is virtually a closed system. Its only source of energy has been the sun. Now we are beginning to add our own production of nuclear energy. This new development is comparable to the development of photosynthesis, which freed life on earth from its earlier dependence on accumulated stores of organic molecules and for the first time made it possible for living organisms using the energy of sunlight to synthesize organic molecules themselves. When we succeed in adding to the thermonuclear reactions of the sun our own controlled thermonuclear reactions (unfortunately still only in the form of explosions), mankind and indeed life on earth will have achieved a new measure of independence.

It is becoming increasingly plain that earth provides the only environment suitable for life in the solar system. We can move about in the solar system by carrying our environment with us. Presumably this will always be necessary. That is why we have to deal with our population problems here. We might conceivably find uses for the other planets, but not as places on which to live.

In a fine flight of imagination a few years ago, Freeman Dyson suggested that a superior technological civilization associated with some other star might find it expedient to smear the substance of the largest available planet so as to form a hollow shell completely enclosing its solar system.[4] It then would capture *all* the energy of its sun, in contrast with the very small fraction of our sun's energy that we capture. It might also use the entire inner surface of the shell for cultivating food, an odd combination of supertechnology with old-fashioned photosynthesis. This makes one wonder about water supplies and also begs the population question. Would such a civilization really want and could it really tolerate a population needing so much food?

We must recognize that now and surely for ages to come the solar system is our home in space and the earth our home in the solar system. This is the New Parochialism. We are not likely to leave the solar system or to be visited from outside it. Nor do I think we should attempt to communicate with our like in outer space. Were they our peers, it might be an interesting and moving experience. But in all likelihood they are either far behind us and hence in no position to communicate with us, or else far ahead and thus able to inflict on us servile dependence at best and catastrophe at worst.

Our dignity and pride as men mean infinitely more to us than answers to technological questions. Our technology is part of that dignity and pride. To begin to subsist on the superior technology of wholly alien creatures in space would finish us off spiritually and perhaps even physically. Such a dependence might mean sudden access to new sources of power that we cannot control to our advantage. We are already threatened by the power we have and still must learn to handle. We need controls much more than further power right now—humane controls, so that our power goes to serve long-range and widely shared human ends.

Technology is part of nature, since it is part of our nature. The only way we can have it fulfill its proper functions and *serve* us rather than defeat and threaten us as it does now is to subordinate it to human nature.

That demands some widely shared view of whence we come, what we are, and where (however tentative) we are to go.

We might try to make a world that most fosters our uniquely human characteristics—our knowing and creating, our science and art. Or what amounts to much the same thing, we might try to make a world in which we most realize our human potentialities, genetic and social. That would mean taking much better care of children than we now do. However complicated the thoughts with which I begin, however complex the social and political programs that seem necessary to me, I find them epitomized in the simple thought: a better world for children. Or to complete the thought: a better world for fewer children.

PANEL DISCUSSION

BROOKS. In this commentary I intend to examine more closely some of the implications of Wald's general propositions. My purpose is not to disagree with him but to indicate that the issues he raises are not as simple and tractable as he makes them appear.

Science versus Technology

Wald sharply differentiates between science, the effort to know, and technology, the effort to use knowledge for human purposes. He also differentiates between creation, the generation of an idea or a prototype, and production, the reproduction of the embodiment of an idea or prototype in repetitive actions or material objects. If his intention is to protect the scientific and creative process from social interference, and in particular from the modern heresy that the generator of new knowledge should suppress knowledge or research that some collective judgment says is likely to be misapplied, then I am in full agreement with him. I associate myself with Sidney Hook when he says:

To suggest that because free enterprise must be subjected to necessary limitations, therefore free inquiry must be subject to limitations is not only false, but mischievously false. . . . The right to pursue truth wherever it leads is far and away of greater significance than the right to pursue free enterprise.[5]

In asserting this proposition it is essential to distinguish between limitations on the subject matter or conclusions of research and limitations on the methods and techniques used. Freedom of inquiry does not preclude limitations on methods of inquiry that violate ethical norms or cause injury or pain to living beings when such injury or pain is out of proportion to the scientific value of the knowledge to be gained.

Freedom of inquiry is more complicated to defend today than it was fifty years ago. The differences between science and technology have been steadily fading. In the nineteenth century science and technology seemed to be two separate, weakly interacting streams of activity. Today they form something more like a continuous distribution, with strong interaction both ways.

In the first place, most science today is sponsored, and the sponsor and performer almost always have different purposes. Even the purest science costs money, so its advance depends on finding some mutual interest between sponsor and performer. This necessity for striking a bargain between patron and scientist has never been wholly absent, but it is accentuated by the current large scale of the scientific enterprise, especially when tax funds are used. Sponsorship creates pressures to use research results in ways that serve the purposes of the sponsor in order to justify continuing patronage. This pressure is aggravated by such actions as the passage of the Mansfield Amendment, which requires direct applicability to military functions as a condition for support of basic research by the Department of Defense.[6] The spirit underlying this amendment is spreading rapidly to other mission-oriented agencies in Washington and in slightly more subtle ways even to the National Science Foundation. To the degree that science has to justify itself directly and continually by the social outcomes of its results, it loses some of its distinctness from technology and its claim to ethical neutrality.

In the second place, science is increasingly dependent on technology for its tools and instruments. Many tools of crucial importance to the advance of pure science have been derived from or at least perfected as a result of military interest. Examples include the computer, satellites for weather or astronomical observations, radars for the study of planetary astronomy, and microwave components for the study of the electromagnetic properties of matter.

The converse is also true; instruments developed purely for research sometimes find applications undreamed of by their originators. The principles of image intensification developed for astronomy, for example, have found their way into night-vision devices for jungle warfare.

In the third place, a whole new area of pure science, the science of the artificial, is developing. This science, often described under the generic term cybernetics, deals not with nature but with the constructions of man. It includes automatic-control theory, information theory, the abstract theory of computing machines, and similar topics. It is truly a pure science, pursued for its own intrinsic intellectual interest. Yet it has important applications from the guidance of missiles to the control of national economies. Is the pursuit of truth less pure in the science of the artificial than in one of the natural sciences? At what point does the science of the artificial become technology rather than science?

Knowledge is, of course, always ambivalent. It can be used for good or ill, and its use can seldom be foreseen with confidence. The greater the potential benefit of knowledge or technology, the greater its potential danger as well. Civilized life cannot continue on earth for more than another century without the exploitation of nuclear energy; yet no other discovery holds as great a threat to the survival of mankind. A single chemical discovery, DDT, has saved half a billion human lives in the last twenty-five years; yet many fear it has brought us to the edge of ecological disaster. Computers and data banks may offer us our only long-term hope of being able to understand and manage our complexly interacting societies; yet they may also hold grave threats to human freedom and individuality. Chemical incapacitating agents offer the possibility of more humane application of force in warfare with reduced loss of life and permanent injury; yet it is reported that in Vietnam tear gas has been used to drive people from protecting caves and bunkers to be slaughtered in large numbers by saturation bombing. Genetic manipulation may become essential in the future to limit the accumulation of an unacceptable burden of genetic defects in a human gene pool no longer exposed to natural selection; yet the possibilities of abuse of this power are enormous.

Thus there seems to be almost a natural complementarity in the powers for good and evil given us by science and technology. The more good we are capable of, the more evil we are also capable of, and the more awesome the burden of choice.

Needs, Goals, and Aspirations of Society

I find this enticing phrase a meaningless abstraction. Society itself is an abstraction, a misleading personification of a collective noun. Does society have any needs, goals, and aspirations apart from the sum of those of the individuals who comprise it? How and by whom are these goals to be ascertained? By a numerical majority? Or by a weighted average of individual views, with the weight assigned according to the degree to which each individual's life is affected, the intensity of his feelings, or his knowledge and wisdom? Who is to assign the weights and by what process? What happens when different groups hold mutually incompatible goals or have conflicting interests? What happens when a single individual has a set of inconsistent aspirations?

Almost all social policies, especially policies for application and dissemination of technology, have redistributive aspects. They redistribute political power, social status, and economic income. One man's gain is another man's loss. Rapid economic growth has kept these redistributive features relatively invisible, but they are now becoming more evident because of worldwide mass communications and transportation. Inequalities in society that have been taken for granted are no longer acceptable, and the improving lot of the lowest social and economic segments of our population lags behind rising expectations and aspirations. Economic growth itself adversely affects common interests such as the environment.

Technology has a way of calling our bluff on inconsistent aspirations. It shows up fuzzy thinking about society and about our own values. Recently I had occasion to review a list of national goals established at the beginning of the Kennedy administration in 1961, most of them involving in one way or another the application of physical or social technology. Many experts at the time regarded these goals as unrealistically ambitious and impractical. But the remarkable thing is that every one of them has been exceeded or improved upon. We landed men on the moon twice within the decade. We exceeded our targets of economic growth and reduced unemployment below what was thought possible, considering the high rate of new entries into the labor force. We secured a stable deterrent posture with the Soviet Union. We even achieved sufficient progress in world food production to make it possible to stave off mass starvation for the twenty-five years necessary to solve the population problem. Public attitudes toward population control have changed drastically, with impressive results in some places. The economic status of the Negro showed more progress in the last ten years than in the previous century, though the progress was less than it justly should have been. We exceeded all our targets for the percentage of young people in higher education and the production of Ph.D.'s in science and engineering. Yet somehow it has all turned sour, not because we failed but because we succeeded. Our successes created new expectations, new aspirations, and unforeseen side effects to the point where today's society resembles the fable of the sorcerer's apprentice.

Our modern urban crisis has been generated in part by a concatenation of several social programs, each one regarded as highly progressive, liberal, and democratic at the time of its introduction. The agricultural research and extension program included the use of DDT, which made it possible to grow cotton in the West; the federal housing program provided cheap money for middle-class home ownership in the suburbs; the federal highway program facilitated the decentralization of industry, and hence jobs, as well as suburban life; minimum wage laws made mechanization of Southern agriculture economically attractive; and the proliferation of social-welfare services in major urban centers made even the squalid life of the ghetto more attractive than Southern rural poverty.

Technology called our bluff by confronting us with the largely unforeseen consequences of policies adopted for the most humane and progressive reasons. That we turned the implementation of each of these social programs over to self-perpetuating bureaucracies, which proceeded in accordance with the narrow goals assigned them, does not basically change the problem. It was largely technology that made these bureaucracies so efficient. In an earlier age they would have failed and we would never have been confronted with the consequences of our success. The same story can be told of hundreds of other progressive aspirations: urban renewal, TVA (which encouraged strip mining), universal higher education (which exaggerated the exclusion of the poor and minorities), and television in every home (which showed the disadvantaged what they were missing). The frightening thing is that today we can set goals and achieve them before we know what has happened to us. We achieve them faster than we can accommodate to the consequences of our success.

This is why I am so allergic to the phrase "needs, goals, and aspirations of society." We can no longer afford the hells we are creating for ourselves by our good intentions. Much has been said recently about anticipating the consequences of technology and acting to avoid them. But I think focusing on technology gives a wrong emphasis. It is not the secondary consequences of technology but the secondary and hidden consequences of achieving our "needs, goals, and aspirations" that are killing us. We must devote a lot more hard intellectual effort to understanding all the implications and inner contradictions of our goals and aspirations; and we must continually adjust them as their achievement brings us new knowledge and insight.

Let me illustrate the problem of conflicting interests and values with an environmental example. We normally mean by the environment the out of doors; yet we spend most of our lives indoors and devote great ingenuity and energy consumption to maintaining the indoor environment. Everything we do to make our life indoors more comfortable adds to our use of power and hence to air pollution. Even our automobiles are air-conditioned, adding about 10 percent to gasoline consumption. New York may suffer an indoor environmental crisis this summer because public concern over its outdoor environment caused a construction delay in two major power plants needed to satisfy its power demands. Technology again called our bluff, confronting us with this dilemma between our indoor comforts and outdoor environment.

Decisions and the Producer

It is true that many decisions about the application and diffusion of technology are in large measure left to the producers. But I think this statement is a misleading oversimplification. Producers make profits because consumers buy their products. In this sense "those who will live with the products" are indeed party to the decision to produce them. Furthermore, the "producer" is another false abstraction. Producers are not only the owners of capital and the managers they employ, but also thousands of employees with a slightly different stake in the operation. The consumer-producer relation is bilateral. It is the third party affected by the outcome of the transaction but not a participant in the bargain whose interests lack representation.

The consumer may have a problem because he has been overpersuaded or because of incomplete knowledge of the product he is buying, a difficulty that increases as products become technologically more complex (for example, the mechanical safety of an automobile or the radiation protection in a color television set). Thus the real problem is to equalize the bargaining of consumer and producer in bilateral consumer-producer transactions and to represent the interests of third parties, including the general public and future generations. This is the well-known problem of external costs, with the classic example being pollution. Pollution is an "external" cost, a cost to society, which normally does not have to be borne by either the producer or the consumer. What is worse, the least responsible producer and the consumer who buys his product at a cheaper price are both rewarded at the expense of the more responsible producer and his customers. Similarly the state or locality whose restrictions on pollution are most lax attracts industry at the expense of more socially responsible states or localities. The geographical relocation of industry is often simply a way of exporting social costs.

There are many ways of internalizing such external costs—through regulatory standards, through taxation of polluting activities, and through judicial interpretation.[7] But these methods require sophisticated knowledge and understanding of manufacturing processes and environmental effects. The external costs must be identified and quantified well enough to be assigned to the producer through decreased profits and to the consumer through increased prices. Whereas in the past science has served primarily as the handmaiden of technology, a source of ideas for new technological development, in the future it will serve increasingly as the conscience of technology, the intellectual basis for the computation of external costs, the prediction of environmental implications, and the estimation of the redistributive effects of technological and social decisions.

Wald is dissatisfied with the representative process because its outcomes are not consistent with his own view of society's needs. But he dodges the question of how and by whom society's true needs are to be determined. Whose interests are to be considered and how much relative weight is to be given to them? In his examples of the ABM and the SST, in addition to the interests of the people who will be affected by the sonic boom or the (speculative and problematical) escalation of the arms race, there are the interests of the employees of the organizations that design and build these systems. These employees often are concentrated in a few areas of the country. The Boeing Company alone accounts for 35 percent of the industrial employment in the Seattle area. More than 35 percent of all federal research and development money is spent in California. These facts are potent hidden factors in the process of technological choice, factors that would exist with equal or greater force if the work were performed by government employees rather than by private industry under contracts. They must also exist in the USSR. These factors should not justify the perpetuation of technological effort that is undesirable in a broader or longer-term perspective, but they cannot be ignored as long as we have representative political processes.

The problem is that large specialized bureaucracies or bureaucratic networks are built up to achieve objectives set for them by society with little regard to their future. Their drive toward self-perpetuation and growth becomes an important political factor in almost all major choices made by our society. We have an ineluctable tendency to find new justifications for continuing to do what we have learned to do well. Consideration of goals tends to take a back seat to the preservation of institutions. I know of no modern society that has found a solution to this problem. Options presented for political decision are strongly conditioned by the capabilities of bureaucracies created in response to earlier decisions and demands. This is an unfortunate aspect of the inherent conservatism of the organic evolution of society, which Wald regards so highly. And it is not only associated with technology. It is a phenomenon of specialization, a price in social inflexibility that we pay for the division of labor—a form of social overadaptation!

We badly need a means for redeployment of technical and other specialized efforts that does not leave resources and manpower unemployed. Certain skills utilized in the ABM program, for example, might be applied to the development of an effective advanced system for controlling air traffic or a sophisticated national system for medical information.

Many people are highly critical of the space program as a waste of resources. Yet the space program may be fully worth its cost to society if it politically facilitates diversion of technical manpower and resources away from projects like the ABM and the SST. At least the secondary effects of the space program are relatively benign. I, together with other scientists, criticized the space program in its early days because I saw it as competing with more humanly useful or intellectually rewarding scientific activity. In the cold light of political reality, I think I should have seen it rather as competing with large weapons systems and further escalation of the arms race.

A Sense of Purpose

I agree with Wald that formulation of "some commonly accepted sense of national meaning and purpose" is one of our pressing psychological needs at the present time. Its lack is what produces boredom and dissatisfaction among the young. Earlier in the twentieth century this sense of purpose was unfortunately provided by two world wars. These wars, horrible as they were in human cost, provided a focus and a sense of community and common purpose beyond individual fulfillment, which youth in every generation seems to require. But the social cost has become entirely prohibitive. Among modern industrial societies only Japan seems to have retained some sense of community and high social morale in a peacetime situation.[8]

The greatest problem of our time is to find a moral and psychological equivalent of war that is constructive rather than destructive.

In the past our society has regarded work highly because it produced material goods that people needed. The ultimate test of useful work has always been the test of the market. Even though employment in the nonprofit sector is now nearly equal to that in the profit sector, services that cannot be submitted to the test of the market are still held suspect. In postindustrial society new tests of the validity of work may have to be found. A test of economic activity may be its ability not only to make its way in the market but also to provide psychologically satisfying work for employees. How can such a test be translated into economic measures? Science clearly would rate very high.

If we are to achieve some sense of common purpose, we will need a great deal of help from science. Science does not by itself provide the values, for it is value free or at least should strive to be so, but it can tell us which values are achievable and at what cost. We need science to tell us both where we are going and where we can go if we will. In achieving the Apollo program's objective, we had not only the political will but also most of the necessary building blocks. The objective was both popularly exciting and scientifically credible. We need a great deal more scientific effort to make other possible goals of our society intellectually credible. This is unfortunately much harder to do with social and political than with technological achievements, in part because we lack the capability to foresee with any confidence the consequences of social policies.

Green Fields and Quiet Rivers

Wald harks back to our pastoral past, but his "privacy and quiet," "clean air and water," and "chance to walk through green fields beside quiet rivers" formerly were reserved for only a tiny minority of the human population. Darwin was independently wealthy and Rayleigh was an aristocrat. But most of humanity lived in abject poverty, misery, moral degradation, and ignorance. Nothing in the modern ghetto compares with conditions at the turn of the century in London. The worst rural poverty in the American South is sheer luxury beside the conditions in Ireland at the time of the potato famine.[9] Unfortunately history is written by and about a tiny fraction of the human population, and today we tend to compare the life of a large majority with the life of a tiny minority several generations ago.

Concern with the deterioration of the natural environment owing to the onrush of industrialization is not new. It was pervasive, even in the United States, throughout the nineteenth century. As early as 1864 a book by George Marsh, recently republished,[10] pointed out the ecological dangers of continuing industrialization. It contains many statements and forecasts reminiscent of today.

Yet the modern threat to the environment is of a new order of magnitude, even though the time scale of the more alarmist predictions is somewhat exaggerated. Extrapolation of current energy and metals consumption and the current output of material goods with current technology leads to catastrophe within several decades. Ecological disaster is a more serious limitation on human population growth than the food supply or the exhaustion of nonrenewable resources.

But I am not one of those who believe that all economic growth should cease forthwith. It seems highly improbable that we can achieve zero population growth (except possibly in a few advanced nations) before the end of the century, considering the extreme youth and lengthening life expectancy of all contemporary populations. I do not believe political stability can be maintained either within developed nations or between developed countries and the rest of the world without continuing economic growth. Indeed I suspect the current revulsion against economic growth and the whole concept of the affluent society is a rather provincial conceit of intellectuals who have attained unprecedented affluence and influence in American society relatively recently.

BELL. In the preface to the *Lyrical Ballads,* Wordsworth wrote that "Poetry is the breath and finer spirit of knowledge; it is the impassioned expression which is in the countenance of all science." Professor Wald's paper breathes that spirit. It is an "impassioned expression." And he makes the claim for science that Wordsworth made for poetry when he said that "Poetry is the first and last of all knowledge." I admire the paper—as poetry—but I cannot accept all of its claims for science.

The paper is full of sweet simplicities. It sketches an Arcadian view of science as full of romance as the pastoral fantasies were of the innocence of youth. Here is science in the single pursuit of truth, science as the forlorn domain of the individual genius, falling before the sorcerer of technology. It is appealing, partly true, and irrelevant.

Wald idealizes science. Science is good because Truth is good. The difficulty with this view is that he treats Truth as an abstract noun, a grail standing at the end of a rocky road. The point is that in life there are many *truths* and they sometimes conflict with each other; also, as William James said, truth is not an entity of state existing unto itself, but a *relational* term referring to something.

Wald tends to "absolutize" science and make it a final good. Yet so many of our difficulties in the past have come from the partisans of absolute truths—particularly religious truths—who brooked no rivals to their conceptions or sanctifications. In the history of moral theology, one lesson that skeptics, stoics, and humanists have learned is that whatever absolutes have been stated, including the Ten Commandments, no man can state with certainty that any particular instance in the here-and-now on earth exemplifies the heavenly absolute. That is why the moral casuists long ago interposed conscience between moral absolute and law and gave conscience the primacy of moral decision. Every moral instance, as Kierkegaard put it in his parable of Abraham and Isaac in *Fear and Trembling*, is a personal decision that each man has to make: was it the Angel of God I heard? As an absolute Wald would like to see a principle of the inviolability of the human germ plasm much like our principle of the inviolability of human life. He wants to see, as we all do, the intrinsic continuity of man. But what do we do about the desire for abortion-law reform and the demand that each woman herself make the decision to retain or abort life? Is there a guide *in science* to this question?

If I were a philosopher, I might say that Professor Wald risks the hubris of scientism. If I were a theologian. I might say that he risks the sin of idolatry. Since I am a sociologist, I can only say that he is guilty of not making correct distinctions. Let me establish some distinctions in the form of a few apothegms:

- Science is a game against nature or things.
- Social life is a game between persons.
- Science deals with knowledge.
- Social life—as politics—deals with interests and values.

If the social world just had to deal with evil and greedy men (as if some men were evil and others not), we would have reached Utopia long ago. But social life has two basic, often intractable problems: people want different things and disagree about how to get them; and a change in one value of an interdependent system levies a cost on some other. The problems are how to adjudicate differences in interests and values (are there rational solutions?) and how to assess the comparative costs of change (can there be trade-offs?).

Let me illustrate these dilemmas from our current concern with pollution and the environment. Agricultural productivity has grown remarkably during the past two decades, averaging 6 to 7 percent a year. Some of the enormous increase in food supply has fed starving areas of the world, such as India. This productivity resulted from the discovery and use of cheap nitrates. But run-off from these nitrates has polluted many rivers. Reducing pollution would probably mean lowering productivity and increasing food costs. How much of a trade-off do we want to make?

Several years ago the Lindsay administration in New York City responded to the pollution problem by barring the use of incinerators in large apartment houses. As a result, the amount of garbage to be collected increased about 40 percent. To deal with the added waste, garbage trucks were concentrated in Manhattan, but when a huge snowstorm smothered the entire city Queens found itself without trucks to carry the snow away and was tied up for almost ten days. John Lindsay almost lost an election because recalcitrant nature refused to recognize the system distribution of garbage trucks.

Finally, the concern with air pollution has prompted much talk of an electric automobile. But this would require greater electrical generating capacity nationally and would increase the likelihood of thermal pollution of the waters.

None of this is a counsel of despair. But it points up the difficulties of a linked ecological-technological-economic system. There are only relative solutions—at costs.

These problems are all embedded in three political-theoretical issues I regard as central to the times:

1. *The rise of nonmarket public decision making.* Increasingly the concerns of social policy (health, housing, environment) cannot be handled by the market but require public decision making. One cannot buy his share of clean air in the market. Housing needs public subsidy. The adjudication of externalities requires governmental mechanisms. The virtue of the market is that it disperses responsibility. If a product does not sell or if the prices of farm products drop because of slackened demand, no one set of persons is to blame. But in nonmarket decision making the decision makers are visible and one knows whose ox will be gored. The results are conflicts over such issues as the location of jetports, the conservation of forests, jobs for a local community, or the routing of new highways.

2. *The increasingly technical character of decisions.* Any of these issues not only has a value component but a technical aspect. A decision regarding a supersonic jet is tied up with the balance-of-payments problem. The reduction of particulate matter in the atmosphere means an increase in solid-waste disposal. The increasingly systemic nature of such decisions brings to the fore the systems analyst, operations researcher, and technologist as expert.

3. *The "impossibility" of a rational social decision.* Any effort at communal consensus is an effort to create a combined social choice out of the discordant individual preferences of individuals. But the idea of a social decision that can satisfy all is an illusion. This has been demonstrated theoretically by Kenneth Arrow in his "impossibility theorem," which shows that no social decision can amalgamate diverse preferences as an individual can rationally order his preferences.[11] Any good social scientist wants to use theory as a benchmark for judging an empirical reality, and the fact that a rational social choice is impossible is deeply disturbing.

Where then do we stand? The relation of technical to political decisions will be a crucial area of public policy in the next decades. The politician and the political public will have to become increasingly versed in the technical character of policy and the ramified impact of decisions as systems are extended. (An econometric study of alternative public investment programs is not as popularly digestible as the views of Adam Smith.) And the technical intelligentsia will have to learn to question the unanalyzed assumptions about efficiency and rationality that underlie their techniques. For in the end, the problems are directly political. The hopes of a particular kind of rationality that says decisions can be reduced to cost-benefit analysis must fall before politics.

Politics, in the sense that we understand it, always precedes and often upsets the rational. The rational, in the administrative and economizing sense of the word, is the routinized, settled, orderly proceeding by rules in an effort to get greatest efficiency of output at least cost. Much of life in a complex society must be rational. We do not haggle with the airline company or railroad over the fare in going to Washington as we might with a taxi driver in the Levant. But politics is haggling, or else it is force. In Washington one haggles over the priorities of the society, the distribution of incomes, and the burden of taxation. In place of a rational, objective scaling of social utilities, there is what every politician knows in his bones —bargaining between persons. Bargaining depends on people's willingness to follow the rules of the game and make trade-offs in their wants and demands. These conflicts of interests and values are games between persons, not games against nature.

What is the role of social science in trying to deal with social change? Professor Wald has posed the issue in what is to me peculiarly strained terms, as between natural selection and technological specification. Since he is deeply suspicious of our ability to design social institutions without becoming overly rigid, he opts for a reliance on the natural processes of adaptation and evolution.

The choice puts him, historically, in peculiar company, for in the period from 1870 to 1900 a species of Darwinism did rule American society. It was the time when Justice Oliver Wendell Holmes accused the Supreme Court of "writing Herbert Spencer's *Social Statics* into the law of the land" because the Court had struck down social regulation of hazardous factory work, child labor laws, regulation of overtime hours, and the like. Darwinism ruled American society during the period of *laissez faire*. It was a period of reckless spoliation of resources against which even our present prodigality pales.

One of the major social problems today is that what an individual wants for himself becomes a nightmare in the aggregate. The individual desires the freedom, mobility, and convenience of a private automobile; yet in the aggregate the roads become choked. If we were to follow the principle of natural selection, the biggest and most powerful cars (and one would then buy tanks) could crowd the small compacts off the highways and the socially fitted would survive. I exaggerate, but the principle is clear.

There are two further and more important sociological reasons why natural selection and evolutionary adaptation are self-defeating. These are the obvious and almost trite points that we live in an age of accelerated technological change and that what distinguishes our social problems from previous generations is a change of scale. We do not have time to adapt to these changes; and if time was our only resource we would truly be living in a Hobbesian world.

I share Professor Wald's skepticism of technological specifications. I do not believe in a technocratic hubris that one can design a world for people. But I do think we can look ahead and sketch *alternative futures*. Rather than drift in a world of change, we can seek to chart the evolutionary possibilities ahead. We need to anticipate problems of population, health, and ecology rather than deal with them *ad hoc* as they arise. We sketch alternative futures not to design a world for people but to widen the sphere of choice and to make people aware of the costs and consequences of whatever choice is made.

Let me give a specific example. The social map of the United States was reworked after World War II by the growth of suburbia. But this was only possible because of public policy, which guaranteed mortgages, gave veterans the privilege of very low down payments, and allowed interest charges to be deducted from income taxes. Public policy presumably reflected a state of social preferences that combined habit with the vested interests of the construction industry. This resulted in a suburbia of unattached, scattered houses with a large waste of land and a costly development of roads, water, and sewerage services. No one sat down and asked as a matter of conscious policy if we wanted to encourage a movement from central cities to suburbs; or if we did, what alternative modes of social and ecological organization were possible; or what would be the alternative costs (utilizing a full social-cost matrix) of a pattern of detached houses, of cluster-type developments, or of high-rise apartments in green parks. I am not saying that people should live in one or another kind of suburbia; that is their choice to make. But I do say that public policy should not be shaped without a conscious debate about choices and alternative social arrangements.

Knowledge is a handmaiden of choice. Its function is to clarify alternatives and specify costs and consequences. The human enterprise is a problem of social organization. Without an effective structure that allows men to organize their lives freely, with a sense of justice and effectiveness, we surely fail. Our problem is to make clear the roads before us and to make conscious our choices. There is an old remark from the Talmud that tells us what will happen if we do not. It says: If you don't know where you are going, any road will take you there.

FISK. Professor Wald has waived the right to respond to the discussants so that we may take questions from the audience. But he does reserve the privilege of bringing up points during the discussion.

GREENBERGER. He is going to have that opportunity, because some of the questions from the audience reopen points made by the discussants. But before getting to those questions, I would like to start with one dealing with computers and communications technology. Dan Ross, president of Ross Telecommunications Engineering Corporation, asks if the use of information systems and telecommunications to improve and spread education is not one of our most urgent national and worldwide goals. If so, why do we tolerate the extraordinary delay (1960 to 1970) in deploying the most useful result of our space program, the geostationary communications satellite?

BELL. I do not share the premise. Technology is not the prime problem today in education. There are many, but the major one is simply that most education is still geared to subject matter and telling people about things rather than teaching them how to conceptualize and continually reorganize knowledge.

BROOKS. I would add that it is wrong to define education as a goal in itself. I think one of the troubles with education today is that we have assumed it was good just because it was education, without examining its purpose.

GREENBERGER. Here is a question addressed to George Wald by Bruce Wolk, a mathematician at the United States Public Health Service. He asks whether the consumer-producer relation as put forth by Harvey Brooks is not a myth. If the producer simply produced what the consumer wanted, why would he bombard the consumer with messages saying he needs more and more?

WALD. I agree! I think there has been a lot of dealing in myths. Right now a plea is being made to the General Motors Corporation to do something more in the way of recognizing the public interest. All that is being asked is that the corporation include the public interest in its statement of purposes and add three public representatives to its board of directors. This is hardly an attack on the General Motors Corporation.

A few years ago there was a blackout throughout the whole Northeast that darkened thirty thousand square miles and made thirty million people helpless. We need to establish a national grid. In certain regions of this country there is an overproduction of power. If the country's power systems were interlinked, no brownout would be necessary next summer in New York.

Why is the country not interlinked? It is vital for national defense, but we are not getting a national grid because: (1) private companies like to take care of their own business and putting them into a grid would force them to cooperate with other businesses; (2) it is an expense, and electric power is in competition with gas and oil and does not want the expense; (3) it would link private and public power, and this private power wants to avoid at all costs. So we accept enormous military vulnerability and do without the national grid because other considerations rule the game.

BROOKS. I do not want to get into a technical discussion of these matters, but I think Wald grossly oversimplifies.

GREENBERGER. I will group the next two questions. Stephen J. Tauber, chief of the Information Science Section at the National Bureau of Standards, asks if Wald includes the experiments in human physiology and pathology conducted in Central and Eastern Europe during the early 1940's in his remark that science is altogether good. Martha Lilienthal, a programmer-analyst at Leasco Corporation, notes that Wald spoke of the inviolability of the human germ plasm and also of science (as the pursuit of knowledge) as not being subject to regulation. Should scientists attempt to understand the control of human germ plasm, even so far as growing a test-tube baby?

WALD. I shall take the second question first. An increase in our knowledge and understanding is always more desirable than ignorance, although there are humanitarian limitations on the kinds of experiments that should be performed. There is a great deal of misconception about test-tube babies. I believe that one of these days, probably within the next twenty-five years, someone, somewhere (perhaps in several places) will put the right molecules in juxtaposition under the right circumstances and will observe them organizing themselves into a little blob of living material. *He* will not have done it; the *molecules* will have done it. The thought that one is going to make amoebas in this way is nonsense. Amoebas make amoebas. And people will go on making people in the good old-fashioned way.

Is birth control essentially incompatible with free human reproduction? No, not at all. We need free, universal contraception and abortion. But this does not violate the evolutionary process unless it is done *selectively,* introducing specifications, and saying who may reproduce, how much, and who may not.

On the first question, those were wretched experiments conducted on hapless persons under Nazi auspices in the 1940's. It is possible to do wretched experiments even on dogs and frogs. There are limitations on experimentation coming out of one's respect for living things and one's reluctance to make them suffer. Recognizing those limitations, those were bad experiments. But I still say all knowledge is good.

BROOKS. I think there is a difference between limitations on the methods by which one gets knowledge and limitations on the pursuit of knowledge itself. I think this is the distinction that George Wald is trying to make.

GREENBERGER. Joel Margolis, a Congressional fellow in Senator Hatfield's office, asks Daniel Bell how we can encourage the public debate (for example, in Congress) on the societal implications of technological changes and scientific discoveries. When we are able to determine the sex of children ahead of time, for example, what will it mean to marriage and career patterns if 70 percent of American families want boys? Or if we develop the ability to implant artificial organs, who will get those organs? The rich? The needy? The physically handicapped? Or the physically well qualified? These are some of the questions. There will be many technological developments with great consequences—some good, some bad. How can we encourage debate on these consequences?

BELL. We face some of these issues already. Today in many hospitals there is a very real problem in kidney transplant operations of who gets the kidneys. Many hospitals have lay boards to decide because doctors do not want the responsibility. The lay boards agonize over these decisions. I do not know any other way it can be done.

The notion that people feel helpless or remote from institutions today always puzzles me. I think it is rather that people before were isolated and that modern mass communications have made us very aware of this. We are so completely aware today of all our problems that we are stunned. We have an overload and must sort out the relevant questions and try to deal with them.

This is being done in a variety of ways. The present symposium is one of them. As another example, the American Academy of Arts and Sciences has sponsored meetings and groups on the year 2000. There is no single process other than the very natural process of debate and the effort to translate the results back through political mechanisms to those who have responsibility for making decisions.

GREENBERGER. This last question is really a point of information. It was submitted by Dale Thomson, director of Canadian studies at The Johns Hopkins School of Advanced International Studies. He refers to Wald's example of an electrical blackout on the East Coast and makes two points: (1) the cause was the grid arrangement with Canada and the breakdown came in Canada; (2) the Canadian power involved was produced by a public corporation, Ontario Hydro.

WALD. Mr. Thomson's remark just demonstrates the inadequacy of present arrangements. The initial cause of the Northeast blackout of 1965, according to the Federal Power Commission, was an improperly set relay at the Adam Beck plant operated by the Hydroelectric Power Commission of Ontario. This relay had not been reset for several years. It shut off, overloading the other lines, which also shut off, sending a power surge into New York State where the "split" occurred, resulting in a cascading blackout. A well-constructed and properly maintained grid would have taken care of the situation. This is exactly what a grid is for.

Since the Northeast blackout in November 1965 there have been thirty-seven other major cascading power failures in this country. Only three areas in the United States apparently have proper grids. They are the Tennessee Valley Authority system, the Bonneville Power Administration, and a grid of private power companies in Ohio and Indiana.

There exist linkages among other power systems, public and private, but those linkages are too weak and frequently too roundabout. I think I have stated the reasons why they remain that way.

DINNER DISCUSSION

GREENBERGER. I would like to ask Raymond Bauer to tell us about the activities and plans of the National Goals Research Staff at the White House, which he serves as senior consultant (chief professional). Many of us are not too well informed about this.

BAUER. Our concepts are still evolving. The original statement of the staff's purpose was drafted for President Nixon by Patrick Moynihan and some people on the Urban Affairs Council. It expressed a desire to establish a unit in the White House giving the executive branch the kind of capability for long-term planning that the *Harvard Business Review* says resides in business. The statement called for the development of better measures of social change, forecasts of problems and options, and the gathering of data relevant to the study of national goals. It did *not* call for a goal-setting mechanism. Previous commissions for setting goals have suffered from being elite groups, and their conclusions have tended to be too abstract and without effect. We hope to encourage and to some extent help responsible outside groups set goals, then synthesize what they say and report back both internally to the White House and externally to the public. We are currently working with the National Industrial Conference Board and the National Planning Association, which both have goal-setting operations, and we plan to work with the Bicentennial Commission and try to stimulate state and local governments to look ahead. Contrary to many people's expectations, we are not going to make our own statement on what national goals should be.

Participants: Raymond A. Bauer, The White House; Daniel Bell, Harvard University; Harvey Brooks, Harvard University; Richard A. Carpenter, The Library of Congress; Larkin H. Farinholt, The Alfred P. Sloan Foundation; James Fisk, Bell Telephone Laboratories; Eugene G. Fubini, private consultant; Sterling Hendricks, Department of Agriculture; Hugh Loweth, Bureau of the Budget; Emanuel G. Mesthene, Harvard University; Charles A. Mosher, House of Representatives; Harold Orlans, The Brookings Institution; S. Fred Singer, Department of the Interior; Joel A. Snow, National Science Foundation; George Wald, Harvard University; James Webb, private practice; Dael Wolfle, University of Washington; Harry Woolf, The Johns Hopkins University; Martin Greenberger, chairman, The Johns Hopkins University.

We are enjoined to make a report each year to the President, who will then probably make a report to the public. We shall be reporting on a whole series of ongoing national debates on the question of how this country should grow. In the area of technology assessment, for example, a decision to have more stringent requirements controlling the introduction of new technology may have an effect on the gross national product. In each of seven such areas we shall detail the policy options and their costs and benefits.

ORLANS. In a press appearance following President Nixon's announcement of the National Goals Research Staff, Patrick Moynihan said that prophetic men have always been able to foresee problems but until now there has been no agency of government to listen. He seemed to be contradicting his own words in the last chapter of *The Maximum Feasible Misunderstanding,* where he asserted that we could not possibly have foreseen all the disasters that befell us in the war on poverty.

BELL. I am not sure what the contradiction is. One can foresee and identify in a broad way certain kinds of problems without being able to predict which option will be taken. One does not know the play of forces on those in a postion to choose, nor what they will decide.

MOSHER. I believe the phrase "technology assessment" was invented in our Subcommittee on Science, Research, and Development, although we use it improperly. What we are really concerned with is assessing the *effects* of technology rather than the technology itself. Congressman Daddario and I are currently in the process of introducing legislation designed to create a new office for technology assessment to aid decision making in Congress. We feel that the Library of Congress, the Legislative Reference Service, and the General Accounting Office are not the right places to put this new office. It would have a staff of about fifty people and a beginning annual budget of about five million dollars. Its staff would not make the assessments themselves, but would administer contracts with many (primarily nongovernmental) sources. Congress now seriously lacks the necessary information for intelligent decisions in areas related to technology.

HENDRICKS. In technological assessment, existing technologies require as much attention as potential ones. Old technologies are better understood with respect to necessary trade-offs and unexpected side effects.

BELL. I do not believe that any technology assessment can be meaningful unless one is prepared to attach tax penalties to certain technological introductions. We accelerate change and growth in our society by allowing tax inducements, such as investment credits, but we are very loath to assess tax penalties when a private profit results from a social cost. If Du Pont introduces Corfam and as a consequence wipes out a section of the leather industry, thereby creating unemployment in particular geographical areas of society (such as Gloversville), then a charge should be levied against Du Pont to cover its part in the overall social cost. Similarly, the natural gas industry should have shared financial responsibility with the federal government for the depression of the coal industry resulting from the widespread adoption of natural gas.

MESTHENE. But if we start adopting a policy of internalizing all social costs, we might wind up killing innovation. We must continue to allow for public subsidies and social payments of the cost when there is a widespread social gain.

BELL. But then it is a matter of social policy as to which costs are internalized and which are not. Someone has to decide.

ORLANS. I have a more generalized criticism of technology assessment as it is practiced today. All of the material I have seen produced by or for the Subcommittee on Science, Research, and Development has been extraordinarily neutral, deliberately avoiding any possibility of criticism for wanting to suppress technology. If technology assessment is to have any public or social value, it must make judgments such as, "on balance this technology is a public good and should be encouraged," or "that technology must be checked until certain specified measures are taken."

FUBINI. I am completely unwilling to accept this dichotomy. The issue is not whether a technology is good or bad. The issue is what are the second-order consequences of the technology. That is what the Congress needs to know.

SNOW. Technology assessments are not only fed to Congress; they are also injected into an interacting sea of special interests. These special interests will pick out of an objective, value-free report those things they want to fight about or push for their own advantage. The reports provide a common base of factual information for discussions that otherwise tend to be largely emotional. Even the most innocuous report on noise from subsonic aircraft is interpreted very differently by someone from an aircraft company and someone living next to an airport. The report provides them with a common base of information to argue about.

SINGER. On Bell's point, we are beginning to internalize social costs in the area where technology affects the environment. We have not gone far enough. We do not yet charge the companies that manufacture aluminum beer cans, for instance, but the trend will, I hope, go to completion within the next few years.

BAUER. I have not yet seen any satisfactory analysis of the range of consequences of internalizing the externalities. A restructuring of industry in this country is one likely result.

SINGER. Yes, this must be the consequence if people are really willing to face the issues. In attacking the problem of air pollution produced by the internal-combustion engine, for example, we are now seeing glowing statements that we have licked the problem. This is just not so. The cost of the little device added to the engine may be only on the order of three hundred dollars, but then there are the costs of inspection and maintenance which, I am told, result in a national cost of six billion dollars a year—year after year. This does not count the cost of taking the car to the inspector or taking it to the garage (and trying to get it back the same day). If we are going to be spending sixty billion dollars in ten years, then the rational view is that we should be devoting a fraction of this to developing or looking for alternatives, maybe radical alternatives.

WALD. I believe current discussions of the environment and pollution are of the highest importance, but they can distract us from other important problems, including the war, the draft, inflation, and the arms budget. There is a particular danger that the interest in antipollution will be turned into a new multibillion dollar industry, supported necessarily with federal funds. Our biggest polluter is the motor car, and that means tackling the auto industry and the oil industry. The lumber industry is a great polluter, as is the power industry. The temptation will be great to allow these industries to go on polluting and to make a great new business of coping with that pollution. Indeed in these days of conglomerates, it could end up being in the same business—one division of it polluting and another removing the pollution, both ultimately at the public expense.

The environment has been called a "motherhood issue." Everybody is for motherhood, though one can even get too much of that! But loving the environment is not enough. The only proper, social way to deal with pollution is to stop it at its source. That will not be easy or pleasant, but it is the only measure that ultimately will work.

WEBB. Much of the discussion of technology assessment seems to suffer from the same kind of mistaken belief as the premise that we can fine-tune the economy. The technology assessments by the National Academies of Sciences and Engineering have fatal weaknesses in not having anyone who had really administered anything think through everything called for in implementation. In our rolling readjustment form of democracy we may eventually find a need for *guidelines*. Maybe the French have something to teach us here. When we decontrolled prices at the end of World War II, some people were badly hurt because the massive array of federal statistics concealed problems rather than revealed them. This is likely to be true with the best of technology assessment. Along with guidelines we need pilot models of action programs so designed that feedback can be used to guide and effect change. In place of our exaggerated concern for finding at the very beginning the best solution to every problem, we need a means to start out in a promising direction with the ability to change course as we learn the terrain.

GREENBERGER. You were very hopeful early in NASA's history that the space program would have socially beneficial fallout.

WEBB. There have been important advances in the specialized uses of computers, the science of simulation, the communication of large masses of data in real time (with automatic switching and automatic monitoring), the art of photography, the scanning capability of the electron microscope, and in many other areas. These advances may not all have come directly out of the space program, but they did come out of the atmosphere produced by the space program.

MESTHENE. I think the greatest argument in support of our going to the moon is the simple achievement of going to the moon. Trying to justify the space program on the basis of fallout strikes me as using the weaker argument. The moment you go to this weaker argument you raise the question, "Is this the most efficient way to have gotten this fallout?"

WEBB. I do not think one raises the question at all. We did not try to justify the moon shot by fallout. We said that to increase the capabilities of the United States for operations in space would require developing every discipline in science and technology to the utmost. This was a second or third order of benefit. We never said it was the justification for the program. We said it was a consequence of the program, and we conducted the program to maximize it.

WOOLF. Webb's reference to French guidelines reminds me of the concern in France in the late eighteenth and early nineteenth centuries about the problem of the French canal system, which the Academy of Sciences addressed by setting up prizes for original work in the mathematics of fluid flow. But the problems were not solved or solvable, and the canal system was built on an *ad hoc* basis using pilot-plant notions. This failure helped to reshape the whole enterprise of science as set by the academy. The problem of technology assessment was faced by the academy and generated an extensive literature that has hardly been explored for its relevance to situations we are currently facing.

WEBB. The guidelines provide a way to get feedback that is essential in the absence of accurate prediction. We got feedback in the space program by using what I call the science of simulation. We put three billion dollars into test and simulation equipment to obtain reliability in our systems.

MOSHER. As a politician I am acutely aware of one type of fallout from the space program: a very heightened level of public expectation of what technology and the art of management can accomplish. The public has a new order of confidence. In a way it is a dangerous expectation. The public is expecting the government to alleviate the problem of water pollution much more rapidly than is possible. People in my district are saying that if we can put a man on the moon and bring him back successfully, as we did in the 1960's, then in the 1970's we ought to be able to put a man in Lake Erie and bring him back healthy. I am afraid this sudden public assurance that we can meet these problems will result in disillusionment and cynicism, perhaps hindering us in carrying through the tremendous long-range effort really required.

REFERENCES

1. "What We Must Do," *Science*, 166 (1969): 1115–21.
2. "Survival of Plants and Man," in *Challenge For Survival*, ed. Pierre Dansereau, Columbia University Press, 1970.
3. Hermann Hesse, *The Glass Bead Game* (*Magister Ludi*), Holt, Rinehart & Winston, 1969 (orig. published in German, 1943); Gunther Stent, *The Coming of the Golden Age: A View of the End of Progress*, Natural History Press, 1969.
4. "Search for Artificial Stellar Sources of Infrared Radiation," *Science*, 131 (1960): 1667.
5. "Barbarism, Virtue, and the University," *Public Interest*, no. 15 (Spring 1969), pp. 23–39.
6. Public Law 91–121, 1969 Department of Defense Authorization, section 203.
7. Milton Katz, "The Function of Tort Liability in Technology Assessment," *University of Cincinnati Law Review*, 38 (1969): 587–662.
8. Howard Van Zandt, "Japanese Culture and the Business Boom," *Foreign Affairs*, 48 (1970): 344–57.
9. Cecil Woodham-Smith, *The Great Hunger*, Harper & Row, 1962.
10. G. P. Marsh, *Man and Nature*, ed. David Lowenthal, Harvard University Press, Belknap Press, John Harvard Library, 1965 (orig. published 1864).
11. *Social Choice and Individual Values*, 2d ed., Wiley, 1963.

BIOGRAPHICAL NOTES

DAVID L. BAZELON was born in Superior, Wisconsin, in 1909 and received a B.S. in law from Northwestern University. He served as assistant U.S. attorney for the Northern District of Illinois and was in private practice for several years before being appointed by President Truman as assistant attorney general of the United States. Judge Bazelon was appointed to the U.S. Court of Appeals for the District of Columbia Circuit in 1949 and became chief judge in 1962. He has lectured in law and psychiatry at several universities and recently served as president of the American Orthopsychiatric Association.

DANIEL BELL was born in New York City in 1919. He received a B.S. from the College of the City of New York and a Ph.D. from Columbia University. Formerly managing editor of the *New Leader* and labor editor of *Fortune,* he also taught at the University of Chicago and was professor of sociology at Columbia before joining the Harvard faculty in 1969. Dr. Bell was cochairman of the Health, Education, and Welfare panel on social indicators and is chairman of the American Academy of Arts and Sciences' Commission on the Year 2000. Among his books are *Work and Its Discontents, The End of Ideology,* and *The Reforming of General Education.* He edited the volume *Toward the Year 2000.*

JOHN E. BERTRAM was born in Bedford, Pennsylvania, in 1927. He received a B.S.E.E. from Washington University, Saint Louis, and a master of science and doctorate from Columbia University. Dr. Bertram joined IBM as a staff engineer with the Research Division in 1958 and was promoted successively to director of experimental machines and director of computer science in the Research Division, associate director of the advanced computing systems project in the Systems Development Division, and general manager of the Advanced Systems Development Division. He is currently corporate director of engineering, programming, and technology.

KINGMAN BREWSTER, JR., was born in Longmeadow, Massachusetts, in 1919. He received an A.B. from Yale University, where he served as chairman of the Yale Daily News, and later took an LL.B. at the Harvard Law School. He was a member of the faculty at the Harvard Law School until 1960, when he accepted an appointment as provost of Yale University. He became president of Yale in 1963. President Brewster is author of *Antitrust and American Business Abroad* and coauthor of *Cases and Materials on the Law of International Transactions and Relations.*

HARVEY BROOKS was born in Cleveland, Ohio, in 1915. He received an A.B. in mathematics from Yale University and a Ph.D. in physics from Harvard University. Formerly associate laboratory head of the Knolls Atomic Power Laboratory of the General Electric Company, he became Gordon McKay Professor of Applied Physics at Harvard in 1950 and dean of engineering and applied physics in 1957. Professor Brooks is currently chairman of the committee on science and public policy of the National Academy of Sciences. He is author of *The Government of Science* and editor in chief of *Physics and Chemistry of Solids*, an international journal which he founded.

RALPH S. BROWN, JR., was born in Federalsburg, Maryland, in 1913. He received B.A. and LL.B. degrees from Yale University and has been a member of the Yale law faculty since 1946. Professor Brown has a long-standing interest in the regulation of intellectual and industrial properties, and is the editor with Benjamin Kaplan of *Cases on Copyright, Unfair Competition and Other Topics.*

JAMES S. COLEMAN was born in Bedford, Indiana, in 1926. He received a B.S. in chemical engineering from Purdue University and a Ph.D. in sociology from Columbia University. After serving on the faculty at the University of Chicago, he went to The Johns Hopkins University in 1959 to found its department of social relations. Dr. Coleman is currently professor of social relations at Johns Hopkins. He is coauthor of the report, *Equality of Educational Opportunity*, and is author of *Community Conflict, The Adolescent Society*, and *Introduction to Mathematical Sociology.*

EMILIO Q. DADDARIO was born in Newton Centre, Massachusetts, in 1918 and received a B.A. from Wesleyan University and an LL.B. from the University of Connecticut. He served as mayor and judge of the Municipal Court in Middletown, Connecticut, before being elected to the House of Representatives in 1958, where he serves on the Committee on Science and Astronautics as chairman of its Subcommittee on Science, Research, and Development and as second-ranking member of the subcommittee which oversees manned spaceflight programs. Congressman Daddario was author of legislation in 1968 to revise the National Science Foundation.

KARL W. DEUTSCH was born in Prague, Czechoslovakia, in 1912. He earned doctorates in Prague and at Harvard and has engaged in teaching or research at a number of universities, including Yale, Princeton, Chicago, Oxford, Heidelberg, Frankfurt, and MIT. Dr. Deutsch is professor of government at Harvard University. He served as president of the American Political Science Association during 1969–70 and is currently vice president of the International Political Science Association. His books include *Nationalism and Social Communication, The Nerves of Government, Arms Control and the Atlantic Alliance, The Analysis of International Relations, Nationalism and Its Alternatives,* and *Politics and Government: How People Decide Their Fate.*

LEE A. DUBRIDGE was born in Terre Haute, Indiana, in 1901. He received an A.B. from Cornell College in Iowa and an A.M. and Ph.D. in physics from the University of Wisconsin. He served on the faculty at the University of Wisconsin and Washington University, Saint Louis, before going to the University of Rochester as professor and chairman of physics and later dean of the faculty of arts and sciences. During the war Dr. DuBridge served as director of the MIT radiation laboratory. In 1946 he was named president of the California Institute of Technology, where he remained until his appointment by President Nixon in 1969 as Science Adviser and director of the Office of Science and Technology. He announced his resignation from this post in August 1970.

ALAIN ENTHOVEN was born in Seattle, Washington, in 1930. He received a B.A. from Stanford University, a B.Phil. from Oxford University, and a Ph.D. from MIT. Formerly an economist with the RAND Corporation and a consultant for the Brookings Institution, Dr. Enthoven was with the Defense Department from 1960 until assuming his current position as vice president of economic planning for Litton Industries in 1969. He is coauthor of *How Much Is Enough: Shaping the Defense Program, 1961–1969,* and he has contributed to *The Economics of Defense in the Nuclear Age, Money in a Theory of Finance,* and *A Modern Design for Defense Decision: A McNamara-Hitch-Enthoven Anthology.*

JAMES B. FISK was born in West Warwick, Rhode Island, in 1910. He received a B.S. and Ph.D. from MIT and was a Proctor traveling fellow at Cambridge University, England. Dr. Fisk joined the technical staff of Bell Telephone Laboratories in 1939 and became president in 1959. He received a Presidential Certificate of Merit in 1946 for his work on magnetrons. He has served on the general advisory committee of the Atomic Energy Commission and was chairman of the United States technical delegation at the Geneva Nuclear Test Ban Conference in 1958 and 1959. He was formerly a member of and is currently a consultant of the President's Science Advisory Committee.

EUGENE G. FUBINI was born in Turin, Italy, in 1913. He attended the Technical Institute at Turin and received a doctorate in physics from the University of Rome. Dr. Fubini is presently a private consultant for industry and government, having previously served as vice president and group executive for the IBM Corporation and as assistant secretary of defense and deputy director for defense research and engineering in the Pentagon. He is on the board of directors of Texas Instruments and is a trustee of The Urban Institute and Fairfield University.

KERMIT GORDON was born in Philadelphia, Pennsylvania, in 1916. He received a B.A. in economics from Swarthmore College and studied at Oxford as a Rhodes scholar. Mr. Gordon taught at Williams College, where he was David E. Wells Professor of Political Economy. He was a member of the Council of Economic Advisers under President Kennedy and Director of the Bureau of the

Budget under Presidents Kennedy and Johnson. He joined the Brookings Institution as vice president in 1965 and assumed his current position as president in 1967. He is editor of *Agenda for the Nation*.

LINCOLN GORDON was born in New York City in 1913. He is a graduate of Harvard College and received a D.Phil. from Oxford University as a Rhodes scholar. His career has been divided between faculty posts at Harvard University and governmental assignments in Washington. Dr. Gordon has served as U.S. ambassador to Brazil and as assistant secretary of state for inter-American affairs. Since 1967 he has been president of The Johns Hopkins University. Among his books is *A New Deal for Latin America*.

MARTIN GREENBERGER was born in Elizabeth, New Jersey, in 1931 and received A.B., A.M., and Ph.D. degrees in applied mathematics from Harvard University. Formerly a member of the MIT faculty, Dr. Greenberger has been at The Johns Hopkins University as professor of computer science and director of information processing since 1967. He is editor of *Computers and the World of the Future* and coauthor of *Microanalysis of Socioeconomic Systems—A Simulation Study* and *On-Line Computation and Simulation—The OPS-3 System*.

CARYL P. HASKINS was born in Schenectady, New York, in 1908. He received the Ph.B. from Yale University and the Ph.D. from Harvard University. Formerly a staff member of the research laboratory of the General Electric Company, Dr. Haskins served as president and director of research of Haskins Laboratories from 1935 to 1955. He has been president of the Carnegie Institution of Washington since 1956 and was a member of the President's Science Advisory Committee from 1955 to 1958. He is author of *Societies and Men*, *The Scientific Revolution and World Politics* and editor of *The Search for Understanding*.

NICHOLAS JOHNSON was born in Iowa City, Iowa, in 1934. He received a B.A. and LL.B. from the University of Texas, where he was article editor of the *Texas Law Review*. He served as law clerk to Judge John R. Brown of the U.S. Court of Appeals for the Fifth Circuit and to Associate Justice Hugo L. Black of the Supreme Court. Mr. Johnson was a member of the University of California School of Law faculty at Berkeley when President Johnson appointed him to the position of Maritime Administrator in 1964. In 1966 he was appointed for a seven-year term as an FCC commissioner. He is author of *How to Talk Back to Your Television Set*.

BENJAMIN KAPLAN was born in New York City in 1911. He received an A.B. from the College of the City of New York and an LL.B. from Columbia University. Mr. Kaplan practiced law in New York for several years. He was appointed to the faculty of the Harvard Law School in 1947 and is now Royall Professor of Law there. The law of literary property has been one of his academic interests. Professor Kaplan is author of *An Unhurried View of Copyright* and coauthor with Ralph S. Brown, Jr., of *Cases on Copyright*.

JOHN G. KEMENY was born in Budapest, Hungary, in 1926 and received a B.A. and Ph.D. in mathematics from Princeton University. He served on the Manhattan Project, later was a research assistant to Albert Einstein, and taught at Princeton until his appointment as professor of mathematics at Dartmouth College in 1953. Dr. Kemeny recently became the thirteenth president of Dartmouth College and remains Albert Bradley Third Century Professor there. Among his books are *A Philosopher Looks at Science, Introduction to Finite Mathematics, Finite Markov Chains, Denumerable Markov Chains,* and *Mathematical Models in the Social Sciences.* He is coauthor of the BASIC computer language and codeveloper of the Dartmouth Time-Sharing Computer System.

DAN LACY was born in Newport News, Virginia, in 1914. He received the A.B. and A.M. in American history and a Litt.D. from the University of North Carolina. Dr. Lacy served as assistant archivist of the United States and became deputy chief assistant librarian for the Library of Congress. From 1953 to 1966 he was managing director of the American Book Publishers Council. He is now a senior vice president of the McGraw-Hill Book Company and chairs the book industry's Joint Copyright Committee. He is author of *Freedom and Communication* and *The Meaning of the American Revolution.*

RALPH NADER was born in Winsted, Connecticut, in 1934. He received an A.B. from Princeton University and an LL.B. from Harvard University. He has lectured at the University of Hartford and at Princeton and has practiced law in Connecticut. Mr. Nader is a well-known consumer advocate and is founder of the Center for Study of Responsive Law. He is author of *Unsafe at Any Speed* and has been involved in a number of studies relating to such public issues as automobile safety, food standards, and the environment.

ANTHONY G. OETTINGER was born in Nuremberg, Germany, in 1929. He received an A.B. and Ph.D. from Harvard University and studied at the University of Cambridge, England. At Harvard he is professor of linguistics, Gordon McKay Professor of Applied Mathematics, and research associate to the Program on Technology and Society. Professor Oettinger is a former president of the Association for Computing Machinery and is current chairman of the Computer Science and Engineering Board of the National Academy of Sciences. He is author of *Automatic Language Translation: Lexical and Technical Aspects,* and *Run, Computer, Run: The Mythology of Educational Innovation.*

DAVID PACKARD was born in Pueblo, Colorado, in 1912. He received an A.B. and an E.E. degree from Stanford University and did graduate work at the University of Colorado. In 1939 he formed the Hewlett-Packard company to design and manufacture electronic measurement instrumentation. He has served as chairman of the board and chief executive officer of the company. Mr. Packard was president of the Stanford board of trustees from 1958 to 1960. President Nixon nominated him to his current post as deputy secretary of defense in 1969.

ALAN J. PERLIS was born in Pittsburgh, Pennsylvania, in 1922. He received a B.S. in chemistry from Carnegie Institute of Technology and an M.S. and Ph.D. in mathematics from MIT. He has been director of the computer center at Purdue University and at Carnegie-Mellon University, where he has also been head of the department of mathematics and is currently head of the department of computer science. Dr. Perlis is a former president of the Association for Computing Machinery and a past editor in chief of its *Communications*.

ITHIEL DE SOLA POOL was born in New York City in 1917 and received an A.B., A.M., and Ph.D. from the University of Chicago. After teaching at Hobart College, Dr. Pool joined the Hoover Institute on War, Revolution, and Peace at Stanford University. He has been a professor of political science at MIT since 1953, working on computer models of social systems and on computer systems for social-science data management. Among his books are *Candidates, Issues and Strategies, American Business and Public Policy,* and *Contemporary Political Science.*

RICHARD A. POSNER was born in New York City in 1939. After receiving a B.A. from Yale University and an LL.B. from Harvard University, Mr. Posner served successively as law clerk to Justice Brennan of the U.S. Supreme Court, assistant to a commissioner of the Federal Trade Commission, assistant to the Solicitor General of the United States, and general counsel of President Johnson's Task Force on Communications Policy, before assuming his present post as professor of law at the University of Chicago. He is author of several articles on government regulation of business.

CHARLES L. SCHULTZE was born in Alexandria, Virginia, in 1924. He received a B.A. and M.A. from Georgetown University and a Ph.D. from the University of Maryland. Dr. Schultze was formerly a staff member of the Council of Economic Advisors, an associate professor of economics at Indiana University, and assistant director and director of the Bureau of the Budget. He is currently a senior fellow at Brookings Institution and a professor of economics at the University of Maryland. He is author of *Recent Inflation in the United States, The Politics and Economics of Public Spending,* and *Setting National Priorities: The 1971 Budget.*

MARTIN SHUBIK was born in New York City in 1926. He received a B.A. in mathematics and an M.A. in political science from the University of Toronto, and an A.M. and Ph.D. in economics from Princeton University. He was at Princeton University, the General Electric Company, and the IBM Watson Research Laboratories, before becoming professor of the economics of organization at Yale University in 1963. He is editor of *Essays in Mathematical Economics in Honor of Oscar Morgenstern* and author of *Readings in Game Theory and Political Behavior, Strategy and Market Structure,* and *Game Theory and Related Approaches to Social Behavior.*

HERBERT A. SIMON was born in Milwaukee, Wisconsin, in 1916 and received an A.B. and Ph.D. from the University of Chicago. Formerly at the University of California at Berkeley and the Illinois Institute of Technology, he is currently professor of computer science and psychology at the Carnegie-Mellon University. Professor Simon has been chairman of the board of directors of the Social Science Research Council and of the Behavioral Sciences Division of the National Research Council, and he serves on the President's Science Advisory Committee. His books include *Administrative Behavior, Organizations, The Shape of Automation, Models of Man,* and *The Sciences of the Artificial.*

PATRICK SUPPES was born in Tulsa, Oklahoma, in 1922. He received a B.S. in meteorology from the University of Chicago and a Ph.D. in philosophy from Columbia University. He has been on the Stanford University faculty since 1950, where he is professor of philosophy, statistics, and education, and director of the Institute for Mathematical Studies in the Social Sciences. Among his books are *Computer-Assisted Instruction: Stanford's 1965–66 Arithmetic Program, Markov Learning Models for Multiperson Interactions, Experiments in Second-Language Learning, Studies in the Methodology and Foundations of Science,* and *A Probabilistic Theory of Causality.*

GEORGE WALD was born in New York City in 1906. He holds a B.S. from New York University and an M.A. and Ph.D. from Columbia University. After holding National Research Council fellowships in Berlin, Zurich, Heidelberg, and Chicago, he joined the faculty of Harvard University in 1934, where he is now Higgins Professor of Biology. For his research in the mechanisms of vision and their evolution, Professor Wald shared the Nobel Prize in Physiology and Medicine in 1967. He is coauthor of *General Education in a Free Society* and a laboratory textbook entitled *26 Afternoons of Biology.*

ALAN F. WESTIN was born in New York City in 1929. He received an A.B. from the University of Florida, and an LL.B. and Ph.D. from Harvard University. Formerly at Yale and Cornell universities, he is now at Columbia University as professor of public law and director of the Center for Research and Education in American Liberties. Professor Westin serves on the board of the American Civil Liberties Union and heads a privacy study for the Computer Science and Engineering Board of the National Academy of Sciences. His books include *Privacy and Freedom, Information Technology in a Democracy, Freedom Now: The Civil Rights Struggle in America,* and *The Autobiography of the Supreme Court.*

LEE C. WHITE was born in Omaha, Nebraska, in 1923. He holds a B.S. in electrical engineering and an LL.B. from the University of Nebraska. Mr. White was legislative assistant to Senator John F. Kennedy, assistant to Hoover Commission member Joseph P. Kennedy, counsel to the Senate Small Business Committee, administrative assistant to Senator John Sherman Cooper, assistant special counsel to President Kennedy, special counsel to President Johnson, and chairman of the Federal Power Commission. He has been engaged in private law practice since 1969.

DAEL WOLFLE was born in Puyallup, Washington, in 1906. He received a B.S. and M.A. from the University of Washington and a Ph.D. from the Ohio State University. He taught at the Universities of Mississippi and Chicago, served with the panel on applied psychology of the Office of Scientific Research and Development, was director of the Commission on Human Resources and Advanced Training, and from 1954 to 1970 was executive officer of the American Association for the Advancement of Science. He is now professor of public affairs at the University of Washington. Among his books are *America's Resources of Specialized Talent, Symposium on Basic Research,* and *Science and Public Policy.*

INDEX

AAAS Commission on the Year 2000, 287
Absolutes, 280–81
Academic institutions, legislative preferences for, 194, 204, 208–11
Access to information: justifying, 101–3, 166, 168; at lower levels, 106 (*see also* Zooming); preventing, 89, 105, 107–9, 179; instead of storage, 45, 54, 57, 64, 66–67, 70–71, 85; unfettered, 84–87, 91–92, 96, 99, 105, 107
Accounting and administrative systems, 78
Acheson, Dean G., 80, 83
Action poverty, 123–24, 137, 145
Active versus passive information systems, 77, 94–95, 104, 109
Administrative Procedure Act, 175
Administrative systems, 153, 155–56, 169; versus statistical systems, 168, 172
ADMINS system at MIT, 95
Adult education, 9
Adversary process, 94, 100–101, 241; limitations of the, 152, 254
Affluence, 123–24, 126, 136, 138–41, 280
Africa, 147

Agriculture: mechanization of, 275; productivity of, 281
Agriculture, Department of, 106
Aiken, Howard H., 67
Aines, Andrew A., 63, 69–70
Air Force, 103, 174
Airline reservation system, 6, 20, 25, 78, 110
Air traffic control, 112, 278
Alameda County, Calif., 159–61
Albert, Carl, 107
Algorithm: versus developed program, 198, 200, 206–7, 215; for doing versus doing, 130–31; of a process, 196–97, 214; protection of an, 200
Alienation, computer, 167, 182
"All channel" legislation, 232
Allocation of frequencies, 230–31, 233, 241, 252
ALTRAN system, 34
American Broadcasting Company, 233
American Chemical Society, 69
American National Standards Institute (ANSI), 34

303

American Telephone and Telegraph. *See* AT&T
Analysis: computer-assisted, 101; and judgment, 96–97, 101; need for, in decision making, 227, 230, 241; open and explicit, 98–99, 101; systems, 96–97, 99–102, 283
Anarchy, nonhierarchical, 111
Antiballistic missile (ABM), 99–100, 112, 229, 261–62, 277–78
Antitrust Division, 169, 245
Antitrust regulation, 204, 210, 216, 252, 256; sanctions, 193, 202, 243
Application right for programs, xvii, 193, 197–99, 207, 209, 211
Apprentice system, 144
Aristotle, 65, 135
Arms race, 277–78, 291
Army: intelligence, Soviet, 94; intelligence, U.S., 186; system-effectiveness estimates by, 99–101
Army, Secretary of the, 99–100
Arrow, Kenneth J., 282
Artificial, science of the, 273–74
Artificial intelligence, 51–52, 59, 77
"Ask a man" system, 112
Assumptions, hidden, 98–101, 103
AT&T, 192, 244, 248, 255; lawsuits against, 228, 234, 245, 250; 1956 consent decree of, 238, 247, 256; problems of, 256; rate study of, 235, 238
Attention: conserving, 42–44, 53–55, 68; measuring capacity of, 41; operations involved in, 55; purpose of, 67; scarcity of, xv, 40–49, 51, 61–64, 79–81
Aufenkamp, Don D., 139, 142
Authoritarian tradition, 154
Authors: protective interests of, 193–95, 201; reliance of, on prior works, 222
Automating, difficulties in, xv
Automobiles: device to assess driving and parking charges, 59; electric, possibility of, 282; pollution from, 18, 50, 229, 276, 290–91; and safety, 172, 229, 277

B-52, 103
Baker, Donald I., 217–218, 222, 254, 256
Baker v. *Selden* case, 197, 206–7
Balance of powers, 75, 89
Ball, George W., 55
Baran, Paul, 25, 28–29
Bargaining, need for, 202–4, 222, 283
Barry, Richard E., 23, 177
BASIC, 3, 15, 24
Batch processing, 2–3, 19, 22–23; express, 19, 22
Bauer, Raymond A., 288, 290
Bazelon, David L., 149–51, 168, 172–73, 185–86, 295

Becker, Joseph, 217
Bell, Daniel, 259, 280–85, 287, 289–90, 295
Bell System, 28–29, 70, 235, 242, 250, 256
Bell Telephone Laboratories, 24, 34, 71
Bender, David, 217, 219–20
Benjamin, Curtis G., 215
Bennett, Robert, 248, 252
Berkeley Barb, 119
Bernhart and Fetter case, 196, 205, 214–15, 218
Bertram, John E., x, 16–18, 24, 31, 34–35, 295
Bicentennial Commission, 288
Big Brother, 23, 58–60, 72, 93, 157
Billing, by computer, 6, 20
Biographical files, 87–90, 93, 104, 112
Biology, modern, 265–66
Birth control, xviii, 281, 286
Bit of information, 41
Black-and-white TV receivers, 232
Blackout, power, 240, 285–88
Black Panthers, 184
Black people: progress of, 275–76; and public schools, 133, 136, 141, 143
Boeing Company, 277
Bonneville Power Administration, 288
Books: versus computers, xiii, xvii, 30, 212–13, 220; cost of, versus microcopies, 213
Borges, Jorge L., 58
Bounds on systems, 110–11
Braille editions, 212
Brandeis, Louis D., 173
Branscomb, Lewis M., 41, 61
Brewster, Kingman, Jr., 225–26, 251, 256–57, 296
Breyer, Stephen G., 217, 221
Briggs, Paul W., 141
Brooks, Harvey, 259, 272–80, 285–86, 296
Brown, Claude, 123
Brown, Ralph S., Jr., xvii, 189–206, 214–17, 222, 296
Brownson, Helen, 104
Bryk, Oliver, 178
Buchwald, Art, 74–75
Buckley, John L., 63, 69–70
Budget Bureau, xvii, 47, 98, 106, 161, 168
Bunker-Ramo, 29, 227–28
Bureaucracies, drive toward self-perpetuation, 278
Burke, Edmund, 68
Business, effects of computer networks on, 10–11
Business Equipment Manufacturers Association, 227
Business Week, 65
Buyer's information service, xiv–xv

Cable television, 203, 218, 221, 229, 254; FCC policy on, 231, 237, 245, 254; offered by telephone carriers, 235–37
California Department of Motor Vehicles, 158–59
California Institute of Technology, 24
California National Guard, 165
Camelot, Project, 66
Carmichael, Stokely, 186
Carnegie, Andrew, xiii
Carnegie unit, 127
Carpenter, Richard A., 288
Carson, Rachel L., 50
Carter, Thomas F., 234
Carterfone case, 234–36, 245, 250
Carver, John A., Jr., 248–53
Case Western Reserve University, 19
Cater, S. Douglass, 106–8, 112
Census Bureau, 42, 159, 169, 171, 182, 184; statistics collected by, 154–55, 170, 184, 213
Central Intelligence Agency, 80, 82, 93–94, 96, 98
Central processor: modest, 95; single large, 4, 16
Change: accelerated technological, 284; feedback in guiding, 291–92; institutional and social, 82, 84, 90, 93, 96, 110, 263–68; slowing the process of, 60–61
Character recognition, 24, 130
Chess-playing: collection of data by wire concerning, 59; program for, 52, 58–59, 62, 64
Chicago Police Department, 158
Chicago Tribune, 119
Chiefs, concept of, versus Indians, xvi, 84–87, 89–90, 108
Children: a better world for fewer, 272; cognitive world of, 118–19; deprived, 126, 133, 136; learning of, 125–127; need for socialization of, 119, 122, 128, 136, 144–45; working and responsibilities of, 123–25, 127–29, 133
Choice, widening, 284
Citizens: as clients, 183; need for informed, 133–34; versus subjects, 167–68
City: computer model of a, 130–31; problems of the, xviii, 10–11, 27, 35, 55, 70, 143, 275–76
Civilizations on other planets, 269–71
Civil liberties: and computerized data systems, 149–87; current relevance of, 151–52; legislative, judicial, and regulatory safeguards of, xvii, 162–68, 175, 187; phases in issues of, 161–63; threat to, 157–58, 169, 274
Civil service, 150, 181

Clearance (permission) from copyright owner, 202, 208, 212, 214–15, 221
COBOL, 15, 24
Cognitive skills: of children, 118–19; teaching of, 119–22, 127, 129–30, 132, 138, 140, 144–45
Cohen, Benjamin V., 217, 223
Cohen, Sheldon S., 217, 221
Coleman, James S., xvi, 115–29, 135–40, 142–45, 296
Coleman report, 116, 121, 133, 136
Collinearity, problem of, 170
Columbia, Md., information system in, 183
Columbia Broadcasting System, 231–32
Commission on the Year 2000, 140
Common carriers: offering computer services, 204, 236–38, 242, 249, 255; specialized, 234–37, 245
Communicate, ability to, with policy makers, 106, 239
Communications: compatibility in, 247–48, 255–56; concentration of time-sharing services in, 29; cost of, 28–29, 57, 71, 227; gap in, 107; industry based on, 29, 221, 243; private overlay in, to unify data services, 247–48; problems of, xviii, 12, 226; processors in, 4–5; rates of, 12, 28–29, 70–71; requirements of, 12, 79, 226; sharing and resale of, 228, 235, 247–48
Communications Act, 226, 230, 252
Community college, 132
Compatible color, 232
Competition: in communications, 242–46, 255; stimulating, xiv
Compunications, 74, 103; as compressing time and space, 76, 82, 88, 105; in crises, 83–84; flexibility in, 83–84, 86, 89–90; growth curve for, 104; in the national decision-making process, 73–114
Computer-aided instruction (CAI), xv–xvii, 120–22, 137, 146, 213–14
Computer industry, 17–18, 192, 216, 221, 238; and communications, xii, xviii, 12, 226–27, 234–37, 238, 242, 243, 244, 245, 255–56; growth of the, xi, 193, 197, 206, 218; and regulation, 226–27, 234–35, 238, 242
Computer inquiry, xviii, 227, 230, 234–39; FCC initiative in the, 228, 245, 251; inappropriateness of the, 244, 246, 249–50; issues in the, 162, 253–55
Comsat, 233, 255
Confidentiality: and Census Bureau, 171, 182; by contract, 199, 219; precomputer rules for, 161–62; of psychiatrist-patient relationship, 186

Conglomerates, 291
Congress: burdens on, 47, 50; on communications, 226, 252, 257; on computer development agency, 23; on copyright protection, 198, 203, 205–6, 217–18, 221–22; decision making in, 289–90; files on members of, 174, 257; on patent protection, 191, 195–96, 200; role of, in formulating basic policy, 241
Congress, Library of, 32, 45, 212, 289
Conservatism, and natural selection, 264–65
Constitution, 74–75, 86, 152; versus common law, 263; on property protection, 191, 195, 200, 205, 210
Consumer: counsel for, 241, 254; legislation concerning, 175; -producer relation, xiv, 277, 285
Content analysis, 95, 104
Control of information, 109; by chiefs, 84–85, 108; by interrogator, 92, 102
Conversational mode, 2
Copying, illicit, 193–94, 201, 209; protection against, 195
Copyright Office, 197, 203
Copyrights, 191, 195, 204–6; in a bookkeeping system, 197–98; for computer programs, 197–98, 206–7, 211, 216–17, 219, 223; for computer textual material, 200–202, 208–12; duration of, 195, 205, 209–10; exemption from, 194, 201, 208; law on, 200, 203, 216, 218–20; limitations of, 197–98, 205; modification of, for educational institutions, 209–10; musical, 198, 203, 205; versus patents, xvii, 195, 197, 215, 217; possible harms of, 221; protected by customer, 219; for published work, 194; revision of law concerning, 201–3, 205–6, 208–10, 217–18, 223; study commission on, 202–3, 205, 209, 217–18, 220, 223; for works in the new technology, 211, 213–15
Cost: external, 277, 281, 289–91; of information systems, 95, 102, 104–5, 110; of producing versus copying a program, 221; sharing, among multiple formats, 213
Council of Economic Advisers, 106
Crawford, David, 25
Creation versus production, 261, 272
Creative activity: decline of, 267–68; for students, 133, 136, 138, 144
Credit bureaus, 156, 174–75
Crime, computer service to fight, 8
Crises: in education, 137; political, 80–81, 95–96; social, 266–68
Crissey, Brian L., 216

Cromlish, Joseph, 138–39
Crop yields, estimates of, 106
Cross-subsidization, issue of, 228, 235–37, 242, 255
Cuban missile crisis, 80, 95, 112
Customers: with manufacturer's copyright, 219; organizing, to avoid copyright, 221
Cybernetics, 273–74

Daddario, Emilio Q., 37–38, 47, 60–61, 289, 296
Dade County, Fla., 164
Dartmouth College, 2; library at, 30; time-sharing system at, 3, 9, 12–13, 18, 22, 24–25
Darwin, Charles R., 262–63, 266, 268, 279
Darwinism, social, 283
Data: marketing of, 220–21; pure theory and raw, 76–79; on race and religion, 173; reference, for computer use, 213; volume of, 110; versus work product, 179
Data bank, xv, 4, 24, 158–61, 204, 213–14; centralized computer service with, 158–59; examples of a, 158–61, 220–21; marginal updating of a, 20; on militants, 165, 167, 186; national, xvii, 161–62, 164, 168, 183; programming the management of a, 17, 24; statistics of inquiries to a, 24; used in decision making, 150
Data collection: administrative versus intelligence versus statistical, xvii, 153–54, 176; as affecting dependent people, 185; in a democracy versus a totalitarian state, 154–55; for personal use versus statistical use, 168, 172, 176
Data communications system, 12, 29, 235–36, 250; unified, 247–48, 255–56
Data systems: benefits of, 173–74; court decisions on, 162, 167; government, 151, 153–56, 161; need for studies of, 167, 173–74; pressure on, 182; regional federated, 164; registry for, 166–67, 178–79; sanctions on use of, 175; stages of computerized, 158–61, 163–64
Datran Company, 250
David, Edward E., Jr., 25, 28–30, 34, 36
DDT, problem of, 45–46, 48–49, 53, 68–69, 274–75
Decentralization: of decision making, 84, 93, 95–96, 102; need for, 55–56, 88
Decision-making process: collegial versus directive, 253–54; decentralization of, 84, 93, 95–96; deficiencies in the, 96–97; implicit, 76, 86, 111; national, xvi,

73–114; by the nonmarket public, 282
Decisions: about computers and communications, 226–27; by computers, 62, 74; inadequate time for, 107–8; by producers, 261–62, 276–77; scientific and technological, 228–29, 227, 282–83, 287, 289; in secret by the few, 95; by thermostat, 75; use of information in, 69, 96–97, 157, 241
Defense, Department of (Pentagon), 22, 96, 98–101, 103–4, 107–8, 229, 273
Defense Intelligence Agency, 96
De Gaulle, Charles, 87
Deintermixture, 232
Democracy: and natural selection, 263–64; representative, inadequacy of, 256–57
Democratic national convention, *1968*, 107
"Derivative work," defined in revision of copyright law, 205, 210
Desalinization, 229
Design, technological versus organic, 262–63, 284
Detroit Social Data Bank, 158–59
Deutsch, Karl W., 37, 52–56, 67–68, 296–97
Dewey, John, 133, 136
Diagnosis, use of computers in, xii–xiii
Domestic communications satellites, 233, 237, 253, 285
Dominance: in aircraft production, 261; biological, 264–65
Doud, Wallace C., 217, 219
Drake, Frank D., 270
DuBridge, Lee A., 1–2, 18, 23–24, 26, 28, 36, 297
Due process, xvii, 151–52, 163; absence of, 154–55; tests of, 155
Dunn, Edgar S., 180, 183
Dyson, Freeman J., 271

Early warning, 65, 68, 112; of unanticipated consequences of innovations, 48–50, 53, 60–61
EC-121 plane incident, 81–83
Economic need, as motivation, 138, 140, 142
Economists versus lawyers, 251–52, 257
Economy, centrally planned, 93
Education: computers in, xvi, 13, 19, 22, 137, 146; continuing and recurrent, xiii, 128–29; driver, 142; financial problems of, 132, 137; goals of, xvi, 125, 127–28, 141, 276, 285; history of, 135; a market for, xvi, 126, 134, 138, 141–42; measurement of performance in, 141, 170; medical, 142; in modern society, 115–147; private contractors in, 120, 134, 140; problems of, from rural past, 126–27; promoting efficiency and innovation in, 126–27, 138, 143; as a public monopoly, 138; record systems for, 155, 161; and technology, xiii, 102, 116, 127, 131; time scale for changes in, 132, 135, 137
Education, Office of, 140, 161
Educational television, 146–47, 233
Eisenhower, Dwight David, 64, 78, 109
Electronics field, 35
Elkes, Joel, 180–81, 183
Employment services, 7
Energy: consumption of, 280; sources of, 270–71; words associated with, 38–39
Engineering: discipline in, 35; on-line computer system for computations in, 215
Enthoven, Alain C., 73, 96–101, 103, 105, 297
Environment: information-processing systems and, 70, 110; leaving information in the, 44, 46, 49, 66; quality of, 18, 260, 271, 276, 279–82, 291
Equality of educational opportunity, 116, 121–22, 133, 136
Equity versus debt financing, 245
Ervin bill, 166
Evans, B. O., 26, 30, 32–33, 137
Evolution, 262–66, 269, 278, 283–84
Executive branch, 75, 82, 101, 288; access to information in, 84–86, 89, 99
Executive Organization, Advisory Council on, 111
Expectations, unrealistic, 97, 274–75, 292
Experiences: direct versus vicarious, 116–18; socializing, 119, 122, 125
Experimentation: limitations on, 272–73, 286; need for, 49, 51–53, 68, 72
"External costs," 277, 281, 289–91

"Face the Nation," 70
Faceless informer, 186
Facts, 97–98, 102; benefits in having, 184–85; learning, 66, 125, 285; and science, 260; "true," 98, 106
Fagg, Helga B., 137
Fair use of copyrighted material, 201, 208–9, 212, 214
Family: changes in the function of the, 119, 132, 135, 145; dissolution of the, 136, 140, 144–45
Fano, Robert M., 26, 28–29, 31–35, 180, 183
Farinholt, Larkin H., 26
Federal Aviation Agency, 112
Federal Bureau of Investigation, 186
Federal Communications Commission (FCC), 12–13, 28–29, 71, 109, 204;

approach to technological problems, 230–34; boundary between Office of Telecommunications Policy and, 254; Common Carrier Bureau of, 228, 236; computer inquiry of (*see* Computer inquiry); lack of policy planning by, 233–34, 237, 239, 241, 244, 253; needs of, 238–39, 241, 247; shortcomings of the, 230, 233–34, 237

Federal Power Commission (FPC), 239–40, 246

Feeney, George J., 26, 29, 32

Fergusson, Stuart, 180

Fermi, Enrico, 269

Filep, Robert T., 139, 141–42, 146

Files, 4–5, 78, 88, 95; amalgamated, 87–88, 160, 176–77; authorship in, 88; computerization of, 157–58; of personal information, 176, 182–84; requirements for on-line, 16, 18; restrictions on the use of, 89, 175

Filing practices, 89–90, 104

Filtering or condensing information, 54–56, 65, 71–72, 91; and decision making, 69, 79, 84–86, 88–89; scarcity of attention to need for, 43–44, 62–64, 82

Fisk, James B., 259–60, 297

Fluoridation, dossiers on people opposing, 174

Flynn, Michael J., 106, 110, 112

Food, world production of, 267, 271, 275, 280, 281

Ford Foundation, 231, 233

Forecasting: of alternative futures, 284; need for, 12, 49, 53; problems of, 289

"Foreign attachments" issue, 234, 236–38

Foreign Office, 43–44

Formulas, computer evaluation of, 213, 215

Forrest, Henry S., 106, 110

Forrester, Jay W., 130–31

FORTRAN, 3, 15, 24, 33–35

Foster, David, 62

Freed, Roy, 194

Freedom of Information Act, 177

Free-enterprise system, 145, 242–44; versus free inquiry, xiv, 272

Fubini, Eugene G., 115, 129–32, 138, 140, 143, 146, 290, 297

Galbraith, John Kenneth, 138

Games by computer, 9, 120–21

Gardner, John W., 38

GE 635, 3

General Electric, 65, 233

General Motors, 285

Genetic manipulation, 265–66, 274

General-purpose computer, as many machines, 196, 205, 215, 219

Germ plasm, human, inviolability of, 266, 281, 286

Gilchrist, Bruce, 139, 142–43

Glassman, Lawrence, 216

Glennan, T. Keith, 139–40

Goals: computer programs seeking, 130–31; educational, 125, 127–28, 141; human, xviii, 262, 271–72; learning to set, 131; national, 52, 62, 275, 279, 285, 288–89; student, 124

Goldberg, Arthur J., 150

Goldberg, Morton David, 217, 222

Gordon, Kermit, 250–52, 297–98

Gordon, Lincoln, 27, 30, 32, 64, 66, 140–42, 145, 251, 253, 298

Government: computer systems for federal, state, and local, 14, 17–18, 70; funding by, 230; rational, 156–57; record keeping by, 153–56; and technology, 228–30, 240

Grants-in-aid, federal, 160, 164, 166

Greenberger, Martin, 29, 33, 62–63, 103, 106, 109, 138, 144–45, 181, 219–20, 246, 248, 251, 255–57, 291, 298

Greenhouse effect (CO_2), 68

Grid: with Canada, 287; national, 285–86

Grooks, 190

Grosch, Herbert R. J., 26, 30, 32, 34

Growth, economic, 275, 280

Guidance counseling service, xv, 8, 17, 26–27

Guidelines, need for, 291–92

Haase, Walter W., 106, 111

Habeas corpus writ, 152, 168

"Habeas data," 168, 179–80

Hand, Learned, 195

Hansen, Alvin H., 180

Hardware: development outpacing software, 34–35, 211; failures of, 16

Harlan, John M., 199

Harvard Business Review, 288

Harvard University: Mark I computer of, 67; Program on Technology and Society at, 158; students at, 105

Haskins, Caryl P., 142, 189–90, 298

Health, Education, and Welfare, Department of, 160

Hearle, E. F. R., 161

Heffner, Hubert, 106, 108, 111–12

Hein, Piet, 190

Helmholtz, Hermann von, 268

Hendricks, Sterling B., 288–89

Heredity, 263, 265–66

Hershey, Robert, 24

Hicks, J. R., 250

INDEX

Hierarchies: dual role of each level in, 76, 79, 85, 87, 112; in government, xvi, 76, 78–85, 111; inertia in, 81–82, 84, 90, 102; information flow in, 78–80, 83, 86; information gathering versus exercise of authority in, 86–87; partitioning in, 80–85, 88, 95, 107–8; shared power and competition in, 81–82, 107–8
Highway program, 275
Hirsch, Phil, 60, 177–78, 247
Hitch, Charles J., 102
Hoak, James, 248
Hobbes, Thomas, 284
Hoffman, Lance J., 180
Hollerith punched card, 42
Holmes, Justice Oliver Wendell, 66, 283
Holt, Charles C., 25–27, 33–34, 181, 184
Hook, Sidney, 272
Hoopes, Townsend, 80
Hopkins, Mark, 120
Hornish, William M., 61–62
House Subcommittee on Science, Research, and Development, 289–90
Housing and Urban Development, Department of, 161, 164
Howard, J. Woodford, 180, 185
Huggins, William H., 139, 146

IBM, 17, 71, 192–93, 216, 219; registration scheme of, 205, 216, 219
Ideas and their expressions: without charge, 220, 222; protection of, 191, 195, 197–98, 205, 215
Identity, protection of, in data systems, 182–84
Ignatius, Paul R., 107
Illiteracy, of the world, 146–47
Indians, concept of, versus chiefs, xvi, 84–87, 89–90, 99, 101, 107
INFO-COM, 228
Information: channels for, 64, 98; cost of, 41; derogatory, collection system requested by Air Force, 174; feedback of, 55–56, 58, 68, 75; indices of, 66; management of, 66–67, 125, 127–30, 133–34; overload of, xv, 21, 42–44, 52–54, 60–61, 72, 79, 82–84, 89, 109, 287; poverty of, 117–19, 122, 126, 136–37; processing of, 40, 42, 51, 77, 120; redundancy in, 45, 55, 66, 69; retrieval of, 32–33, 46, 49, 54, 93, 110, 112, 268; richness of, xvi, 37–72, 116–19, 123–26, 133, 136–37, 151; systems for, computerized, 38, 69, 95, 103, 104, 151; theory of, 45, 57
"Information": versus "data," 56–57, 61; meaning of, 39–40, 57, 61
Ingram, Glenn, 26

Innovation: monopolies and technological, 250; need for creativity and, 55–56; stimulating, xvii, 191–93, 204, 210
Institutions: changes in, xvi, 82, 84, 90, 93, 96, 110; merging economic and educational, 128–29, 138; problems of, xiii–xvi, 76, 97; self-preservation of, 278
Integration, program for symbolic, 65
Intellectual property, 190, 210–11, 222
Intelligence: compilation of dossiers by government for, 154–56, 169, 174; function of, 48, 80–82, 87, 91, 94; process for gathering, 93; systems of, 43–44, 53, 94, 153–56; as threat to privacy, 186
"Intelligence," meaning of, 77, 84
Interaction: in the classroom, 145–46; real-time, 2, 9, 121
"Interconnection" issue, 234, 236–38, 243–44, 248, 255–56
Interests: conflicting, 252, 257, 274, 276, 282–83; consumer, xiii–xiv, 254; special, 227, 230, 234, 290
Internal Revenue Service, 186, 221; files of, 158, 169, 177; sample data of, 171
Interstate Commerce Act, 252
Interstate Commerce Commission, 226
Intimidation of employees and customers, use of information files for, 175–76
Inventor, protecting the, 195
Irreversible phenomena, 48–49, 60–61, 68, 72
Isaacs, H. H., 161

James, William, 280
Job placement service, xv, 6–7, 14, 20, 25–26, 159; in Baltimore, 7; and maintaining privacy, 182
Johns Hopkins University, 30, 142; library at, 32
Johnson, Leland L., 231, 248, 250, 255
Johnson, Lyndon B., 54, 63–64, 80, 83, 233
Johnson, Nicholas, xviii, 64, 70–71, 109, 112, 225–39, 244–47, 249–51, 254, 298
Johnson, Wendell, 112
Joint Chiefs of Staff, 80, 99
Joyce, Charles, 104
Jumpers and lateral communication in organizations, 80, 84–86, 88, 106–7
Justice, Department of, 186, 228, 236, 246, 255–56

Kaplan, Benjamin, 189, 206–10, 215–17, 233, 298
Kayton, Irving, 214, 217–19
Keats, John, 195

Kemeny, John G., xv, 1–15, 18, 22–28, 30, 32–35, 298–99
Kennedy, John F., 78, 92, 275
Kennedy, Robert F., 80–81
Kent, Sherman, 82, 87
Kessler, Myer M., 33
Khrushchev, Nikita S., 87, 104, 112
Kierkegaard, Søren, 281
"Know": meaning of, 45, 56, 59, 64–67; need to, 44, 67, 89, 99, 102–3
Knowledge: dissemination of, 191, 210–11; as a handmaiden of choice, 284; as power, 86, 105, 109–11, 183; production of, 54–55, 63; quest for, 260–61, 272; from theory and data, 76–79, 81; used for good or ill, 274
Knox, William, 216
Koller, Herbert, 217–19

Labor Statistics, Bureau of, 159
Lacy, Dan M., 189, 210–14, 222, 299
Laissez faire, 283
Lancaster, Joseph, 134
Land, Edwin H., 199
Language: high-level computer, 3, 15, 19, 24, 33–35, 67; technical, 106
Lappin, S. S., 117, 123
Law, codified versus common, 263
Lawyers: versus economists, 251–52, 257; and Nader's concept of serving the public interest, 172
Learning: individualistic, 125, 145; to learn, 129–31, 134, 140–41; machine, 130–31; outside schools, 120–21, 126–28, 139–40
Lear v. *Adkins* case, 199–200, 220
Legal rights, versus economic results, 251–52, 254; systems, 68
Legislative Reference Service, 289
Leontief, Wassily, 140
Liberman, Yevsei G., 93
Libertarian tradition, in contrast to authoritarian, 154–55
Libraries: automated, xv, 10, 14, 30, 194, 209; copyright interests of the, 194; problems of the, 10, 30, 45–46
Licenses: broadcasting, 229, 232, 245, 252; compulsory, 202–4, 208, 212–13
Life: improving the quality of, xv, 6–9, 20; on other planets, 268–71
Lilienthal, Bruce, 179
Lilienthal, Martha, 286
Lindsay, John V., 281–82
List processing, 52
LITE, Project, 32
Lockheed Corporation, 120, 164
London, J. Phillip, 105
Longitudinal data files, 170, 183
Loring, William T., 138

Los Angeles, Calif., 161, 164
Loweth, Hugh, 288
Ludgin, Quentin, 60

MacBride, Robert, 164
McGraw-Hill, 215
McGreer, W. Lester, 105
Machine: creation and use of a, 190; and man, 130, 259–93; meaning of, 39–40
Machlup, Fritz, 191
McLuhan, Marshall, 62, 85
McNamara, Robert S., 98–100, 107
Madison, James, 155
Man: and machine, 259–93; place of, in space and time, xviii, 265, 268–72; as a technological product, 265–66; understanding of, 51–52, 58–59, 62
Management information systems (MIS), xv–xvi, 44, 83, 95, 97, 102–4; government-integrated, 164, 178–79; and implicit decision making in staff echelons, 76, 104, 108
Manipulation: of computer programs, 207, 216–17, 219, 221; of copyrighted material, 201, 208, 220
Manning, Winton H., 139–41
Mansfield Amendment, 273
Marden, Ethel, 247
Margolis, Joel, 286–87
Market, role of, in growth of computer industry, 17, 242, 279
Marland, Sidney P., 139–40, 143–47
Marsh, George, 280
Marshall, Alfred, 250
Mason, Edward S., 251
Mason, R. J., 161
Mass media, 93, 105, 118–19, 185
Matching data, 169–72
Mating algorithm, 27
Maxwell, James Clerk, 268
Mays, John M., 139, 143
Medical application, of computers, xii–xiii, xv, 8, 14, 30, 278; in assignment of interns, 27; in record keeping, xiii
Melody, William, 236
Memory: core, 4–5; in designing information filters, 55–56, 67; mass, xvi, 16, 18, 31, 51, 110
Messages, 57, 75
Message switching, 238
Mesthene, Emanuel G., 288, 290, 292
Microcopies, 209, 213
Microwave Communications Incorporated (MCI) case, 235–36, 245
MIT: students at, 64; time-sharing system of, 24–25, 31
Mobile radio, 229–230, 233 234, 250
Models, in social science, 78, 90, 170–71
Monopoly: objections to, 251; patent and

INDEX

copyright as a partial, 191–92, 194, 221; profit maximization of a, 244–45; regulated, 204, 242, 249, 255; unregulated, 242
Moore, William, 60
Morrill, William A., 248, 254, 256
Morton, W. Brown, Jr., 217–18
Moses, Joel, 64–65
Mosher, Charles A., 26, 289, 292
Motivation: economic, 138–42; to learn, xiii, 22, 133, 139; for teachers, 141
Moynihan, Daniel Patrick, 288–89
Multiprocessing system, 4, 16
Mumford, Lewis, 267
Municipal information systems, 161

Naddor, Eliezer, 62
Nader, Ralph, xiii–xiv, 50, 149, 172–77, 183, 185, 254, 299
National Academy of Engineering, 50, 291
National Academy of Sciences, 47, 50, 238, 291
National Aeronautics and Space Administration (NASA), 146–47, 291
National Bureau of Standards, 23, 41, 61, 139, 213
National Computer Development Agency (NCDA), 14–15, 17–18, 22–23, 33–35
National data center, xvii, 164, 171; opposition to, 161–62, 168, 170, 181–82
National Industrial Conference Board, 288
National Planning Association, 288
National Research Library, proposal for, 10, 30
National Science Foundation, 13, 273
Natural selection: versus artificial, 266; of organisms, 262–63, 274; in society, 263–66, 278, 283–84
Nature: as a laboratory, xv, 47, 49–50, 64; versus nurture, 263
Negrin, David A., 24
Networks: ARPA, 28–29, 33; educational, xiii; financial information, xiv; large time-sharing, xv, 1–36, 51, 77, 121, 204; national computer, 6–8, 11–14, 33; nonprofit communications, 25; odor-sensing, xiv; problems of, 240; for reporting data within governmental jurisdictions, 164; separate, data communications, 12, 29, 235–36
Network signaling, 236
Neustadt, Richard E., 74–75, 81, 84, 90
New Haven, Conn., 164
Newspaper: automated, 8–9, 21–22; daily, 66, 69; personalized, 8–9, 21–22, 31, 71

New York City: brownout in, 285; educational problems of, 137, 143; environmental problems in, 276, 281–82
New York State Identification and Intelligence System, 158, 160–61
New York Times, 21, 42, 57, 65, 69
Nixon, Richard M., 74, 87, 104, 184, 288–289; administration of, 143, 262

Obedin, Neale, 137
Oettinger, Anthony G., xvi, 64, 73–91, 101–6, 108–12, 137, 140–42, 144–45, 182, 184, 202, 207, 212, 299
Office of Emergency Preparedness, 240
Office of Science and Technology, 47, 50
Okun, Arthur M., 106
Ombudsman for ensuring privacy, 180
Ontario Hydro, 287
Organizations, 41, 65, 80, 111–12; arrangements in, 96–97, 101–2, 247; designing, xv, 37–72; power problem in, 105, 112
Orlans, Harold, 139–40, 145, 289–90
Overhage, Carl F. J., 217, 220

Packard, David, 73–74, 91, 96, 101, 104–5, 299
Palme, Olof, 128–29
Parkinson, C. Northcote, 138
Patent Office, 196
Patents, 191–93, 195, 199–200, 204–6, 218; for computer programs, 195–97, 206–7, 211, 214, 219–20, 223; versus copyrights, xvii, 195, 197, 215, 217; doubt about efficacy in stimulating new ideas, 191; duration of, 195; novelty as requirement for, 207, 214–15, 218–20; for principles and equations, 196–97, 205, 218
Pease, Billie J., 23–24
Pechman, Joseph A., 63, 171
Perle, Edgar G., 194, 210–11
Perlis, Alan J., x, 1, 18–25, 27, 30, 299–300
Personality tests, as part of data systems, 155–56, 178
Picturephone, 11, 28, 76
Piore, Emanuel R., 180–84
PL-1, 24, 35
Platt, John R., 53, 63, 65, 69, 71, 266
Polling by computer, 9
Pollution, xviii, 70, 229, 277, 281; of air, 18, 261, 276, 282, 290; commercializing, 291; detecting, xiv; by insecticides, 45–46, 48–50; of water, 292
Polygraphs, 156, 162
Pool, Ithiel de Sola, 73, 91–96, 104–5, 108–9, 300

Population problem, xviii, 68, 267–68, 271, 275, 280
Posner, Richard A., 225, 242–51, 255–56, 300
Postley, J. A., 161
Post Office, 42
Power: blackout of (*see* Blackout); control of, 271; new sources of, 271
Power industry, xi, 248, 256, 286
Pragmatism, 53, 56, 68
Prater and Wei case, 195–96
President of the United States: access to information by, 78, 80–81, 83–86, 88–92, 94–95, 98, 101, 106; attention scarcity in office of, 47, 56, 64–65, 69–70; cabinet of, 69, 78; leadership of, 107–9; and national decision making, 74–76
Press, as source of information, 65–66, 108, 165
Pricing: average-cost, 243; mechanism for, 42, 52, 70–71; predatory, 243, 245, 250, 255; telephone, 70, 243
Privacy: in computer systems, 25, 59, 151; cost of, 178; FCC interest in, 162, 235, 237–38; functions of, 150, 152, 181, 185–86; meaning of, 150, 152, 173, 177, 180–81, 185; of organizations, 174, 177–80 (*see also* Secrecy); problem of, 105, 162, 169–70, 173; right of, 151–52, 155, 166, 173, 176; versus security, 163, 177–78; tactics to overcome desire for, 184–85; threats to, xvii, 51, 156, 169, 186
Private-line rate case, 235, 245
Processes, patent protection of, 214, 218
Production versus creation, 261, 272
Profit: maximization of, 245; versus nonprofit, 194–95, 211, 279
Programming, computer, 19, 35, 46, 144, 146; as engineering, 219; errors in, 19, 22; inventiveness in, 219, 223
Programming-planning-budgeting system (PPBS), 78, 141
Programs: applications versus systems, 192, 219; cost of producing versus copying, 221; as improvements to a computer, 196, 205, 219; modification of, to circumvent copyright, 207, 216–17, 219, 221; proprietary, 193, 198; tailoring of, to users, 221; as writings of an author, 199, 221
Property, meaning of, 190–91, 204
Property rights: in computer programs, 192, 195–99, 206–7, 209, 211, 219; creating or extending, 192; in information, 190–91; interests affected by, 222; need for negotiation on, 202–4; under the new technology, xvii, 189–224; reasons for protecting, 222–23; state and common-law protection of, 199–200; transaction costs of, 207–8, 221; view of academic institutions on, 194
Proprietary programs, 193, 198
Proxmire-Sullivan bills, 166
Public, the: alarm of, over uncontrolled circulation of information, 157, 182; rights of, to information, 89, 177
Public Health Service, 174
Public interest, xv, 172, 222, 226–27, 241, 251, 285
Public message system, 228
Publishers, 210–12, 221; and computing firms, 194, 201–2; protective interest of, 193–94, 201, 209, 214
Pueblo, U.S.S., 81–82

Raborn, William F., Jr., 80
Radio: communication with other planets by means of, 269–70; instruction by, 147
Radio spectrum, 230–31
Radio Corporation of America, 194, 232
Ramparts, 119
RAND Corporation, 27, 50, 231
Ransom, Harry H., 81–82
Rayleigh, third baron, 279
Reader's Digest, 119
Reagan, Ronald, 165
Records: attitudes about the significance of, 150–52, 165; criminal, 160–61, 165, 170; driver, 160; employee, 155, 175; health, education, and welfare, 155, 160–61; history of written, 153; matching, consolidating, and circulating, 155, 157, 169–72, 179; separation or amalgamation of administrative, intelligence, and statistical, 155, 159–61, 165, 176–77; updating of, 183–84
Recreation, use of computer in, 8–9
Regulation, 204, 254; anticipating problems of, 227–34; of communications, 226, 234; and computing, 227; versus free market, 242–43; justification of, xviii, 166, 209, 244–46, 249–52, 256; need for analyses as basis for, 227, 233–34, 237, 241; statutes for, 251–54, 257
Regulatory agencies: as forums, 240; problems of, 172, 239, 252–53
Resources, natural, supply of, 267, 280
Resources for the Future, 50
Response time, 3
Responsibility, delegating or abdicating, 74–75, 79–80, 91; social, of scientists and engineers, 21, 60–61, 260
Rich, Giles S., 214, 217, 222–23
Richardson, John M., 104
Rights: of access, 89, 155, 175; of citi-

zens, in data systems, xv, 150, 154, 157, 161, 166, 178, 179; of free inquiry, 272–73, 286; of individuals versus groups, 190; of third party, 180–81
Rights, Bill of, 173, 185
Ringer, Barbara A., 217–18
Roberts, Lawrence G., 26, 28, 33, 247, 255–56
Roosevelt, Franklin D., 78
Rose, David J., 106, 110
Ross, Dan C., 285
Rostow, Walt W., 80
Rouse, Andrew, 106, 110
Rowe, James E., 26, 31
Royalties: and compulsory licenses, 203; for computer programs, 198–99, 202–3, 208, 212, 214, 220; for original versus subsequent use, 210; setting a price for, 203; for unpatented inventions, 199
Rule-making inquiry, 246

Sadowsky, George, 26
Safeguard system, 99, 262
Salant, Walter S., 180, 184–85
Sample data, 170–72
Santa Clara County, Calif., 159–61
Sarnoff, David, 194
Satellite transmission, 71, 146–47, 233
Scammon, Richard M., 180, 182, 184
Schools: changes in, xiii, xvi, 116, 128–29, 132, 135, 137, 142; commercial and private, 120, 134–35, 140–42; versus computer terminals, 121; constraints on location of, 121–22; functions of, xvi, 117–22, 124, 127–29, 131–37, 145; program for experimental, 143–44; test scores of, as a means of measuring performance, 126
Schultze, Charles L., 149, 168–72, 178–79, 181–82, 186, 230, 300
Schumpeter, J. A., 250
Science, 31
Science: meaning of, 260, 281; versus technology, 260–61, 272–74, 277; and values, 261–62, 264, 279–80, 286
Science Citation Index, 221
Scientific research: goals of, 136; results of, 273
Scientists: computer, xvi; declining productivity of, 267–68; and engineers, responsibility of, 21, 60–61, 260
Sears-Compco cases, 200
Secrecy, 89, 150, 154, 163; property protection through, 191, 199–200, 210
Security: versus privacy, 163, 177–78, 182, 184; time aspect of, 182
Semiconductor technology, xii
Sentinel system, 99

Serial devices, one-at-a-time, 41, 47, 56, 59
Servomechanisms, 130
Shannon, Claude E., 41, 45
Shredding standards, need for, 175
Shubik, Martin, 37, 56–60, 66, 71, 141, 300
SICOM, 228
Silk, Leonard S., 63, 65, 221–22
Simon, Herbert A., xv–xvi, 37–52, 56, 59–66, 71–72, 109, 300
Simulation, 291–92; computer, 121, 131–32; as a pedagogical tool, 131–32, 146; of the universe, 132
Singer, S. Fred, 288, 290
Sniffers, xiv
Snow, C. P., 39, 229
Snow, Joel A., 288, 290
Social change, 93, 110, 260, 263–68
Social management, 12, 169–70, 183–85
Social programs, consequences of, 275–76
Social-science data, 59, 76, 155, 157; needed on performance and production functions, 169
Social Security data, 159, 169
Society: affluent (*see* Affluence); communication structure of, xiv, 116, 119, 129, 132; information-rich (*see* Information, richness of); natural selection in, 263–66; needs of, 38, 218, 260–62, 264, 274–77; polarization of, 105; role of privacy in, 152; technological, 38, 60–61, 146
Software: machine-independent, 15; in manufacturing, 216; problems of, 16; production of, 34–35, 192–93, 211; protection of, 192, 195–99, 204, 216; special-purpose, 32
Software firms, independent, versus large integrated computer companies, 18, 192–93, 197, 216
Solomon, Richard A., 246
Solutions in closed form, 131
"Solve," meaning of, 131
Sonic boom, 229, 261, 277
Sophar, Gerald, 217, 220–21
Sources, information, identification of, 88, 91, 101, 112, 163, 186
Soviet Union, 174, 233, 261, 275, 278; elitist communications in, 96; intelligence system of, 94; reaction of, to the ABM, 99–100, 262
Space program, 278–79, 291–92
Space travel, 260, 270, 275
Specialization, 62–63, 278; anatomical, 265; of universities, xiii
Spencer, Herbert, 283
SST, 229, 261, 277–78
Standards, xiii, 14–15, 33–34, 207

Stanford Research Institute, 236, 247, 249
State, Department of, 43, 92, 98
Statistical data systems, 154–56, 162, 169, 213; versus administrative systems, 168, 172; aggregation in, 159, 170, 177–78; privacy safeguards in, 170–71, 181; in social-science research, 168–70; updating records in, 183–84; used for intelligence, 161, 169–71, 177, 184
Strassburg, Bernard, 26–29, 249, 255–56
Subordinates: competing, 107–8; making knowledgeable, 83–84, 86, 88, 90, 102, 104, 111; personal review of, 181
Subroutines, 67
Subsequent use: of an author's work, 210; of material put into a computer, 208, 215–16
Sullivan case, 173
Suppes, Patrick, 115, 120, 132–38, 140, 147, 301
Supreme Court: on copyright, 197–98; as influenced by social Darwinism, 283; on patents for computer programs, 205, 218–19; on privacy, 155, 180–81; on trade-secret protection, 199–200, 220
Switching systems, telephone, 28, 42
Symbols: versus concrete experience, 146; inventions of, 196
Systems designer, essential concerns of, xvi-xvii
Systems Development Corporation, 22

Talsky, Barry, 23
Tauber, Stephen J., 61, 286
Teachers: as adult models, 141, 146; inadequately rewarded, 141; limitations of, 121
Technology: dangers of, 51, 60, 229, 260–62; distrust of, xviii, 72, 75, 260; incentives for work in, xiii, xv, xvii, 192, 206, 209–14; meaning of, 261; need for, xviii, 61, 72; not primary problem, 101–2, 147, 158, 165, 167, 285; as part of nature, 269, 271; policy decisions concerning, 226–30, 289; versus science, 260–61, 272–74, 277; secondary effects of, 47–49, 275–78, 287, 289–90; stages in using new, 131–32, 157
Technology assessment, 38, 47–51, 56, 276, 289–92; of information processing, 50–51
Telecommunications, Office of, 247, 253–54
Telecommunications policy: Johnson task force on, 233; Nixon review of, 233, 237

Telegraph investigation, 228, 235, 245
Telephone, 9, 32, 77, 83, 120; and cost of directory assistance, 34; EKG signals by, xii; elitist ("key") system, 96; gaining information by, 46, 49, 70–71, 112; long distance, 70, 88, 243
Telephone company, 12, 28–29, 71, 238; CATV offered by a, 235–37; costs of, 28–29, 71; New England, 28; rates of, 12, 70, 243, 252; revenue of, xi, 230; Southern Bell, 28
Television, 58, 70, 107, 109–10, 116–19, 133, 230, 276; allocation of channels, 252; color, 231–32, 241, 277; diversity in, 252; educational, 116, 146–47, 233; effects of, on social environment, 70, 107, 109–10, 116–19, 133; for executives, 71; industry based on, 9–10; licenses for, 229, 232, 245, 252; as means of interaction, 58, 76–77; UHF, 232–33
Telex, 228
Telpak case, 235–37, 245
Tennessee Valley Authority (TVA), 276, 288
Terminals: with graphic abilities, 31; for homes, 8–9; mass production of, 31; time-sharing, 4, 8–9, 31
Test scores and measures, 126–27, 129, 139, 142
Texarkana, Ark., project in, 120, 140, 143
Theory: of the behavior of firms, 244; physical, 77; pure, and raw data, 76–79; scientific, 45–46
Thermostat, 75
"Think," meaning of, 39–40
Thomson, Dale, 287
Thurman, Ronald, 214
Timberg, Sigmund, 216
Time-sharing systems, 2–4, 19, 22, 41, 120; cost of, 4, 16, 19, 29; dedicated (or "limited"), 19, 24, 32–33; design alternatives for, 4–6, 16; general-purpose, 19, 32–33; large (1,000 users), xv, 3–8, 15–16, 18, 24, 29, 121; medium (100 to 200 users), 3, 6, 9; protection of access to, 25; response time of, 3, 19; small (10 to 30 users), 3, 24; for students, 6, 19, 22
Toynbee, Arnold, 60
Trade-secret protection, 199–200, 260
Traffic, control of, 8
Transportation: communications as an extension of, 226; regulation of, 249
Treble damages, 243
Triangle Universities Computing Center (TUCC), 28

Truman, Harry S, 81
Trust, 181, 183–84, 186
Truth, as a relational term, 280–81
Turnaround time, 2, 19, 22, 56
Turner, Donald F., 248, 250, 252, 256
Two cultures, problem of the, 229

UHF television, 232–33, 248
Ultramicrofiche, 209, 213
Unbundling, 193, 211, 219
United Auto Workers, 166
United Computing Systems, 215
Universities: change in, xiii; as resources for policy analysis, 257
University Microfilms, 212
Users: burden on copyright, 209; concerns of computer, 201–2; groups of computer, 221; programs tailored to, 221
Utility, computer (or "information"), xviii, 204, 228, 235

Values: personal versus communal, 145; science and, xv, 261–62, 264; shaping of, 119, 133, 144
VHF TV channels, 232
Vietnam, 53, 56, 63, 80, 95, 98, 162; bomb shortage in, 107; war in, 156, 186, 274, 291
Vouchers, xvi, 126–27, 129, 138–43; doubts about, 134–35, 140–42; in higher education, 142; medical, 143; need for empirical critique of, 134, 140, 142–43

Wald, George, xviii, 259–72, 285–88, 291, 301
Walsingham, Sir Francis, 154
Warren, Samuel D., 173
Washington, Booker T., 123
Washington, D.C., Real Property Data Bank, 158
Washington Post, 41, 69
Waterloo University, 19, 22
Webb, James E., 288, 291–92
Weintraub, Stanley, 25
Weizenbaum, Joseph, 63–65
Welfare payments, computerizing, xv, 185
Western Union, xviii, 29, 228, 242, 247–49, 255–56
Westin, Alan F., xvii, 149, 151–68, 176–83, 185–87, 301
Westinghouse, 120
Westmoreland, William C., 107
Whaley, Barton, 94
White, Lee C., 225, 239–41, 246, 248, 251, 301
Whitehead, Clay T., 248, 250, 253, 256
Wilensky, Harold L., 81
Wiretapping, 151, 156, 162, 178, 181, 186
Wolfle, Dael, 31–32, 108, 115–16, 144, 254, 301
Wolk, Bruce, 285
Women, new opportunities for, provided by home terminals, 11
Woolf, Harry, 288, 292
Words: legal, 251–52; technical meanings of, 38–40, 51, 57
Wordsworth, William, 280
Work: child's need for, 123–25, 144–45; integrating education and, 127–29, 133, 137–38, 141, 144; validity of, 279

Xerox machine, 45, 49, 70–71, 93, 209, 229

Zooming (reach) for details by executives, 75–76, 83–90, 95–96, 102, 104, 108, 111
Zurkowski, Paul G., 217

THE JOHNS HOPKINS PRESS

Designed by Arlene J. Sheer

Composed in Times Roman text and display by Monotype Composition Company

Printed on 60 lb. Perkins and Squier, R and bound in Columbia Riverside Linen RL-3425 by The Maple Press Company

QA
76.5
C6143

DEC 8 1972